U.S. Laws, Acts, and Treaties

U.S. Laws, Acts, and Treaties

Volume 3

1970-2002

edited by
Timothy L. Hall
University of Mississippi School of Law

co-editor
Christina J. Moose

Salem Press, Inc.
Pasadena, California   Hackensack, New Jersey

Parts of this publication previously appeared in the following publications, copyrighted by Salem Press, Inc.: *Great Events from History: Human Rights* (© 1992), *Great Events from History: Business and Commerce*
(© 1994), *Great Events from History: Ecology and the Environment* (© 1995),
Ready Reference: American Justice (c 1996), *Great Events from History: Revised North American Series* (c 1997), *Ready Reference: Censorship* (© 1997),
Ready Reference: Women's Issues (© 1997), *Natural Resources* (© 1998),
Encyclopedia of Family Life (© 1999), *Racial and Ethnic Relations in America*
(© 1999), *The Sixties in America* (© 1999), *Aging* (© 2000), *Encyclopedia
of Environmental Issues* (© 2000), *Encyclopedia of the U.S. Supreme Court*
(© 2001), *Magill's Choice: American Indian History* (© 2002), and *Magill's
Choice: The Bill of Rights* (© 2002). New material has been added.

Library of Congress Cataloging-in-Publication Data
U.S. laws, acts, and treaties / edited by Timothy L. Hall.
    p. cm. — (Magill's choice)
Includes bibliographical references and index.
    ISBN 1-58765-098-3 (set : alk. paper) — ISBN 1-58765-099-1 (vol. 1 :
alk. paper) — ISBN 1-58765-100-9 (vol. 2 : alk. paper)— ISBN
1-58765-101-7 (vol. 3 : alk. paper)
    1. United States. Laws, etc. 2. Law—United States. 3. United
States—Foreign relations—Treaties. I. Title: US laws, acts, and
treaties. II. Hall, Timothy L. III. Series.
    KF385.A4U152 2003
    348.73'2—dc21

                                                            2002156063

Third Printing

CONTENTS

Contents

CONTENTS BY POPULAR NAME

U.S. Laws, Acts, and Treaties

RESOURCE RECOVERY ACT

DATE: October 26, 1970
U.S. STATUTES AT LARGE: 84 Stat. 1227
PUBLIC LAW: 91-512
CATEGORIES: Environment and Conservation; Natural Resources

An amendment to the Solid Waste Disposal Act of 1965, this law funded recycling programs and mandated extensive reassessment of solid waste practices.

On October 26, 1970, President Richard M. Nixon signed the Resource Recovery Act, which amended the 1965 Solid Waste Disposal Act. The amendment was a bipartisan effort emerging from the Senate, particularly the subcommittee on air and water pollution. By redefining solid waste disposal as "resource recovery," the legislation indicated a shift in federal policy on how to manage garbage, refuse, rubbish, solid waste, and hazardous waste. The act also shifted emphasis from simple regulation of interstate commerce to the regulation of individual businesses.

The initial Solid Waste Disposal Act of 1965 had supported the demonstration, construction, and applications of solid waste management and resource-recovery systems that preserved the other environmental resources. That act had underwritten technical and financial assistance for the planning and development of the necessary facilities, and it had established a national research and development program for safe treatment and disposal of nonrecoverable residues and for the collection, separation, and recovery of recyclable solid waste. The emphasis was on organization and management rather than on the actual processes.

PROVISIONS

The new act gave the secretary of health, education, and welfare broad powers to carry out research and demonstration projects on recovering solid wastes and on deriving energy from such materials. An important aspect of the act was the assessment of resource-recovery methods. Other policy shifts included trying to improve recovery means and identifying potential markets for the recovered materials; gauging the impact of increased recovery; and encouraging a reduction of packaging, a truly revolutionary concept.

The secretary was made responsible for studying the effects of existing public policies and of the incentives proposed in the legislation to change some of those policies.

Government agencies were encouraged to apply for grants to study existing practices, make plans and propose new initiatives. Grants were also made available for demonstration projects for resource-recovery systems in which the federal share was to range between 50 and 75 percent of the cost.

The act also gave the secretary authority to fund research, an activity that was especially important given the state of the solid waste management system at the time. A 1968 survey by the U.S. Public Health Service had reported that the nation's collection system was largely controlled by local government or its contractors and that disposal was likewise under local control. All methods of disposal had associated problems; the vast majority of landfills were frighteningly inadequate, as were the incinerators.

With the 1970 Resource Recovery Act, the federal contribution to solid waste management shifted to a new emphasis on recycling, resource recovery, and energy conversion of wastes. The baseline data on which the legislation was based had been gathered by a 1968 Public Health Service survey summarized in a 1971 report entitled *The Third Pollution: The National Problem of Solid Waste Disposal.* That publication reported political problems with the efforts to control solid waste pollution; the Environmental Protection Agency (EPA) had suggested a broader approach to the issue, with greater emphasis on resource issues.

Implementation of the act was, however, delayed. The act had given the Department of Health, Education, and Welfare the means and authority to revolutionize solid waste management systems, but designated funds were not expended, and the various innovations and provisions for technical assistance to local governments fell behind schedule. The Nixon administration did not favor funding construction of demonstration facilities, instead proposing to tax products that were harmful to the environment. The Boggs Amendment proposed a national policy to continue the program of trying to reduce waste rather than to develop new ways of disposing of it.

SANITARY LANDFILLS

At about the time the act was passed, combined garbage-collection systems were beginning to come into use, in which both rubbish and garbage—both puetrescible and nonpuetrescible materials—were removed weekly by local authorities and disposed of in publicly owned facilities. The increasing amount of trash was a serious problem. Although hydraulic compaction was an important technological advance, the amount of trash—fast-food detritus, disposable baby diapers, combined and single-serve packaging—increased more rapidly than could be dealt with by even this new technique.

The problems associated with disposal in open dumps, still a common practice at the time, were brought to public attention by the death of a child, Kevin Mock, in a dump fire. This resulted in a major innovation, the sanitary landfill, which reduced the health problems as well as the burning and scavenging associated with the open dumps. A ban on open burning emerged as a component of air pollution laws. The development of stronger compaction equipment led to less loose material. Individual households invested in trash compaction devices and garbage grinders in the sink, and some effort was made to encourage diversion of solid waste into the sanitary sewage. Daily coverage of the dumps with dirt reduced visual pollution and eliminated some of the vermin associated with open dumping. Subsequent analyses of sanitary landfills—such as William Rathje's Garbage Project excavations—revealed that materials disposed of this way remained close to their original state for decades because the new conditions retarded decomposition.

INCINERATORS AND PYROLYSIS

At the time the act was passed, there were nearly two hundred incinerators in the United States, half of them located in the New England and Mid-Atlantic states. The 1970 act subsidized major trash-burning projects in Menlo Park, California; Franklin, Ohio; and St. Louis, Missouri. The act also funded two important demonstration projects that involved pyrolysis of solid waste in San Diego and Baltimore; pyrolysis uses heat without oxygen to decompose solid waste to produce a fuel-like substance. The federal and local or state governments invested millions to study and demonstrate new technologies. According to the EPA, these grant-funded facilities were a small number of the nearly four dozen incinerators that came into use during this period.

RECYCLING

Interest in recycling, other than industrial recycling, developed in a grassroots fashion. Early, informal recycling efforts were followed by more serious efforts, often handled by the Boy Scouts, Camp-Fire Girls, or religious organizations, which interested individuals in the reuse and recycling of materials.

The results of research funded by the 1970 amendment were published by the federal government and circulated widely. Some ideas—such as how to organize rural collection systems—were inexpensive and practical, others were more costly and highly technical, such as information about how to use refuse in power plants or recover material in new ways.

IMPACT AND LATER LEGISLATION

The 1970 act continued the tradition of circulating information and requesting responses. The EPA eventually issued reports to Congress on the state of resource recovery and waste reduction. Eventually, the 1965 and 1970 acts were modified by the Resource Conservation and Recovery Act of 1976. The earlier acts also initiated surveys of public and private solid waste management efforts (one publication even summarized possible methods for dealing with abandoned cars). Information on state-of-the-art efforts and equipment came from the National Center for Resource Recovery, Inc., which was funded by federal grants. All this information would not have been available without the initiatives of the 1970 act.

Nancy R. Bain

SOURCES FOR FURTHER STUDY

Melosi, Martin V. *Garbage in the Cities: Refuse, Reform, and the Environment, 1880-1980.* College Station: Texas A&M University Press, 1981.

Rathje, William, and Cullen Murphy. *Rubbish! The Archaeology of Garbage.* New York: HarperCollins, 1992.

Small, William E. *The Third Pollution: The National Problem of Solid Waste Disposal.* New York: Praeger, 1971.

Udall, Stewart L. *The Quiet Crisis.* New York: Holt, Rinehart and Winston, 1963.

SEE ALSO: Solid Waste Disposal Act (1965); Hazardous Materials Transportation Act (1974); Toxic Substances Control Act (1976); Resource Conservation and Recovery Act (1976); Low-Level Radioactive Waste Policy Act (1980); Superfund Act (1980); Nuclear Waste Policy Act (1983).

COMPREHENSIVE DRUG ABUSE PREVENTION AND CONTROL ACT

DATE: October 27, 1970
U.S. STATUTES AT LARGE: 84 Stat. 1242
PUBLIC LAW: 91-513
U.S. CODE: 21 § 801
CATEGORIES: Crimes and Criminal Procedure; Food and Drugs; Health and Welfare

This law consolidated previous drug-control legislation and enlarged the scope of federal jurisdiction over drug laws; it was "comprehensive" in that it contained provisions for treatment, control, and enforcement in a single law.

Legislation to control the use of drugs has existed in various forms throughout the twentieth century. By 1970, public opinion polls indicated that the American public cited use of illegal drugs as one of the most important public concerns. The federal government estimated that between 800,000 and 1.2 million Americans were using marijuana on a daily basis. The availability of other drugs, particularly heroin, had increased public anxiety about drug use. Federal law enforcement officials and the Nixon administration sought to strengthen and clarify the large number of federal laws that governed controlled substances.

The 1970 act distinguished among several categories of drugs based on the potential for abuse and medicinal uses. Heroin, lysergic acid diethylamide (LSD) and other hallucinogens, and marijuana were outlawed, and any medicinal uses were subject to approval by federal officials. Title I of the act clarified the definition of a "drug dependent person" and provided structures for rehabilitation treatment.

The main effect of the act on the structure of law enforcement was the expansion of federal jurisdiction over drug laws. Prior to the 1970 act, the federal role had been confined primarily to enforcing prohibitions of the interstate transport of drugs, enforcing laws against tax violations, and prohibiting illegal imports. The act granted federal officials greater search powers and permitted the attorney general to utilize paid informants. Many states have used the 1970 federal act as a model for state drug laws.

Lawrence Clark III

SOURCES FOR FURTHER STUDY

U.S. Food and Drug Administration. *Milestones in U.S. Food and Drug Law History.* Washington, D.C.: Government Printing Office, 1985.

Temin, Peter. *Taking Your Medicine: Drug Regulation in the United States.* Cambridge, Mass.: Harvard University Press, 1980.

SEE ALSO: Opium Exclusion Act (1909); Harrison Narcotic Drug Act (1914); Eighteenth Amendment (1919); Marihuana Tax Act (1937); Kefauver-Harris Amendment (1962); National Narcotics Act (1984).

FAMILY PLANNING SERVICES AND POPULATION RESEARCH ACT

DATE: December 28, 1970
U.S. STATUTES AT LARGE: 84 Stat. 1504
PUBLIC LAW: 91-572
U.S. CODE: 42 § 201
CATEGORIES: Children's Issues; Health and Welfare; Women's Issues

> *Birth control proponents, feminists, and social planners, after decades of advocacy, effected federal legislation making family planning services available to all American women.*

Since the beginning of the twentieth century, when the modern birth control movement emerged under the leadership of Margaret Sanger, feminists, social planners, and health care professionals have campaigned for public policy that would first acknowledge and then advance the legitimacy and importance of contraception and its practice. The Family Planning Services and Population Research Act of 1970 brought this effort to fruition by legislating a central agency to direct "population affairs" and by designating monies to support and extend family planning services to all Americans regardless of their ability to pay. The act made it possible for considerable numbers of American women, especially poor women, to have access to birth control information and reproductive health care. Viewed by supporters as a legislative watershed in advancing enlightened health care for women, as well as affording poor women the same opportunities or rights as the wealthy, the bill's most controversial elements, such as abortion, continued to be debated thirty years after its passage and implementation.

BIRTH CONTROL: HISTORY AND ATTITUDES

During the late nineteenth century and for the greater portion of the twentieth, information about contraception as well as contraceptive aids and procedures, including abortion, were banned in various ways on both the state and federal levels.

Feminists, beginning with Elizabeth Cady Stanton, advocated a woman's right to control the frequency of conception. This then-controversial position contributed to divisions in the women's rights movement and was eventually abandoned by the mainstream of female suffrage reformers at the turn of the century.

The cause of legal contraception was revived in the twentieth century by the personality and activism of Margaret Sanger. A trained nurse and avowed socialist, Sanger educated herself about "birth control," as she was the first to call it, and then turned to the task of educating American society. She spoke of what she saw daily in New York City's lower East Side, of the women who worked in the sweatshop industries, and their ill health, fatigue, and desperate dread of frequent pregnancies. Sanger's graphic descriptions of these conditions and circumstances, especially the common resort to self-induced and often fatal abortion, awakened a growing number of Americans to the importance of legal birth control. For Sanger and her movement, which grew in size and effectiveness during the first half of the twentieth century, making legal the availability of birth control information, aids, and practice was more than a woman's right: It was essential to ensuring sound public health policy for women and children specifically, and for the American family generally.

During the 1930's, the courts' lifting of the federal ban on birth control combined with the actualities of the Depression to encourage policies that incorporated birth control counseling and reproductive health care into national and federally subsidized state programs. By the end of the decade, two pieces of legislation, Title V of the Social Security Act amendments of 1938 and the Venereal Disease Control Act of 1939, designated several million dollars for maternal and child health services as well as the prevention of sexually transmitted disease. As administered by the Children's Bureau and the United States Public Health Service, these programs offered, to married women only, public health programs that recognized and advanced the legitimacy of birth control practice.

EARLIER LEGISLATIVE EFFORTS

Attitudes about birth control and family planning shifted after World War II. During this period of peace and prosperity, concerns about population growth diminished and the ethos of traditional family values prevailed, despite the ever-increasing number of women entering the labor market. Although the presidential administrations of Harry S. Truman and Dwight D. Eisenhower rhetorically endorsed family planning research and reproductive health services, little actual progress was made until the 1960's, when Congress turned national attention once again to issues of poverty and social welfare. In 1963, Senators Ernest Gruening and Joseph Clark introduced legislation calling on the president to increase family planning research programs within the National Institutes of Health and to make widely available the results of such efforts. Two years of extensive hearings followed, heightening public awareness and concern regarding reproductive health care, population growth, and declining resources.

Committed to making war on poverty, President Lyndon B.

Johnson promoted federally financed family planning services, and in his 1966 "Message on Domestic Health and Education" endorsed the idea of each American's "freedom to choose the number and spacing of their children within the dictates of individual conscience." In 1967, he appointed a Presidential Committee on Population and Family Planning led by John D. Rockefeller III and Secretary of the Department of Health, Education, and Welfare (HEW) Wilbur Cohen. In the same year, as part of the Johnson legislative agenda, Congress passed amendments to the Social Security Act and the Economic Opportunity Act, extending reproductive health care programs. Under Social Security, more monies were to be directed specifically to family planning, and all states were required to extend family planning services to any recipient of Aid to Families with Dependent Children (AFDC) who requested such services.

At the Office of Econommic Opportunity (OEO), project grants for family planning became a special priority. The report of the presidential committee recommended an expenditure of $150 million by 1973 for family planning to reach all women who wanted but could not afford services, a consolidated Center for Population Research, and appropriations of an additional $130 million for research in 1970 and 1971.

PROPOSAL AND PASSAGE

President Richard M. Nixon endorsed, in principle, the recommendations of the Rockefeller Commission, and in 1969, Senator Joseph Tydings and twenty-three cosponsors introduced the Family Planning Services and Population Research Act (S. 2108). The Tydings bill primarily sought to consolidate all extant family planning and population-related programs scattered throughout HEW in a National Center for Population and Family Planning which would also coordinate comparable programs of in OEO and other departments, and report to Congress. In this regard, the bill responded to what many believed had been the slowness of HEW to implement the 1967 amendments. Testimony in hearings on the bill emphasized the persistent inadequacy of reproductive health care for poor and near-poor women in the United States. HEW's own surveys estimated that fewer than 800,000 of an eligible 5.4 million women were receiving family planning assistance, and Tydings argued that as of late 1969 "it was unlikely that any woman had yet received family planning services through Title V." The bill also specified monies, $89 million more than that recommended by the commission, to be spent in various project grants for family planning services, research, and training. The Nixon administration introduced its own bill (S.3219), which avoided any administrative reorganization, but also proposed various project grants as amendments to the Public Health Services Act, although no appropriations were specified.

For most who supported the bill, the issue of federal family planning services was a matter of equal opportunity. They strongly believed that poor women should have the same "fundamental individual rights" as already enjoyed by the affluent. Allowing poor women to exercise their reproductive rights was understood as a way of attacking the poverty cycle as well. The bill was also designed to address the larger issue of unwanted births, especially those resulting from ineffective contraception, which most agreed contributed to family instability for rich and poor alike. Not only did the bill encourage more aggressive research in the field of safe and effective contraception, but it tacitly responded to the arguments of a small group of feminists who held that women had an absolute right to control all phases of reproduction, including the option of abortion. Representative Shirley Chisholm calling the laws prohibiting abortion "compulsory pregnancy laws," argued for the legalization of abortion and that it be recognized in the proposed legislation as an acceptable method of family planning. Neither Senate bill mentioned abortion, leaving the option open for its recognition.

The House received the Senate bills and, although enthusiastically supporting the Tydings version in principle, found reason to propose alternative legislation. The modifications concerned the authorization for the project grants, stipulating these as amendments to the Public Health Services Act at a significantly smaller doller amount, and the provision that no federal monies used in the context of family planning be expended on abortion. Although the preponderant testimony before the House endorsed all aspects of the Tydings bill, the National Right to Life Committee, an anti-abortion organization making its public debut, joined the traditional Catholic opposition and argued against any federal acknowledgment of abortion as legitimate. The House clearly did not want to have to defend the expenditure of tax money on this controversial and still illegal practice of birth control. Nor did the Senate, which, after conferees met, agreed to the House version. On December 28, 1970, President Nixon signed into law the Family Planning Services and Population Research Act making contraception, excluding abortion, available to all American women as a vital means for improving the quality of life for all.

With the passage of the Family Planning Services and Population Research Act considerable amounts of money were directed to reproductive health care for the first time. In 1973, when Congress considered extending the bill for three more years, close to three million American women were receiving comprehensive family planning services under its provisions, although it was estimated that close to seven million women still remained to be served. Throughout the 1970's and 1980's, women's groups, public health leaders, and the Planned Parenthood Federation of America lobbied for increased appropriations, with minimal success. In 1991, federal grants to clinics, administered by the Public Health Service's Office of Population Affairs, amounted to $144 million. Twenty years after the bill's passage, various family planning programs were conducted in four thousand voluntary clinics, community health centers, county health departments, and hospitals around the country, serving more than four million women. Most of the women served by these programs were poor or had low income; one-third were adolescents. As a result of the 1970 law, poor and unmarried women had access to the same reproductive health care available to the affluent and married.

ABORTION CONTROVERSY

From its inception, the most controversial aspect of the legislation was the role abortion should play in federally subsidized family planning services. After the Supreme Court's 1973 ruling in *Roe v. Wade*, the issue became particularly vexing for policymakers whose intent was to extend to poor women the same reproductive health care available to the nonpoor. As long as state law and court dicta recognized the legality of abortion as defined by the guidelines of *Roe*, poor women not served by public programs or whose contraception failed had little recourse in terminating unwanted pregnancies. In 1975, the Hyde amendment was passed, denying Medicaid reimbursements for elective abortions, and in 1977, Congress liberalized this restriction somewhat by allowing for Medicaid reimbursements only in cases of rape, incest, or endangerment of the woman's life. These restrictions left millions of poor women the choice of forced motherhood or "back-alley" abortion.

After 1973, pro-life groups, primarily from the religious right, proliferated and increasingly put pressure on Congress and the courts to undermine and overturn the *Roe* decision. Public clinics often were targeted for protest demonstrations. By the 1980's, violent confrontation of this type was a common occurrence. Despite this activity and the modified Hyde amendment, the family planning programs operated during the first seventeen years under regulations that allowed clinic employees to provide information about abortion as well as about childbirth. Title X of the law was interpreted as referring only to abortions themselves, not to advice or information about abortion.

In 1988, the Reagan administration openly embraced the right-wing agenda on reproduction and issued new regulations prohibiting federally financed family planning clinics from all discussion of abortion with their patients, even if the patient so inquired. Although never implemented because of various court challenges, on May 24, 1991, the Supreme Court upheld the regulatory prohibition in *Rust v. Sullivan* on the grounds that federal and state governments were not constitutionally required to pay for abortions, even if they chose to subsidize childbirth. Soon after the *Rust* decision, legislation was introduced in Congress to remove the restrictions of Title X.

With the *Rust* decision and the conservative bent of the Supreme Court, family planning advocates and feminists expressed fear that the progress made since the 1960's on the front of women's and reproductive rights might be eroded seriously. Such fears were renewed in the year 2000 when, after the hotly contested election narrowly won by the conservative George W. Bush, questions of Supreme Court succession and inroads by social conservatives seemed more likely than ever.

Nancy A. White

SOURCES FOR FURTHER STUDY

Baer, Judith A., ed. *Historical and Multicultural Encyclopedia of Women's Reproductive Rights in the United States.* Westport, Conn.: Greenwood Press, 2002.

Gordon, Linda. *Woman's Body, Woman's Right: Birth Control in America.* New York: Penguin Books, 1990.

Leavitt, Judith Walzer. *Women and Health in America: Historical Readings.* Madison: University of Wisconsin Press, 1999.

Rengel, Marian. *Encyclopedia of Birth Control.* Phoenix, Ariz.: Oryx Press, 2000.

Rothman, Barbara Katz. *Encyclopedia of Childbearing: Critical Perspectives.* Phoenix, Ariz.: Oryx Press, 1993.

Tobin, Kathleen A. *The American Religious Debate over Birth Control.* Jefferson, N.C.: McFarland, 2001.

SEE ALSO: Pregnancy Discrimination Act (1978); Child Support Enforcement Amendments (1984); Family Violence Prevention and Services Act (1984); Family Support Act (1988); Family and Medical Leave Act (1993).

OCCUPATIONAL SAFETY AND HEALTH ACT

DATE: December 29, 1970
U.S. STATUTES AT LARGE: 84 Stat. 1590
PUBLIC LAW: 91-596
U.S. CODE: 29 § 651
CATEGORIES: Health and Welfare; Labor and Employment

Commonly known by its acronym OSHA, this law required employers to furnish their employees with workplaces that are safe from recognized life-threatening hazards and work-related diseases.

The Occupational Safety and Health Act was enacted to ensure safe and healthful working conditions for approximately 57 million workers employed in businesses affecting interstate commerce at the time the act became effective. Immediate responsibility for ensuring compliance with the act's provisions fell upon more than 4.1 million employers nationwide.

PROVISIONS AND ENFORCMENT

Establishment and enforcement of the act's safety and health standards were charged to the U.S. secretary of labor. Standards were numerous and complex, covering more than eight hundred pages in the *Code of Federal Regulations* and numbering about forty-four hundred; twenty-one hundred of these regulations applied to all industries nationwide, including agriculture, and the remaining twenty-three hundred regulations applied specifically to the construction and maritime industries. State, local, and federal governments, although they represented major employers themselves, were exempted from the act.

Established federal standards such as those previously imposed by the government on federal contractors and suppliers under the Walsh-Healey Public Contracts Act of 1936 initially provided partial guidelines for preliminary standards established under the act. Other extant standards originated from prevalent consensus standards, which derived from rules defined by the American National Standards Institute and the National Fire Protection Association. One authority estimated that 45 percent of the first forty-four hundred standards established under the act were copied from the standards of these two organizations; later standards were drawn from those created by federal legislation such as the Walsh-Healey Act, the Construction Safety Act of 1962, and the Longshoremen's and Harbor Worker's Compensation Act of 1953.

After setting preliminary safety and health rules in place, the act allowed additional standards to be issued by the secretary of labor. This could be done after a careful review, a process that allowed the secretary to request recommendations from the National Institute of Occupational Safety and Health (NIOSH); the agency had been set up within the Department of Health, Education, and Welfare to conduct research on occupational safety and health. The labor secretary could also propose standards after consulting with an advisory committee about the feasibility of a proposed new standard, any fresh scientific information about it, and consideration of experience gained under other relevant laws. In instances in which the labor secretary found that employees were in grave danger and required immediate protection, he or she could issue temporary standards pending procedures for the design of permanent ones. Such initiatives were granted to the labor secretary, but the act was routinely administered by the Occupational Safety and Health Administration (OSHA) within the Department of Labor.

The entire burden of compliance with new procedures and standards fell upon employers, who were required to furnish their employees with jobs that were "free from recognized hazards that are causing or are likely to cause death or serious physical harm." Employers could secure a variance from the law if, after hearings and investigation, they demonstrated that their workplaces were as safe and healthy as they would be if they complied with federal standards. In cases in which employers were doing their best to comply with the act but were unable to do so immediately for economic reasons, temporary variances of up to two years could be granted. The act's administrators were nevertheless barred from considering the economic impact of OSHA standards upon employers.

EARLIER LEGISLATION

The first federal efforts to affect occupational safety and health began in the 1890's with legislation that addressed the safety of railroads and coal mines. In 1910, a Bureau of Mines was established within the Interior Department, followed in 1914 by creation of an Office of Industrial Safety and Hygiene under the Public Health Service. In 1916, injured federal workers were covered by a Federal Employees' Compensation Act. Until passage of the Walsh-Healey Act of 1936, however, little more was accomplished, and the beginning of World War II aborted most congressional health and safety bills. During the 1950's, liberal senators such as Hubert Humphrey of Minnesota and Jacob Javits of New York unsuccessfully sought extensions of federal health and safety regulations. A new series of federal regulations occurred in the 1960's, marked by the passage of the McNamara-O'Hara Public Service Contract Act and new federal safety regulations that applied to coal mining.

As part of his Great Society campaign, President Lyndon B. Johnson proposed the nation's first comprehensive occupational safety and health legislation in 1968. Despite support from congressmen such as James O'Hara of Michigan, senators such as Ralph Yarborough of Texas, and consumer advocate Ralph Nader, opposition from national business associations and the indifference of trade-union leaders defeated Johnson's proposals.

An increasing number of public and private studies, reports, and publications indicated that between the 1950's and 1970 a health and safety crisis had developed in the American workplace. The Department of Labor's Bureau of Labor Statistics reported in 1972 that between 1956 and 1970 the industrial accident rate rose 29 percent. Approximately 3 percent of the civilian work force, or 2.2 million workers, were disabled every year, and work-related deaths were estimated to average fourteen thousand per year. In addition, despite less information on worker health than on safety, authorities during these same years annually recorded 390,000 fresh cases of occupational disease, noting that only one-fourth of workers exposed to occupational health hazards were protected. Costs to America's overall economic performance were calculated at over 100,000 person years of labor lost annually, equivalent to $25 billion lost to the economy. Many official and unofficial observers perceived that this trend toward occupational disease and injury worsened during those years.

OCCUPATIONAL SAFETY AND HEALTH ADMINISTRATION
Created during more than a decade of tumultuous public and private campaigns for social and related environmental reform, the Occupational Safety and Health Administration (OSHA) began operations with considerable vigor. It did so amid persistent public conflicts over the authorizing act's necessity and significance. Criticism focused on the effectiveness of the act's authority and methods. By 1977, OSHA had a budget of $125 million (or $160 million if the NIOSH budget is factored in) and employed 1,250 safety and health inspectors to cover the nation's 4.1 million employers. To this force, 900 additional inspectors were added by the twenty-three states that operated their own OSHA-approved safety and health programs.

Within the first four years of its operations, OSHA conducted 213,400 inspections, in the course of which it cited 145,300 employers for a total of 750,700 violations. More than three-quarters of these inspections and subsequent citations concentrated on safety hazards such as danger of fire, explosion, and electrocution, as well as danger from stationary machinery and from industrial operations that produced excessive noise, heat, vibration, and stress to workers' sight. OSHA further sought to locate and reduce ergonomic hazards, that is, workplace situations that caused employee discomfort and fatigue and increased the likelihood of accidents.

Because of the broad legislative scope of the act's provisions, OSHA launched a target industry program designed not only to make inspections more specific and thus more effective but also to increase the pressure on other businesses to begin implementing safety procedures. Target industries were deemed to be those in which injury frequency rates exceeded the national average of 14.8 disabling injuries per million employee hours worked. In descending order, these workplace dangers occurred in longshoring, roofing and sheet metal work, the meat industry, work involving mobile homes and other transportation equipment, and the lumber and wood products industries. OSHA's target industry program (which was directed solely at industries with more than twenty employees) emphasized collaborative efforts on the part of labor, management, and the National Safety Council. Nearly all industries targeted were also subject to OSHA inspections.

Nearly three-fourths of OSHA's efforts were concentrated on ensuring remedial safety measures; all other efforts were aimed at discovering the causes of work-related disease. Many experts believed that the country's workplaces generated many more dangerous diseases than industrial accidents. Health standards were often hard to define precisely, but OSHA instituted about four hundred standards aimed at minimizing occupational health hazards. Many industrial diseases were caused by high-decibel noises that triggered serious heart, glandular, and nervous disorders. Other serious diseases stemmed from the inhaling of harmful dusts such as coal, asbestos, cotton, and beryllium. Still other health hazards were associated with workers' proximity to toxic gases, poisonous metals, some of the approximately sixty thousand chemicals used by industry, and cancer-causing agents (carcinogens), among them coal tar, aniline dyes, X rays, radioactivity, arsenic, asbestos, paraffin, and hydrocarbon derivatives such as vinyl chloride.

Ongoing Criticism of OSHA

OSHA continued to be controversial into the mid-1990's. Experts noted, for example, that between 1972 and 1974, OSHA's target industries program cut injuries by 3 percent; thereafter, however, the decline slowed to 1 percent, that is, to a statistically meaningless level. Some observers estimated that strict enforcement of OSHA safety standards might have reduced injuries by as much as 22 percent. Congress had, however, given OSHA weak enforcement powers. Twenty years after its creation, several respected authorities concluded that OSHA's overall impact had been nil.

Some critics opposed OSHA on more fundamental grounds. They did not oppose the principle of improving workers' safety and health (as long as the concepts safety and health could be precisely defined), but they argued that OSHA represented a misguided attempt by the federal government to solve problems that would otherwise have been solved far more effectively and cheaply by private initiative. These critics suggested replacing the costly federal intervention with simpler laws allowing workers to sue employers when they suspected they were being exposed to undue safety hazards and health risks. The threat of lawsuits, these critics believed, would be more likely to encourage employers to improve the workplace than a 10 percent chance that their businesses would be inspected or fined an insignificant sum. Other experts declared that it was the prerogative of employees—and the general public—to determine whether they preferred to accept higher wages in risky workplaces or take lower wages in less hazardous ones.

OSHA was condemned by many critics for requiring industries to accept detailed, highly specific standards for equipment and facilities rather than allowing performance standards to prevail. As a result of the objections and criticisms, more than one hundred bills were introduced in the Ninety-second Congress and thirty more in the opening days of the Ninety-fourth Congress to repeal, amend, or otherwise modify the Occupational Safety and Health Act.

Clifton K. Yearley

Sources for Further Study

Ashford, Nicolas A. *Crisis in the Workplace.* Cambridge, Mass.: MIT Press, 1976.

Nelkin, Dorothy, and Michael S. Brown. *Workers at Risk: Voices from the Workplace.* Chicago: University of Chicago Press, 1984.

Noble, Charles. *Liberalism at Work: The Rise and Fall of OSHA.* Philadelphia: Temple University Press, 1986.

Northrup, Herbert R., et al. *The Impact of OSHA.* Philadelphia: University of Pennsylvania Press, 1978.

Smith, Robert Stewart. *The Occupational Safety and Health Act.* Washington, D.C.: American Enterprise Institute for Public Policy Research, 1976.

United States. Congress. Senate. Committee on Labor and Public Welfare. Subcommittee on Labor. *Legislative History of the Occupational Safety and Health Act of 1970.* 92d Congress, 1st session. Washington, D.C.: Government Printing Office, 1971.

SEE ALSO: Federal Coal Mine Health and Safety Act (1969); Equal Employment Opportunity Act (1972); Noise Control Act (1972); Comprehensive Employment Training Act (1973); Age Discrimination Act (1975); Pregnancy Discrimination Act (1978); Women in Apprenticeship and Nontraditional Occupations Act (1992).

CLEAN AIR ACT AMENDMENTS OF 1970

DATE: December 31, 1970
U.S. STATUTES AT LARGE: 84 Stat. 1707
PUBLIC LAW: 91-604
U.S. CODE: 42 § 7401
CATEGORIES: Environment and Conservation; Natural Resources

The 1970 Clean Air Act Amendments were enacted to abate the ambient air pollution problem in the United States.

The Clean Air Act Amendments of 1970 were signed into law on December 31, 1970. Before this legislation, U.S. air quality control efforts were largely decentralized. Various federal and state agencies reacted to situations addressing local concerns. This legislation was the federal government's first effort to protect air quality in a comprehensive way, and enforcing this policy was the Environmental Protection Agency's first major responsibility.

EARLIER LEGISLATION

The federal government's role in protecting air quality became more prevalent with the Air Pollution Control Act of 1955. This act assigned research, technical assistance, and training programs to the Public Health Service division of the Department of Health, Education, and Welfare (HEW). Five years later, the Public Health Service established an air pollution division that dealt with legal, administrative, economic, and social concerns. In 1963, the Public Health Service was given authority over interstate air pollution problems and federal sources of air pollution under the Clean Air Act. Pollution control and abatement were emphasized.

The federal government became progressively more assertive in protecting the nation's ambient air quality in the 1960's. The 1963 Clean Air Act received its impetus from the notion that the nation's population had become more concentrated in expanding metropolitan and urban areas. In formulating this policy, it was asserted that air pollutants had increased in complexity and posed a greater danger to the public health and welfare. It was further asserted that the prevention and control of air pollution at its source were primary responsibilities of states and local governments. Two years later, however, with the Clean Air Act Amendments of 1965, the federal government began setting emission standards and controlling more categories of sources.

In 1967, the Air Quality Control Act was passed. Its major purpose was to prevent individual states from establishing their own standards for new motor vehicles. It also expanded air pollution research programs, provided for planning and controlling programs on a regional basis, and required states to set air quality standards conforming to criteria set by HEW. Authorization was given to the secretary of HEW to designate air quality control regions throughout the country, even though states were still given primary responsibility for enforcing air pollution standards within their geographic areas. The unsatisfactory progress under this approach, coupled with Earth Day activities in April, 1970, provided the impetus for the Clean Air Act Amendments of 1970.

ENVIRONMENTAL PROTECTION AGENCY

The Clean Air Act Amendments of 1970 paralleled the establishment of the Environmental Protection Agency (EPA). The EPA was given the authority to establish standards and to require states to develop implementation plans to meet those standards. The EPA was also given control over emissions from new stationary sources in an attempt to prevent polluting industries from migrating to less polluted states where standards might not be as stringent as in the more industrialized states. Prior to this legislation, federal air pollution legislation had always viewed state and local governments as having the primary responsibility for dealing with air pollution problems. Under the 1970 amendments, this power was limited to implementation plans to meet the national ambient (outdoor) air quality standards.

Initially, the EPA resisted drawing up regulations to preserve air quality until it was ordered to do so by the courts following a suit initiated by the Sierra Club. Each state was given responsibility for ensuring that air quality standards would be met within its geographic area. State Implementation Plans (SIPs) specified the manner in which ambient air quality standards would be achieved and maintained. The EPA administrator was given the responsibility for approving the SIPs. Public input into SIPs was required. If a state did not hold public hearings on the SIPs in compliance with the legislation, the administrator was instructed to provide an opportunity for a hearing within the state.

EMISSIONS STANDARDS

An important feature of the 1970 Clean Air Act Amendments dealt with emissions standards for automobiles. It specified that 1975 model cars had to satisfy carbon monoxide and hydrocarbon standards by emitting no more than 10 percent of the emissions allowable for 1970 models, and that 1976 model cars had to have nitrogen-oxide emissions no more than 10 percent of those actually measured in 1971. The administrator of the EPA was empowered to permit a suspension of the standards for one year if necessary. After public hearings in 1973 at which the U.S. automobile manufacturers claimed they would be unable to meet the 1975-1976 standards, the EPA postponed compliance for one year even though three foreign manufacturers had vehicles that would meet the standards. Still another one-year postponement was obtained in 1974, to 1977-1978 models, by a section of the Energy Supply and Environmental Coordination Act; this provided for the nitrogen-oxide standard to be lowered. In 1975, Russell E. Train, the EPA administrator, postponed the standards yet another year, to 1978-1979 models. Train requested that Congress legislate postponement to 1982 models and recommended that the 1975-1976 interim standards apply to models through 1979. In return, the automobile industry would increase the fuel efficiency for models from 1974 to 1980.

To achieve the national ambient air quality standards, in 1974 the EPA divided air areas into three classes: class 1, in which very little air quality deterioration would be allowed; class 2, in which only moderate air quality deterioration would be allowed; and class 3, in which more significant deterioration would be allowed as long as ambient standards were not exceeded. Mandatory class 1 areas were international parks, natural wilderness areas, national memorial parks that exceeded five thousand acres, and national parks that exceeded six thousand acres.

The 1970 amendments also had geographic implications. Increments and ceilings for pollutant concentrations over baseline air quality levels were established for particulate matter and sulfur dioxide. In class 3 areas where baseline levels were low, the pollutant increments could be sustained, allowing growth to occur. Additional growth would be difficult in class 3 areas close to the national standards, as in older industrialized urban centers. No provision was made to allow construction of new sources or substantial expansion of old sources in nonattainment areas, areas that exceeded ambient air quality standards, after 1975. The lack of such a provision would have impeded economic development in some areas. An emission-offset policy to deal with the problem of new or expanded sources proposed by the EPA was not adopted until 1975.

IMPACT ON AIR QUALITY

In response to the Clean Air Act Amendments of 1970, the EPA set national standards for the six most prevalent air pollutants: sulfur dioxide, nitrogen oxides, carbon monoxide, particulate matter, hydrocarbons, and lead. According to a report by the National Council on Environmental Quality, annual emissions of lead declined by 96 percent between the 1960's and the 1990's, mainly because of the phaseout of leaded gasoline. Progress was also made in reducing sulfur dioxide, particulate matter, hydrocarbons, and carbon monoxide. Although emissions of sulfur dioxide and particulate matter had been increasing rapidly before 1970, the total national annual emissions of sulfur dioxide declined by 28 percent, and the emissions of particulate matter declined by 61 percent. Furthermore, total national hydrocarbons and carbon monoxide emissions declined by 28 percent and 38 percent, respectively. This prog-ress in controlling air pollution is especially noteworthy because the motor-vehicle population has grown faster than the human population—between 1970 and the mid-1990's, the number of vehicle miles traveled doubled from one trillion to two trillion miles.

The 1970 amendments also helped change the national attitude toward the environment and the federal government's role in protecting the environment. This new attitude suggested that environmental protection and economic development could be accomplished concurrently. The law changed the way government does business with the private sector. The 1970 act allowed indirect enforcement power by prohibiting federal agencies from obtaining goods, materials, or services from a source convicted of intentional violation of emission standards. In 1971, President Richard Nixon issued a presidential order prohibiting federal assistance to facilities not complying with the standards. Agencies such as Housing and Urban Development (HUD) and the Federal Highway Administration required that construction be compatible with the 1970 Clean Air Act.

With the responsibility for reaching the air quality standards resting largely with each state, the states slowly assumed more control over local municipalities and governments in an effort to meet those standards. States may prevent the construction or modification of sources the emissions of which are incompatible with attainment or maintenance of national ambient air quality standards. This is accomplished through a permit-letting process.

Major air-polluting industries have changed their location strategies. These industries are required to make relatively large investments in pollution-control equipment and maintenance. This is sometimes an important cost factor in the industrial site-selection process. For some firms, pollution-control requirements have resulted in the decision to close a plant or build a new facility, frequently at a different location. This is especially true in heavily industrialized nonattainment areas.

The 1970 Clean Air Act Amendments evolved from many earlier attempts to solve a national problem, the declining quality of the nation's air resources. Because the 1970 act was the first national effort to control and, when necessary, enforce air quality standards, there was some apprehension about the policy's success, but air quality monitoring data indicate that the nation's air quality has been improving since the enactment of the 1970 Clean Air Act Amendments.

Jasper L. Harris

SOURCES FOR FURTHER STUDY

Berry, Brian, and Frank E. Horton. "Managing Air Resources." In *Urban Environmental Management: Planning for Pollution Control*. Englewood Cliffs, N.J.: Prentice Hall, 1974.

Council on Environmental Quality. *Fourth Annual Report on Environmental Quality*. Washington, D.C.: Government Printing Office, 1973.

Greenberg, Michael J., et al. "Air Resources." In *A Primer on Industrial Environmental Impact*. Piscataway, N.J.: Center for Urban Policy Research, Rutgers University, 1979.

Library of Congress. Environmental Policy Division. *A Legislative History of the Clean Air Amendments of 1970*. 93d Congress, 2d session. Washington, D.C.: Government Printing Office, 1974-1980.

Paul, John A. "Urban Air Quality: The Problem." *EPA Journal* 17 (January/February, 1991): 24-26.

Rogers, Paul G. "The Clean Air Act of 1970." *EPA Journal* 16 (January/February, 1990): 21-23.

Thierman, Alan. "Air Pollution and the Expanding Consumption of Fuels in Internal Combustion Engines." In *Environmental Side Effects of Rising Industrial Outputs*, edited by Alfred J. Van Tassel. Lexington, Mass.: D. C. Health, 1970.

SEE ALSO: Air Pollution Control Act (1955); Clean Air Act (1963); Clean Air Act Amendments of 1977 (1977); Clean Air Act Amendments of 1990 (1990); Pollution Prevention Act (1990).

MINING AND MINERALS POLICY ACT

DATE: December 31, 1970
U.S. STATUTES AT LARGE: 84 Stat. 1876
PUBLIC LAW: 91-631
U.S. CODE: 30 § 21
CATEGORIES: Environment and Conservation; Land Management; Natural Resources

Congress approved a short, clear policy statement "to foster and encourage private enterprise" in the mining of minerals and metals while ensuring appropriate reclamation.

On the last day of 1970, Congress established the Mining and Minerals Act. It reaffirmed several concepts, including the United States' reliance on private enterprise to develop economically sound and stable mining industries as well as the need to consider reclamation and recycling. It did not essentially amend previous U.S. mining laws.

PREVIOUS MINING LAWS: FAVORING PRIVATE INDUSTRY

The General Mining Act of 1872 had stated that mineral reserves on public land were open to exploration and purchase by private individuals. This early law established guidelines for persons to stake out and acquire a claim. The Mineral Leasing Act of 1920 recognized that some deposits were impossible to work as small claims and allowed the federal government to lease public lands to developers. This promoted the mining of coal, oil, gas, oil shale, sodium, phosphate, potash, sand, clay, gravel, and sulfur on public lands. As a result of these early laws, mining in the United States remained a private industry. Transfer of property rights remained a matter of negotiation and mutual agreement. States provided additional regulations concerning mineral rights, right of access, and similar issues.

PROVISIONS OF THE 1970 LAW

The 1970 act confirmed that private enterprise was to continue to mine and reclaim minerals and metals. The rationale for further development was to serve the needs of industry, national security, and the environment. The act also encouraged the private sector to continue research in these fields, including research on recycling, disposal, control, reclamation of waste products and mined land, and other adverse impacts from mining on the environment. After asserting this policy position, the short act concluded by giving the secretary of the interior the responsibility for reporting to Congress on the state of domestic mining in a regular annual report.

By keeping the costs for mineral exploration, mine development, and eventually reclamation in the private sector, the Mining and Minerals Act kept the government from becoming deeply involved in an expensive and risky business. Regulatory agencies with inspectors, however, and research on health and safety unrelated to the development of mineral resources fell outside the private sector and required a funding source. Many of the acts that followed the 1970 Mining and Minerals Act therefore relied on general tax funds, although some expenses were charged to companies where appropriate. Some states levied property taxes, severance taxes, or production royalties. Because taxes were, however, often based on assessed value, companies could limit their exploration to minimize payments, which led to an underestimation of proven reserves.

Another aspect of keeping mining private was international economics. Private companies generally managed to produce and trade in a fluid and sometimes volatile international market, regardless of revolutions and diplomatic disputes. Occasionally, mineral-producing countries banded together to form consortia to control the supply and thereby the price of various commodities; this was done by the oil-producing countries of OPEC (Organization of Petroleum Exporting Countries) and the diamond-trading companies of deBeers. Although the United States desired to maintain mineral mining under private enterprise and free trade, many other nations preferred to run nationalized industries or to establish subsidies. Therefore, private-sector management of mining continued to be a very complex matter with both positive and negative effects.

ENVIRONMENTAL CONCERNS, ECONOMIC REALITIES

Although the 1970 policy statement was fairly clear in expressing the congressional intention to keep development of mining, reclamation, and recycling in the private sector, a substantial number of other acts and executive orders placed restrictions on the purchase of public lands and the disposition of certain permitted activities. Developers had to follow provisions of the Reclamation Act of 1902, the Wilderness Act of 1964, the Wild and Scenic Rivers Act of 1968, the National Trails System Act of 1968, the Coastal Zone Protection Act of 1972, a Protection of Wetlands order, the National Wildlife Refuge System Administration Act of 1966, the Forest and Rangeland Renewable Resources Planning Act of 1974, the Antiquuities Act, the Archeological and Historical Preservation Act, the National Historic Preservation Act of 1966, and others.

For example, with the implementation of the Wilderness Act of 1964, more than two-thirds of public lands were eventually closed or in some way restricted from mineral exploration and development. This was particularly true in Alaska, where public lands were a major portion of the land's purchase from Russia in 1867. Across the United States, mineral policy was altered. Private enterprise was still responsible for developing mineral resources, but the private sector had to supply minerals from an ever-shrinking portion of available public land.

In addition, more than one dozen environmental laws were enacted between 1970 and 1980 that restricted some mining activities to protect air and water quality. These included the Clean Air Act Amendments of 1977, the Water Pollution Control Act Amendments of 1972, the Noise Control Act of 1972, the Safe Drinking Water Act of 1974, the Federal Resource Conservation and Recovery Act of 1976, and the Uranium Mill Tailings Radiation Control Act of 1978. Acts that required disposal of wastes or discharges from mining operations included the Refuse Act of 1899, the Resource Conservation and Recovery Act of 1976, the Water Quality Improvement Act of 1970, the National Environmental Policy Act of 1969, and the very important Surface Mining Control and Reclamation Act of 1977.

Nevertheless, any good environmental intentions that could be read into the Mining and Minerals Policy Act were far less important than the day-to-day economic considerations. The volatile international energy market of the 1970's played havoc with any policies that lacked provisions for implementation. The price of coal, for example, fluctuated dramatically with the price of oil; in 1974, coal prices averaged $15 per ton but ranged from $7 to as high as

$70 per ton. When oil prices soared, the Federal Energy Administration required seventy-four power plants in operation to convert to coal fuel, and forty-seven plants under construction were required to incorporate coal-burning units that would meet Environmental Protection Agency (EPA) pollution controls. Consideration was also given to developing the technology to extract fluid fuels from coal. When, within a decade, oil prices dropped and coal prices fell as well, conversion systems were no longer cost-effective and the need for coal decreased. The only regulations that could survive in this era were those that recognized such economic realities.

LATER LEGISLATION

Standards for effective reclamation of surface coal mines were established in 1977 by the Surface Mining Control and Reclamation Act, which was in agreement with the policy of the 1970 Mining and Minerals Act. An average of twelve units of waste overburden was generated for every unit of coal removed, and the 1977 act required that all surface mining wastes, including the highwall and drainage patterns, be reclaimed. Acid drainage from abandoned underground mines was a major environmental problem; in Pennsylvania, however, surface mining of some of those areas effectively controlled much of that acid drainage. The real costs of reclaiming surface mines were difficult to assess but could range from $500 to $2,000 for regrading and from $300 to $1,000 for seeding and fertilizer. Over time, it became apparent that in some regions, particularly those where agriculture was not practiced, areas reclaimed from surface mining often become more valuable than adjacent nonmined areas.

Noncoal minerals usually generated far more than the twelve units of waste per unit of product, but most wastes were generated at smelters and mills where it could be more easily handled. Mineral wastes were generally "fluffed" in the extraction process to take up a larger volume of space, so a reclamation process that merely required backfilling often left huge amounts of wastes or spoils to be moved and disposed somewhere else. Many minerals generated toxic materials in the waste tailings that required special care in reclamation of mined areas; the Uranium Mill Tailings Radiation Control Act of 1978 addressed this problem.

John Richard Schrock

Sources for Further Study

Dennen, W. H. *Mineral Resources: Geology, Exploration, and Development.* New York: Taylor and Francis, 1989.

Fung, R., ed. *Surface Coal Mining Technology: Engineering and Environmental Aspects.* Park Ridge, N.J.: Noyes Data, 1981.

Hoppe, R., ed. *E/MJ Operating Handbook of Mineral Surface Mining and Exploration.* New York: E/MJ Mining Informational Services, 1978.

Rowe, James E. *Coal Surface Mining: Impacts of Reclamation.* Boulder, Colo.: Westview Press, 1979.

Schaller, F. W., and P. Sutton, eds. *Reclamation of Drastically Disturbed Lands.* Madison, Wis.: American Society of Agronomy, 1978.

Wali, M. K., ed. *Ecology and Coal Resource Development.* Vols. 1 and 2. New York: Pergamon Press, 1979.

See also: General Mining Act (1872); Mineral Leasing Act (1920); Wilderness Act (1964); Surface Mining Control and Reclamation Act (1977).

Lead-Based Paint Poisoning Prevention Act

Date: January 13, 1971
U.S. Statutes at Large: 84 Stat. 2078
Public law: 91-695
U.S. Code: 42 § 4801
Categories: Children's Issues; Health and Welfare

Alarmed by the widespread incidence of lead poisoning, particularly among children, Congress passed legislation limiting lead content in paint and authorized funds for cleanup.

The Lead Paint Poisoning Prevention Act authorized $30 million for the fiscal years 1971 to 1973, to be spent in three specific areas. The secretary of housing and urban development would receive approximately $5 million to determine the extent of lead-paint poisoning and evaluate methods by which lead-based paint might be removed from residential housing; $15 million would go to local governments for elimination of lead-paint hazards; and approximately $10 million would be provided for local governments to detect and treat lead-paint poisoning. The events that led up to the bill's passage were complex, and the aftermath of the bill's passage was disheartening for supporters.

THE DANGERS OF LEAD

The dangers of lead have been known since ancient times: The Roman scholar Pliny, for example, warned against using lead pots for winemaking. An outbreak of adult colic in Devonshire in the eighteenth century was traced to the use of lead vats for cider. The same ailment, exhibited in chronic form in tinkers and printers, was described by Benjamin Franklin. Painter's colic was widespread as late as the 1940's, when lead-based paint pigments began to be replaced by titanium oxide. Other adult manifestations of lead poisoning are high blood pressure, nephropathy (a condition in which the blood vessels of the kidneys are weakened), and at high lead levels permanent kidney damage. Acute lead poisoning can cause vomiting, cramps, dizziness and confusion, coma, and death.

Sources of lead exposure for adults are drinking and cooking water from lead plumbing or even copper plumbing, if joints have been carelessly soldered; canned foods, if cans are lead-soldered; air (less significant since alkyl lead antiknock additives have been banned from gasoline); upper layers of soil, which in some locations can still show the results of past use of lead arsenate as a pesticide; and paint, in both application and, more important, removal. Lead is present in paint as white lead, the basic carbonate, which was used for a century or more for its covering power and ease of tinting, and red lead, widely used in steel construction for its rustproofing properties. Many acute poisonings, in fact, are reported from the shipbreaking and building-wrecking industries, in which cutting of structures with welding torches vaporizes red lead into the atmosphere. Without effective protection, worker exposure is immediate and considerable. Lead is also found in paint, in relatively minor quantities, as the lead salts of certain organic acids, which are used as driers in oil-based paint.

Risks to Children

For children, the single most important source of lead is paint—
old paint, from pretitanium years. Such paint is found on walls and
woodwork, furniture, handles of tools and cooking utensils, and
floors, and even in the dirt at foundation edges, where rain has
washed chalking paint from exterior walls. Children are uniquely
at risk from these things, particularly young children up to about
the age of five years, because they chew things, put things into
their mouths, or in the case of those with a disorder called pica, in-
gest various nonfood materials such as dirt or paint chips. A well-
layered paint chip can contain many milligrams of lead. Intestinal
absorption is not complete, averaging about 20 percent, the rest
being excreted; ingestion of many chips by an organism the size of
a two-year-old, however, can raise blood-lead levels to the range of
40 micrograms per deciliter, where poisoning effects are noted in a
matter of weeks or even days.

The earliest and mildest symptoms in childhood lead poisoning
are, unfortunately, all too easily mistaken for many typical childhood diseases: vomiting and stomach pains, headaches, listlessness,
or irritability. A physician who is not familiar with lead poisoning
may diagnose a virus or anemia. Only when neurological symptoms,
such as loss of muscle movement, begin to manifest does it become
clear that something more is wrong. Blood tests at this point can
show lead levels in excess of eighty micrograms per deciliter, and
hospitalization for lead-lowering treatment is indicated. Such treatment can mean simply a period in the lead-free hospital environment or treatment of blood with chelating agents to remove lead.
Beyond this level, coma and an extended hospital stay are likely. Of
the children who have recovered from lead poisoning, most return
to the environment that they came from, and second and third
bouts of poisoning are not uncommon. As one physician sourly
noted, this cycle in effect puts the children in the position of being
test instruments to diagnose a problem that is not medical but environmental: The house or apartment is lead-poisoned and should
be treated. The only effective treatment is removal of paint down
to the underlying structural surface. New paint or wallpaper does
not suffice because the child often chews right through it.

The immediate effects of lead poisoning are not its only consequences. The majority of lead-poisoned children show long-term
neurological damage that includes attention-deficit disorder, im-

pulsive or disruptive behavior, lowering of academic performance, and sometimes deterioration of vision. Hearing loss has been demonstrated at blood-lead levels that show no threshold, only a progressive loss at greater levels. One carefully controlled study showed a statistically significant drop in intelligence quotient (IQ) at blood levels as low as eleven micrograms per deciliter. In very severe circumstances of loss of intellectual capacity, children must be committed to public institutions—a final irony, because many such facilities are housed in ancient buildings with decades of lead-paint buildup on the walls, thus presenting the children with the means to exacerbate their problems.

PASSAGE AND IMPLEMENT OF THE LAW

All these factors were known or suspected at the time the Lead Paint Poisoning Prevention Act was passed. For this reason, it proceeded handily through both houses of Congress and was signed into law two weeks later by President Richard Nixon.

With the passage of the act, the scientific input effectively ceased, and the political and economic issues surfaced. The first roadblock to enforcement of the act was Health, Education, and Welfare Secretary Eliot Richardson's refusal to ask Congress to appropriate any of the authorized $30 million. He was categorically opposed to giving targeted funds to states, preferring block grants that could be used according to local priorities, thus avoiding construction of a new bureaucracy with the targeted funds. It was not made clear how lead-clearance money administered through local health and housing authorities would lead to a separate bureaucracy, but Richardson held up appropriations until fiscal 1973. For that year, he proposed an appropriation of only $2 million; the eventual appropriation was only $7.5 million, or one-half of the original provision of the act. As a side issue at the time, Representative William Ryan, one of the lead-paint bill's sponsors, and a number of interested private citizens filed a petition with the Food and Drug Administration asking it to invoke its existing authority under the Hazardous Substances Act to limit amounts of lead in new paint to trace quantities, a proposal eventually adopted.

COMMUNITY ACTION AND STATE LAWS

Meanwhile, many states were beginning to enact their own lead-control legislation, particularly eastern states with old, crowded cities such as Boston, New York, Detroit, and Chicago (although it should be pointed out that lead-paint poisoning was never confined to inner-city tenements; children in reasonably affluent suburbs suffered as well). The experience of the Commonwealth of Massachusetts serves as an example. As early as the 1960's, Boston newspapers uncovered hospital records showing the extent of lead-paint poisoning among children. Testing and lead-removal programs were called for, but the Housing Inspection Department refused to do more than provide educational leaflets, thus shifting the burden of protection to relatively powerless individual citizens. Pressure on the department eventually resulted in its bringing a number of landlords to court for sanitary-code violations, but they were released with minuscule fines and no requirement to remove the lead found in their properties.

Citizen groups and the Boston Department of Health began to call for state legislation to correct the problem. A screening program on children's blood-lead levels had been conducted using funds from the National Institutes of Health and the City of Boston, and it was agreed that this was a good if minimal start to a state program. When it became clear in 1971 that the federal government would offer little, if any, help, the Lead Poisoning Prevention and Control Act was pushed through the Massachusetts legislature by the end of that year.

This did not solve the problem. It was more than a year before a director of the prevention program was appointed; the entire program sagged from administrative inaction, and in the second year its budget was cut by nearly one-fifth. A combination of refusal by landlords to spend large amounts of money for complete lead removal and the unwillingness of local authorities to take the time and money to take violators to court slowed the program to a near halt. Over the years, the situation has improved somewhat, with landlords cooperating voluntarily or with a minimum of prodding from the slowly strengthening local health and housing administrations. Children, however, are still being poisoned in large numbers by lead paint.

LONG-TERM EFFECTS

The Massachusetts pattern has been repeated, with variations, in many other states, and it is reflected at the national level. Textbooks on the hazards of lead in the 1980's and 1990's still cite lead paint as the main source of childhood lead poisoning. When, during his first administration, President Bill Clinton's health reform bill was being formulated and debated, medical authorities said that any bill that was enacted should provide funds for routine screening of children's blood-lead levels. Federally mandated programs were proposed for that purpose, but the only related action appears to have been a computer tracking system to correlate existing data.

An entire industry has grown up that specializes in the removal of lead paint in housing of all kinds. The fact that a large-scale commercial operation exists suggests that the demand for such services is fairly widespread. A new source for childhood lead poisoning has been discovered, however: paint dust from removal activities. A number of verified cases have been reported, and in early 1994 a Milwaukee child won a settlement of $1.5 million for his poisoning as the result of paint removal. Lead paint and its removal pose threats to health and must be monitored to ensure ongoing progress in the battle against contaminants.

Robert M. Hawthorne, Jr.

SOURCES FOR FURTHER STUDY

Craig, Paul P. "Lead, the Inexcusable Pollutant." *Saturday Review* 54 (October 2, 1971): 68-70, 75.

Featherstone, Joseph. "The 'Silent Epidemic.'" *New Republic*, November 8, 1969, 13-14.

Jones, Hubert E., ed. *State of Danger: Childhood Lead Paint Poisoning in Massachusetts.* Boston: Massachusetts Advocacy Center, 1974.

Lansdown, Richard, and William Yule. *Lead Toxicity: History and Environmental Impact.* Baltimore: The Johns Hopkins University Press, 1986.

Needleman, Herbert L., ed. *Human Lead Exposure.* Boca Raton, Fla.: CRC Press, 1992.

Oskarsson, Agneta. *Exposure of Infants and Children to Lead.* Rome: Food and Agriculture Organization of the United Nations, 1989.

SEE ALSO: Hazardous Substances Labeling Act (1960); Consumer Product Safety Act (1972); Toxic Substances Control Act (1976).

TWENTY-SIXTH AMENDMENT

DATE: Ratified July 1, 1971; certified July 5, 1971
U.S. STATUTES AT LARGE: 85 Stat. 825
PUBLIC LAW: 91-285
CATEGORIES: Constitutional Law; Voting and Elections

The Twenty-sixth Amendment awarded voting rights to those aged eighteen and older, infusing a powerful new constituency into the U.S. electorate.

In the colonial America, most colonies adopted the English practice specifying twenty-one years of age as the minimum voting age. A lower age was allowed only for men voting on militia officers. A uniform lowering of the voting age was debated as early as the New York Constitutional Convention of 1897. By 1942, when the U.S. Congress discussed it in relation to lowering the draft age to eighteen years of age, the notion had acquired significant public support. Between 1925 and 1964, nearly sixty proposals had been introduced in Congress.

PROS AND CONS

The argument most often advanced for lowering the voting age— and the principal argument during the first period (1941 to 1952) of the thirty-year movement—was youth's forced military participation. In 1942, the Selective Service and Training Act lowered the draft age to eighteen years. Between fall, 1942, and October, 1944, several joint resolutions were introduced in Congress to lower the voting age by amending the Constitution, and forty resolutions were introduced in thirty states. The 1944 Democratic National Convention included voting age as a plank in the party platform, and the issue was the 1943-1944 national school debate topic. Interest escalated; from 1945 to 1952, nearly one hundred bills were introduced in the legislatures of more than forty states.

President Dwight D. Eisenhower endorsed the measure in his January, 1954, state of the union message. In 1956, he again urged a constitutional amendment. During this period, youth's military service was still a major argument. In Senate debate on the issue, in April, 1943, it was argued that because the nation had interrupted the careers and jeopardized the lives of eighteen-year-olds, it should honor their sacrifices by extending them the vote. Senator Hubert H. Humphrey argued that the measure would get youth to participate in politics at a point when they were interested in and enthusiastic about government, lessen voter apathy, and broaden the base of democracy by adding a large number of voters.

Several widely varying arguments against lowering the voting age were advanced in 1953: Youth younger than twenty-one years of age did not have the wisdom and experience to evaluate political issues and would espouse the views of their parents; youth should obtain both schooling and experience before exercising the vote, rather than learning from the experience of voting; the parallel between military service and voting is false, because soldiers need only uncritical obedience and physical, not intellectual, maturity; youth do not have enough knowledge of the country's history and are susceptible to the appeal of radicalism; since the U.S. government is representative, the voice of youth could be heard through their elders, who elect legislators; and the argument "old enough to fight, old enough to vote" does not enfranchise women and suggests that those too old to fight should lose the right to vote.

During the second phase of the movement (1953 to 1960), arguments generally related to youths' cognizance of their political place in society. In 1954, a quiz was conducted by the American Institute of Public Opinion. On seven questions testing basic political knowledge, persons between eighteen and twenty-one years of age did much better than adults.

THE 1960's YOUTH VOTE MOVEMENT

In 1967, Senator Jennings Randolph of West Virginia introduced his eighth joint resolution for a constitutional amendment to lower the voting age to eighteen years; his first had been in 1942. That same year, more than one hundred measures were introduced in thirty-six state legislatures, and a Gallup poll showed support at an all-time high: 64 percent of adults and youth. In 1968, President Lyndon Johnson proposed that Congress submit a constitutional amendment for ratification by the states—the second such proposal from a president. Richard Nixon, in his 1968 campaign for president, promised youth "a piece of the action." Late that same year, a youth movement called Let Us Vote (LUV) was founded by Dennis Warren, a student at the University of the Pacific in Stockton, California. In six weeks, the sophisticated, widely publicized campaign expanded to more than three thousand high schools and four hundred colleges in all states. The Youth Franchise Coalition (of which LUV was a member) was organized on February 5, 1969. It used the multiple strategies of working through state legislation, a constitutional amendment, and separate campaigns mounted by member organizations. In 1968, the Republican Party called for state action to lower the voting age, while the Democratic platform endorsed a constitutional amendment. In April, 1969, a survey found that 93 percent of U.S. representatives favored the cause, as well as most federal and state senators. In this final phase of the movement, youth's strategy of active insistence on being enfranchised was making a difference.

Additional rationales for the measure surfaced during this period. Those who defended the existing age restrictions, it was argued, should prove that eighteen-year-olds, as a group, lacked the knowledge and maturity to vote responsibly and that allowing them to vote would damage the system of responsible government. Others argued that the real objective of the states should not be to limit the vote to those best informed but to see that all voters were reasonably well informed. Statistics and surveys showed that, as a result of improvements in education and mass communication, eighteen-year-olds were at least as well informed as twenty-one-year-olds had been when that minimum age was established. Voting rights cases had argued that all who have a stake in an election should be allowed to vote. This point added relevance to the "old enough to fight, old enough to vote" rhetoric. Men between eighteen and twenty years of age were the most vulnerable to conscription and to career disruption, injury, and death in wars; and elections arguably have an impact on war and peace.

Public Law 91-285 and the Amendment

On March 11, 1970, Senate Majority Leader Mike Mansfield introduced Amendment 545 to the Voting Rights Act of 1965. The amendment, cosponsored by Senator Edward Kennedy, would lower the voting age to eighteen years in all elections. Kennedy's support was buttressed by the opinions of several esteemed constitutional lawyers—in particular, Archibald Cox, whose 1966 article in the *Harvard Law Review* suggested a statutory amendment, as opposed to the cumbersome constitutional amendment process.

The bill passed, and President Nixon signed Public Law 91-285 into law on June 22, 1970. A test case against the law was filed in district court that same day. In 1970, seventeen states, three jurisdictions, and the U.S. Supreme Court assessed youth's suitability for the vote. On December 21, 1970, the latter upheld in law in respect to presidential and congressional elections, but found it unconstitutional for state and local elections. Nevertheless, on January 1, 1971, millions of youth gained the right to vote in national elections when they turned eighteen years of age.

On January 25, 1971, Senator Jennings Randolph introduced a joint resolution to amend the Constitution to allow eighteen-year-olds to vote. On March 10, the Senate passed the resolution unanimously. The House passed it on March 23, by a vote of 400 to 19. In eight days, ten states had ratified the amendment. On June 30, 1971, Ohio became the thirty-sixth state to ratify the amendment; thus the Twenty-sixth Amendment to the U.S. Constitution became law.

Glenn Ellen Starr

SOURCES FOR FURTHER STUDY

Congressional Digest. "The Question of Lowering the Voting Age to Eighteen." 33, no. 3 (March, 1954): 67-95.

Cultice, Wendell W. *Youth's Battle for the Ballot: A History of Voting Age in America.* New York: Greenwood Press, 1992.

Johnson, Julia E., comp. *Lowering the Voting Age.* New York: H. W. Wilson, 1944.

Roth, Robert. "A Rapid Change of Sentiment." *Annals of the American Academy of Political and Social Science* 397 (September, 1971): 83-87.

Vile, John R. *Encyclopedia of Constitutional Amendments, Proposed Amendments, and Amending Issues, 1789-1995.* Santa Barbara, Calif: ABC-CLIO, 1996.

SEE ALSO: U.S. Constitution: Provisions (1787); Direct democracy laws (1913); Voting Rights Act of 1965 (1965).

ALASKA NATIVE CLAIMS SETTLEMENT ACT

DATE: December 18, 1971
U.S. STATUTES AT LARGE: 85 Stat. 688
PUBLIC LAW: 92-203
U.S. CODE: 43 § 1601
CATEGORIES: Land Management; Native Americans

Native Alaskans received compensation in return for relinquishing their claims to lands they had historically occupied.

The Alaska Native Claims Settlement Act (ANCSA) was signed into law by President Richard M. Nixon on December 18, 1971. It represented the culmination of a long struggle over native land claims that was compounded by the immediate need to construct a pipeline to carry oil from Prudhoe Bay to Valdez through lands claimed by Native Alaskans.

NATIVE RIGHTS

In 1960, Native Alaskans constituted roughly 20 percent of the Alaskan population. For those living in native communities or villages, life consisted of subsistence hunting and fishing, which necessitated access to large amounts of land. Many were seasonally employed and lived in poverty. Seventy percent had less than an elementary education, and only ten percent had received a secondary education. Owing to disease, alcoholism, and impoverished conditions, the life span of Native Alaskans was about thirty-five years of age, half the national average. Many Native Alaskans believed that existing laws, rather than protecting them, stripped them of rights to lands that they claimed. They generally did not consider either the state or the federal government to be supportive of their concerns.

Land claims had long been a disputed issue between Native Alaskans and the U.S. government. A Supreme Court ruling in 1955 declared that the Fifth Amendment to the Constitution did not protect native land rights. When Alaska became the forty-ninth state of the Union in 1959, it was granted the right to select 103.3 million acres of land over the next twenty-five years without any acknowledgment of claims by Native Alaskans. Between 1959 and 1969, the state claimed nineteen million acres. By comparison, Native Alaskans owned only five hundred acres and had restricted title to another fifteen thousand acres. Since the state claimed nearly 28 percent of Alaskan territory, fears arose that there would be little valuable land remaining to satisfy native claims, and native opposition to state land claims intensified.

Some Native Alaskans believed that proposed use of their lands by the state or federal government would violate traditional rights enjoyed by the native inhabitants. The Atomic Energy Commission, for example, sought to use Cape Thompson as a nuclear testing site; it was situated near an Eskimo village, with a population of three hundred, at Point Hope and the ancestral lands the villagers used for hunting. Another issue under dispute was the proposed Rampart Dam, a hydroelectric project that was to be built on the Yukon River in the north-central region of the state. Opponents of the dam argued that it would damage wildlife breeding grounds, displace twelve hundred natives from seven small villages, and endanger the livelihood of five thousand to six thousand others who depended on salmon in that area. Finally, the state was beginning to legislate hunting restrictions on state-owned land, which natives believed would threaten their traditional way of life. In the early 1960's, native groups began to take action to protect their interests. Between 1961 and 1968, Alaskan natives filed claims protesting the state's use of 337 million acres of Alaskan territory.

FISHERIES, CANNERIES, AND OIL FIELDS

Two other groups who entered the contest over land claims were developers and environmentalists. Developers desired the construction of more fisheries and canneries, as well as highways and industries that would enable Alaska's natural resources to be fully developed. Environmentalists sought protection of certain lands as parks, natural wilderness areas, and wildlife refuges. By 1966, land disputes had become so hotly contested that Secretary of the Interior Stewart Udall ordered a freeze on all transfers of land claimed by the natives until a mutually acceptable agreement could be reached.

Following the discovery at Prudhoe Bay, on the North Slope of Alaska, of one of the largest oil fields ever found, the federal government proposed that a pipeline be constructed across the state to transport the oil to Valdez, a city easily accessible for loading petroleum because of its position as a year-round ice-free port on Prince William Sound. The proposed route of the eight-hundred-mile Trans-Alaska Pipeline included twenty miles of land that was claimed by Native Alaskans, who feared that construction of the pipeline would likely lead to other infringements of their land claims. By this time, however, the Alaska Native Brotherhood and the Alaska Federation of Natives, among other native groups, were well organized to press for their interests. It became evident that the land issue would have to be resolved before the pipeline was built.

Walter Hickel, Udall's successor as secretary of the interior, extended the land-freeze in 1970. A federal restraining order halted the project until a settlement could be reached. Because developers and oil companies were anxious to get the project under way, pressure was applied to settle the issue quickly. Other interested parties anticipated benefits from the construction of the pipeline, which promised lower petroleum prices to the federal government, revenue to the state, land preservation to environmentalists, and previously denied rights to natives, particularly title to land that they believed was theirs. British Petroleum, one of the interested parties, agreed to lobby for a bill that would protect native land interests. A joint Senate-House conference committee drew up the final bill, which gained widespread support. It passed Congress and was signed into law by Nixon on December 18, 1971.

PROVISIONS AND IMPLEMENTATION OF ANCSA

ANCSA granted forty-four million acres of land and $962.5 million to Native Alaskans in exchange for the relinquishment of their claims to the remaining nine-tenths of the land in Alaska. The law provided for an equitable distribution of funds among the three primary native groups (the Aleuts, Inuits, and Eskimos) and allowed first village corporations and then the regional native corporations, formed by the ANCSA, to select their lands. The Alaska Federation of Natives, speaking for the Alaskan native groups, accepted the settlement by a vote of 511 to 56, despite concerns about how it would affect traditional native patterns of hunting and fishing.

Twelve regional corporations were established between 1972 and 1974 (to which a thirteenth was added for natives not living in Alaska) in order to manage the funds and organize land selection. Every Alaskan native became a member of a regional corporation, in which he or she was given one hundred shares of stock. In addition, about 220 village corporations were formed to oversee the distribution of land at the local level. Native reservations were abolished, and sixteen million acres of land were set aside for selection by the village corporations.

The village corporations were allowed to select their land over a three-year period and the regional corporations over four years. Beneficiaries of the land claims were required to be one-quarter native Alaskan (either Inuit, Aleut, or Eskimo) and had to be born on or before December 18, 1971. While the land selection involved a lengthy process, native corporations eventually selected 102 million acres instead of the allotted 44 million. For twenty years after the passage of the act, Native Alaskans were not permitted to sell their stock to non-natives, and their undeveloped land was not to be taxed. In 1987, Congress passed the "1991 amendments," which preserved the tax-exemption benefits on undeveloped lands indefinitely and allowed new stock to be issued to Native Alaskans born after December 18, 1971.

IMPACT

ANCSA was, in many respects, a watershed in the history of Native Alaskans that promised to change their way of life permanently. The act began the transformation of Alaskan native cultures from a subsistence economy based on traditional hunting and fishing patterns to one based on ownership of modern business-for-profit ventures. Many Native Alaskans embarked on a difficult transition from life on reservations to membership in native corporations that undertook a variety of commercial enterprises. These corporations invested in banking, hotels, fisheries, real estate, and mineral exploration. Some were successful and some were not. Nevertheless, the acquisition of land and income gave Native Alaskans a position of influence in state politics that they had never had before.

Anne-Marie E. Ferngren

SOURCES FOR FURTHER STUDY

Anders, Gary C. "Social and Economic Consequences of Federal Indian Policy." *Economic Development and Cultural Change* 37, no. 2 (January, 1989): 285-303.

Arnold, Robert D., et al. *Alaska Native Land Claims.* Anchorage: Alaska Native Foundation, 1978.

Berger, Thomas R. *Village Journey: The Report of the Alaska Native Review Commission.* New York: Hill & Wang, 1985.

Berry, Mary Clay. *The Alaska Pipeline: The Politics of Oil and Native Land Claims.* Bloomington: Indiana University Press, 1975.

Case, David S. *Alaska Natives and American Laws.* Fairbanks: University of Alaska Press, 1984.

Flanders, Nicholas E. "The ANCSA Amendments of 1987 and Land Management in Alaska." *The Polar Record* 25, no. 155 (October, 1989): 315-322.

Strohmeyer, John. *Extreme Conditions: Big Oil and the Transformation of Alaska.* New York: Simon & Schuster, 1993.

SEE ALSO: Alaska National Interest Lands Conservation Act (1980).

FEDERAL ELECTION CAMPAIGN ACT

DATE: February 7, 1972
U.S. STATUES AT LARGE: 86 Stat. 3
PUBLIC LAW: 92-225
CATEGORIES: Voting and Elections

> *This act regulated the financing of campaigns, primaries, general elections, and political conventions, placing limits on advertising and contributions that were nevertheless circumvented later.*

The Federal Election Campaign Act (FECA) replaced and consolidated earlier federal law related to elections, especially the 1925 Federal Corrupt Practices Act, which included provisions for public disclosure of all campaign spending and contributions of more than fifty dollars, limitations on total campaign spending, and prohibitions of offers of patronage and government contracts to supporters. The 1925 act, which was enacted because of the Teapot Dome scandal, also prohibited all corporate contributions to political candidates.

FECA was proposed in 1971 and passed on February 7, 1972. This followed a decade of discussion of the issue following President John F. Kennedy's 1962 Commission on Campaign Costs, which urged full campaign disclosure to a new agency that would enforce violations. Later in the 1960's, President Lyndon Johnson recommended tax incentives for small contributions, and some proposed limited public financing of campaigns.

The 1971 act created a comprehensive framework of regulation of campaign financing of primaries, runoffs, general elections, and conventions. It required full and periodic disclosure of campaign contributions and spending to be filed with the House clerk and the Senate secretary. Presidential candidates and national parties were required to file with the comptroller-general. The act established limits on media advertising; established limits on contributions from candidates and their families; permitted unions and corporations to solicit voluntary contributions from members, employees, and stockholders; and allowed union and corporate treasury funds to be used to operated political action committees (PACs).

Related to the FECA was the Revenue Act of 1971. This act created limited public funding for presidential campaigns and allowed individuals a fifty-dollar tax deduction for contributions to political campaigns (eliminated in 1978).

The 1974 Federal Election Campaign Act Amendments substantially changed the 1972 act. With these changes, brought about by the Watergate scandal, the law now limited how much a campaign could spend as a whole as well as how much as individual or organization working independently of a candidate could spend on a particular race. Individuals could only give one thousand dollars per election per candidate and a total of twenty-five thousand dollars in federal elections. The 1974 amendments also established the Federal Election Commission.

In 1976 a divided Supreme Court ruled in *Buckley v. Valeo* that limits on campaign spending (but not limits on campaign contributions) were unconstitutional. This ended the limits imposed on candidates and family members in the 1972 act. The Court ruled that limits on spending could reduce "the number of issues discussed, the depth of their explanation, and the size of the audience reached."

There were amendments to the FECA in 1976 and 1979. The amount of money spent on political campaigns and the source of contributions continues to generate political controversy. This led the House and Senate to pass the Bipartisan Campaign Reform Act of 2002, which limited large contributions by individual donors to political parties.

Michael L. Coulter

SOURCES FOR FURTHER STUDY
Adamany, David, and George Agree. "Election Campaign Financing: The 1974 Reforms." *Political Science Quarterly* 90, no. 2 (Summer, 1975): 201-220.
Levit, Kenneth J. "Campaign Finance Reform (Case Note)." *Yale Law Journal* 103, no. 2 (November, 1993): 469-503.

SEE ALSO: Federal Corrupt Practices Act (1925); Bipartisan Campaign Reform Act (2002).

SEABED TREATY

DATE: Ratified February 15, 1972; in force May 18, 1972
CATEGORIES: Environment and Conservation; Foreign Relations; Treaties and Agreements

The treaty prohibited nuclear and other weapons of mass destruction on the seabeds of oceans and other bodies of water not within the twelve-mile territorial limits of a country.

Throughout the 1960's the two main rivals in the Cold War, the United States and the Union of Soviet Socialist Republics (or Soviet Union), negotiated a series of treaties and agreements that were believed to be mutually beneficial and conducive to more peaceful relations. One type of treaty sought to limit the competition from expanding into new areas. In 1967, the Outer Space Treaty was ratified to keep countries from using outer space for military purposes. Also in that year, a proposal was put forward by Malta to do the same for the ocean floor. The General Assembly of the United Nations established a committee to examine this proposal.

The committee, originally composed of eighteen members, was expanded in 1969. Although it was a multilateral committee, progress was dependent upon negotiations between the United States and the Soviet Union. As was typical of treaty proposals during this era, the initial proposal by the Soviet Union was for a broader and more comprehensive treaty, while the United States proposed a more specific, limited treaty. Once the initial statements were on the table, progress between the two countries was made fairly quickly, and a joint proposal was made in October, 1969, less than seven months after the initial Soviet proposal. However, as this was not to be a bilateral treaty, the needs and desires of the other members of the committee had to be considered in the final treaty.

It took another year to settle the concerns of the other countries. These dealt with how far out on the seabed territorial claims should be allowed (twelve miles) and how smaller countries could verify that the treaty was being observed without disregarding the rights of other countries to make legitimate use of the seabed (countries may request the assistance of other countries or international bodies to assist in the verification process). In December, 1970, a draft of the treaty was approved by the General Assembly. A process was established for the treaty to enter into force when more than twenty-five countries had ratified it. As of 2002, more than 110 countries had taken official action on this treaty.

The treaty was developed to prohibit the stationing of nuclear and other weapons of mass destruction on the seabeds of oceans and other bodies of water not within the territorial limits of a country. Within the twelve-mile limit defined in the treaty, countries may place any type of facility or weapons system desired. Beyond that limit, however, all facilities are subject to observation to determine if weapons of mass destruction are being placed. Mechanisms for reviewing the treaty and for coming into compliance with the treaty were established. The first meeting to make these determinations was scheduled five years after the treaty went into force, and meetings have been held periodically since that time.

Donald A. Watt

SOURCES FOR FURTHER STUDY

Keesing's Research Report. *Disarmament: Negotiations and Treaties 1946-1971.* New York: Charles Scribner's Sons, 1972.

Larson, Thomas B. *Soviet-American Rivalry: An Expert Analysis of the Economic, Political, and Military Competition Which Dominates Foreign Relations.* New York: W. W. Norton, 1978.

SEE ALSO: Outer Space Treaty (1967); Law of the Sea Treaty (1982).

WATER POLLUTION CONTROL ACT AMENDMENTS OF 1972

DATE: March 1, 1972
U.S. STATUTES AT LARGE: 86 Stat. 47
PUBLIC LAW: 92-240
U.S. CODE: 33 § 1251
CATEGORIES: Environment and Conservation; Natural Resources

These amendments to the original 1948 act (as amended in 1956) demonstrated Congress's willingness to continue to expand its protection of the national water supply.

Water-quality standards were initially established to control waterborne diseases, such as typhoid fever and cholera, and contamination of public water resulting from the careless use of chemicals and the heedless disposal of wastes. To combat these problems, early water-quality acts focused on the need to help local governments build water-treatment plants to filter out some pollutants and chemically neutralize others. The laws also allowed the federal government to take action against companies and local governments whose wastewater adversely affected other areas.

EARLIER LEGISLATION

The Federal Water Pollution Control Act of 1948, which was first amended in 1956, was implemented to protect public health and welfare and to improve the quality of the nation's water. The act increased the amount of federal money allocated to local governments to build water-treatment plants, and during the 1960's and 1970's many new sewer systems were funded by the federal government. The states had the primary responsibility for setting water-quality standards, which had to be approved by the Environmental Protection Agency (EPA). The state standards could be stricter than those of the EPA; conversely, the EPA could set a state's standards if they were not consistent with the act.

PROVISIONS OF THE 1972 AMENDMENTS

The Federal Water Pollution Control Act Amendments of 1972 were passed to "restore and maintain the chemical, physical, and biological integrity of the nation's waters." The amendments focused mainly on the control of surface water and the pollutants dumped therein, but they also included provisions to halt local development in wetlands. The amendments had three declared aims: to eliminate pollutant discharge by 1985; to restore water quality to the point that would enable safe fishing, swimming, and recreation by 1983; and to ensure that toxic pollutants were no longer dumped in large amounts. The amendments set limits for pollutants from a single source and standards for overall water quality, as well as inaugurating pollution records through National Pollutant Discharge Elimination System (NPDES) permits.

The 1972 amendments had five principal provisions that covered research and demonstration projects; grants for sewage-treatment plants; processes for implementing standards, inspections, and enforcement; establishment of the National Pollutant Discharge Elimination System (NPDES); and judicial terms and actions.

PERMITS FOR DUMPING OF EFFLUENTS

The most effective provision of the 1972 law was the establishment of NPDES permits for dumping effluents into the water supply; dumping of pollutants without a permit was prohibited altogether. The permits, which were administered by state environmental agencies and intended for direct point-source dischargers only, limited the amounts of pollutant to be dumped and enforced terms and conditions depending on the type of pollutant and the measures needed to restore water quality according to FWPCAA standards.

The NPDES permit process unfortunately had a significant loophole that allowed relaxed restrictions on renewed or modified permits. The relaxed standard went into effect if, for example, a plant's design changed or even simply if a polluter was unable to meet the original standard. A company could also seek a variance in the NPDES permits by arguing that potential cleanup costs would be too high.

The 1972 law defined several important concepts. The first was that a single source of pollution, also called a point source, is a specific and confined object that dumps pollutants into a stream or river; a point source could be a pipe, ditch, feedlot, boat, landfill, or other specific source. The second definition was that pollutants are any change in the water quality brought about by humans, whether harmful or not. Pollutants could be soil, sewage, garbage, chemicals, wrecked equipment, rock, sand, or even heat. Sewage and oil from ships were not included, nor were the chemicals injected into oil and gas wells to help the production process, or water from oil and gas production that was disposed legally in wells.

Discharged pollutants were defined as one of two types of effluent: those dumped directly into streams and rivers and those dumped into publicly owned treatment plants. The amendment established national standards for effluents considered unsuitable for normal treatment at water plants.

The 1972 amendments awarded grants to statewide waste-treatment and water-quality management plans. These grants ended in 1990, but new upgrading programs were started in 1989 in which local governments received loans for the construction of publicly owned treatment plants. The loans could also be used to control urban and agricultural runoff and to protect estuaries. Public water-treatment plants were required to meet secondary treatment levels of effluent by mid-1977; an extension of one year was possible if the plants were still under construction or if no federal money had been used for the treatment plant.

After the end of 1981, no further permits were issued for dumping sludge into the ocean. Public treatment plants could, however, get a variance from the regulation and dump sludge if the materials did not interfere with water-quality standards. The EPA had begun to set national standards for industrial-effluent discharges, but it had done so without considering the quality of the water that received the discharge. During one of its periods of understaffing, the EPA also omitted to regulate industrial discharge according to type of industry.

Effluent discharge was regulated nationwide in one of two ways. The less restrictive method, usually for the removal of conventional pollutants, was by the so-called "best practicable technology," or BPT. The standard set by the BPT was the average of the best technology in use at the time the law took effect. Before mid-1977, all effluents, except those from publicly owned water-treatment plants, had to be treated with that technology before being dumped. The more restrictive method was to remove toxic and nonconventional pollutants from wastewater by the "best available technology" or BAT. BAT standards were designed to raise the level of pollutant removal using the best current technology, and after 1983, BAT was the standard for all pollutant removal.

LATER LEGISLATION

Passage of the Federal Water Pollution Control Act Amendments of 1972 marked a turning point for increased federal involvement in national water-quality protection. The act was succeeded and strengthened by amendments in 1977, 1981, and 1987 as well as by a related law that targeted drinking water. Additional amendments were proposed but not passed in 1994.

In the 1987 Water Quality Act, Congress turned its attention to lakes, bays, and estuaries where fresh water meets the ocean. The act established the National Estuary Program, which called for comprehensive plans to protect certain estuaries, and various other programs to clean the Great Lakes and Chesapeake Bay. The 1987 act also addressed the problem of waters polluted with toxic chemicals and heavy metals, which despite BAT requirements had remained polluted. The act made states responsible for developing programs for dealing with toxic "hot spots," including specialized control strategies for individual areas. Each state was required to send the EPA a list of its problematic waters, as well as a plan for pollution control that included public water-treatment plants, river basins, and an overall water-quality inventory. The plans were to show the locations of the point sources that continued to contaminate.

A similar program was established for cleanup of polluted water from chemicals caught in runoff from rain. Large areas that contribute to water pollution, so-called nonpoint sources, include large mining and construction facilities, farms, and urban streets. Nonpoint-source pollution can account for between 45 and 75 percent of all water pollution.

An aspect of pollution that had not been addressed sufficiently in the original 1948 Clean Water Act was the problem of urban stormwater runoff. Because some city stormwater systems were connected to the general sewer systems, the sudden accumulation of water after heavy rains could result in untreated household wastes contaminating drinking water supplies. After the 1987 act, large and medium-sized cities were required to apply for stormwater permits. Cities with populations of more than 250,000 had to establish control plans and apply for the permit by early 1990; cities with populations between 100,000 and 250,000 were given until 1992 to design their plans and apply for the permit. In addition, most heavy industries were from then on required to have stormwater permits.

The revisions proposed to the Clean Water Act in 1994 included requiring smaller cities of 50,000 to 100,000 to obtain stormwater permits. The proposed amendment also expanded the definition of a body of water so as to include all wetlands, mudflats, wet meadows, and generally any water that could be used for recreation, fishing, or industrial use. Another proposed modification focused on controlling almost all excavations, no matter how small or temporary.

A federal law closely related to the Clean Water Act was the Safe Drinking Water Act of 1974, in which the EPA established standards for drinking water from any source that served more than twenty-five people or had more than fifteen connections to one water source. The drinking-water standards also limit the injection of chemicals into groundwater sources. It was possible for local governments to request a variance to the Safe Drinking Water Act on the grounds that a listed contaminant in the water did not pose a health risk, the water required no treatment, the city was using alternative treatment techniques with equally good results, or the city was unable to pay the costs. The EPA set up regulations for the entire nation, but the individual states developed their own plans for implementing and enforcing the regulations. They were also required to protect aquifers and the area around wells.

Because of the EPA's cumbersome process of implementation, most of the Safe Drinking Water Act's new standards for contaminants did not become effective until after the passage of amendments in 1986 that streamlined the process of implementation. The strengthened law also required that all chemicals known or expected to occur in drinking water be listed and that the water-treatment methods employed be the best affordable technology.

Elise M. Bright

SOURCES FOR FURTHER STUDY

Bonine, John E., and Thomas O. McGarity. *The Law of Environmental Protection: Cases—Legislation—Policies.* St. Paul, Minn.: West, 1984.

Freeman, Warren. *Federal Statutes on Environmental Protection—Regulation in the Public Interest.* Westport, Conn.: Quorum Books, 1987.

Library of Congress. Environmental Policy Division. *A Legislative History of the Water Pollution Control Act Amendment of 1972.* 4 vols. 93d Congress, 1st session. Washington, D.C.: Government Printing Office, 1973-1978.

Ortolano, Leonard. *Environmental Planning and Decision Making.* New York: John Wiley & Sons, 1984.

Tabb, William Murray, and Linda A. Malone. *Environmental Law—Cases and Materials.* Charlottesville, Va.: Michie, 1992.

SEE ALSO: Water Pollution Control Act (1948); Water Pollution Control Act Amendments of 1956 (1956); Water Resources Research Act (1964); Clean Water Act and Amendments (1965); Wild and Scenic Rivers Act and National Trails System Act (1968); National Environmental Policy Act (1970); Safe Drinking Water Act (1974); Marine Plastic Pollution Research and Control Act (1987).

EQUAL EMPLOYMENT OPPORTUNITY ACT

DATE: March 24, 1972
U.S. STATUTES AT LARGE: 86 Stat. 103
PUBLIC LAW: 92-261
U.S. CODE: 42 § 2000e
CATEGORIES: Education; Labor and Employment;

> *The Equal Employment Opportunity Act of 1972 was an omnibus bill appended to Title VII of the Civil Rights Act, which had been enacted on July 2, 1964, to meet a need for federal legislation dealing with job discrimination on the basis of "race, color, religion, sex or national origin."*

The 1964 Civil Rights Act was charged to enforce the constitutional right to vote, to protect constitutional rights in public facilities and public education, to prevent discrimination in federally assisted programs, and to establish an Equal Employment Opportunity Commission. Title VII did not, however, give comprehensive jurisdiction to the EEOC.

PREVIOUS LEGISLATION

A series of laws and executive orders had built up over the years to add to the momentum against discrimination in all areas of American life. With enactment of the Fourteenth and Fifteenth Amendments, the Civil Rights Acts of 1866 and 1875, and a series of laws passed in the mid- and late 1880's, the government and the president, in theory at least, gained sufficient authority to eradicate racial discrimination, including employment bias. No president, however, used his constitutional power in this regard. With the peaking of the Civil Rights movement in the early 1960's, the pace of progress toward equal opportunity accelerated. President John F. Kennedy's Executive Order 10925 established the Committee on Equal Employment Opportunity, the predecessor of the EEOC. Numerous other executive orders by succeeding presidents followed, each chipping away at discrimination in employment.

The first modern federal legislation to deal specifically with employment discrimination, however, was the Equal Pay Act of 1963.

As a result of this act, more than $37.5 million was subsequently found to be due to 91,661 employees, almost all of them women, for the years between 1963 and 1972. Then followed the momentous Civil Rights Act of 1964, which contained the provision for equal employment opportunity that would be expanded with the 1972 law.

DISCRIMINATION IN THE WORKPLACE

The push for the Equal Employment Opportunity Act was a natural result of many forces in the early 1970's: The economic disparity between white men, on one hand, and minorities and women, on the other, had become more apparent and disturbing. Women and minorities were generally last hired and first fired, with little chance for promotion. Yet, one-third of the U.S. workforce were women. Although most women worked in order to support themselves and their families, many people still considered their employment to be expendable and marginal. This was especially true for poor women, minority women, and female heads of households. Female college graduates earned only slightly more per year than the average white man with an eighth-grade education. In the 1960's, female heads of households were largely black women with one thousand dollars less than their white counterparts in annual median income. The median annual income for white women in 1971 was slightly more than five thousand dollars, and for nonwhite women, four thousand dollars. Blacks in general suffered more from lower salary and lower job security and benefits because, in part, they either were discouraged from joining or, in many cases, were not permitted to join labor or professional unions. In 1972, some 88 percent of unionists—about 15 million—were white, while only 2.1 million were from minority groups.

RESPONSE TO UNEMPLOYMENT

Another motivation to push for the act was unemployment. In 1971, the general unemployment rate was close to 6 percent as compared to 3.4 percent as recently as 1969. Rates of joblessness were highest among the veterans returning from Vietnam (12.4 percent), and in cities with high minority populations such as Jersey City (9 to 11.9 percent) and Detroit (6 to 8.9 percent). The U.S. Department of Labor reported in 1972 that one-fifth of all wage and salary earners were unionized and males outnumbered females four to one. The unemployment issue had plagued government and business ever since Congress passed the Employment Act of 1946, which declared, among other things, that it was federal policy to promote "maximum employment."

PASSAGE AND PROVISIONS

On March 13, 1972, the act was passed by Congress, and on March 24, it was signed into law by President Richard Nixon. Primary responsibility for eliminating employment discrimination was entrusted to the Equal Employment Opportunity Commission (EEOC). Congress increased EEOC's authority dramatically by giving it power to issue cease-and-desist orders, to receive and investigate charges, and to engage in mediation and conciliation regarding discriminatory practices. Jurisdiction of the EEOC was extended to cover all companies and unions of fifteen or more employees, private educational institutions, and state and local governments. The EEOC found broad patterns of discrimination. It resolved most of them and referred unresolved cases to the attorney general, who had authority to file federal lawsuits.

Affirmative action became one means to promote equal employment opportunity. It was a controversial measure from the start. Opponents of affirmative action viewed it as preferential treatment or "reverse discrimination," often invoking the decision in *Griggs v. Duke Power Company* (1971), in which the Supreme Court noted that Congress did not intend to prefer the less qualified over the better qualified simply because of minority origin. Proponents of affirmative action believed that when properly implemented, the policy did not do away with competition but, rather, leveled the playing field to create equal *opportunity* for jobs in hiring, on-the-job treatment, and firing policies. Affirmative action, according to proponents, meant a conscious effort to root out all types of inequality of employment opportunity, such as unrealistic job requirements, non-job-related selection instruments and procedures, insufficient opportunity for upward mobility, and inadequate publicity about job openings.

The U.S. Civil Service Commission provided technical assistance to state and local governments in developing affirmative action plans and provided training manuals for the purpose. The thrust of the act's guidelines, however, was that gender, racial, ethnic, national origin, or religious status alone should be avoided as an employment consideration. Women and minorities had taken the lead in getting the equal employment opportunity proposal through Congress, thus making it a women's and minority issue.

The act dealt with areas where discrimination had been blatant, such as hiring and promotion by small businesses and by police and fire departments, as well as admission to local unions such as branches of the longshoremen in the Northeast and Southeast. Discrimination in some areas was so blatant that the federal appeals courts actually had to order hiring of minorities to rectify the situation. For example, after the passage of the EEO, Minneapolis hired its first minority-group fireman in twenty-five years.

The act also dealt with various forms of discrimination against women, such as denying employment because there were no toilet facilities for women. The act required that women receive equal opportunities for sick leave, vacation, insurance, and pensions. It also became illegal to refuse to hire or to dismiss an unmarried mother as long as unwed fathers were holding jobs. Newspaper classified sections were no longer permitted to segregate help-wanted listings under male and female headings. Only a few jobs, such as that of actor, could be proved to have a *bona fide* occupational qualification on the basis of sex.

RESPONSE AND IMPACT

Opposition forces focused on the confusion created by the passage of the act. Many of the existing labor laws protecting women and minorities seemed to become invalid in the context of the act. For example, the classic prohibition on work that would require a woman to lift more than a specified maximum weight could not stand. Qualification for employment would have to be based on ability to meet physical demands, regardless of gender. Banning women from certain jobs because of the possibility of pregnancy appeared to be impermissible. Leaves or special arrangements for the rearing of children would have to be available to the father, if the couple decided he was to take over domestic duties. In fact, "Men's Lib" became a new trend in the 1970's. Women's campaigns for full equality prompted men to reassess their own situation. The result was that "liberation" was becoming an issue for both men and women.

Men began moving into jobs once reserved for women, seeking alimony from wives, and demanding paternity leaves. The Supreme Court ruled that airlines could not limit flight attendant jobs to women, and most airlines began hiring some male stewards. AT&T had filled 25 percent of its clerical positions and 10 percent of its telephone operator positions with men by 1974. More men enrolled in nursing schools. On the other hand, by the time the law was enacted in 1972, the fastest-growing type of family was that headed by a black woman. One decade later, in 1982, this figure had grown to 45 percent as compared to 14 percent for the white families headed by women in the same year.

The act worked in tandem with or initiated investigations into other areas of discrimination, such as education. For example, by the late 1960's, more than a decade after the Court struck down "separate but equal" laws, more than 75 percent of the school districts in the South remained segregated. This meant markedly disproportionate employment opportunities for blacks.

Armed with its new authority, field investigators, and two hundred newly hired lawyers, the EEOC was able to respond effectively to complaints of discrimination. Within a few weeks of assuming its new, authoritative position, the EEOC had filed suits against many big companies. The actionable charges of sex discrimination surged from 2,003 cases in 1967 to 10,436 by June of 1972. Sex discrimination cases, in only three years from 1970 through 1972, increased by nearly 300 percent. By June 30, 1972, however, only 22 percent of cases involved sex discrimination and 58 percent racial and ethnic discrimination, with 11 percent involving national origin and 2.5 percent religious discrimination. In 1972, the EEOC forced employers to give raises to some twenty-nine thousand workers, mainly women, after finding violations of the law. The total underpayment of wages amounted to about fourteen million dollars.

Much of the business sector objected to the EEOC's efforts, contending that the new law would permit employees to file class-action suits without the employer's being given fair notice of the identity of its accusers. Such criticism protested that as many as eight different laws gave employees an unfair advantage in pressing charges. Nevertheless, companies—including many large corporations that did work for the government—were forced to change their employment policies to comply, and the composition of the workforce began to change. The Equal Employment Opportunity Act, along with subsequent follow-on legislation, opened the door for many women, African Americans, and ethnic minorities to rise out of poverty and begin a movement toward middle- and upper-middle-class status that later would begin to change the power structure in the United States.

Chogollah Maroufi

Sources for Further Study

Belknap, Michal R., ed. *Equal Employment Opportunity.* New York: Garland, 1991.

Buckley, John F. *Equal Employment Opportunity Compliance Guide: 2002 Edition.* New York: Aspen Publishers, 2002.

Bureau of National Affairs. *Equal Employment Opportunity Act of 1972.* Washington, D.C.: Bureau of National Affairs Books, 1973.

Burstein, Paul. *Discrimination, Jobs, and Politics: The Struggle for Equal Employment Opportunity in the United States Since the New Deal.* Chicago: University of Chicago Press, 1997.

Downing, Paul M. *The Equal Employment Opportunity Act of 1972: Legislative History.* Washington, D.C.: Library of Congress, Congressional Research Service, 1977.

Sedmark, Nancy J., and Chrissie Vidas. *Primer on Equal Employment Opportunity.* 6th ed. Washington, D.C.: Bureau of National Affairs Books, 1994.

Shulman, Stephen N., and Charles F. Abernathy. *The Law of Equal Employment Opportunity.* Boston: Warren, Gorham & Lamont, 1990.

U.S. National Labor Relations Board. *Titles VII and XI of Civil Rights Act of 1964 and the Equal Employment Opportunity Act of 1972.* Buffalo, N.Y.: William S. Hein, 1978.

See also: Equal Pay Act (1963); Civil Rights Act of 1964 (1964); Title VII of the Civil Rights Act of 1964 (1964); Economic Opportunity Act (1964); Pregnancy Discrimination Act (1978); Women in Apprenticeship and Nontraditional Occupations Act (1992).

SALT I TREATY

DATE: Signed May 26, 1972
CATEGORIES: Foreign Relations; Treaties and Agreements

The negotiation of SALT I marked the beginning of the end of the Cold War between the United States and the Soviet Union.

When détente (literally, "relaxation") became the prevailing framework of Soviet-U.S. relations in the early 1970's, neither its meaning nor its implications were clear. On the surface, its most important result was a series of nuclear arms agreements—with corollaries in trade, education, space research, and more—between the United States and the Soviet Union, beginning with the first Strategic Arms Limitation Talks (SALT I) Treaty signed by President Richard M. Nixon and Soviet leader Leonid I. Brezhnev in Moscow in May, 1972. At a deeper level, it reflected a new and more pragmatic turn in the long history of the Cold War: Among European and Middle Eastern peoples, détente aggravated fears that the two superpowers would freeze their strategic options, thus precluding genuinely credible deterrence to protect them. By its very nature, détente, as manifested in SALT I, was encouraging to some and troublesome to others. Two other SALT treaties followed, culminating in the SALT III pact. SALT III was signed by President Jimmy Carter and Brezhnev in 1979 but never ratified by the U.S. Senate because of Soviet suppression of Jews and dissidents.

HISTORICAL PERSPECTIVE

From the beginning, the SALT treaties, and even the notion of détente between the vastly different nuclear age superpowers, appeared contradictory and one-sided to those who considered it another ruse by the communists to lull the United States into dangerous passivity. Others, notably Senator Henry "Scoop" Jackson and exiled Soviet dissident writer Aleksandr Solzhenitsyn, believed that détente lowered the Soviet Union's risks of conflict while allowing it to continue building up its military and suppressing all political and ideological opposition at home. That the Soviet Union signed the 1975 Helsinki Accords, thus ostensibly endorsing the section called Basket III, which theoretically guaranteed basic human and civil rights in the contracting countries, did not convince those who did not trust Soviet sincerity.

Détente was a significant chapter in the history of global politics. Fundamental changes have marked the world of diplomacy in the twentieth century, including a steady and dramatic reduction in the number of true world powers. In 1900, the power bases in world politics were multipolar: Germany, Austria-Hungary, czarist Russia, Great Britain, France, and the United States all were engaged in empire-building. Similarly, between the two world wars, Nazi Germany, Japan, Great Britain, and the temporarily isolationist United States occupied prominent positions as world powers. World War II, however, narrowed the field effectively to two major world powers—the United States and the Soviet Union—thus marking the advent of a bipolar world after 1945.

Bipolarism dominated the diplomacy of the Cold War years following World War II. Although the Soviet Union under Joseph Stalin's regime had been allied with the United States and Great Britain during the war, it was clear to most contemporaries of the war years that the alliance was one of convenience. At war's end, the world split into two basic camps, one allied with the Soviet Union, one with the United States. Tension increased markedly as the Communist Bloc was expanded by force in Eastern Europe and China. By the 1950's, the Cold War had erupted into a real conflict in Korea (1950-1953) and in the military alliances of Western nations in the North Atlantic Treaty Organization (NATO) and Eastern nations in the Warsaw Pact. Both sides ultimately were backed by the awesome power of nuclear weapons.

The Cold War, with its periodic military outbursts (the Bay of Pigs, Laos, Vietnam), had been characterized by military expenditures on both sides of the conflict throughout the 1950's and 1960's. This arms race had been the most massive in all of human history. The Soviet Union had given top social and economic priorities to military spending during these decades, at the obvious expense of civilian, consumer-oriented production. At the same time, the United States had given top priority to its defense expenditures, at the expense of its own social needs. This had led since the late 1960's to attempts by both Soviet and U.S. leaders to effect a rapprochement, or détente. The primary aim of this policy was to reduce the arms race and military tension in the world between the United States and the Soviet Union. In general, mistrust prevailed and worked against thorough cooperation. As long as the Soviet Union was ruled by an oppressive communist political structure, the United States and other supporters of détente had serious reservations, as did the Soviet leadership. Any concessions by one side or the other were viewed from the framework of national rather than mutual interest. Therein lay the greatest weakness of détente.

NIXON, KISSINGER, AND LINKAGE

The first active application of the détente policy originated during the presidency of Richard M. Nixon. Although Nixon clearly initiated the policy, detailed negotiations were the work of Henry A. Kissinger, the key diplomatic figure of the Nixon presidency. Kissinger came to the administration from an academic background. A German-Jewish refugee from Nazi Germany, Kissinger had fully assimilated himself through the United States Army and as a student and faculty member at Harvard, where he gradually developed into an activist scholar who sought to influence foreign policy with his theory. He came to the public limelight through his friendship with Nelson Rockefeller. Based on his loyalty to Richard Nixon, once he entered Nixon's administration, Kissinger came to dominate the foreign policy of the Nixon years, both as national security adviser and as secretary of state.

Nixon and Kissinger both had excellent credentials for redirecting United States policy toward the Soviet Union. Both were conservatives and arch-foes of communism. If a liberal Democratic administration had proposed détente in earlier decades, it likely would have faced a massive Cold War backlash in public opinion. Liberals, in effect, could not push for Soviet-U.S. agreements without suffering politically. A conservative such as Nixon, on the other hand, could strike up negotiations with the Russians without fanning domestic fears that he was "soft on communism."

The key concept launched by Kissinger and carried through in the presidency of Jimmy Carter was the insistence of the United States on linkage in any agreements with the Soviet Union. "Linkage" meant that any trade agreement, exchange program, credit—in effect, any concession—must be accompanied by (linked to) changes in Soviet policy. During the Kissinger years, the United States insisted on the elimination of ideology from Soviet foreign policy decisions. In negotiating the first Strategic Arms Limitation Treaties (SALTs I and II), the United States used its improved relations with Chairman Mao Zedong's China as leverage with Brezhnev's negotiators. In addition, the United States obtained Soviet aid in ending the Vietnam War through negotiations by tying the negotiations to SALT's prospects.

FORD AND CARTER

After SALT I, the United States linked ties with the Soviets to human rights for people in the Soviet sphere, but this effort bore little fruit until the rise of Mikhail Gorbachev as Soviet leader in 1985. Official commitment to détente waned after Nixon was forced to resign in 1974 in the wake of the Watergate scandal. His successor, Gerald Ford, visited the Soviet Union and continued the SALT negotiating process, but with less success than Nixon and Kissinger. President Carter's policy of upholding and reaffirming human rights had few tangible results in the short run, which contributed to the Senate's refusal to ratify SALT II. The Soviet Union further eroded détente by deploying large numbers of its new, mobile SS-20 missiles targeted on all major European cities. That, more than the Soviet invasion of Afghanistan in December, 1979, disillusioned Carter and prompted him to cancel U.S. participation in the Olympics in Moscow in 1980.

REAGAN, GORBACHEV, AND START

Linkage, the cornerstone of détente, seemed to have reached its limits. The Soviet Union would not eliminate ideological considerations in either its domestic or foreign policies until the advent of Gorbachev as Soviet leader in March, 1985, and even then, only on a limited basis. Despite the 1975 Helsinki Accords, Soviet suppression of dissidents continued almost unabated until Gorbachev's *perestroika* (restructuring) opened the door to *glasnost* (publicity or openness), which invited public discussion and criticism of government policies. Under Gorbachev, détente took new turns, notably a more intense U.S. and Soviet interest in arms reduction. President Ronald Reagan, an old-style Cold Warrior, moved from his first term's blistering rhetoric, such as calling the Soviet Union an "evil empire," to a more accommodating position. This was reinforced by his projected Strategic Defense Initiative (SDI, popularly known as "Star Wars"), which aimed to protect the world from nuclear weapons through an elaborate system of space and land-based lasers that would provide a shield against incoming missiles.

Reagan proposed START (the Strategic Arms Reduction Talks) to replace the faltering SALT agreements, but a series of Reagan-Gorbachev summits in the middle 1980's foundered on Soviet fears that SDI would neutralize their nuclear deterrence and violate earlier SALT agreements. Nevertheless, the détente process continued as Gorbachev and his popular foreign minister, Eduard Shevardnadze, pursued arms reductions, and the subsequent administrations of Ronald Reagan and George H. W. Bush remained open to credible, adequately guaranteed and equitable reductions. The most important tangible products were the INF (Intermediate Nuclear Force) Treaty of late 1987, which eliminated an entire class of nuclear weapons; the START Treaty of July, 1991; and the START II Treaty (January, 1993), negotiated by Bush and implemented early in the administration of President Bill Clinton.

The Soviet Union was officially dissolved on December 26, 1991, with its East European Warsaw Pact allies already in disarray as communist regimes crumbled in that region. Détente outlived the Soviet Union, and the vision of a world safe from nuclear war again gained ground.

More than a declining Soviet system and U.S. vigilance, however, contributed to this radically new and unexpected twist of history. In retrospect, it is clearly important that Gorbachev and Shevardnadze made substantive changes of a scope that few would have believed possible in the early days of détente. The role that détente played in the overall process is not easy to estimate. What is clearer is that the long détente process contributed to new thinking about world peace and the national interests of the Soviet Union, the United States, and their allies. If the future of arms control has been uncertain in the post-Soviet period, there is little doubt that it will remain a pivotal concern of most nations, because of the continuing existence of thousands of nuclear weapons and the possibility that they might fall into the hands of states or individuals less restrained by Cold War considerations than the United States and the Soviet Union were for decades.

Edward A. Zivich, updated by
Thomas R. Peake

SOURCES FOR FURTHER STUDY

Gorbachev, Mikhail. *Perestroika: New Thinking for Our Country and the World.* Updated ed. New York: Perennial Library, 1988.

Kissinger, Henry A. *American Foreign Policy.* New York: W. W. Norton, 1969.

_____. *Diplomacy.* New York: Simon & Schuster, 1994.

Landau, David. *Kissinger: The Uses of Power.* Boston: Houghton Mifflin, 1972.

Nixon, Richard M. *RN: The Memoirs of Richard Nixon.* New York: Grosset & Dunlap, 1978.

Ulam, Adam B. "Forty Years of Troubled Coexistence." *Foreign Affairs* 64, no. 1 (Fall, 1985): 12-32.

SEE ALSO: SALT II Treaty (1979); INF Treaty (1987); START II Treaty (1993); U.S.-Russia Arms Agreement (2002).

INDIAN EDUCATION ACTS

DATE: June 23, 1972; November 1, 1978
U.S. STATUTES AT LARGE: 86 Stat. 343 (1972), 92 Stat. 2329 (1978)
PUBLIC LAW: 92-318 (1972), 95-561 (1978)
CATEGORIES: Education; Native Americans

These acts represent the first legislative victories for Native American peoples under the policy of Indian self-determination.

The Indian Education Act of 1972 was an attempt to remedy some of the problems in Indian education identified in the National Study of American Indian Education (carried out from 1967 to 1971) and in the hearings of the Special Senate Subcommittee on Indian Education that summarized its findings in 1969 under the title *Indian Education: A National Tragedy, a National Challenge* (also known as the Kennedy Report). Both studies found that Indian people wanted a better education for their children, wanted schools to pay more attention to Indian heritage, and wanted more to say in how their children's schools were run.

The 1972 act pertained to public schools on and off reservations and provided supplemental funding for schools with ten or more Indian students in order to meet their special needs. All public schools with Indian students could get this quasi-entitlement funding and were required to involve Indian parents and communities in designing the supplemental programs. Grant money was also provided.

Part A of the act required parental and community participation in impact-aid programs (programs that provided federal money to local school districts to make up for tax-exempt federal lands such as Indian reservations). Part B authorized a series of grant programs to stress culturally relevant and bilingual curriculum materials. Part C provided money for adult-education projects. Part D established an Office of Indian Education within the U.S. Office of Education (now the Department of Education). Part E provided funds for training teachers for Bureau of Indian Affairs (BIA) schools, with preference to be given to Indians. The act also established the National Advisory Council on Indian Education.

The Indian Education Amendments of 1978 established standards for BIA schools, institutionalized BIA school boards, required formula funding of BIA schools, and provided for increased Indian involvement in the spending of impact-aid funds.

Jon Reyhner

SOURCES FOR FURTHER STUDY

Cleary, Linda Miller. *Collected Wisdom: American Indian Education.* Boston: Allyn & Bacon, 1998.

Dejong, David H. *Promises of the Past: A History of Indian Education.* Golden, Colo.: North American Press, 1993.

Deloria, Vine, and Daniel Wildcat. *Power and Place: Indian Education in America.* Golden, Colo.: American Indian Graduate Center, Fulcrum Resources, 2001.

Stein, Wayne J., ed. *Renaissance of American Indian Higher Education: Capturing the Dream.* Mahwah, N.J.: Lawrence Erlbaum, 2002.

Szasz, Margaret Connell. *Education and the American Indian: The Road to Self-Determination.* 1928. Rev. ed. Albuquerque: University of New Mexico Press, 1999.

SEE ALSO: Higher Education Act (1965); Bilingual Education Act (1968); Equal Employment Opportunity Act (1972); Comprehensive Employment Training Act (1973); Education for All Handicapped Children Act (1975); Indian Self-Determination and Education Assistance Act (1975).

TITLE IX OF THE EDUCATION AMENDMENTS OF 1972

DATE: June 23, 1972
U.S. STATUTES AT LARGE: 86 Stat. 373
PUBLIC LAW: 92-318
U.S. CODE: 20 § 1681
CATEGORIES: Education; Women's Issues

This law was the first federal legislation in the United States to prohibit sexual discrimination in educational institutions and agencies.

Title IX of the Education Amendments of 1972 states that "No person in the United States shall, on the basis of sex, be excluded from participation in, be denied the benefits of, or be subjected to discrimination under any education program or activity receiving Federal financial assistance." Male and female students must be given equal opportunity and treatment in admissions, curricular and extracurricular programs and activities, student benefits and services, and employment.

WHY TITLE IX?
Testimony at congressional hearings before the passage of Title IX documented the pervasiveness of direct and indirect sexual discrimination in educational institutions

For example, secondary vocational schools were often completely segregated on the basis of gender. Financial assistance was distributed unevenly, with women less likely to receive awards. At some colleges, rules required female students to live on campus while male students could live off campus. Discriminatory policies affected hiring and promotions so that women with advanced degrees were not working in jobs that matched their qualifications. Men's and women's athletic programs were not equal in size or quality, availability of coaching, equipment, or facilities.

OBJECTIVES

The regulations to implement Title IX, which became effective on July 21, 1975, specified five tasks for educational institutions: first, to state the policy of sexual nondiscrimination in all school and employment documents; second, to appoint an employee to coordinate compliance efforts; third, to develop a grievance procedure for student and employee complaints; fourth, to conduct an institutional self-evaluation to assess current practices and institute new policies; and, fifth, to submit an assurance form of the Office for Civil Rights with all applications for federal financial assistance. Institutions were required to take both remedial and affirmative action if sexual discrimination was determined to exist. Exemptions applied to schools that were traditionally single-sex or that held religious tenets that prevented compliance.

IMPACT

Title IX has eliminated the most blatant discriminatory practices in education, especially in admissions. Colleges can no longer set higher admission standards for women than for men, and graduate schools cannot use the "equal rejection rate" system that ensured acceptance of equal numbers of men and women even when women might be more highly qualified. Placement in courses in all subjects, including vocational, technical, and advanced courses, cannot be determined by sex, and institutions are required to take remedial action through recruiting and course revisions to ensure that access is open.

Title IX was especially felt in athletics. There was a tremendous increase in the number of women participating in school sports. The percentage of female high school athletes increased from 7 percent to 35 percent between 1972 and 1982, and girls' teams were included in local, state, and national high school organizations. In 1971, the Association for Intercollegiate Athletics for Women was formed as an independent organization; eventually, membership grew from 278 to 973 institutions by 1979-1980. Between 1971 and 1980, the percentage of female college athletes increased from 15 percent to 30 percent. Many institutions voluntarily expanded their women's athletic programs prior to the passage of Title IX or following the self-studies required for implementation in 1975-1976. Teams were created, schedules were expanded, and more money was budgeted for travel and equipment. State, regional, and national championships were added. Coaches of female teams began to be compensated at a higher level, although they were usually required to also fill teaching and administrative roles. Perhaps most significant, there was a general change in attitude about the importance of sports activities for girls and young women.

LIMITED SUCCESS

Beyond admissions and athletics, Title IX has had limited impact on other sources of gender bias: curriculum, classroom procedures, the interaction between male and female students, and faculty support. Assumptions that female students are gifted verbally and male students are gifted in science and mathematics prevail, and most young women are not encouraged to take courses that provide entry to scientific and technical fields. Many vocational programs are still segregated by sex, with change stymied by the virtual lack of role models for women or men outside of a narrow range of occupations. Moreover, although sexual harassment is prohibited under Title IX, schools often do little to prevent such behavior.

By the mid-1990's, women still did not have equal opportunity in sports programs and may have actually lost ground. While women generally formed 50 percent of the student body at various institutions, they made up only 33 percent of college athletes. At the high school level, women accounted for 39 percent of athletes. The number of female coaches had declined significantly. With improved salaries, men applied for jobs coaching female teams. In 1972, more than 90 percent of the coaches for women's college teams were women; in 1990, only 47.3 percent were women. Traditional female sports such as volleyball or field hockey were being coached by men or eliminated from the schedule. The two fastest growing sports between 1977 and the 1990's were soccer and cross-country running, but the percentage of female coaches in these sports continued to decline. Women had not moved into jobs coaching male teams; in the 1995, 99 percent of male college teams were coached by men. Women also lost leadership roles: When men's and women's athletic departments were combined, often the head of the men's department became the chief administrator. The same was true for sports officials. As the payment for officiating at an athletic contest increased for women, the number of female officials decreased, especially in women's basketball, softball, and volleyball. In sports media, women have a limited, usually insignificant role. Women are writing about and broadcasting women's sports, but they have made little progress in covering male sports, often because they lack access to the locker room.

WOMEN'S REACTION

Despite the opening of opportunities by Title IX, many women believe that real progress can only be made by changing the practices that limit women and men to traditionally accepted areas of study, work, and play, which requires effective monitoring of programs and strong enforcement of Title IX. Women are calling for a renewed commitment to this law in order to improve the quality of public education for everyone. Schools and teachers need to use methods that promote gender equity and include the experiences of women in the curriculum. National boards and professional organizations should include women as part of reform efforts.

Female athletes must continue to work to overcome the same problems that existed in 1972. Reformers call for compliance with Title IX as a precondition for membership in the National Collegiate Athletic Association (NCAA). They also seek more scholarships for women and the appointment of female athletic administrators to regulate and evaluate women's athletic programs.

Jeanne M. McGlinn

SOURCES FOR FURTHER STUDY

Durrant, Sue M. "Title IX: Its Power and Its Limitations." *Journal of Physical Education, Recreation, and Dance* 63 (March, 1992): 60-64.

Hoepner, Barbara J., ed. *Women's Athletics: Coping with Controversy.* Washington, D.C.: American Association for Health, Physical Education, and Recreation, 1974.

National Foundation for the Improvement of Education. *Title IX: Selected Resources.* Washington, D.C.: Government Printing Office, 1977.

Wellesley College. Center for Research on Women. *How Schools Shortchange Girls: A Study of Major Findings on Girls and Education.* Washington, D.C.: AAUW Educational Foundation and National Education Association, 1992.

Westervelt, Esther Manning. *Barriers to Women's Participation in Postsecondary Education: A Review of Research and Commentary as of 1973-74.* Washington, D.C.: Government Printing Office, 1975.

SEE ALSO: Economic Opportunity Act (1964); Higher Education Act (1965); Bilingual Education Act (1968); Equal Employment Opportunity Act (1972); Comprehensive Employment Training Act (1973); Women in Armed Services Academies Act (1975); Women's Educational Equity Act (1978).

FEDERAL ENVIRONMENTAL PESTICIDE CONTROL ACT

DATE: October 21, 1972
U.S. STATUTES AT LARGE: 86 Stat. 975
PUBLIC LAW: 92-516
U.S. CODE: 7 § 136
CATEGORIES: Environment and Conservation

This law was passed to protect the environment from the effects of toxic chemicals.

The prosperity and the relative good health of the U.S. population are based in part on the nation's ability not only to grow an abundance of basic crops but also to store harvests effectively. Crop losses resulting from insect activity, fungal infections, and rodent invasion are often as devastating to the human population as is a lack of productivity. Insecticides, fungicides, and rodenticides have been critical to the maintenance of the quantity and quality of grains, fruits, and vegetables produced, stored, and transported in the United States. In addition, pesticides are vital to the protection of wooden homes from termites, clothing from clothes moths, and museum artifacts from a wide array of fungal and insect agents.

THE FEDERAL INSECTICIDE, FUNGICIDE, AND RODENTICIDE ACT

The Federal Insecticide, Fungicide, and Rodenticide Act of 1947 (FIFRA) established basic requirements for the labeling of pesticide products. This act was an attempt to ensure that pesticides were effective as claimed and to protect users, mainly farmers, by requiring that specific safety instructions be posted on product labels.

At the time that FIFRA was enacted, the use of dichloro-diphenyl-trichloroethane (DDT) had prevented repetition of the World War I-era deaths from louse-born typhus and had offered some hope of dramatically reducing malaria worldwide. Increasing numbers of chemical agents, particularly chlorinated hydrocarbon insecticides, were becoming available for farm use. Using chemicals to reduce crop losses was viewed by the general public hardly different from the use of penicillin to overcome infections. The 1947 act was thus primarily intended to protect the safety of farmers, who were the main applicators of pesticides, and to provide some degree of truth in labeling. The long-term environmental effects of some pesticides that persist in the environment was not well understood until much later, following the 1962 publication of Rachel Carson's *Silent Spring.*

PROVISIONS OF THE 1972 LAW

In 1972, the Federal Environmental Pesticide Control Act (FEPCA) made substantial revisions in FIFRA that gave it an environmental dimension. The critical change was the provision that the pesticide, "when used in accordance with widespread and commonly recognized practice will not generally cause unreasonable adverse effects on the environment." Such "unreasonable adverse effects" were further defined in the act as "any unreasonable risk to man or the environment, taking into account the economic, social, and environmental costs and benefits of the use of any pesticide." FIFRA was no longer viewed as an act to protect farmers from harm; adverse effects on humans became simply one of many environmental effects.

The 1972 FEPCA revision continued to control pesticide sales by way of label requirements and required the administrator of the Environmental Protection Agency (EPA), formed two years earlier, to consider the environmental impact of the use of pesticides for the uses proposed on the label. This addition expanded FIFRA from an act regulating pesticide use to an environmental protection act by way of controlling the labeling and registration process. In 1972, Congress directed that each pesticide be classified as either "restricted" or "general use." In addition, specific uses of pesticides could be classified as either "general" or "restricted."

GENERAL VS. RESTRICTED USE

If used according to the label instructions, general-use pesticides can be applied by anyone, and no additional training or certification is required of the user. A general-use pesticide, however, is often restricted in the sites where it can be used. For example, paradichlorobenzene moth balls are registered for home use, in which a few moth balls are usually isolated in closets and drawers away from people; however, the same chemical is not legal for use in museums, where employees would constantly be working around higher concentrations built up in often-used specimen cabinets.

Restricted-use pesticides may be applied only by certified applicators or persons working under their direct supervision. Pesticides that are highly toxic require specially trained applicators. A pesticide may also be restricted, however, if it persists in the environment for a long period. Common insecticides thus disappeared from store counters because they were too persistent in the environment, because they were found to have adverse health effects, or because they required specialized application gear.

DEFINITION OF "PEST"

According to FIFRA, the term "pest" encompasses not only insects, rodents, and fungi but also roundworms, weeds, and any other aquatic or terrestrial animal, plant, or microorganism declared by the EPA administrator to be a pest because of its effects on health or the environment. Viruses, bacteria, and other microorganisms on or in humans or other animals are not considered pests. A pesticide is thus defined as any substance that prevents, repels, or destroys such pests. Pesticides may be chemical or biological substances; a pesticide may be merely considered as active ingredient or may consist of a complex formulation. Attractants, repellents, defoliants, and plant regulators are all pesticides.

LABELING REQUIREMENTS

The pesticide registrant has specific duties to label the product after it is produced. It is a violation to remove or deface the usage instructions that are required on a pesticide container. If pesticides are purchased in large quantity, the label is to be copied and transferred to the containers to be used in application.

Because the major leverage for regulating pesticides centers on labeling, the contents of the label are set by regulation. The nine items that must appear on the label include the product name, the name of the producer, the net contents, the product registration number, the producer-identifying number, the ingredient statement, exact warning statements, directions for use, and use classifications.

The ingredient statement lists active and inert ingredients of the pesticide, similar to the ingredient labels often seen on food packaging in grocery stores. The warning statement is considerably more complex than the ingredient statement, because a chemical can pose different levels of damage if exposed to skin or eyes, or if inhaled or ingested. Pesticides, therefore, must be extensively evaluated in animal tests to establish levels of 50 percent lethal dosage for skin contact or ingestion (a level known as LD) or lethal concentration if inhaled (known as LC). With four levels of toxicity for each of five hazards, a pesticide must be labeled with warnings indicating the highest hazard. The large signal words used to flag the level of danger range from the most dangerous, "poison," to the least alarming, "caution."

All pesticides rated category 1 poisons must also provide a statement of practical treatment or first aid on the front panel of the product label; products in other categories may print the treatment elsewhere on the label. Warnings of potential hazard to humans and domestic animals must also be included on labels, as must a notice stating if other nontarget organisms are particularly endangered. Because some pesticides are petroleum-based or pressurized, warnings about flammability and danger from explosion may also be required.

The directions for use must include legible and simple instructions that protect the public from injury and fraud and that avoid adverse effects on the environment. Such directions include site of application, target pests, dosage or rate of application, method of application, frequency of application, and limitations on re-entry to the area where the pesticide has been applied. Storage and disposal instructions are particularly critical for preventing environmental contamination. The statement of use classification advertises boldly whether the pesticide is classified for general use or restricted use. This last designation requires a follow-up statement that clearly states that the pesticide is for retail sale only to certified applicators.

Storage-facility criteria are provided for the most toxic pesticides. Mobile equipment must follow general procedures for decontamination, maintenance, and inspection. Safety precautions are mandated, including both accident-prevention measures and ongoing safety measures for persons working in the distribution and handling of pesticides. For specific highly toxic pesticides, periodic physical examinations, including cholinesterase tests, are required of persons working with pesticides. Fires involving pesticides can present particularly dangerous scenarios, and storage of large quantities of pesticides require the notification of local fire-fighting personnel to ensure preparedness.

EXEMPTIONS

Exemptions from the complex FIFRA regulations are allowed when a pest outbreak occurs posing dramatic economic or health threats and when there is not enough time to seek registration of an appropriate pesticide. With the increasing availability of fast international travel and the rise in pesticide resistance, such problems seem more likely to arise in the future.

CERTIFICATION STANDARDS

Most important, FIFRA established standards for certification of commercial applicators for the use of restricted pesticides. The testing of an applicator's competency is based on problems and situations relevant to the applicator's certification. In addition to the use of the pesticide in various formulations, certified applicators must be knowledgeable about the label data, safety procedures, environmental concerns, and laws and regulations relating to the pesticide being used. There are provisions for experimental-use permits for the purpose of gathering data on new pesticide formulations and applications.

SUBSEQUENT LEGISLATION

Minor amendments to the act were made in 1975, but in 1978 the Federal Pesticide Act changed FIFRA considerably, establishing a generic registration procedure that required a standardized evaluation of the benefits and risks of active ingredients of pesticide products. The prior act had required registration of each chemical based on its brand name; however, the same chemical is often marketed under many brand names.

Additional extensive amendments in 1988 fine-tuned procedures for registration of pesticides and for canceling or removing pesticide registrations. The 1988 amendments empowered the EPA to set deadlines for manufacturers to reregister pesticides containing newly regulated ingredients. A fee based on market factors was also assessed pesticide applicants to help underwrite a portion of the cost of reviewing pesticide reapplications.

Congress authorized the use of a scientific advisory panel to assist the EPA in evaluating and regulating pesticides. Subpanels of this group review major scientific studies relevant to pesticides and consult in the reclassification of pesticides. It is sometimes necessary to take immediate action when new research reveals that a pesticide has unexpected harmful effects. The EPA administrator can promptly suspend or change registration on a pesticide; this is called an emergency suspension action. Any emergency suspension, however, requires an immediate peer review. In cases in which such an action leaves a registrant holding a large quantity of pesticide, the administrator is authorized to compensate the registrant for the loss.

Procedures exist for the recall of pesticides determined by the EPA to be more hazardous than first recognized. In such cases, producers must notify the EPA administrator of the location and the amount of the canceled or suspended pesticide. Pesticide containers and rinsing agents are also regulated, and penalties for falsifying records or data submitted in support of applications are defined in the act.

IMPACT

FIFRA, FEPCA, and their amendments provided uniform criteria for pesticide regulation on a nationwide scale. The responsibility for registering a pesticide is with the manufacturer, not with the user. No person in any state may sell, ship, or receive any pesticide that is not registered with the EPA, regardless of whether the activity is carried out within a state or across state lines. (There are provisions allowing a manufacturer to transport a nonregistered pesticide for disposal when it has been canceled or while it is in an experimental stage of development.) States retain the right to register pesticides in each state, and a state may impose more stringent restrictions. States may not, however, allow sale or use of a pesticide if the pesticide is prohibited under the law.

The act directs enforcement power to the EPA. For those states that hold a cooperative agreement with the EPA, the state assumes primary enforcement responsibility. Provisions of these acts allow the administering government agency to seek both criminal and civil sanctions against companies, individuals, and organizations that violate provisions of the law. The EPA may inspect for violations, issue orders to require compliance, and seek court injunctions to require compliance. Knowingly violating provisions of the law is a misdemeanor.

Examples of violations include failure to submit required information, falsification of records, and failure to observe the various orders canceling or suspending pesticide use. Individuals who advise pesticide applicators to use illegal pesticides are considered to be in violation of the law. It is also unlawful to use any registered pesticide in a manner inconsistent with its label, although it is legal to dilute pesticides to lower concentrations or to use them against alternative pests or by other methods of applications if such uses are not specifically prohibited. As with any system that must deal with the complexity of the environment and the limitations in scientific knowledge, however, the enforcement of these laws is open to considerable prosecutorial discretion.

Passage of FIFRA and its amendments was a response to the real need for effective insecticides, fungicides, and rodenticides as well as to the need to protect the populace and the environment from the damaging effects of toxic and long-lasting chemicals. The law mandates the use of the current expertise of the scientific community to maintain a fair and reliable system of regulation for the pesticide industry.

John Richard Schrock

SOURCES FOR FURTHER STUDY

Carson, Rachel. *Silent Spring.* Boston: Houghton Mifflin, 1962.

Edwards, Clive A. *Persistent Pesticides in the Environment.* 2d ed. Cleveland, Ohio: CRC Press, 1973.

McGregor, Gregor I. *Environmental Law and Enforcement.* Boca Raton, Fla.: Lewis, 1994.

Russell, Irma S. "Federal Statutes and Regulations Governing the Use of Pesticides and an Annotation of Federal Pesticide Regulations." In *A Guide to Museum Pest Control,* edited by John R. Schrock and Lynda A. Zycherman. Washington, D.C.: Association of Systematics Collections and Foundation of the American Institute for Conservation of Historic and Artistic Works, 1988.

Ware, George W. *Pesticides: An Auto-tutorial Approach.* San Francisco: W. H. Freeman, 1975.

SEE ALSO: Hazardous Substances Labeling Act (1960); Solid Waste Disposal Act (1965); Toxic Substances Control Act (1976).

MARINE MAMMAL PROTECTION ACT

DATE: October 21, 1972
U.S. STATUTES AT LARGE: 86 Stat. 1027
PUBLIC LAW: 92-522
U.S. CODE: 16 § 1361-1421h
CATEGORIES: Animals; Environment and Conservation; Natural Resources

This legislation provided safe environments for marine mammals.

The United States Marine Mammal Protection Act (MMPA) prohibits ownership or importation of any marine mammal or any of their products. However, it does allow a limited catch by Eskimos, American Indians, and Aleuts for purposes of material survival or cultural heritage. An amendment was added in 1994 to restructure jurisdiction and enforcement of laws and to establish guidelines for transportation of marine mammals. Controversies exist among fishing interests, environmentalists, and cultural societies as to the interpretation and effects of the MMPA.

When the MMPA became law in 1972, the Fish and Wildlife Service (FWS), which is part of the Department of the Interior, became responsible for manatees, dugongs, polar bears, walruses, and sea otters. The National Marine Fisheries Service (NMFS), a division of the Department of Commerce, was assigned management of whales, dolphins, sea lions, fur seals, elephant seals, monk seals, true northern seals, and southern fur seals.

AMENDMENTS

The 1994 amendment stipulated stronger fishing regulations, especially the use of improved equipment to reduce the number of accidental killings of marine mammals and to exclude the by-catch of turtles, nontarget fish, and undersized fish of the targeted species. Before the amendment, jurisdiction over care and transport of captive marine mammals was jointly shared by the NMFS and the Department of Agriculture's Animal and Plant Health Inspection Service (APHIS). The amendment eliminated the NMFS's part of the administration and enforcement, which has caused concern in the environmental community because the Department of Agriculture officials do not have much experience working with marine mammals.

The Humane Society of the United States appealed for reinstatement of the NMFS as a joint authority, but APHIS was delegated as sole authority. Zoos and aquariums supported APHIS control, since that agency made it easier for marine mammals to be captured and transported. Public facilities that already own a marine mammal need only to send a notice to APHIS after acquiring additional mammals, whereas previously it was necessary to obtain a permit. Other changes brought about by the amendment ease regulations on scientists and researchers, who no longer need permits unless there is the potential of harm to a marine mammal. Ecologists also approve of the amendment because it places emphasis on maintaining healthy ecosystems, particularly in the northwestern and northeastern coasts of the United States where the seal and sea lion populations are declining at an alarming rate.

IMPACT ON SEA LIFE
Many of the human activities that threatened marine mammals in the past are now violations of the MMPA. Sea otters were over-hunted for their skins, but government protection has allowed their populations to recover around Prince William Sound and off the California coast. Whales are completely protected by the MMPA and the International Whaling Commission (IWC). However, the natural renewable resources on which the whales feed may be endangered since some countries are harvesting large quantities of krill, which is the mainstay of many whales' diets and is an important link in the marine food chain. As human populations increase worldwide and become more industrialized, demands on the oceans as a food source and a place to dump chemicals also increase. Noise disturbances come from sonic testing and boat traffic. Continued publicity and pressure from environmental advocates such as Greenpeace and the World Wildlife Fund (WWF) have led wildlife managers, fishers, animal rights supporters, and scientists to work together under the terms of the 1994 MMPA amendment.

Dale F. Burnside with
Aubyn C. Burnside

SOURCES FOR FURTHER STUDY

Reinke, Danny C., and Lucinda Low Swartz, eds. *Endangered Species: Legal Requirements and Policy Guidance.* Columbus, Ohio: Battelle Press, 2001.

Rodgers, William H. *Environmental Law.* 2d ed. St. Paul, Minn.: West Publishing, 1994.

Twiss, John R., Jr., and Randall R. Reeves, eds. *Conservation and Management of Marine Mammals.* Washington, D.C.: Smithsonian Institution Press, 1999.

SEE ALSO: Oil Pollution Act of 1924 (1924); Animal Welfare Act (1966); Endangered Species Preservation Act (1966); Coastal Zone Management Act (1972); Endangered Species Act (1973); Convention on International Trade in Endangered Species (1975); Convention on the Conservation of Migratory Species of Wild Animals (1979); Alaska National Interest Lands Conservation Act (1980); Marine Plastic Pollution Research and Control Act (1987).

COASTAL ZONE MANAGEMENT ACT

DATE: October 27, 1972
U.S. STATUTES AT LARGE: 86 Stat. 1280
PUBLIC LAW: 89-454
U.S. CODE: 16 § 1451
CATEGORIES: Environment and Conservation; Land Management

> *This act, along with the Marine Protection, Research, and Sanctuaries Act (1968), involved the federal government in environmental protection that had previously been considered an issue of local land use.*

In response to the increasing environmental awareness of the 1960's, Congress began to consider land-use issues that earlier would have been local decisions. By the close of the twentieth century, more than 75 percent of the U.S. population lived within one hour's drive of a coast. Over time, development had destroyed various aspects of the coastal environment through toxic contamination and an intrusion of saltwater into bodies of fresh water.

In 1972, Congress passed the Coastal Zone Management Act to protect the nation's valuable but threatened coastal areas. Congress cited several reasons for its decision to implement federal management, protection, and development of the coastal zones, including that the continued survival of the coastal areas was in the national interest; that the areas' rich resources would be valuable to future generations for natural, recreational, aesthetic, commercial, and industrial purposes; and that population growth and economic expansion had caused the disappearance of natural habitats for fish, wildlife, and plants, as well as permanent and adverse ecological changes. Coastal zone ecosystems are fragile and extremely vulnerable to human activities, and poorly planned developments and land-use regulations then in place had been inadequate to protect the coastal ecological systems from competing demands.

REGIONS OF JURISDICTION AND PROVISIONS

The act covered the coasts along the Pacific and Atlantic oceans, the Gulf of Mexico, the Great Lakes, Puerto Rico, the Virgin Islands, Guam, and American Samoa; the three-mile territorial waters also fall under the jurisdiction of the act, as well as parts of the Continental Shelf, which in some areas extends more than two hundred miles into the ocean. Coastal zones were broadly defined to include shoreland in areas where the land may have a direct impact on the coastal waters; the individual states were authorized to determine how much area to include in this category. In addition, the act allowed estuarine sanctuaries to be developed for research in areas where the rivers flow into the ocean.

The act established restrictive zoning—extremely intensive land uses, such as industrial uses, were, for example, generally prohibited—and it allocated federal grants to establish and administer programs in the individual states. States were made responsible for developing plans for the effective use of their coastal land. Congress mandated that the states were to implement conservation laws with unified policies and defined standards and methods, and that they were to work together with federal, local, and private interests in the protection of coastal lands and water.

GRANTS FOR COASTAL MANAGEMENT

Federal grants to states for establishing coastal management programs had a three-year limit; annual grant renewal required that the state identify the boundaries of the coastal zone in question; define the land and water uses permitted in the zone; develop an inventory and zone the critical areas; control the land and water use through relevant laws; indicate land uses in order of priority; and describe the interrelationships among local, regional, and state agencies responsible for the coastal zone.

A second federal grant to cover operating costs was to become available once a state's coastal management program was approved by the secretary of commerce. Both grants had certain rules about when and how much money could be spent in the state programs. States were required to hold public hearings, to be announced thirty days in advance; at the time of the announcement, all information on the coastal zone management program had to be made available to the public. The secretary of commerce was made responsible for reviewing the individual state programs, and he was empowered to terminate the grant of a noncompliant state.

MARINE PROTECTION, RESEARCH, AND SANCTUARIES ACT

The Marine Protection, Research, and Sanctuaries Act was passed by Congress in the same year as the Coastal Zone Management Act in response to the routine and continuous dumping of sewage sludge and industrial waste in offshore waters near major U.S. cities. To combat dumping and control pollution in waters within the United States, Congress had in 1899 enacted the Rivers and Harbors Act, and in 1948 the Water Pollution Control Act. These laws did not, however, directly address the problems resulting from dumping into the oceans, which was harmful to both human health and the marine ecosystems.

The Marine Protection, Research, and Sanctuaries Act specifically protected the ocean and some of the coastline areas, and it limited ocean dumping of any materials transported from the United States or transported in a U.S. ship or plane. The act defined "ocean" as the area beyond the three-mile territorial water surrounding the United States, Puerto Rico, the Panama Canal, and the U.S. Pacific Islands held in trust. Proscribed material included oil taken on by a ship or plane for the sole purpose of dumping and included, but was not limited to, garbage, sewage, industrial waste, military ammunition (including biological and chemical warfare agents), discarded equipment, chemicals, and excavation debris. Oil and sewage that ships or planes normally carry were excluded, as were radioactive materials regulated by the Atomic Energy Act and fish wastes resulting from commercial fishing.

The act required that anyone transporting materials for the purpose of dumping them in the ocean apply to the Environmental Protection Agency (EPA) or the Corps of Engineers for a permit; the two agencies were authorized to issue permits only for materials that do not harm the environment and only after holding public hearings on the application. The act made provisions for different categories of permits, and for different times and places for allowing dumping. The agencies were given a list of criteria to observe, including consideration of the possible effects on human health, marine life, and various ecosystems. If the secretary of the Corps of Engineers should disagree with the EPA administrator on the effects of proposed dumping, the EPA decision would go into effect. Individual permits were required to include precise information as to the nature and amount of the material to be dumped, and the dumping site. Violation of any of the specified guidelines carried stiff criminal and civil fines and penalties, including prison sentences.

The Marine Protection, Research, and Sanctuaries Act revoked all previous permits, unless the permit was under the 1899 Rivers and Harbors Act. The act also made provisions for research of the short- and long-term effects of ocean dumping, pollution, over-fishing, and changes to the ocean's ecosystems. In the last section of the act, the secretary of commerce was empowered to preserve parts of the marine environment as sanctuaries so as to conserve or restore them for their recreational, ecological, or aesthetic values.

IMPACT AND COURT DECISIONS
The Coastal Zone Management Act had an enormous impact in protecting U.S. coastlines. Although participation in the state programs was entirely voluntary, all states to which the act applied except Illinois developed coastal zone management plans and restrictions on coastal development. In some cases the federal legislation prompted state legislation with similar environmental protection. The California Coastal Act of 1972, for example, established a coastal commission with the authority to make land-use decisions in coastal areas even if the local government opposed the decisions.

The funds provided by the Marine Protection, Sanctuaries, and Research Act for the establishment of sanctuaries led to the designation of twelve new sanctuaries, with other areas expected to be considered for sanctuary status at a later time. The act also established centers for marine conservation; every year, center volunteers spent one day clearing tons of debris from the coastlines.

The Coastal Zone Management Act withstood a number of court challenges in the first dozen years. In the late 1980's, however, several legal decisions placed limits on the act's ability to restrict development. In the 1987 case *Nollan v. California Coastal Commission*, for example, the U.S. Supreme Court ruled that a building permit could not be denied simply because the landowner refused to grant public access across his beach; by requiring that the landowner be paid for the access easement, the Court laid the foundation for future challenges. In the 1993 case *Lucas v. the South Carolina Coastal Commission*, the Supreme Court ruled that a beachfront landowner must be paid when a new regulation is passed that prohibits the landowner from building. Although both of these cases limited the extent of protection provided by the act, it was expected that over time the federal legislation would save millions of acres of vulnerable marine life and shoreline lands.

Elise M. Bright

SOURCES FOR FURTHER STUDY
Bureau of National Affairs. *U.S. Environmental Laws.* Washington, D.C.: Author, 1988.
Fulton, William. *Guide to California Planning.* Point Arena, Calif.: Solano Press Books, 1991.
Gray, Oscar. *Cases and Materials on Environmental Law.* 2d ed. Washington, D.C.: Bureau of National Affairs, 1973.
Mandelker, Daniel R., and Roger A. Cunningham. *Planning and Control of Land Development: Cases and Materials.* Charlottesville, Va.: Michie, 1990.
Tabb, William Murray, and Linda A. Malone. *Environmental Law—Cases and Materials.* Charlottesville, Va.: Michie, 1992.
Weinberg, Philip. *Environmental Law: Cases and Materials.* Port Washington, N.Y.: Associated Faculty Press, 1985.

SEE ALSO: Oil Pollution Act of 1924 (1924); Water Pollution Control Act (1948); Water Pollution Control Act Amendments of 1956 (1956); Seabed Treaty (1972); Water Pollution Control Act Amendments of 1972 (1972); Port and Tanker Safety Act (1978); Marine Plastic Pollution Research and Control Act (1987); Oil Pollution Act of 1990 (1990).

CONSUMER PRODUCT SAFETY ACT

DATE: October 27, 1972
U.S. STATUTES AT LARGE: 86 Stat. 1207
PUBLIC LAW: 92-573
U.S. CODE: 15 § 2051
CATEGORIES: Business, Commerce, and Trade; Health and Welfare

The Consumer Product Safety Act established an independent agency of the federal government to investigate the causes of product-related injuries and to develop regulations to control their occurrence.

The Consumer Product Safety Act of 1972 (CPSA) established the Consumer Product Safety Commission (CPSC) as an independent agency of the federal government. The CPSC was given authority to identify unsafe products, establish standards for labeling and product safety, recall defective products, and ban products that posed unreasonable risks to consumers. In order to ensure compliance with its directives, the CPSC was given authority to impose civil and criminal penalties, including fines and jail sentences.

PRIOR STANDARDS, ACCIDENTS

Prior to the enactment of the CPSA, attempts to reduce hazards associated with consumer products were fragmented and produced uneven results. Federal, state, and local laws addressed safety issues in a limited, piecemeal manner. Industry self-regulation was occasionally attempted by trade associations, testing laboratories, or other standards-making groups. Competitive economic forces often delayed or weakened the establishment of standards, and the inability of the industry legally to enforce standards once they were set often made these attempts little more than window dressing. In 1967, members of Congress decided that there had to be a consistent approach to the problems of injuries resulting from the use of consumer products.

The House of Representatives and the Senate enacted Public Law 90-146 in June, 1967, creating the National Commission on Public Safety (NCPS). The commission was given the responsibility of identifying products presenting unreasonable hazards to consumers, examining existing means of protecting consumers from these hazards, and recommending appropriate legislative action. In June, 1970, the commission reported the magnitude of the problem: 20 million people were injured each year because of incidents related to consumer products; 110,000 people were permanently disabled from such accidents; and 30,000 deaths resulted each year. The cost to the country was estimated to be more than $5.5 billion a year. The commission suggested that consumers were in more dangerous environments in their own homes than when driving on the highway.

The commission outlined sixteen categories of products as providing unreasonably hazardous risks to the consumer. Architectural glass used for sliding doors in homes caused approximately 150,000 injuries a year; the commission recommended that safety-glazed materials be required for this use. Hot-water vaporizers that were capable of heating water to 180 degrees repeatedly caused second- and third-degree burns to young children. High-rise bicycles with "banana" seats, high handlebars, and small front wheels encouraged stunt riding and frequently resulted in injuries. Furniture polish with 95 percent petroleum distillates were packaged in screw-cap bottles, colored to resemble soft drinks, and attractively scented; many children who drank these suffered fatal chemical pneumonia. Power rotary lawn mowers sliced through fingers and toes and sent objects hurtling toward bystanders. Other products that the commission identified as posing unreasonable potential hazards to consumers included color television sets, fireworks, floor furnaces, glass bottles, household chemicals, infant furniture, ladders, power tools, protective headgear (especially football helmets), unvented gas heaters, and wringer washing machines.

WHOSE RESPONSIBILITY?

The commission maintained that it was not entirely the responsibility of consumers to protect themselves, because they could reasonably be expected neither to understand all the existing hazards nor to know how to deal effectively with the hazards. Although consumers were becoming increasingly successful at receiving compensation for injuries through common law, manufacturers in general had not responded by taking preventive measures.

The commission suggested that a national program was needed to prevent further accidents and injuries. At hearings before the U.S. Senate Committee on Commerce on June 24, 1970, the National Commission on Public Safety recommended that an independent agency, the Consumer Product Safety Commission, be formed. Hearings were held between May of 1971 and February of 1972. These hearings allowed individuals representing both businesses and organizations concerned with health and safety issues to testify. Competing legislation included proposals to give the responsibility for oversight to the existing secretary of health, education, and welfare rather than to an independent agency. One proposal would have permitted the adoption of an existing private standard as a federal safety standard; this proposal, however, was criticized on the grounds that it might result in the acceptance of private standards that were inadequate or anticompetitive.

Witnesses at the hearings testified on the problems of hazardous household products, the function and effectiveness of state and local laws, and the role of advertising and the need for public education and debated whether the American economy would reward or punish producers of safe consumer products, which were likely to carry higher prices. Manufacturers, legislators, college professors, attorneys, publishers, representatives of trade and professional associations, engineers, and physicians provided information and opinions on the proposed legislation.

PASSAGE AND PROVISIONS

The process brought about intense lobbying and heated debates. Companies saw the CPSC as a potential source of harassment, with government decisions affecting their industries. Sponsors of the legislation complained that regular government agencies listened too closely to the very industries that they were directed to regulate and ignored the voice of the consumer. Long filibustering sessions and angry accusations nearly killed the legislation. Observers claimed that key sponsors could have brought the issue to a vote sooner but were not present when votes on stopping the filibustering were taken. The administration of President Richard M. Nixon publicly supported the legislation, but key aides supported the filibustering. The Grocery Manufacturers of America, a business lobby, distributed information kits on how to fight the bill in Congress, calling the legislation a threat to free enterprise. Opponents warned of the authority the agency could have, claiming that it had the potential to turn against the consumer, side with big business, and increase the costs of products to consumers.

As it was passed in 1972, the Consumer Product Safety Act charged the CPSC with four main tasks: to protect the public from unreasonable risks of injury associated with the use of consumer products; to be of assistance to consumers in evaluating and comparing the safety of consumer products; to develop uniform safety standards for consumer products; and to encourage research and investigation into the causes and prevention of product-related deaths, illnesses, and injuries. "Consumer products" were defined both as things sold to customers as well as things distributed for the use of customers (such as component parts). Specifically excluded were tobacco and tobacco products, motor vehicles and equipment, pesticides, firearms and ammunition, aircraft, boats and equipment, drugs, cosmetics, and foods, as these fell under the jurisdiction of other existing agencies. Responsibility for a product was extended to include producers, importers, and, basically, anyone who handled the product in the stream of commerce.

IMPLEMENTATION AND IMPACT

The CPSC established a National Electronic Injury Surveillance System (NEISS) in order to collect and investigate information on injuries and deaths related to consumer products. NEISS was a computer-based system tied into more than one hundred hospital emergency rooms that allowed the commission to compute a product "hazard index." Products with the highest hazard indices—such as cleaning agents, swings and slides, liquid fuels, snowmobiles, and all-terrain vehicles—were targeted for further studies and possible regulation.

The CPSC was authorized to perform in-depth studies on accidents and to investigate the effects and costs of these injuries to individuals and the country as a whole. If the CPSC believes there to be significant cause, it is empowered to investigate the industry and product in question with the goal of encouraging voluntary industry safety standards or initiate mandatory safety standards of its own. If CPSC investigators believe that safety standards are required, they research the product, develop test methods if necessary, and propose an appropriate safety standard. Proposals for appropriate standards are also solicited from the affected industry. Interested organizations, individuals, and industry representatives testify during open hearings on the proposed standards. After the hearings, the standards may be modified or enacted as proposed. Products that fail to meet the standards within a set period of time (from one to six months) may be pulled from store shelves, and manufacturers may face fines as well as jail sentences. If adequate safety standards cannot be designed, court action may be taken to have the products banned. So that unreasonable demands are not placed on a small company, fines for violations may be limited, or establishments of particular sizes may be given extensions of time in which to comply with regulations.

The establishment of specific standards is a process that is frequently viewed with concern by the manufacturers involved. When changes in manufacturing, product design, or labeling are suggested, manufacturers' associations respond with proposals, which include estimates of the additional costs necessary to implement the changes. Cost/benefit criteria are considered to determine if the benefits of a proposed action can be justified by the attendant costs. This not an easy issue to revolve. For example, the changes that were contemplated in the design of power lawn mowers included locating pull cords away from chokes and throttles, installing footguards, redesigning exhaust systems, and installing automatic cutoffs. The enacted changes increased the price of the power lawn mower to the consumer by an average of twenty-two dollars.

Manufacturers, legislators, and administrative figures all were aware of the potential power of CPSC. The establishment and enforcement of standards had the potential to raise the costs of manufacturing and, consequently, increase prices to consumers. Regulations had the potential to limit the types and quality of consumer products on the market. Passing the Consumer Product Safety Act did not bring an end to the debate. The CPSC's first action was to establish flammability standards for mattresses. As soon as the new regulations were established, the CPSC was promptly taken to court both by manufacturers' associations and by consumer groups unhappy with the standards. Manufacturers claimed that they were being unfairly asked to absorb the costs of switching materials and conducting new testing procedures; the problem, the manufacturers alleged, was really caused by careless cigarette smokers. Consumer groups claimed that the standards were not strict enough, since small manufacturers were given additional time during which they could sell mattresses that did not meet the flammability standards if such mattresses were prominently so labeled. Consumer groups wanted only safe mattresses on the market, without a time delay. In spite of the potential for unlimited power claimed by opponents, the CPSC—a watchdog agency—soon became the watched.

Critics of regulatory agencies argue that solutions to safety problems cost money and that these costs will be passed along to consumers. Direct costs, such as those involved in retooling, testing, labeling, and changes in personnel and material, are relatively easy to determine. Trade associations and manufacturers argue that government standards actually limit consumers' freedom of choice, increase costs, put people out of work, and lead to excessive governmental control. Many associations advocate self-regulation in order to preempt government involvement. Consumer-protection advocates contend that if self-regulation could solve the problem, there would not be any problem. They also argue that costs are inevitable when safety is concerned. Indirect costs, including hospital and doctors' fees, time lost from work, and pain and suffering from injuries, must be paid, whether by injured consumers, insurance companies, or manufacturers. Regardless of who pays directly, the ultimate cost is passed on, whether to the consumer or to the public as a whole.

Sharon C. Wagner

SOURCES FOR FURTHER STUDY

Evans, Joel R., ed. *Consumerism in the United States An Inter-Industry Analysis.* New York: Praeger, 1980.

Heffron, Howard A. *Federal Consumer Safety Legislation: A Study of the Scope and Adequacy of the Automobile Safety, Flammable Fabrics, Toys, and Hazardous Substances Programs.* Washington, D.C.: Government Printing Office, 1970.

Katz, Robert N., ed. *Protecting the Consumer Interests.* Cambridge, Mass.: Ballinger, 1976.

Mayer, Robert N. *The Consumer Movement Guardians of the Marketplace.* Boston: Twayne, 1989.

U.S. Consumer Product Safety Commission. *Regulatory Responsibilities of the U.S. Consumer Product Safety Commission Study Guide.* Washington, D.C.: Government Printing Office, 1976.

SEE ALSO: Pure Food and Drugs Act (1906); Food, Drug, and Cosmetic Act (1938); Food Additives Amendment (1958); Hazardous Substances Labeling Act (1960); National Traffic and Motor Vehicle Safety Act (1966); Child Protection and Toy Safety Act (1969); Child product safety laws (1970's); Magnuson-Moss Warranty Act (1975).

NOISE CONTROL ACT

DATE: October 27, 1972
U.S. STATUTES AT LARGE: 86 Stat. 1234
PUBLIC LAW: 92-574
U.S. CODE: 42 § 4901-4918, 49 § 44715
CATEGORIES: Environment and Conservation

> *The first major piece of federal legislation in the area of noise control, this act directed the U.S. Environmental Protection Agency to identify major noise sources and to define permissible levels.*

The Noise Control Act sets noise-emission standards for commercial products, as well as aircraft, railroads, and motor vehicles. It also specifies that the Environmental Protection Agency (EPA) is empowered to coordinate all federal programs regarding noise research and noise control, as well as to act as a federal clearinghouse for noise regulations. The EPA was also given the authority to require environmental noise impact studies for new highways and industrial manufacturing plants. If deemed that the resulting environmental noise would be too great, project approval could be denied until the potential problem was addressed satisfactorily.

NEED FOR THE LAW

Although the detrimental effects of noise had been discussed for many years, the only measures passed by Congress prior to the Noise Control Act of 1972 were the Aircraft Noise Abatement Act of 1968 and a section of the Clean Air Act of 1970. This section required the Environmental Protection Agency to conduct a study of noise, hold public hearings, and report its results and recommendations to Congress.

The EPA report was duly submitted on January 26, 1972. The gist of this report was that noise had a significant negative impact on U.S. citizens, causing both physiological and psychological disturbances such as hearing impairment, interference with sleep, and stress reactions. Research also suggested that repeated exposure to high intensity noise would cause permanent hearing loss, while less intense noises could produce irritation and annoyance. The report concluded that noise adversely affected approximately eighty million U.S. citizens (40 percent of the population), and was costing $4 billion annually as a result of noise-induced accidents, absenteeism, inefficiency, and compensation claims for hearing loss.

PROPOSAL AND PASSAGE

The Interstate and Foreign Commerce Committee reported out H.R. 11021, the Noise Control Act, drafted by Florida congressman Paul G. Rogers, on February 19, 1972. This legislation was based on the EPA report and upon hearings held by Rogers's Subcommittee on Public Health and Environment during the previous summer. The testimony received indicated that most major sources of noise pollution affecting the population of the U.S. could be reduced using the available technology. The major sources of noise to be addressed by the bill were transportation, machinery, appliances, and other commercial products. Additionally, H.R. 11021 would coordinate federal research and activities, establish federal noise-emission standards for commercial products, and provide the noise characteristics of these products to the public. H.R. 11021 was passed by the House on February 29 after several amendments attempting to regulate aircraft noise and sonic booms were rejected.

On April 12 and 13, the Senate Public Works Subcommittee on Air and Water Pollution held hearings on a Senate noise-control bill (S. 3342) cosponsored by Senators John V. Tunney and Edmund S. Muskie. The three important provisions of this bill were regulation of aircraft noise emissions by the EPA, rather than the Federal Aviation Administration (FAA); development of criteria that indicate levels of noise that adversely affect public health and welfare; and a provision that federal regulation for new-product noise-emission standards not prohibit cities or states from enacting more stringent standards, if deemed necessary.

On September 19, the full Public Works Committee reported out a revised bill S. 3342, which was a combination of the original S. 3342 and the House-passed bill H.R. 11021. Although endorsed by eight environmental organizations, the modified bill left the final setting of aircraft noise standards with the FAA, but the EPA could provide input. The Senate passed S. 3342 on October 13, after two days of debate and after adopting four amendments. They then passed H.R. 11021, which was modified by the insertion of the language of S. 3342. The House agreed to the Senate amendments on October 18. The Noise Control Act of 1972 became the first major piece of legislation aimed specifically at reducing most forms of environmental noise detrimental to humans.

PROVISIONS AND ENFORCEMENT

The Noise Control Act of 1972 was designed to help alleviate four major sources of noise: transportation, construction, engines and motors, and electrical and electronic equipment. This was to be accomplished by requiring manufacturers to produce quieter products by legislating maximum allowable noise levels. Also, in addition to requiring environmental impact studies, the EPA was empowered to conduct and finance research, to develop and publish information on hazardous noise levels, to disseminate public information on noise control, to identify major noise sources, and to define permissible noise levels for each source. As a direct result of the act, the EPA prepared model noise ordinances which specified a sound level that was not to be exceeded. These sound levels depended upon the zoned use of the area (residential, commercial, or industrial), and the time of day. The actual values depended on the particular community and usually take into account typical background noise levels. Even so, in some regions, the levels were initially set so low that local crickets were in violation. The EPA is also directed to coordinate all federal noise research, to control programs, and to provide technical assistance to state and local governments.

Among the major sources of noise that have been targeted by the EPA are portable air compressors, medium and heavy trucks, motorcycles, buses, garbage trucks, jackhammers, railroad cars, snowmobiles, and lawnmowers. The EPA strategy for abating noise from these sources has included writing noise-emission standards that encourage proper maintenance or encourage the modification of existing devices, and the setting of more stringent requirements for new equipment so that noise levels will be reduced as the older models are replaced.

Although the EPA has the primary responsibility for most federal efforts to control noise, other agencies are now concerned with special areas of noise control. The FAA sets criteria and standards for aircraft noise, with the EPA providing technical information and pertinent advice. Most of the research and testing are performed for the FAA by the National Aeronautics and Space Administration (NASA) and the U.S. Air Force. The Federal Highway Administration has legislated noise-control standards for motor vehicles, and the Bureau of Motor Vehicle Safety shares the responsibility for enforcement with state and local agencies.

The Occupational Safety and Health Administration (OSHA) sets and enforces regulations to protect workers' hearing for all companies engaged in interstate commerce. OSHA standards set the limits of permissible noise exposure on a sliding scale so that the maximum allowable time of exposure is reduced as the sound intensity level increases. The Department of Housing and Urban Development (HUD) has enacted sound-insulation standards for the walls and floors of multifamily residences that qualify for HUD mortgage insurance. HUD also sets guidelines for maximum permissible noise levels at housing construction sites. The National Institute for Occupational Safety and Health (NIOSH) has mandated that workers in underground mines be provided with hearing protection devices. These rules are enforced by the Mining Enforcement and Safety Administration. The National Bureau of Standards continues to be actively engaged in a program of research and testing to help control noise in factories and commercial work areas, as well as in homes and offices. Their basic recommendations for quieting are available in a published handbook.

While the Noise Control Act of 1972 leaves the primary responsibility for controlling noise with state and local governments, noise guidelines and regulations for interstate road transportation fall under the jurisdiction of the EPA. The EPA also requires that protective measures such as walls or buffer zones be used wherever interstate highway noise would be above seventy decibels on adjoining residential property more than 10 percent of the time. Even stricter standards apply where highways pass schools, hospitals, and libraries.

IMPACT

Many cities have now adopted noise regulations, and there is a nationwide trend to include noise standards in building codes. Although noise regulation is important, the wise planning of land use is perhaps more basic. By zoning residential areas to be well separated from industrial areas, airports, railroad rights-of-ways and highways, expensive noise-protecting walls are rendered unnecessary. Also, commercial zones can be utilized as buffer zones between residential regions and industrial zones or airports.

Since many consumers prefer to buy quieter products, and because it is very difficult to compare the noise output of different brands, the EPA has proposed requiring noise labels on all appliances. The acoustic basis for this labeling procedure already exists. Known as the Product Noise Rating (PNR), it is expected to allow the careful consumer to accurately compare products without the misleading hype that usually accompanies appliance advertising.

The Noise Control Act has done much to ensure auditory comfort and to protect the hearing of the general population as well as to guard against auditory hazards in the workplace. As the twenty-first century begins to unfold, and as new methods of transportation and communication, heavy machinery, and domestic labor-saving devices make their debut, the Noise Control Act will continue to be employed to safeguard the auditory environment.

George R. Plitnik

Sources for Further Study
Baron, R. A. *The Tyranny of Noise.* New York: St. Martin's Press, 1970.

Berendt, R. D., E. L. R. Corliss, and M. S. Oljavo. *Quieting: A Practical Guide to Noise Control.* Washington, D.C.: Government Printing Office, 1976.

Kryter, K. D. *The Effects of Noise on Man.* 2d ed. New York: Academic Press, 1985.

Miller, R. K. *Handbook of Industrial Noise Management.* Atlanta: Fairmont Press, 1976.

Still, H. *In Quest of Quiet: Meeting the Menace of Noise Pollution.* Harrisburg, Pa.: Stackpole Books, 1970.

Strong, W. J., and G. R. Plitnik. *Music, Speech, and Audio.* Provo, Utah: Soundprint, 1992.

U.S. Environmental Protection Agency. Office of Noise Abatement and Control. *Public Hearings on Noise Abatement and Control.* Washington, D.C.: Government Printing Office, 1971.

See also: Aircraft Noise Abatement Act (1968).

WAR POWERS RESOLUTION

DATE: November 7, 1973
U.S. STATUTES AT LARGE: 87 Stat. 555
PUBLIC LAW: 93-148
U.S. CODE: 50 § 1541
CATEGORIES: Military and National Security

> *This congressional joint resolution placed certain restrictions and reporting requirements on the president's deployment of military forces during hostilities.*

Article I, section 8, of the Constitutions stipulates, "The Congress shall have Power . . . to declare War. . . ." Article II, section 2, designates the president as "Commander in Chief of the Army and Navy of the United States, and of the Militia of the several States, when called into the actual Service of the United States." As the United States' commander in chief, the president has played a major role in the declaration as well as the conduct of war.

WAR POWERS: CONGRESS OR THE PRESIDENT?

The War Powers Resolution was an effort by Congress to regain lost influence in U.S. military policy. Specifically, the act, passed on November 7, 1973, over a veto by President Richard M. Nixon, established certain requirements for the president to meet and follow when acting to deploy military forces in a hostile environment. No president has ever accepted the act as a legitimate constraint on the presidential war powers. Still, presidents in most circumstances have followed the form, if not the spirit, of the act's reporting requirements. Despite protracted political and academic debates as to the law's constitutionality, the Supreme Court has never ruled directly on that issue.

THE TONKIN GULF RESOLUTION

The War Powers Act can be viewed as a congressional reversal of its Tonkin Gulf Resolution in 1964. That resolution, which marked the full commitment of the U.S. military to aiding South Vietnam, came in direct response to a plea by President Lyndon B. Johnson after an attack on U.S. ships by North Vietnamese planes. Through the resolution, Congress expressed that it "approves and supports the determination of the president, as commander in chief, to take all necessary measures to repel any armed attack against the forces of the United States and to prevent further aggression."

The Tonkin Gulf Resolution was viewed as the functional equivalent of transferring to the president Congress's constitutional power to declare war. Although the United States never formally declared war against North Vietnam, the ensuing decade saw an enormous, escalating commitment of U.S. troops, aircraft, and other military material to fighting the North Vietnamese. The mounting numbers of U.S. casualties and the dwindling hope of military or political success made the Vietnam War a source of heated political battles in the United States, as well as popular demonstrations, civil unrest, and other attacks on the political establishment.

As public sentiment increasingly turned against the war in the late 1960's, members of Congress felt more and more frustrated by their relative powerlessness to call a halt to a war Congress never formally declared. Out of this growing frustration emerged the 1973 War Powers Act. Coming near the beginning and end of major U.S. involvement in the Vietnam War, the Tonkin Gulf Resolution and the War Powers Act serve as bookmarks to the era of Congress's near-delegation of its war powers.

PROVISIONS OF THE 1973 ACT

The War Powers Act includes four major provisions limiting the president's power to deploy forces into hostilities: First, the president shall consult with Congress "in every possible instance" prior to introducing forces into actual or imminent hostile situations; second, the president must report to the Congress in writing within forty-eight hours after introducing forces in such situations; third, the president must withdraw those forces within sixty days of that report, unless the president judges that the troops' safety requires a thirty-day extension or Congress specifically authorizes their continued deployment; and fourth, Congress may, with a concurrent resolution, direct the president to withdraw those forces earlier than the sixty to ninety days provided in the third provision.

President Nixon vetoed the act, deeming it an unconstitutional intrusion in the president's role as commander in chief. However, Congress overrode the president's veto, and the act became law.

CONSTITUTIONAL CHALLENGES

Congress and the president have repeatedly clashed over the constitutionality and interpretation of the act since its passage. Members of Congress in particular have charged that presidents have failed to abide by the various provisions, most particularly the "consultation" provision. Although presidential notification of Congress only hours before an attack might be difficult to define as "consultation," the law gives little direction as to the amount of advance notice that is required to make "consultation" meaningful. In addition, the "in every possible instance" clause seems to allow for circumstances when consultation is not possible.

The forty-eight-hour reporting requirement is less vague but also imposes little congressional control over presidential war powers. Even when notifying Congress of military deployments into hostile situations, presidents have been careful not to directly link the notification to the War Powers Act in order to avoid a tacit endorsement of the alleged constitutionality of the law.

The fourth provision of the act, permitting Congress to force the president to withdraw military forces, has drawn the most significant constitutional objections. Congressional action on this provision is claimed to amount to a legislative veto.

COURT CASES

Elements of the War Powers Act have been examined by federal courts, including, for example, a district court's consideration of the act's definition of "hostilities" and other matters. In that case, *Crockett v. Reagan* (1982), the court found the "hostilities" question to be a matter for congressional, and not judicial, investigation. It also avoided a direct judgment of the sixty-day withdrawal requirement. Courts all the way up to the Supreme Court have been reluctant to address the various aspects of the act that many consider to be political questions.

However, the Court's decisions on other cases have been subsequently considered by scholars in the context of the act. For example, in the *Prize Cases* of 1863, the Court declared that determining whether national security considerations justify a president's military response is a matter "to be decided by him." More recently, the *Immigration and Naturalization Service v. Chadha* decision of 1983, which concerns legislative vetoes, has been considered by some to signal the unconstitutionality of the War Powers Act's provision permitting Congress to demand the withdrawal of troops.

Steve D. Boilard

SOURCES FOR FURTHER STUDY
Fisher, Louis. *Constitutional Conflicts Between Congress and the President.* 4th ed. Lawrence: University Press of Kansas, 1997.
_____. *The Politics of Shared Power: Congress and the Executive.* 4th ed. College Station: Texas A&M University Press, 1998.
Hall, David Locke. "The War Powers Resolution." In *The Reagan Wars: A Constitutional Perspective on War Powers and the Presidency.* Boulder, Colo.: Westview Press, 1991.
U.S. Congress. *The War Powers Resolution: Relevant Documents, Reports, Correspondence.* Washington, D.C.: Government Printing Office, 1994.

SEE ALSO: Formosa Resolution (1955); Tonkin Gulf Resolution (1964).

MENOMINEE RESTORATION ACT

DATE: December 22, 1973
U.S. STATUTES AT LARGE: 87 Stat. 770
PUBLIC LAW: 93-197
U.S. CODE: 25 § 903
CATEGORIES: Native Americans

The federal policy of termination, which sought to dissolve the government's special legal relationship with tribes, was effectively destroyed when the Menominee tribe was restored to full federal status.

In June, 1954, the United States terminated its relationship with the Menominee Tribe of Wisconsin, in part because the tribe was so successful in managing its resources. The Menominee owned their own sawmill and operated a hospital and utility company on their reservation. The government decided the Menominee could be self-sufficient. Termination caused an abrupt change of fortune for the tribe. The reservation became Menominee County. Property taxes were high, unemployment rose, and the hospital and utility companies closed. Most devastating, while the tribal lands, assets, and sawmill were formed into a corporation composed of all former tribal members, non-Indian shareholders, who managed the shares of minors and incompetents, dominated the corporation.

The corporation began to sell valuable Menominee lakefront property and mismanaged the sawmill operation, and soon Menominee County became the poorest county in Wisconsin. In 1969, Menominee activists organized DRUMS, Determination of Rights and Unity for Menominee Shareholders, to prevent further land sales and to seek restoration of federal recognition. Both the State of Wisconsin and Congress supported restoration. In 1973, Congress passed Public Law 93-197, which repealed termination, granted federal status to the Menominee, and returned their lands to full trust status.

Carole A. Barrett

SOURCES FOR FURTHER STUDY

Davis, Thomas. *Sustaining the Forest, the People, and the Spirit.* Albany: State University of New York Press, 2000.

Ourada, Patricia K. *The Menominee Indians: A History.* Norman: University of Oklahoma Press, 1979.

Peroff, Nicholas C. *Menominee Drums: Tribal Termination and Restoration, 1954-1974.* Norman: University of Oklahoma Press, 1982.

Wilkinson, Charles F. *The Menominee Restoration Act.* 93rd Congress, 1st session. Boulder, Colo.: Native American Rights Fund, 1973.

SEE ALSO: Termination Resolution (1953); Public Law 280 (1953); Indian Civil Rights Act (1968).

COMPREHENSIVE EMPLOYMENT TRAINING ACT

DATE: December 28, 1973
U.S. STATUTES AT LARGE: 87 Stat. 879
PUBLIC LAW: 93-203
CATEGORIES: Education; Labor and Employment

> *This legislation provided opportunities for economically disadvantaged people who were unemployed or underemployed to secure job training and employment opportunities.*

In response to the growing concern with civil rights and equal opportunity in the United States in the early 1970's, Congress passed the CETA legislation. Its goal was to increase the income of the entire spectrum of disadvantaged, unemployed, and underemployed: youth, older workers, minority groups, and others, including those receiving public assistance. Under CETA, the secretary of labor made block grants to state and local governments, which in turn identified employment needs in their areas and operated the necessary training centers. The act also authorized national programs for special groups such as American Indians and established the Job Corps for disadvantaged youth. Funds were used for job-related skills as well as for such supportive services as medical and child care.

Although these support services should have given women equal access to training, administration of the act depended largely on the quality of state and local participation. Wide variances in services occurred between urban areas and small towns in both northern and southern regions of the country. The act was amended numerous times, completely revised in 1978, and repealed on October 13, 1982, when its funding ran out and its programs incorporated into statutes such as Title I that have similar objectives.

Louise M. Stone

SOURCE FOR FURTHER STUDY

Franklin, Paul L. *Comprehensive Employment Training Act.* New York: Henry Holt, 1979.

SEE ALSO: Employment Act (1946); Equal Pay Act (1963); Economic Opportunity Act (1964); Age Discrimination in Employment Act (1967); Equal Employment Opportunity Act (1972).

ENDANGERED SPECIES ACT

DATE: December 28, 1973
U.S. STATUTES AT LARGE: 87 Stat. 884
PUBLIC LAW: 93-205
U.S. CODE: 16 § 1531
CATEGORIES: Animals; Environment and Conservation; Natural Resources

This act provided for conservation of threatened and endangered species of animals and plants by outlining a process for the listing of protected species, identifying appropriate regulations surrounding such species, and providing state subsidies and funding for habitat acquisition.

Congress first demonstrated concern for the conservation of species in the Lacey Act of 1900, which prohibited the transportation in interstate commerce of any fish or wildlife taken in violation of national, state, or foreign laws. Following the extinction of passenger pigeons, the Migratory Bird Treaty Act of 1918 authorized the secretary of the interior to adopt regulations for the protection of migratory birds.

In the Endangered Species Preservation Act of 1966, Congress declared that the preservation of species was a national policy. The statute authorized the secretary to identify native fish and wildlife threatened with extinction and to purchase land for the protection and restoration of such species. The Endangered Species Conservation Act of 1969 further empowered the secretary to list species threatened with "worldwide extinction" and prohibited the importation of any listed species into the United States. The only species eligible for the list were those threatened with complete extinction. Although the 1966 and 1969 statutes did not include any penalties for destroying species on the list, at the time the legislation was the most comprehensive of its kind enacted by any nation.

In legislative hearings of 1973, it was reported that species were being lost at the rate of about one per year and that the pace of disappearance seemed to be accelerating, with potential damage to the total ecosystem. The majority of Congress concluded that it was necessary to stop a further decline in biodiversity, and President Richard Nixon signed the ESA into law on December 28, 1973.

ENDANGERED VS. THREATENED

The Endangered Species Act (ESA) provides that any species of wild animals or plants may receive federal protection whenever the species has been listed as "endangered" or "threatened." The statute defines "endangered" to mean that the species is currently in danger of becoming extinct within a significant geographical region. The term "threatened" means that the species probably will become endangered within the foreseeable future. The definition of a "species" includes any subspecies or any distinct population that interbreeds within a specific region. Species found only in other parts of the world are eligible for inclusion on the U.S. list. The only creatures not eligible for inclusion are those insects that are determined to pose an extreme risk to human welfare.

The act makes it a federal offense to take, buy, sell, or transport any portion of a threatened or endangered species. Listed animals, however, may be taken in defense of human life, and Alaskan natives are allowed to use listed animals for subsistence purposes. Additional exemptions may be granted for special cases involving economic hardship, scientific research, or projects aimed at the propagation of a species. Individuals may be fined thousands of dollars for each violation of the law committed knowingly and lower amounts for a violation committed unknowingly. Harsher criminal penalties are available in extreme cases.

ENFORCEMENT

The ESA assigned most enforcement and regulatory powers to the heads of two executive departments. The secretary of commerce, through the National Marine Fisheries Service (NMFS), has responsibility over threatened and endangered marine species. The secretary of the interior exercises formal responsibility for the protection of other species, but the secretary delegates most of the work to the U.S. Fish and Wildlife Service (FWS), which is assisted by the Office of Endangered Species (OES). As of 1994, the regulations under the act took up 350 pages in the *Code of Federal Regulations*.

THE PROCESS OF LISTING SPECIES

In order to benefit from the ESA, the species must be officially designated as either endangered or threatened. The courts have consistently ruled that the act cannot be used to protect an unlisted species. Species may be proposed for listing by the NMFS, the FWS, private organizations, or citizens. Species are listed only after comprehensive investigations, open hearings, and opportunities for public involvement in the decision.

The first list of endangered species, published in 1967, included 72 species. By 1976 the list had grown to 634 species. As of 1995, 1,526 species of plants and animals were listed, including more than 500 that were foreign, and there were almost 4,000 candidate species awaiting a listing determination. Although the FWS is required to prepare a recovery plan for each listed species, only a few have recovered sufficiently to be taken off the list.

The act requires that critical habitat for threatened or endangered species be designated whenever possible. All federal agencies have special obligations to determine whether their projects or actions jeopardize the continued existence of a species. Following the Supreme Court's controversial ruling in *Tennessee Valley Authority v. Hill,* Congress passed the amendments of 1978, which allow consideration for economic factors in the designation of critical habitat. Especially controversial is the section of the act requiring the FWS to formulate and enforce regulations on private lands that provide habitat for listed species. The government must compensate owners in those rare cases when regulations eliminate almost all productive and economic uses of their property, but not when landowners continue to have partial productive use of their land.

ATTITUDES AND IMPACT

Many people in western and rural states are highly critical of the ESA, and they charge that it causes a significant loss of jobs to protect minor subspecies, such as the northern spotted owl. In 1995-1996, a conservative coalition of Republican congressmen tried to pass the Young-Plombo bill, which would have weakened the ESA. The controversy demonstrated, however, that the existing law enjoyed considerable support, and the proposed bill was never passed. Most experts argue that the economic impact of the ESA is minimal on the national economy but that it does cause hardship for small landowners in some instances. Many environmentalists would support revisions of the law that would give less emphasis to particular species and place more concern on the need for sufficient habitat to support a healthy biodiversity, but others fear that such complexity would make the law ineffective.

Thomas T. Lewis

SOURCES FOR FURTHER STUDY

Bean, Michael J. *The Evolution of National Wildlife Law.* Rev. ed. New York: Praeger, 1983.

Clepper, Henry, ed. *Origins of American Conservation.* New York: Ronald Press, 1966.

Galen, Mark. *There's Still Time: The Success of the Endangered Species Act.* Hanover, Pa.: National Geographic Society, 2001.

Kohm, Kathryn, ed. *Balancing on the Brink of Extinction: The Endangered Species Act and Lessons for the Future,* 1991.

Littel, Richard. *Endangered and Other Protected Species: Federal Law and Regulation.* Washington, D.C.: Bureau of National Affairs, 1992.

Lund, Thomas A. *American Wildlife Law.* Berkeley: University of California Press, 1980.

Mann, Charles, and Mark Plummer. *Noah's Choice: The Future of Endangered Species,* 1995.

Noss, Reed. Michael O'Connell, and Dennis Murphy. *Habitat Conservation Under the Endangered Species Act,* 1997.

Regenstein, Lewis. *The Politics of Extinction,* 1975.

Rohlf, Daniel. *The Endangered Species Act: Protection and Implementation,* 1989.

Stanford Environmental Law Society. *The Endangered Species Act.* Palo Alto, Calif.: Stanford University Press, 2000.

See also: Migratory Bird Act (1913); Migratory Bird Treaty Act (1918); Migratory Bird Hunting and Conservation Stamp Act (1934); Animal Welfare Act (1966); Endangered Species Preservation Act (1966); Convention on International Trade in Endangered Species (1975); Convention on the Conservation of Migratory Species of Wild Animals (1979).

CHILD ABUSE PREVENTION AND TREATMENT ACT

DATE: January 31, 1974
U.S. STATUTES AT LARGE: 88 Stat. 5
PUBLIC LAW: 93-247
U.S. CODE: 42 § 5101
CATEGORIES: Children's Issues; Health and Welfare

This law brought child maltreatment to national attention and mandated that states report cases of child abuse and neglect.

Sponsored by Senator Walter Mondale, the Child Abuse Prevention and Treatment Act provided small grants to states for research and demonstration projects to prevent and treat child abuse and neglect. States were required to mandate the reporting of known or suspected cases of child abuse and neglect, provide immunity for reporting, provide guardian ad litem representation for children, ensure confidentiality of records, provide public education on abuse and neglect, develop tracking, and investigate systems. The act created the National Center on Child Abuse and Neglect, which established regulatory standards for prevention and treatment programs, including twenty-four-hour response services. This act led to the Adoption Assistance and Child Welfare Act of 1980, which mandated that the special needs of children with disabilities, sibling groups, and older-aged children be met. The impact of the Child Abuse Prevention and Treatment Act of 1974 produced services to preserve, strengthen, and reunite families. Its passage resulted in states establishing reporting and tracking systems and coordinated information systems that are essential to permanency and placement procedures.

Karen V. Harper

Sources for Further Study

Briere, John, et al., eds. *The APSAC Handbook on Child Maltreatment.* Thousand Oaks, Calif.: Sage Publications, 1996.

The U.S. Advisory Board on Child Abuse and Neglect. *The Continuing Child Protection Emergency: A Challenge to the Nation.* Washington, D.C.: Department of Health and Human Services, 1993.

See also: Child Support Enforcement Amendments (1984); Family Violence Prevention and Services Act (1984); Missing Children's Assistance Act (1984); Child Care and Development Block Grant Act (1990); Megan's Law (1996).

Forest and Rangeland Renewable Resources Planning Act

Date: August 17, 1974
U.S. Statutes at Large: 88 Stat. 476
Public law: 93-378
U.S. Code: 16 § 1601
Categories: Agriculture; Land Management; Natural Resources

The law directed the Forest Service to assess resource needs and capabilities, define alternatives, and recommend a program of management and investment.

On August 17, 1974, President Gerald Ford signed the Forest and Rangeland Renewable Resources Planning Act (RPA) into law. The RPA resulted in the first complete legislative revision of the Forest

Service's mission since the early 1900's. The act addressed the need for an assessment of forest inventories and of the demands for products and services of forests and rangelands.

TIMBER MANAGEMENT

Although the public supported the measure once it was enacted, it started as one of the most controversial issues in land management. Industry pressure for more attention to timber management was amplified by increasing criticism from economists about the inefficient allocation of public resources in national forest management. Timber prices rose to extreme heights in 1969, resulting in public concern. The timber industry used the price increases as an opportunity to call congressional attention to the fact that a steady supply of timber was needed and that the issue of timber management needed to be placed on the legislative agenda.

In 1973, President Richard Nixon appointed the President's Advisory Panel on Timber and the Environment (PAPTE), an advisory board, to make recommendations concerning timber-management problems as they related to environmental concerns. The PAPTE called for a comprehensive forest development plan. The RPA, incorporating a complex planning process, resulted from the congressional attempt to balance industry needs with environmentalists' concerns about the Forest Service.

PROVISIONS

Under the RPA, the Forest Service is required to prepare and publish a revised program every five years and a revised assessment every ten years, both of which must be responsive to changes anticipated in the years ahead. The assessment explains the agencies and the regulations involved in forest resource activities. It presents an evaluation of the opportunities available to improve the yield of goods and services produced from forest resources. The goal of the assessment is to provide a factual basis from which to formulate future renewable resource management programs. In order to do this, the assessment provides information on projected population and income levels; forest and rangeland area; location and type of vegetative cover; supply and demand conditions of forest resources; social, economic, and environmental implications of projected demands and supplies; and opportunities for responding to the implications of such projections.

The program component of the RPA is similar to an Environmental Impact Statement. It provides a physical inventory and a description of the overall resource situation, including the problems and opportunities, potential supply and probable demand, prices at various output levels, and anticipated impacts. With the assessment as a foundation, the secretary of agriculture recommends a program of action for the Forest Service to employ in order to solve the problems and to take advantage of the opportunities identified in the assessment.

The Resources Planning Act requires the president to submit the program and a statement of the national forest-management policy to Congress. In doing so, he declares his budget request and provides justification. Congress will then either accept or amend the president's program in the consideration of funding. This structural process allows for checks and balances between Congress and the president.

In the past, the Forest Service had failed to receive increased funding from the government's executive branch. The RPA legislation was viewed as an opportunity for the Forest Service to submit its funding proposals directly to Congress and the public. The public was invited to examine these reports and to recommend changes or additions. The chief forester, John McGuire, lauded for his ability to negotiate, achieved his first significant accomplishment with the passage of the RPA. The new legislation provided an opportunity for the chief forester to employ his mediation skills with the public.

RESPONSE
While the RPA did appeal to the public, it did not eliminate all public disapproval of Forest Service activities. The caustic debates during the late 1960's and 1970's over the Forest Service program of clear-cutting timber in the Monongahela National Forest in West Virginia resulted in a judicial decision to halt all clear-cutting, ruling that new national forest management legislation would be needed. As a result, the National Forest Management Act (NFMA) was passed by Congress in 1976. The act demanded that clear-cuts be reduced and resource management guidelines be set up for controversial management practices.

With the passage of the National Forest Management Act in 1976 came changes in the RPA. The NFMA made significant amendments to the RPA, resulting in a restructuring of the planning process. It set new standards for national forest resource planning. The function of the RPA was expanded beyond that of a mere budget-setting device. A comprehensive plan would be developed and used for a whole forest and would not include separate plans for land and timber use. The Forest Service adopted planning rules that required the RPA program to define regional objectives for forest-range grazing, minerals, timber, water, and other resources. In turn, these objectives would be applied to each individual forest by the regional plans. The NFMA also called for an economic classification of specifically recorded alternative management strategies for each land area, with a balanced consideration of the potential combination of all goods and services produced from the land. It essentially mandated multiple-use planning for all forests.

Significance and Impact

The 1974 RPA and the 1976 NFMA were passed at a time when the Forest Service was concerned about the inconsistencies in the forest-planning process. These acts gave the agency a legislative mandate to administer the forest in ways that maximized the advantages from sustained-yield multiple-use production, while still considering the potential production of the land. The RPA became a pivotal policy in the history of U.S. forestry legislation, along with the NFMA the primary law governing U.S. forest policy. This legislative achievement is important, but the ultimate meaning is unclear, because Congress did not identify priorities. The RPA is considered to be consistent with most congressional legislation, because it promotes compromise rather than radical change. The fact that the initial act defines procedures rather than specific goals is a major characteristic of 1970's legislation. It directs land-managing agencies to consider all factors, but it does not provide a framework for prioritizing them.

Since 1974, there have been several assessments conducted under the RPA. According to the Forest Service, figures concerning demand and supply of renewable resources depend primarily upon population growth, income levels, economic activities, changes in technology and institutions, the cost of energy, availability of capital, and the investment levels in resource management and utilization.

The long-term trend of the U.S. economy has been continued growth; the population and the economy are expected to continue to grow in the future. Renewable resources in the United States meet the needs of nearly fifty million more people than when the RPA was first instituted, and overall increases in demand are greater than the levels that are supplied using 1990's management methods. As the country continues to grow, society's view of renewable resources is likely to change to reflect the problems, opportunities, and management of these resources.

Sandra Harrison and
Ruth Bamberger

SOURCES FOR FURTHER STUDY

Bowes, Michael D., and John V. Krutilla. *Multiple-Use Management: The Economics of Public Forestlands.* Washington, D.C.: Resources for the Future, 1989.

Clary, David A. *Timber and the Forest Service.* Lawrence: University Press of Kansas, 1986.

Cubbage, Frederick W., Jay O'Laughlin, and Charles S. Bullock III. *Forest Resource Policy.* New York: John Wiley & Sons, 1993.

Ellefson, Paul V. *Forest Resources Policy.* New York: McGraw-Hill, 1991.

President's Advisory Panel on Timber and the Environment. *Report.* Washington, D.C.: Government Printing Office, 1973.

SEE ALSO: National Park Service Organic Act (1916); Multiple Use-Sustained Yield Act (1960); Wilderness Act (1964); Wild and Scenic Rivers Act and National Trails System Act (1968); National Environmental Policy Act (1970); Eastern Wilderness Act (1975); Resource Conservation and Recovery Act (1976); National Forest Management Act (1976).

EMPLOYEE RETIREMENT INCOME SECURITY ACT

DATE: September 2, 1974
U.S. STATUTES AT LARGE: 88 Stat. 832
PUBLIC LAW: 93-406
U.S. CODE: 29 § 1001
CATEGORIES: Business, Commerce, and Trade; Labor and Employment

> *By establishing fiduciary, funding, vesting, and disclosure rules and plan termination insurance, ERISA attempted to protect employees' rights to retirement and other benefits.*

On September 2 (Labor Day), 1974, President Gerald Ford signed the Employee Retirement Income Security Act of 1974 (ERISA) into law. ERISA established complex rules concerning employee benefit plan disclosure, fiduciary responsibility, funding, and vesting. Vesting refers to an employee's nonforfeitable right to a pension, a right earned, for example, after a fixed number of years of service. The law also established pension plan termination insurance and the Pension Benefit Guaranty Corporation.

ERISA was the culmination of eight years of investigations, hearings, and legislative proposals that responded to reports of abuse in the private pension and group insurance system, particularly with respect to the absence of vesting and funding standards in some plans. ERISA mandated practices that had become increasingly common among large corporate plans. The law's supporters thus included a wide range of interests, such as the American Bankers' Association and the United Auto Workers union. ERISA was moderate in scope and did not include certain reforms, such as the mandating of private employee benefit coverage for everyone in the workforce, that were advocated at the time by Ralph Nader and other public interest advocates.

HISTORY AND PREVIOUS LEGISLATION

The American Express Company adopted the first pension plan in the United States in 1875. By 1940, more than four million American employees were covered by private pensions. The Revenue Act of 1942 allowed a company to receive a guarantee that pension contributions would be tax-deductible, and this provision encouraged growth in coverage. The War Labor Board also encouraged growth during World War II by exempting employee benefit plans from wage freezes. A similar provision was made during the Korean War. Furthermore, in 1948 the Seventh Circuit Court of Appeals upheld a ruling in a case involving the Inland Steel Company that pensions are mandatory subjects of collective bargaining. This decision opened the door to collective bargaining by unions for employee benefits. Pension assets rose from $2.4 billion in 1940 to $52 billion in 1960. By 1970, more than twenty-six million American employees were covered by private pensions.

In 1958, the Welfare and Pension Plan Disclosure Act (WPPDA) established disclosure requirements for employee benefit plans. The WPPDA was amended in 1962 to establish criminal sanctions. The WPPDA's disclosure requirements, however, were limited in scope.

In 1963 and 1964, pension plans gained public attention when Studebaker's factory in South Bend, Indiana, closed. About forty-five hundred Studebaker employees under the age of sixty received only 15 percent of the retirement benefits they had earned, and many received no benefits at all. President John F. Kennedy had appointed a Committee on Corporate Pension Funds in 1962, and in 1965 the committee recommended stricter standards for plan funding and vesting of employees' pension benefits. This recommendation led to a 1968 House bill that would have established fiduciary standards for administrators of employee benefit plans, but the bill died.

PASSAGE THROUGH CONGRESS

In a message to Congress on December 8, 1971, President Richard M. Nixon proposed legislation to establish vesting and fiduciary standards and to permit individual retirement accounts (IRAs). A House Banking and Currency Committee task force investigated pension reform that year as well. In 1972, the National Broadcasting Company encouraged popular support for pension reform legislation by airing a television news documentary, *Pensions: The Broken Promise*, that depicted abuses in the pension system.

The House Ways and Means Committee, chaired by Wilbur Mills, held hearings in 1972 on H.R. 12272, the Nixon administration's bill. H.R. 12272 included provisions on disclosure, fiduciary responsibility, and vesting, but not on funding and plan termination insurance. The most controversial part of the bill was its proposal for increasing the limits on the tax deductibility of pension benefits for self-employed individuals and their employees (Keogh or HR 10 plans) and IRAs. More than twenty national and local bar associations and the American Medical Association testified in favor of the Keogh plans and IRAs. The American Federation of Labor-Congress of Industrial Organizations (AFL-CIO) strongly opposed the Nixon bill because of these provisions. The bill died in the House.

In September, 1972, the Senate Labor and Public Welfare Committee, chaired by Harrison Williams, reported out a bill that would have regulated pension plans, but the bill died when Senator Russell Long argued that it was primarily tax legislation and so was the province of his Senate Finance Committee. The Senate Finance Committee reported the bill out only after removing its provisions concerning vesting, funding, and termination insurance.

By early 1973, public support for pension reform was widespread, and jurisdictional disputes were to be swept aside. Congressman Carl Perkins, chairman of the Education and Labor Committee, testified that he had received several thousand letters in support of pension reform. Later that year, Ralph Nader and Kate Blackwell published *You and Your Pension,* a book that encouraged popular support for pension reform by providing examples of insufficiently funded plans, the absence of vesting rules, and excessively complex plan provisions.

In September, 1973, the Senate Labor and Public Welfare Committee reported out a bill cosponsored by Jacob Javits and chairman Harrison Williams. At the same time, the Senate Finance Committee sponsored a complementary bill. The two bills were merged into S. 4, which passed the Senate. The bill set minimum fiduciary, funding, portability, and vesting standards, established plan termination insurance, established IRAs, and extended limits on Keogh plans. (Portability refers to allowing employees to transfer pension assets to a new employer or to a centralized trust fund when they change jobs). Weeks later, in October, 1973, the House Education and Labor Committee reported H.R. 2, which omitted S. 4's provisions on portability, Keogh plans, and IRAs but was similar to it in other respects.

During 1972 and 1973, the House Ways and Means Committee held hearings concerning H.R. 12272; the Senate Labor and Public Welfare Committee held hearings concerning S. 4; and the General Subcommittee on Labor, chaired by John H. Dent, held hearings concerning H.R. 2. In the course of these hearings, organized labor gave only mixed support to pension reform legislation. For example, a representative of the Amalgamated Clothing Workers Union testified that jointly sponsored labor-management trusts should be exempt from retirement legislation. In fact, industry groups such as the national Chamber of Commerce and the American Bankers' Association, along with Towers, Perrin, Foster, and Crosby, a consulting firm, gave stronger support to the proposed vesting, disclosure, and fiduciary rules than did the AFL-CIO. The AFL-CIO did not testify during the S. 4 and H.R. 2 hearings. The United Steelworkers, the United Auto Workers, and other industrial unions, along with some craft unions, did not support the proposed legislation, especially its termination insurance provisions, probably because pension funds in the steel and auto industries were underfunded. In testimony concerning H.R. 2, Ralph Nader excoriated the labor movement for its weak support of pension legislation.

In February, 1974, the House Ways and Means Committee passed a revised H.R. 2 bill that included improvements to Keogh plans and established IRAs. The House-Senate conference committee reported a final compromise version of H.R. 2 and S. 4 in August, 1974. The conference committee's bill passed the Senate unanimously, 85-0. In the House, only two representatives voted against ERISA. President Ford signed the bill on September 2, 1974.

PROVISIONS OF ERISA

ERISA established new rules on disclosure, vesting, eligibility, funding, and fiduciary responsibility. It established individual retirement accounts and increased the amount that self-employed individuals could contribute to their own pension plans. It established limits on contributions and benefits to highly paid individuals and restated the Internal Revenue Code's rules on integration of pensions with Social Security benefits. It also established the Pension Benefit Guaranty Corporation and a $1 per participant tax on single-employer plans to cover the newly created plan termination insurance.

With respect to disclosure, ERISA required that plan sponsors (both single employers and multiemployer trusts that sponsor benefit plans) provide participants with a summary of the formal, relatively technical, plan document that governs their pension plan. The summary, called a summary plan description, was required to be written in a manner calculated to be understood by the average plan participant. ERISA required that each plan administrator produce a detailed annual report that, in the case of pension and profit sharing plans, was required to be audited by a certified public accountant. It also required plan administrators to provide each plan participant with a summary of this annual report. Furthermore, the law required that the plan administrator provide an estimate of a participant's benefit upon request.

With respect to eligibility, ERISA required that plans could not require more stringent eligibility requirements than participants being twenty-five years of age or older, with at least one year of service, although with full immediate vesting, plans could require three years of service. Plans could no longer exclude employees because they were too old unless those employees began work within five years of the normal retirement age for the plan.

With respect to vesting, ERISA allowed plan participants to vest according to one of three rules: full vesting at ten years, the five to fifteen rule (25 percent vesting at five years of service increasing by 5 percent in the following five years and by 10 percent for five more years) and the rule of forty-five (50 percent vesting when the sum of age and years of service equals forty-five, increasing 10 percent per year thereafter). It also required that pension plans' normal form of benefit be a 50 percent joint and survivor benefit, that is, a pension amount at normal retirement age that has been actuarially reduced to provide a 50 percent benefit to the participant's spouse in the event of the participant's death.

With respect to funding, ERISA required that plans fully fund the cost accruing each year and that unfunded past service liabilities be funded over thirty years, with the exception of pre-existing past service liabilities, which could be funded over forty years. With respect to fiduciary standards, ERISA required that plans name a fiduciary and that the named fiduciary and any cofiduciaries must act exclusively for the benefit of plan participants. The law required that fiduciaries act as would a prudent person in like capacity. The law also required that fiduciaries diversify assets and prohibited the exchange of property or lending of money between a plan and a party-in-interest, defined as a fiduciary or the relative of a fiduciary, a person providing services to a plan, an employer, or a related union.

With respect to Keogh plans and IRAs, ERISA raised the tax-deductible amounts that a self-employed person could contribute to $7,500, or 15 percent of earnings if less. It also allowed individuals not otherwise covered by a pension plan to establish an IRA. With respect to limitations on contributions and benefits, it limited contributions to profit-sharing plans (such as 401k's) to $25,000 or 25 percent of compensation, whichever was less, and limited benefits under pension plans to $75,000 or 100 percent of final average earnings, whichever was less. Both limits were indexed for inflation and were intended to prevent highly paid individuals from taking undue advantage of tax deductions for qualified pension plans. Rules on these amounts have been adjusted with passing years.

CRITICISMS

Several writers, including Nader and Blackwell, raised important concerns about ERISA's efficacy. One characteristic of America's private system of pension and other benefits is that coverage is skewed toward higher-paid employees and employees of large firms. For example, in 1978, those whose preretirement income was more than 43 percent in excess of the median worker's had pensions worth 93 percent more than the median amount, as pointed out by Teresa Ghilarducci. Similarly, according to another study, in 1988, 65 percent of workers in firms with more than five hundred employees were covered by pension plans, while only about 12 percent of workers in firms with fewer than twenty-five employees were covered. By failing to mandate benefits and doing little to tighten restrictions on offsetting Social Security benefits from pension benefits (called integration), ERISA did little to alleviate the skew in coverage toward higher-paid workers.

The additional disclosures and plan termination insurance that ERISA required were costly, and administrative costs associated with compliance with ERISA may have had a depressing effect on plan adoption rates, especially among small firms. Although coverage rates of private pension plans grew from 15 percent of the work force in 1940 to 45 percent in 1970, the coverage rate remained constant at about 45 percent from 1970 to 1987. In particular, coverage among firms with fewer than twenty-five employees declined by about 15 percent from 1979 to 1988.

SUBSEQUENT REGULATION

ERISA opened a floodgate for regulation of employee benefit plans. From 1974 through 1992, fifteen laws regulating employee benefit programs were passed. For example, the Tax Equity and Fiscal Responsibility Act of 1982 reduced the limitations on contributions and benefits, the Retirement Equity Act mandated further spousal benefits, and the Tax Reform Act of 1986 reduced the minimum years of service for vesting to five. The premium required for plan termination insurance increased dramatically, twentyfold for some plans. As of 1993, approximately half of the American workforce lacked private pension coverage, and much of the remainder expected only modest benefits from the private pension system.

Mitchell Langbert

SOURCES FOR FURTHER STUDY

Ghilarducci, Teresa. *Labor's Capital: The Economics and Politics of Private Pensions.* Cambridge, Mass.: MIT Press, 1992.

Ippolito, Richard. *Pensions, Economics, and Public Policy.* Homewood, Ill.: Dow Jones-Irwin, 1986.

Mamorsky, Jeffrey D. *Employee Benefit Law: ERISA and Beyond.* New York: Law Journal Seminars Press, 1992.

Nader, Ralph, and Kate Blackwell. *You and Your Pension.* New York: Grossman, 1973.

Rosenbloom, Jerry S., ed. *The Handbook of Employee Benefits.* Homewood, Ill.: Dow Jones-Irwin, 1984.

Turner, J. A., and D. J. Beller, eds. *Trends in Pensions 1992.* Washington, D.C.: Government Printing Office, 1992.

Ziesenheim, Ken. *Understanding ERISA: A Compact Guide to the Landmark Act.* Columbia, Md.: Traders' Library, 2002.

SEE ALSO: Dependent Pension Act (1890); Social Security Act (1935); Emergency Price Control Act (1942); G.I. Bill (1944); Tax Reform Act of 1986 (1986).

JUVENILE JUSTICE AND DELINQUENCY PREVENTION ACT

DATE: September 7, 1974
U.S. STATUTES AT LARGE: 88 Stat. 1109
PUBLIC LAW: 93-415
U.S. CODE: 42 § 5601 et seq.
CATEGORIES: Children's Issues; Crimes and Criminal Procedure

This law attempted to reduce juvenile delinquency through prevention programs and reforms to the existing juvenile justice system. It emphasized education and counseling over punishment.

Stating its finding that juveniles accounted for about half of the arrests for serious crimes, Congress enacted the Juvenile Justice and Delinquency Prevention Act as a broad attack on juvenile delinquency. The main provisions of the act provided federal block grants to states. The grants were intended for reforming juvenile justice procedures and for providing resources such as counseling and school programs to prevent delinquency. The act sought to decriminalize youth "status offenders," whose offenses would not be considered crimes if they were adults. Alternative sentences such as placement in a halfway house would be offered. The act also coordinated research on juvenile delinquency and established the Office of Juvenile Justice and Delinquency Prevention within the Department of Justice. This legislation was complemented by another measure from 1974, the Runaway and Homeless Youth Act. The act was amended and authorization extended in 1974, 1980, and 1984.

Steve D. Boilard

SOURCE FOR FURTHER STUDY

United States. Congress. House. Committee on Education and the Workforce. Subcommittee on Early Childhood, Youth, and Families. *Juvenile Justice and Delinquency Prevention Act: Hearing Before the Subcommittee on Early Childhood, Youth, and Families of the Committee on Education and the Workforce, House of Representatives.*

105th Congress, 1st session. Washington, D.C.: Government Printing Office, 1997.

SEE ALSO: Child Abuse Prevention and Treatment Act (1974); Parental Kidnapping Prevention Act (1980); Child Support Enforcement Amendments (1984); Family Violence Prevention and Services Act (1984); Missing Children's Assistance Act (1984); Family Violence Prevention and Services Act (1984); McKinney Homeless Assistance Act (1987).

PARENS PATRIAE ACT

DATE: September 30, 1974
U.S. STATUTES AT LARGE: 90 Stat. 1394
PUBLIC LAW: 94-435
U.S. CODE: 15 § 15x
CATEGORIES: Business, Commerce, and Trade

This law authorizes state attorneys general to sue violators of antitrust laws on behalf of citizens of their states.

The Latin phrase *parens patriae* means "the state as parent" and is more commonly used to described the powers of government in relation to juveniles in its custody. The assumption underlying this term is that anything the state does to a juvenile is done on the juvenile's behalf.

In the context of antitrust legislation, this act authorizes the attorneys general of individual states to sue violators of antitrust laws on behalf of citizens of their states and request reasonable attorney fees as well as triple damages for consumers. The Hart-Scott-Rodino Antitrust Improvement Act of 1976 expanded this authority of state attorneys general, although this 1976 law is much better known for establishing in law a "prenotification" requirement that large firms give the Department of Justice advance notice of planned mergers.

Gayle Avant

SOURCE FOR FURTHER STUDY
Business Week. "The First Big Test of a New Antitrust Law." September 12, 1977.

SEE ALSO: Interstate Commerce Act (1887); Sherman Antitrust Act (1890); Federal Trade Commission Act (1914); Clayton Antitrust Act (1914); Wheeler-Lea Act (1938); Celler-Kefauver Act (1950); Antitrust Procedures and Penalties Act (1974).

EQUAL CREDIT OPPORTUNITY ACT

DATE: October 28, 1974
U.S. STATUTES AT LARGE: 88 Stat. 1521
PUBLIC LAW: 93-495
U.S. CODE: 15 § 1691
CATEGORIES: Banking, Money, and Finance; Women's Issues

This law requires financial institutions to make credit available without discrimination on the basis of sex or marital status.

In 1968, Congress passed the Consumer Credit Protection Act. One provision of the law created the National Commission on Consumer Finance. In 1972, as a member of the commission, Congresswoman Leonor K. Sullivan persuaded the commission to investigate discrimination against women in the consumer credit industry. During commission hearings on the subject, testimony was presented about instances in which married women were denied credit cards and charge accounts except in their husbands' names, and about the fact that widows and divorced and separated women often were denied any sort of credit. Widows often continued to use their dead husband's name in order to continue to have credit, as if a live widow had less credit than a dead spouse. As a result, many women could buy neither cars nor houses on credit, even if they had been the bill payers in their families before the departure of their husbands.

PASSAGE

The commission's report galvanized Congresswoman Bella S. Abzug to introduce a series of bills in 1972 to make credit discrimination illegal. Hearings were held in 1973, when a related bill, sponsored by Senator William E. Brock, passed the Senate, but more hearings in 1974 did not bear fruit in the House of Representatives. The issue was overshadowed by rampant inflation and developments in electronic bank transfers, which required a congressional reexamination of regulations in the banking and finance industry.

Congress was then working on the Depository Institutions Amendments of 1974, the most important provision of which was to raise the amount of federally guaranteed bank deposits from twenty thousand dollars to forty thousand dollars. On May 14, 1974, Brock and several cosponsors (Wallace F. Bennett, Edward W. Brooke, Alan Cranston, Robert W. Packwood, William Proxmire, and John G. Tower) attached to the larger bill a provision known as Title V, which amended the Consumer Credit Protection Act by adding a new section, known as the Equal Credit Opportunity Act. When the larger bill was adopted overwhelmingly, the Equal Credit Opportunity Act of 1974 passed as well, going into effect on October 28, 1975.

PROVISIONS AND OVERSIGHT

The law prohibited any creditor from discriminating against any applicant on the basis of sex or marital status with respect to any aspect of a credit transaction. Although the Federal Reserve Board was empowered to issue implementing regulations, administrative enforcement by way of complaint investigation was assigned to many agencies. For national banks, enforcement is by the Comptroller of the Currency. The Federal Reserve Board handles all of its member banks, other than national banks. The Federal Deposit Insurance Corporation enforces the law for all banks that it ensures, other than members of the Federal Reserve System. The Federal Home Loan Bank Board, acting directly or through the Federal Savings and Loan Insurance Corporation, has jurisdiction over financial institutions subject to provisions of the Home Owners' Loan Act, the National Housing Act, and the Federal Home Loan Bank. The administrator of the National Credit Union enforces the law for any federal credit union. The Interstate Commerce Commission regulates any common carrier under its jurisdiction. The Civil Aeronautics Board monitors any air carrier subject to the Federal Aviation Act of 1958. The secretary of agriculture handles complaints regarding activities subject to the Packers and Stockyards Act of 1921. The Farm Credit Administration plays a similar role for any federal land bank, federal land bank association, federal intermediate credit bank, and production credit association. The Securities and Exchange Commission has jurisdiction over brokers and dealers. The Small Business Administration looks after small business investment companies. For all other matters, the Federal Trade Commission has responsibility under the law. In all cases, agencies can respond to complaints by initiating investigations; alternatively, they can monitor statistical patterns of reported loans for evidence that certain groups are disproportionately denied credit. If discrimination is documented, the agency can refer a case to the Department of Justice for legal action against the offending financial institution.

The bill put a cap on the amount to be obtained by victims of discrimination. Individuals could sue only up to $10,000, and class complaints were limited to $100,000 or 1 percent of net worth for willful violations. According to Sullivan, this provision made the law less effective, even diluting the force of the Truth in Lending Act by reducing the penalty for infractions.

AMENDMENTS

Passage of the Equal Credit Opportunity Act was an easy victory: There were no public hearings and no opposition in Congress. After the law was signed by President Gerald R. Ford, Jr., on October 28, 1975, Sullivan urged Congress to amend the bill to remove the monetary caps and to broaden coverage so that credit discrimination based on race, color, religion, national origin, and age also would be illegal. She soon introduced an expanded bill. Senators Joseph R. Biden, Jr., and William Proxmire assumed leadership on the bill in the Senate, modifying its text somewhat. On March 23, 1976, the Equal Credit Opportunity Act Amendments of 1976 passed, expanding coverage as Sullivan had recommended, with a new cap of $500,000 for class-action suits; the statute of limitations for infractions was extended from one to two years.

The purpose of the law, as amended, is to require financial institutions to determine creditworthiness on the basis of finances, rather than on such nonfinancial grounds as age, sex, marital status, race, color, religion, or national origin. The law also protects recipients of public assistance funds from credit discrimination. The law immediately enabled millions of women to obtain credit cards, charge accounts, car loans, and home loans from financial institutions. However, the law had no effect on policies of insurance companies, and serious systemic credit discrimination has continued, especially based on race.

Michael Haas

Sources for Further Study

Burns, James A., Jr. "An Empirical Analysis of the Equal Credit Opportunity Act." *University of Michigan Journal of Law Reform* 13 (Fall, 1979): 102-142.

Cronin, Lisa. "Equal Credit Opportunity Act: Some Good News, Some Not So Good." *Ms.* 5 (March, 1977): 95-97.

Matheson, John H. "The Equal Credit Opportunity Act: A Functional Failure." *Harvard Journal of Legislation* 21 (Summer, 1984): 371-403.

Rogers, Laura L., and John L. Culhane, Jr. "Developments Under the Equal Credit Opportunity Act and Regulation B." *The Business Lawyer* 43 (August, 1988): 1571-1583.

Schafer, Robert T., and Helen F. Ladd. *Discrimination in Mortgage Lending.* Cambridge: MIT Press, 1981.

Smith, Dolores S. "Revision of the Board's Equal Credit Regulation: An Overview." *Federal Reserve Bulletin* 71 (December, 1985): 913-923.

Taibi, Anthony D. "Banking, Finance, and Community Empowerment: Structural Economic Theory, Procedural Civil Rights, and Substantive Racial Justice." *Harvard Law Review* 107 (May, 1994): 1463-1545.

See also: Consumer Credit Protection Act (1968); Truth in Lending Act (1968); Fair Credit Reporting Act (1970).

HAZARDOUS MATERIALS TRANSPORTATION ACT

DATE: November 21, 1974
U.S. STATUTES AT LARGE: 88 Stat. 2156
PUBLIC LAW: 93-633
U.S. CODE: 5 § 552a
CATEGORIES: Business, Commerce, and Trade; Environment and Conservation

This law regulated commerce by improving the protection afforded the public against risks connected with the transportation of hazardous materials by air, sea, rail, and road.

In 1975, President Gerald Ford signed the Transportation Safety Act of 1974, which was designed to overcome long-standing problems in transportation safety statutes. The law represented a declaration of congressional discontent over inadequate coverage provided by existing regulations; this discontent had been heightened by increased hazardous materials movements and accidents in the early 1970's and by a corresponding lack of enforcement of such regulations then in place as the Hazardous Materials Control Act of 1970 and the Railroad Safety Act of 1970.

PRIOR HAZARDOUS MATERIALS REGULATION
The history of hazardous materials regulation dates back to the Civil War. In 1866, the first federal law was passed regulating explosives and flammable materials. It was not until the establishment of the Interstate Commerce Commission in 1887 that the federal government began a concerted effort to impose some degree of regulatory uniformity on all modes of transportation. The first real regulatory attempt was the Explosives and Combustibles Act of 1908, which addressed safety on railroads, the most popular domestic mode of transportation of the time.

In 1966, authority to regulate the transportation of hazardous materials was transferred to the newly formed Department of Transportation. The secretary appointed to head the department held a cabinet-level position and had responsibility for all transportation safety standards, including those governing hazardous materials. Under this system, the Federal Aviation Administration, the Federal Highway Administration, the Federal Railroad Administration, and the U.S. Coast Guard were each allowed to promulgate its own independent regulations, which were published in different parts of the *Code of Federal Regulations.* The National Transportation Safety Board was also created to determine and report causes of transportation accidents and to conduct research into accident prevention. The Department of Transportation secretary formed the Hazardous Materials Regulations Board, which was staffed by the Office of Hazardous Materials to coordinate hazardous materials activities within the department.

Even with the passage of the Hazardous Material Control Act in 1970, persistent departmental, administrative, and organizational difficulties prevented the enforcement of the Hazardous Materials Transportation Act. Accidents during the early 1970's convinced Congress that Department of Transportation mismanagement and poor allocation of resources were contributing to the failure. In spite of the Railroad Safety Act of 1970, rail safety did not improve, largely because the rail industry was unwilling or unable to repair substandard tracks and structures. Economic insolvency and reorganization of rail carriers, inflation, and lack of tax incentives prevented capitalization for significant rail-line infrastructure repair. The energy crisis also contributed to the problem by necessitating greater dependence on train traffic along decaying and neglected rail beds and tracks.

PROVISIONS: THREE TITLES

In an effort to consolidate regulatory activities and to give the secretary authority over all modes of transportation, Congress passed the Hazardous Materials Transportation Act of 1974. The final House of Representatives bill, as amended by Senate conference action, consisted of three major sections, or "Titles." Title I, the Hazardous Materials Transportation Act, was perhaps the most important of the three sections. Title II was essentially designed to amend and improve the Railroad Safety Act of 1970. Title III, which was designed to divorce the National Transportation Safety Board from any political influence, made that investigative body separate from the Department of Transportation and answerable only to Congress.

The major provisions of the Hazardous Materials Transportation Act expanded the Department of Transportation's jurisdiction to include all interstate or foreign trade, traffic, and commerce. (The act has been interpreted so that intrastate movements also fall within the department's regulatory sphere.) The act also authorized the classification and designation of "hazardous materials"—a term that had not been legally defined before—as materials in quantities and forms that the secretary of transportation determines may pose an "unreasonable risk" to health, safety, or property when transported in commerce. (These materials explicitly included, but were not limited to, explosives, radioactive materials, etiologic agents, flammable liquids or solids, combustible liquids or solids, poisons, oxidizing or corrosive materials, and compressed gases.) In addition, the act prohibited transportation of radioactive materials on passenger aircraft, except for medical and research isotopes. The Department of Transportation was also authorized to issue regulations related to packing, handling, labeling, and routing of hazardous materials; this provision significantly expanded the definition of "transportation community" to include those who manufacture, test, maintain, and recondition containers or packages used to transport hazardous materials. The act also provided for registration of shippers, carriers, and container manufacturers and reconditioners and spelled out procedures for regulatory exemptions. The Department of Transportation was empowered to conduct surveillance activities, conduct inspections, establish record-keeping requirements, and assess civil and criminal penalties for violations. Lastly, the act defined the relationship between federal regulations and those of state and local governments, preempting local rules found to be inconsistent with the federal programs.

IMPLEMENTATION

One of the first implementations of the act was in the form of regulatory rule-making. A major provision of the act was the empowerment of the Department of Transportation to make rules and regulations in accordance with the Administrative Procedure Act. This has led to a plethora of "dockets" dealing specifically with hazardous materials transportation as technology and circumstances warranted. In 1976, one year after the passage of the act, the process produced Docket No. HM-112, a massive new regulatory framework for the transportation of hazardous materials.

Shortly after the Hazardous Materials Transportation Act was enacted, the secretary of transportation created the Materials Transportation Bureau within the Research and Special Programs Administration of the Department of Transportation, replacing the old Office of Hazardous Materials of the Hazardous Materials Board. This bureau became the lead agency for hazardous materials regulations, while the various administrations continued to be responsible for their individual safety regulations. The inspection and enforcement authority, however, was divided between the bureau and the administrations. The exception to this new organization is the carriage of hazardous materials in bulk by water, which is completely regulated by the U.S. Coast Guard.

In 1985, the Materials Transportation Bureau was abolished, and its responsibilities were transferred to the Office of Pipeline Safety and the Office of Hazardous Materials Transportation. The latter office became the major entity in establishing both national hazardous materials regulations and safety and training programs that reach state and local governments. The impact of this organization over the years has been to create huge industries in training programs, safety equipment manufacturers, database and information companies, and other safety-related activities.

In response to increased international, interstate, and intrastate movements of hazardous materials, state and local governments have taken greater regulatory roles in the effort to protect their respective publics. Although the Hazardous Materials Transportation Act authorized the Department of Transportation to regulate intrastate movements, the department has been hesitant to do so, and this reluctance has motivated the states to enact their own regulations. The Department of Transportation was also empowered to begin a national registration but elected to leave this up to the states. The regulatory role for state and local governments is preserved under the Hazardous Materials Transportation Act section 112, as long as local regulations do not conflict with federal standards. It is clear that Congress intended to preclude a multiplicity of state and local regulations when enacting this provision, but the preemption of federal standards and uniformity has frequently occurred. There has been no comprehensive effort by the Department of Transportation to resolve these inconsistencies and interjurisdictional differences.

IMPACT

The Hazardous Materials Transportation Act is considered the grandfather of modern hazardous materials regulation. The act consolidated several earlier, fragmented regulations, and it authorized Department of Transportation officials to define a "hazardous material." This regulatory basis constituted the foundation of many future regulations and was referenced in several subsequent statutes.

The law, however, has resulted in state and local governments creating a huge regulatory environment that requires licensing, registration, permits, routing, and emergency-response programs and organizations. Many of these regulations are inconsistent with the spirit of the act and vary from state to state, and the lack of uniformity in state laws has contributed to an insurance crisis. Transportation frequently involves multiple jurisdictions, making insurance for movement of hazardous materials sometimes impossible to obtain.

The empowerment of the Department of Transportation to enforce its own regulations through civil and criminal penalties was a major provision of the act. Rather than have infraction citations adjudicated and engage in lengthy and costly criminal litigation, however, the department in practice usually elects to mete out civil penalties.

The Hazardous Materials Transportation Act produced a new regulatory climate. It created vast new federal, state, and local infrastructures and industries and helped to bridge the gap to international intermodal shipments. Its effect on environmental protection, moreover, can only be estimated. Safety is difficult to quantify, and cost-benefit analyses seem inappropriate in regard to human life or ecological disaster. Clearly, however, the Hazardous Materials Transportation Act in many ways improved public and environmental well-being in a growing chemical-industrial society.

Paul Leyda

SOURCES FOR FURTHER STUDY

Bierlein, Lawrence. *Red Book on Transportation of Hazardous Materials.* 2d ed. New York: Van Nostrand Reinhold, 1988.
Congressional Quarterly Almanac. "Transportation Safety." 30 (1975): 698-703.

Keller, J. J., and Associates. *Hazardous Materials Guide: Shipping, Materials Handling, and Transportation.* Neenah, Wis.: J. J. Keller, 1977.

U.S. Congress. *Statutes at Large.* Washington, D.C.: Government Printing Office, 1976.

U.S. Congress. House. *United States Code—Congressional and Administrative News.* St. Paul, Minn.: West Publishing, 1974.

U.S. Congress. Office of Technology Assessment. *Transportation of Hazardous Materials.* OTA-SET-304. Washington, D.C.: Government Printing Office, 1986.

U.S. Congress. Office of Technology Assessment. *Transportation of Hazardous Materials: State and Local Activities.* OTA-SET-301. Washington, D.C.: Government Printing Office, 1986.

University of Texas at Austin. Highway Safety Policy Research Project. *Hazardous Materials Transportation in Texas.* Lyndon B. Johnson School of Public Affairs Policy Research Project Report 82. Austin, Tex.: The Project, 1987.

SEE ALSO: Interstate Commerce Act (1887); Hazardous Substances Labeling Act (1960); Federal Environmental Pesticide Control Act (1972); Toxic Substances Control Act (1976); Low-Level Radioactive Waste Policy Act (1980); Superfund Act (1980); Nuclear Waste Policy Act (1983); Emergency Planning and Community Right-to-Know Act (1986); Marine Plastic Pollution Research and Control Act (1987).

SAFE DRINKING WATER ACT

DATE: December 16, 1974
U.S. STATUTES AT LARGE: 88 Stat. 1660
PUBLIC LAW: 93-523
CATEGORIES: Environment and Conservation; Natural Resources

The U.S. Environmental Protection Agency was given authority to establish minimum safety requirements for pollutants such as arsenic, barium, cadmium, chromium, fluoride, lead, mercury, nitrates, pesticides, radioactivity, and silver.

On December 16, 1974, President Gerald Ford signed the Safe Drinking Water Act, which empowered the Environmental Protection Agency (EPA) to control the quality of drinking water by establishment of standard regulations and other techniques.

PRECIPITATING EVENTS

Prior to the law's passage, a trend toward increasing discharges of agricultural, industrial, and domestic wastewater from a growing population and economy, which in some cases exceeds natural replenishment, caused a "mining" of water, which can have a deteriorating effect on water purity. In addition, the increasing complexity of chemicals used in industry that potentially can make their way into the water supply posed new challenges for pollution abatement.

On November 7, 1974, a study by Dr. Robert Harris was released by the Environmental Defense Fund (EDF), which claimed that cancer deaths were associated with chemicals in New Orleans drinking water. Suspicion was directed toward chlorinated organics, which were either added from chlorination of the water supply system or by chlorinating upstream sewage. Chlorination had been employed for about seventy years as a protective antibacterial measure. Robert B. Hilbert, president of the American Water Works Association (AWWA), denied there was a crisis regarding water supplies and believed the federal role should involve training and research, not enforcement and surveillance. Despite such objections, the SDWA was eventually passed, 296 votes to 84 votes.

PROVISIONS

The primary intent of the SDWA was to establish uniform drinking-water quality in all parts of the United States. Its regulations mainly apply to water after it has been treated, as opposed to surface water or groundwater. The SDWA required the EPA to develop two types of standards for water consumed by humans: recommended maximum contaminant levels (RMCLs) and maximum contaminant levels (MCLs). An RMCL quantifies a maximum contaminant concentration based only on scientific and health-related concerns. This is an informational standard and a long-term goal. In contrast, an MCL is a legal limit which, if exceeded, will require action to lower the pollutant concentration to the compliance value.

The SDWA gives the EPA the power to regulate injection of wastes underground and to protect vulnerable and essential aquifers that are a community's sole source of drinking water. Also, the SDWA requires research on economic, technical, and health-related aspects of drinking water, a rural water supply survey, and funding to enhance the quality of state drinking-water programs. The SDWA created a three-stage process to develop comprehensive drinking-water quality standards. National Interim Primary Drinking Water regulations were promulgated based on generally available technology at the time, the National Academy of Sciences (NAS) was empowered to conduct a survey of health effects stemming from exposure to drinking water pollutants, and Revised Primary Drinking Water Regulations based upon NAS findings were to be established. The SDWA provides uniform, stringent standards for pollutants in water which apply to several hundred thousand water supplies. After the law's passage, starting with interim standards in 1975, the EPA established MCLs for twenty-two pollutants by 1987, and more were added later.

The development of standards was guided by the NAS report completed in 1977 and later updated. Close to one thousand chemicals were identified in the nation's water supplies, and some believed that this number represented only a fraction of those present. The implementation of the SDWA therefore has not proceeded without controversy. The EDF has sued the EPA for foot dragging, the AWWA has sued the agency for being overzealous, and attempts have been made in Congress to weaken the law. In the early 1980's, the AWWA suit was settled. The EPA backed off from requiring installation of activated charcoal filters to lower TTHM levels and instead agreed to deal with TTHM MCL compliance on an individual water-utility basis.

MCLs for Inorganic and Organic Chemicals

Inorganic chemicals regulated are arsenic, barium, cadmium, chromium, lead, mercury, nitrate, selenium, silver, and fluoride. For all the inorganics except fluoride, the MCLs are straightforward limits ranging from 2 (for mercury) to 10,000 (for nitrate) parts per billion depending upon the pollutant in question. Fluoride is a water additive for dental caries prevention. Fluoride MCLs depend upon water temperature. Since people drink more water in hotter climates, the fluoride limits attempt to maintain a uniform dose of fluoride throughout the nation. Organic chemicals regulated are: Endrin; Lindane; Methoxychlor; 2,4-D; 2,4,5-TP (Silvex); Toxaphene; and total Trihalomethanes (TTHM), none of which are naturally occurring substances. The first four are insecticides; the next two are herbicides, typically employed to limit aquatic growth.

Organic chemicals can enter the water supply from industrial discharge during manufacture or from rain water runoff. Inorganic chemicals can enter the water supply from industrial activity or from natural action such as soil leaching. Trihalomethanes are water disinfection by-products consequent to chlorine, iodine, or bromine additions. Additional standards were promulgated for turbidity, microbiological contaminants, and radioactivity. Not all water comes under SDWA purview. Public drinking-water supplies serving twenty-five or fewer individuals are exempt, as is tap water used for purposes other than drinking, such as irrigation and industrial process water.

RMCLs FOR "NUISANCE" SUBSTANCES
The RMCLs, also sometimes called secondary maximum contaminant levels (SMCLs), have been established for substances that are nuisances to the consumer. These substances degrade the aesthetic qualities of water, such as color and odor, and may interfere with water uses such as washing of clothes. At high concentrations, such substances can have health implications. RMCLs have been established for chloride, color, copper, corrosivity, foaming agents, iron, manganese, odor, pH (a measure of water acidity), sulfate, total dissolved solids, and zinc. Monitoring for sodium is mandatory. Corrosive action, mainly a function of pH, must be checked, since corrosive action can leach hazardous materials from the distribution system. Water utilities must examine their distribution systems for components such as lead-soldered pipes and asbestos cement pipes. Also, the EPA has published no adverse response levels (SNARLs) for a variety of organics. These are not legal standards, but some municipalities and states have adopted them for well closures.

IMPLEMENTATION AND ENFORCEMENT
The SDWA's provisions are implemented by the EPA, the states, and local water facilities in partnership. The EPA provides overall

national guidance. Section 1446 of the SDWA provided for an advisory council, including representatives from private organizations, state and local government, and the general public, to advise the EPA administrator on matters related to the act.

The states have primary SDWA enforcement responsibility within their borders, and the regulations were crafted to be nonduplicative and administratively compatible with existing state activities. This was deemed necessary because of many differences among states in the use and availability of water, geological conditions, underground injection practices, among other things. By 1988, fifty out of fifty-seven states and territories had been granted primacy, or full control, over their water programs. The EPA can intervene, however, if a state's regulations are not as stringent as federal law or if the regulations are not being enforced. This was a major departure from previous practice. Prior to the act, the U.S. government only regulated water on interstate carriers such as trains, although the U.S. Public Health Service provided water-quality guidelines. State programs went into effect in June, 1977. The activity levels in states vary widely. Between 1977 and 1983, for example, Ohio officials estimated that $35,000 was spent on groundwater protection efforts, while California's expenditures were $5,160,000 and Texas spent $22,969,700. The 1985 SDWA reauthorization required each state to formulate a groundwater drinking-water source protection plan including land-use pattern and aquifer mapping.

The first aquifer granted sole source protection was the Edwards underground reservoir near San Antonio, Texas, which achieved this status on December 16, 1975, one year after passage of the SDWA. Nearly fifty principal sole source aquifers have been designated; about half are located in the Northeast.

IMPACT

The SDWA has resulted in a decline in drinking-water pollution in many localities, although problems remain. For example, a National Research Council study reported in 1980 that thirty to forty states, including almost all states east of the Mississippi River, had serious drinking-water problems. Problems occur mostly in water systems serving fewer than 10,000 people, since larger systems can afford better water-treatment technology and better-trained personnel. In 1981, for example, more than five years after the law's passage, 4,430 people became ill from polluted drinking water in thirty-two different disease outbreaks. Most outbreaks were caused by bacterial contamination.

A 1982 survey of rural America revealed that one-third of households, most of which used well water, had bacterial contamination in their water. High lead, mercury, selenium, and cadmium concentrations also were noted. The SDWA, which originally exempted well water, was amended in 1986. A unique groundwater protection measure was introduced, the Wellhead Protection Program, the first congressionally mandated environmental protection tool to comprehensively deal with groundwater resources. Later provisions have called for an EPA evaluation of other drinking-water pollutants, including many synthetic organic chemicals.

Kirk J. Bundy

SOURCES FOR FURTHER STUDY

Cheremisinoff, Paul N. *Water Management and Supply.* Englewood Cliffs, N.J.: Prentice Hall, 1993.

Cotruvo, Joseph A. "Implementation of the Safe Drinking Water Act." In *Drinking Water Quality Enhancement Through Source Protection,* edited by Robert B. Pojasek. Ann Arbor, Mich.: Ann Arbor Science Publishers, 1977.

Faust, Samuel D., and Osman M. Aly. *Chemistry of Water Treatment.* Boston: Butterworths, 1983.

National Research Council. Committee on Ground Water Quality Protection. *Ground Water Quality Protection: State and Local Strategies.* Washington, D.C.: National Academy Press, 1986.

Re Velle, Penelope, and Charles Re Velle. *The Environment: Issues and Choices for Society.* 3d ed. Boston: Jones and Bartlett, 1988.

Sheaffer, John R., and Leonard A. Stevens. *Future Water: An Exciting Solution to America's Most Serious Resource Crisis.* New York: William Morrow, 1983.

Smith, V. Kerry, and William H. Desvousges. *Measuring Water Quality Benefits.* Boston: Kluwer-Nijhoff, 1986.

Speidel, David R., Lon C. Ruedisili, and Allen F. Agnew, eds. *Perspectives on Water Uses and Abuses.* New York: Oxford University Press, 1988.

Viessman, W., and Mark J. Hammer. *Water Supply and Pollution Control.* 4th ed. New York: Harper & Row, 1985.

Williams, Robert B., and G. L. Culp. "Criteria and Standards for Improved Potable Water Qualities." In *Handbook of Public Water Systems.* New York: Van Nostrand Reinhold, 1986.

SEE ALSO: Water Pollution Control Act (1948); Water Pollution Control Act Amendments of 1956 (1956); Water Resources Research Act (1964); Clean Water Act and Amendments (1965); Wild and Scenic Rivers Act and National Trails System Act (1968); Water Pollution Control Act Amendments of 1972 (1972).

ANTITRUST PROCEDURES AND PENALTIES ACT

ALSO KNOWN AS: Tunney Act
DATE: December 21, 1974
U.S. STATUTES AT LARGE: 88 Stat. 1708
PUBLIC LAW: 93-528
CATEGORIES: Business, Commerce, and Trade

Although this act had little effect on the way the Department of Justice prosecutes antitrust actions, it did require that consent decrees issued in such actions be in the public interest and be publicly disclosed.

In the early 1970's the Antitrust Division of the Department of Justice settled several important cases with consent decrees. Rather than taking a case to court, the Department of Justice negotiated a settlement with the firm accused of violating antitrust laws. Some decrees, notably the 1971 International Telephone & Telegraph decree (IT&T), were criticized for not requiring the accused firm to make sufficient changes to its business practices. Some antitrust violators, such as IT&T, are major firms wielding considerable economic influence and political power in Washington, D.C. Senator John Tunney claimed that added opportunity for the public to comment on proposed consent decrees would lessen the political pressure these companies might bring on elected officials favoring "pro-business" consent decrees.

Seeking to make the negotiation process more open to the public and stiffen the resolve of the Department of Justice to apply the law vigorously, the Antitrust Procedures and Penalties Act required (1) determination by a court that the proposed consent decree was in the public interest, (2) preliminary publication for public comment on the proposed decree, and (3) disclosure of the firm's lobbying efforts, culminating in a proposal for a consent decree.

A study conducted in 1981 showed that this act had relatively little effect on the operation of the Antitrust Division of the Department of Justice. Although a consent decree is no longer a private matter between the Department of Justice and the accused company, as of 1978 approximately 80 percent of the antitrust lawsuits filed by the Department of Justice were settled by consent decrees. Opting for a consent decree saves the government and the accused time and money in the same sense that a guilty plea by a criminal defendant saves both parties to the criminal suit time and money.

Gayle Avant

SOURCES FOR FURTHER STUDY
Branfman, Eric J. "Antitrust Consent Decrees." *Antitrust Bulletin* 27, no. 2 (Summer, 1982): 303-355.
Kalodner, Andrea. "Consent Decrees as an Antitrust Enforcement Device." *Antitrust Bulletin* 23, no. 2 (Summer, 1978): 277-301.

SEE ALSO: Interstate Commerce Act (1887); Sherman Antitrust Act (1890); Federal Trade Commission Act (1914); Clayton Antitrust Act (1914); Wheeler-Lea Act (1938); Celler-Kefauver Act (1950); Parens Patriae Act (1974).

NAVAJO-HOPI LAND SETTLEMENT ACT

DATE: December 22, 1974
U.S. STATUTES AT LARGE: 88 Stat. 1723
PUBLIC LAW: 93-531
U.S. CODE: 25 § 640
CATEGORIES: Land Management; Native Americans

> *This act was designed to settle land disputes between the Hopi and Navajo; it triggered tremendous controversy surrounding the removal and relocation of several thousand Navajos.*

The Navajo-Hopi Land Settlement Act was enacted by Congress in 1974 primarily to clarify rights of the Navajo and Hopi tribes in the 1882 "Executive Order Reservation" established by President Chester A. Arthur. This executive order set aside 2,472,095 acres "for the use and occupancy of the Moqui [Hopi] and such other Indians as the Secretary of the Interior may see fit to settle thereon." At the time, both Hopis and Navajos were living in the set-aside area. Disputes increased as the Navajo population in the area expanded.

LAND DISPUTES

In 1934 Congress consolidated the boundaries of the Navajo Reservation without altering the 1882 Executive Order Reservation. The Bureau of Indian Affairs then established grazing districts on both reservations. District 6, exclusively for Hopi use, consisted of about 25 percent of the 1882 reservation. The remainder was occupied largely by Navajo stock raisers. Disputes between members of the two tribes continued.

In 1958 Congress authorized a lawsuit to settle conflicting claims to the 1882 reservation. In 1962 a federal court, in *Healing v. Jones*, held that for the area outside District 6, the Hopi and Navajo had "joint, undivided and equal interests." Because the Navajos occupied most of the area, however, they controlled the most surface resources in the Joint Use Area (JUA). Negotiations between the two tribes concerning management of the JUA were unsuccessful. In the early 1970's the Hopis sought and obtained a court order for livestock reduction in the area. The continuing controversy stimulated congressional interest, and the Navajo-Hopi Land Settlement Act was enacted in 1974.

PROVISIONS AND AMENDMENTS

The act was comprehensive. It directed that a mediator make recommendations to the district court, which would then partition the surface rights of the JUA. In 1977 each tribe received half of the JUA. Money was appropriated for livestock reduction and boundary fencing. The act, and a 1980 amendment, allowed for the transfer of some federal lands to the Navajos to help offset lost JUA land. In 1983 about 370,000 acres of "new lands" along the southern edge of the Navajo Reservation were selected.

The act required the removal of members of one tribe living on lands transferred to the other tribe. This involved a relatively small number of Hopis but thousands of Navajos. An independent commission was created to administer the relocation program, but it was inept, contributing to the hardships of relocatees. The $52,000,000 initial appropriation was inadequate. Congress belatedly responded in the 1980's, amending the act to restructure the commission and authorizing hundreds of millions of additional dollars for relocation.

As a final touch of irony, one section of this legislation, designed to resolve controversy over the 1882 reservation, allowed the tribes the right to sue to settle rights in lands within the 1934 Navajo Reservation. In 1992 a federal district court decided that the Hopis and San Juan Southern Paiutes (who had intervened in the lawsuit) had rights in portions of the Navajo Reservation long used by tribal members.

Eric Henderson

SOURCES FOR FURTHER STUDY

Benedek, Emily. *The Wind Won't Know Me: A History of the Navajo-Hopi Land Dispute.* New York: Knopf, 1992.

Brugge, David M. *The Navajo-Hopi Land Dispute: An American Tragedy.* Albuquerque: University of New Mexico Press, 1994.

Clemmer, Richard O. *Roads in the Sky: The Hopi Indians in a Century of Change.* Boulder, Colo.: Westview Press, 1995.

SEE ALSO: Navajo-Hopi Rehabilitation Act (1950).

PRIVACY ACT

ALSO KNOWN AS: Buckley Amendment
DATE: December 31, 1974
U.S. STATUTES AT LARGE: 88 Stat. 1896
PUBLIC LAW: 93-579
U.S. CODE: 5 § 552a
CATEGORIES: Civil Rights and Liberties; Privacy

> *The Privacy Act required the federal government to open to individuals their government records, to correct inaccurate records, and allowed citizens to sue the federal government for violations of the act.*

The right to privacy is not specifically contained in the U.S. Constitution, so in the past an individual had limited abilities to know that a violation of his or her privacy had occurred. Government conducted its business in secret, and citizens knew only what government wanted them to know. The Freedom of Information Act of 1966, of which the Privacy Act later became a part, changed the manner in which government operated. The Privacy Act reflects the need to balance individual privacy concerns with the institutional practice of storing information. The act does not prevent the government from gathering information about people and thereby invading their privacy. Instead it allows a citizen to learn what the government knows about his or her private life.

PROVISIONS

The act guarantees three basic rights: (1) the individual's right to review his or her records; (2) the individual's right to amend inaccurate records; and (3) the individual's right to file a federal lawsuit against the government for violations of the act. Disclosure of any record contained in the system of a federal agency to any other person or agency without the written request or consent of the individual is prohibited. Information gathered for one purpose cannot be used for another purpose absent the individual's consent. Under the act, federal agencies are obliged to store only such personal information as is relevant and necessary. Other restrictions include a requirement to maintain accurate and complete records and to establish appropriate administrative and technical safeguards that assure the security of the records. To confirm compliance with these limitations, the Privacy Act allows an individual access to, and an opportunity to amend, government records of which he or she is the subject. An individual may request correction of information which is not timely, accurate, or complete. Should the agency fail to comply with the request, a review of the agency decision is available.

The act provides for civil remedies against federal agencies, including (1) an order instructing the agency to amend the record, (2) reasonable costs and attorneys fees, (3) an injunction from withholding records from an individual, and (4) actual damages sustained by an individual in cases of willful or intentional agency action.

STATE LEGISLATION

The Privacy Act applies only to the federal government; most states have similar legislation. Where federal statutes are lacking, citizens are left with the protections at the state level, which lack uniformity and are generally inconsistent with overlaps and critical gaps. Generally speaking, however, privacy law is not well developed and has generated relatively little litigation. It has emerged in a sector-by-sector manner; that is, specific laws exist to protect specific types of records (banking), but in some areas (such as health care records), specific protections either do not exist or are inadequate.

Marcia J. Weiss

SOURCES FOR FURTHER STUDY

Privacy Protection Study Commission. *Personal Privacy in an Information Society.* Washington, D.C.: Government Printing Office, 1977.

Regan, Priscilla M. *Legislating Privacy: Technology, Social Values, and Public Policy.* Chapel Hill: University of North Carolina Press, 1995.

Schwartz, Paul. "Privacy and Participation: Personal Information and Public Sector Regulation in the United States." *Iowa Law Review* 80 (1995), 553-618.

SEE ALSO: Ninth Amendment (1789); Freedom of Information Act (1966); Consumer Credit Protection Act (1968); Privacy Protection Act (1980).

EASTERN WILDERNESS ACT

DATE: January 3, 1975
U.S. STATUTES AT LARGE: 88 Stat. 2096
PUBLIC LAW: 93-622
CATEGORIES: Agriculture; Environment and Conservation; Land Management

The Eastern Wilderness Act significantly increased the area preserved as wilderness in Eastern national forests and confirmed that areas no longer pristine might be added to the wilderness system and allowed to recover their wilderness character.

On January 3, 1975, President Gerald R. Ford signed Public Law 93-622, which is known informally as the Eastern Wilderness Act. The law established sixteen new wilderness areas in the Eastern United States and designated seventeen others for further study and possible later inclusion in the National Wilderness Preservation System. It represented a victory for conservation organizations interested in enlarging the wilderness system and a defeat for the U.S. Forest Service, which had championed strict standards of naturalness for admission to the wilderness system.

PREVIOUS LEGISLATION

Although the term "wilderness" logically applies to any area that is wild and undeveloped, in the United States the term is generally applied to an area of reasonably undisturbed natural land owned by the government and specifically set aside and protected against development. Before 1964, some wilderness areas in the national forests were protected by administrative rules of the U.S. Forest Service. Many other areas of wild land were within the boundaries of national parks, national monuments, and national wildlife refuges and enjoyed the degree of protection available to the park, monument, or refuge of which they were a part. These areas all had some level of legal protection against development, but none was protected by law as wilderness until Congress passed and President Lyndon Johnson signed the Wilderness Act of 1964.

The Wilderness Act defined wilderness in law and designated national forest wilderness areas comprising 9.1 million acres, including four east of the one hundredth meridian. It established a process under which the Forest Service, the National Park Service, and the Fish and Wildlife Service would review undeveloped lands within their respective jurisdictions and recommend those that might in the future be added to the National Wilderness Preservation System.

In the process of studying undeveloped areas and making recommendations, the Forest Service evolved what came to be called its "purity policy." Under this policy, the Forest Service declined to recommend areas for wilderness status unless they were very nearly pristine.

The purity policy was based on a controversial interpretation of the Wilderness Act. Congress had written relatively flexible admissions standards into the Wilderness Act but required relatively strict management of areas once admitted. In an apparent effort to limit the impact of the wilderness review process on its commodity programs, Associated Chief John R. McGuire articulated the Forest Service's conclusion that the Wilderness Act's strict management standards applied to admission as well. Insistence that wilderness areas must be pure to be considered for inclusion in the system reduced the potential for growth in the wilderness system nationwide. In the East, the impact of the policy was most dramatic. McGuire asserted that there were no areas east of the Rockies that could qualify for inclusion in the wilderness system. Yet the Forest Service was not unmindful of the growing demand for primitive recreation in national forests near centers of population.

To meet the demand without comprising its view that no areas in the East met the standards of the Wilderness Act, the Forest Service developed a proposal for a new system of wild areas. The proposal originated with the regional foresters in Atlanta and Milwaukee. These wild areas were to be primarily recreational. Mining and grazing would be prohibited, but otherwise the Forest Service would have broad latitude in administration. The proposal became public in the fall of 1971, when Associate Chief McGuire addressed the Sierra Club's Biennial Wilderness Conference. McGuire recognized the need for primitive recreational opportunities in the East but asserted that this need would have to be met through some alternative to the Wilderness Act. Virtually all candidate areas in the East had at some time been logged, roaded, or farmed. They did not qualify under the Wilderness Act as areas of "undeveloped Federal land retaining [their] primeval character."

McGuire's speech precipitated extended discussions involving the Forest Service and the national conservation organizations. At first, influential members of the Izaak Walton League and the Sierra Club were disposed to favor the Forest Service proposal. It seemed a practical way to preserve the areas they favored. The Wilderness Society and most of the other national conservation organizations were opposed to the proposal. To accept the plan would be to accept the Forest Service's interpretation of the Wilderness Act: To be admitted to the wilderness system an area must be—and must always have been—pristine. Acceptance of this interpretation would sharply limit the possibility of future wilderness designations all over the country.

Pressure to act was building. In February, 1972, President Nixon delivered an environmental message to Congress bemoaning the lack of wilderness areas in the East and ordering the secretary of agriculture to accelerate efforts to identify candidate areas.

Senators George Aiken and Herman Talmadge, members of the Senate Agriculture Committee and political allies of the Forest Service, introduced legislation to implement a wild area system of the sort the agency was promoting. Several wild area bills were directed to the Senate Committee on Agriculture and Forestry, which Talmadge chaired. One was reported from the committee and passed by the Senate, catching the national conservation organizations off guard. Doug Scott of the Wilderness Society quickly drafted an alternative bill based on the Wilderness Act and convinced Senators James Buckley and Henry Jackson to sponsor it.

The battle lines were clearly drawn. The Forest Service preferred Aiken-Talmadge, which was based on its own proposal. The bill created only one instant wilderness. It was being handled by the committee on agriculture and forestry, on which the Forest Service had considerable influence, and it would write the purity policy into law. The national conservation organizations were by now reasonably united in their support for Buckley-Jackson. As eventually approved by the interior committee, it would have created nineteen wilderness areas and an additional thirty-nine wilderness study areas under the authority of the Wilderness Act. It would reassert the interior committee's dominant role in wilderness legislation and the environmental community's more flexible interpretation of admissions standards under the Wilderness Act. Congress adjourned without passing any Eastern wilderness bill.

In 1973, both the Aiken-Talmadge and Buckley-Jackson proposals were reintroduced with the understanding that the competing committees would share jurisdiction. After each committee had finished its work, negotiations began to produce a compromise bill. The differences were deep, and the negotiations might well have broken down. Those involved credited Senator Aiken for making sure they did not. The compromise bill created nineteen wilderness areas and forty wilderness study areas. It was approved by the Senate on May 31, 1974.

Consideration in the House was anticlimactic. National attention was focused on the Watergate investigations. The House interior committee deleted wilderness areas that appeared controversial and reported a bill that created sixteen wilderness areas and seventeen wilderness study areas. The House passed it on December 18, 1974, and the Senate agreed to the House version. President Ford signed the Eastern Wilderness Act on January 3, 1975.

The Eastern Wilderness Act designated sixteen new wilderness areas covering about 207,000 acres in thirteen Eastern states: Alabama, Arkansas, Florida, Georgia, Kentucky, New Hampshire, North Carolina, South Carolina, Tennessee, Vermont, Virginia, West Virginia, and Wisconsin. The largest was the 34,500-acre Cohutta Wilderness, which spans the border between Georgia and Tennessee in the Appalachian Mountains and protects a land of rocky gorges, plunging waterfalls, and virgin forest. Other significant additions to the wilderness system ranged from the 20,380-acre, near-arctic Presidential Range-Dry River Wilderness in New Hampshire to the 22,000-acre swamp-forest of Bradwell Bay Wilderness in the panhandle of Florida. The smallest of the sixteen new wilderness areas was the 2,570-acre Gee Creek Wilderness in Tennessee's southern Appalachian Mountains.

The act designated seventeen additional areas for study and potential designation at a later date. By March, 1994, twelve of those seventeen areas had been approved by Congress, adding another 122,000 acres to the national forest wilderness system.

The importance of the designation of the additional wilderness areas may be overshadowed by the Eastern Wilderness Act's implicit policy conclusion about wilderness admissions standards. The legislative battle over Eastern wilderness ended the Forest Service's purity policy. If the purity policy had been left unchecked, it might have curtailed the growth of national forest wilderness nationwide and could have ended it altogether east of the Rocky Mountains. Congress declared, in effect, that areas will be added to the National Wilderness Preservation System when the national interest is better served by the area's protection as wilderness than by its development for other uses. Old roads, buildings, and other evidences of past development may be overlooked in areas being considered for designation as national forest wilderness areas.

As if to underscore its repudiation of the purity policy, in the final days of 1974 Congress passed Public Law 93-632, establishing eleven wilderness areas totaling nearly 85,000 acres of national wildlife refuge lands in eight Eastern states. These lands were administered by the Fish and Wildlife Service, which did not share the Forest Service's purity policy, but few of these areas could have been admitted to the wilderness system if Congress had adopted the strict admissions requirements advocated by the Forest Service. Public Law 93-632 became law contemporaneously with the Eastern Wilderness Act on January 3, 1975.

Congressional repudiation of the purity policy was a landmark in the history of wilderness law, but it was not a change in policy. An examination of the initial national forest areas approved in the Wilderness Act of 1964 reveals many deviations from pristine wilderness. In passing the Eastern Wilderness Act, the Congress simply declined to accept the view advocated by the Forest Service that an area must be pristine to be admitted to the wilderness system. Congress's rejection of purity preserved its own freedom of action on wilderness admissions and preserved the possibility that many more areas in the Eastern national forests might eventually be given wilderness status.

The precedent established by the Eastern Wilderness Act has dramatically altered federal land-management practices in the East. It has encouraged advocates to study relatively undeveloped tracts and to propose wilderness designations. Since passage of the Eastern Wilderness Act, the efforts of wilderness advocates have produced remarkable results.

At the close of 1984, a decade after the passage of the Wilderness Act, Congress had added thirteen wilderness areas in the East, all on national wildlife refuge lands and five encompassing less than thirty acres each. In the national forests of the East there remained only the four original wilderness areas: Linville Gorge and Shining Rock in North Carolina, Great Gulf in New Hampshire, and the Boundary Waters Canoe Area in Minnesota.

In the decade after the Eastern Wilderness Act, the number of Eastern wilderness areas grew rapidly, and national forest lands constituted most of the addition. The process continues, albeit at a diminishing pace. By mid-1994, there were 173 wilderness areas in national forests, national parks, and national wildlife refuges. Together, these wilderness areas protected 4.2 million acres in 31 of the 37 states east of the Rockies. Most of these wilderness areas are less than pristine, but they provide an increasingly valuable resource for history, science, and recreation.

Craig W. Allin

SOURCES FOR FURTHER STUDY

Allin, Craig W. *The Politics of Wilderness Preservation.* Westport, Conn.: Greenwood Press, 1982.

Costley, Richard J. "Wilderness: An Enduring Resource." *American Forests* 78 (June, 1972): 7-11, 54-56.

Frome, Michael. *Battle for the Wilderness.* New York: Praeger, 1974.

Hendee, John C., George H. Stankey, and Robert C. Lucas. *Wilderness Management.* Rev. ed. Golden, Colo.: North American Press, 1990.

Kulhavy, David L., and Richard N. Conner, eds. *Wilderness and Natural Areas in the Eastern United States: A Management Challenge.* Nacogdoches, Tex.: Center for Applied Studies, School of Forestry, Stephen F. Austin University, 1986.

Roth, Dennis M. *The Wilderness Movement and the National Forests.* College Station, Tex.: Intaglio Press, 1988.

SEE ALSO: National Park Service Organic Act (1916); Wilderness Act (1964)

SPEEDY TRIAL ACT

DATE: January 3, 1975
U.S. STATUTES AT LARGE: 88 Stat. 2076
PUBLIC LAW: 93-619
U.S. CODE: 18 § 3161
CATEGORIES: Civil Rights and Liberties; Judiciary and Judicial Procedure; Crimes and Criminal Procedure

To put teeth into the Sixth Amendment's guarantee of speedy trials for accused persons, this act, which applies only to federal courts, sets specific time limits for indictment, arraignment, and trial.

It is believed that the speedy trial concept had its source in the Magna Carta (1215), the "Great Charter" of England that set forth, among other principles, the right of a man to a trial by his peers. Contained in the Sixth Amendment of the U.S. Constitution, the speedy trial clause was made to apply to the states through the Fourteenth Amendment. Prior to the 1960's the notion of a speedy trial was rarely discussed, because courts generally proceeded in a timely manner.

In 1970, however, a backlog of cases began to appear, and lawyers questioned the constitutionality of lengthy delays. There was disagreement and debate over when the clock started ticking—from the time of commission of the offense or the time of indictment when formal charges were filed. While prosecutors could publicly announce that indictments were forthcoming, they could take years to file charges. This delay compromised the rights of accused individuals by making them wait sometimes as long as two or three years for formal charges to be filed.

In *Barker v. Wingo* (1972) the Supreme Court considered the constitutionality of long delays in bringing someone to trial. Ruling that the right to a speedy trial is relative rather than absolute, the justices refused to interpret the Sixth Amendment as requiring any specific length of time, but instead formulated a balancing test for determining unreasonable delay, assessing the conduct of both the prosecution and the defense in regard to the following: (1) the length of the delay, (2) the reasons for the delay, (3) the point at which defendants assert their right, and (4) whether the delay prejudices the defendant because, for example, a favorable witness has died or memories have blurred.

In the uproar that followed that vague decision, Congress passed legislation called the Speedy Trial Act of 1974 (amended in 1979) in order to put teeth into the guarantee. Applying only to federal courts, it sets specific time limits, requiring indictment within thirty days of arrest, arraignment within ten days after indictment, and trial sixty days after arraignment. Time periods such as those associated with pretrial motions and mental competency are excluded. The right to a speedy trial is a safeguard to prevent undue and oppressive pretrial incarceration, minimize anxiety and concern accompanying public accusation, and ensure that the defendants maintain the ability to defend themselves. It is also supposed to satisfy the societal interest in minimizing the necessity to support persons in jail at public expense as well as upholding the deterrent and rehabilitative effects of criminal law.

Speedy trial statutes exist in all fifty states. If the time limits are not respected, the case is to be dismissed. Realistically, however, only in extraordinary circumstances have criminal charges been dismissed for lack of timely trial, and most states as well as the federal government have enacted exceptions to their Speedy Trial Acts. Efforts to mandate speedy trials lack specifics and are not based on the reasons for the delay in question. They do not provide for additional personnel to aid the courts in complying, and conflicts in the court calendar often occur. Enforcement can also be a problem.

Marcia J. Weiss

SOURCES FOR FURTHER STUDY

Misner, Robert. *Speedy Trial: Federal and State Practice.* Charlottesville, Va.: Michie, 1983.

Neubauer, David W. *America's Courts and the Criminal Justice System.* 6th ed. Belmont, Calif.: Wadsworth, 1999.

SEE ALSO: Sixth Amendment (1789).

INDIAN SELF-DETERMINATION AND EDUCATION ASSISTANCE ACT

DATE: January 4, 1975
U.S. STATUTES AT LARGE: 88 Stat. 2203
PUBLIC LAW: 93-638
U.S. CODE: 25 § 450
CATEGORIES: Education; Native Americans

> *This act marked a significant swing away from the overt assimilationist policies of the federal government and supported the basic concepts of tribalism and Native American sovereignty.*

The 1970's were marked by support of federal officials for broadening Indian participation in programs that affected them and to lessen the paternalism that had guided federal Indian policy for so long. The Indian Self-Determination and Education Assistance Act of 1975 marked a radical change in federal policy—the assimilationist philosophy of the federal government was replaced by policies favoring tribalism and Native American sovereignty. This law enabled and encouraged tribes to take over and run their own programs.

The act clearly endorsed Indian decision making, and the preamble declared that the United States recognized its obligation "to respond to the strong expression of the Indian people for self-determination by assuring maximum participation in the direction of educational as well as other federal services to Indian communities so as to render such services more responsive to the needs and desires of those communities." It also stated that Congress confirms its commitment to maintain "the Federal Government's unique and continuing relationship with and responsibility to the Indian people through the establishment of a meaningful Indian self-determination policy."

The Self-Determination and Education Assistance Act consists of three major sections. In the first part, Congress outlines the basic federal policy toward native people, denounces federal paternalism, and affirms tribal rights to control their own affairs. Second, Congress asserts it will work for Indian self-determination particularly in education, while maintaining and preserving the trust relationship. Third, Indians will receive hiring preference in all federal government contracts affecting Indian tribes.

The most significant drawback to the act is that, even though decision making and administrative authority seemed to pass to tribal councils, the Bureau of Indian Affairs maintained the power to decide which tribal contracts it would accept. This reserved power included determining budget allocations provided to tribes who seek to run their own programs. Yet despite limitations placed on tribal authority, many tribes throughout the United States contract and run many programs that were formerly run by the Bureau of Indian Affairs. The most dramatic impact of the act has been in the area of education. A majority of former Bureau of Indian Affairs schools are now run by tribes, and many higher education scholarship programs are tribally run. The act is important in that it supports the basic concept of tribal self-determination.

Carole A. Barrett

Source for Further Study

Castile, George Pierre. *To Show Heart: Native American Self-Determination and Federal Indian Policy, 1960-1975.* Tucson: University of Arizona Press, 1998.

See also: General Allotment Act (1887); Burke Act (1906); Indian Citizenship Act (1924); Indian Reorganization Act (1934); Termination Resolution (1953); Public Law 280 (1953).

Magnuson-Moss Warranty Act

Date: January 4, 1975
U.S. Statutes at Large: 88 Stat. 2193
Public law: 93-637
U.S. Code: 15 § 45
Categories: Business, Commerce, and Trade

The Magnuson-Moss Warranty Act imposed important requirements on manufacturers and sellers that offer written warranties to consumers.

The Magnuson-Moss Warranty Act of 1975 imposed important disclosure requirements upon sellers that provide written product warranties to consumers, addressed and sought to simplify the procedures for enforcing such warranties, and limited or proscribed certain common practices of product warrantors. This act, the first major federal effort to reform warranty law, represented the culmination of several years of federally prescribed studies of consumer-directed written warranties.

THE UNIFORM COMMERCIAL CODE

Prior to 1975, state law, in the form of the Uniform Commercial Code (UCC), governed the creation, interpretation, and enforcement of product warranties. The UCC was the law in virtually all states and, in Article 2, included several provisions governing warranties. For example, the UCC governed express warranties or oral or written statements by sellers that they will stand behind the goods they sell. It also governed implied warranties, warranties arising because of the sales contract and existing regardless of the presence of an express warranty.

The two most important implied warranties are the implied warranty of merchantability and the implied warranty of fitness for a particular purpose. The implied warranty of merchantability arises in sales by merchants or dealers in a particular type of good. It requires that the goods be fit for their ordinary use or purpose. For example, under the UCC, merchant sellers by implication warrant that automobiles are generally safe to drive and that washing machines are capable of washing clothes. In both cases, the sellers are warranting that their product meets general industry standards. The implied warranty of fitness for a particular purpose requires that sellers select appropriate goods in those cases in which buyers rely on the sellers' expertise to do so. For example, a contractor needing a certain type of exterior paint to complete a project might inform the seller that he or she is relying on the seller's expertise in identifying suitable paint. The implied warranty of fitness for a particular purpose would arise in that sale. If the paint is unfit for the stated purpose, then the seller has breached the implied warranty.

LIMITATIONS TO UCC WARRANTIES

Although the UCC's regime of express and implied warranties represented the most comprehensive product warranty rules ever adopted, a number of federal studies in the 1960's and 1970's revealed the UCC's shortcomings, particularly in its rules related to written warranties. These studies suggested that some written warranties were so general that they communicated nothing about product quality, were often misleading, and were usually imposed by the product seller or manufacturer rather than being the result of bargaining between the seller and buyer.

The studies' more specific observations identified some of the key problems with written warranties. For example, it became evident that in many sales of durable goods such as automobiles and large appliances, sellers were not communicating their warranties to buyers. Instead, buyers would often learn of a warranty after having received the product. The warranty in those cases was largely unimportant in the sale because the buyer knew nothing of it until after agreeing to purchase the product. In those cases in which the buyer knew of a written warranty, the seller often would include a disclaimer of implied warranties and/or a limitation of consequential damages (damages other than the reduced worth of a defective product; for example, the damages from a basement flood caused by a defective valve on a hot water heater). The net result of such a warranty was that the buyer would lack the benefits of the implied warranties and consequential damages. Buyers often were confronted with conditions of qualification for warranty protection. These conditions might include a requirement to send a warranty card to a manufacturer to ensure coverage, a provision that the defective product be sent to a distant manufacturer for service, or a requirement that the buyer take the product to a local retailer for service despite the manufacturer's unwillingness to compensate the retailer adequately for the services provided. Another conclusion of the federal studies was that many purchasers who enjoyed rights under the UCC's warranty provisions were unwilling to litigate because the amount of the claim, often only the difference between the actual and warranted value of the product, would not justify pursuing an action against the manufacturer or seller of the product.

PROVISIONS OF MAGNUSON-MOSS

On January 4, 1975, Congress's effort to correct these problems, the Magnuson-Moss Warranty Act, became law. In general, the act requires manufacturers and sellers who use written product warranties to disclose to purchasers the scope, effect, and limitations, if any, of a warranty; requires warrantors to establish informal dispute resolution programs for consumers who have claims based on written warranties; and prohibits warrantors from using a written warranty to disclaim the UCC's implied warranties. It is important to note that the act does not require that product sellers make written warranties; it applies only to those sellers that elect to use such warranties.

DISCLOSURE PROVISIONS

The disclosure provisions of the Magnuson-Moss Warranty Act were likely its most significant provisions. These provisions were intended to respond to the less-than-clear language often used by sellers in their written warranties and to provide consumers with more information, with which they could make better choices. The most important disclosure requirement is that warrantors clearly label written warranties as either "full" or "limited." A full warranty requires the warrantor or its designated representative to repair the defective product at no cost to the consumer, and, if repair is not possible, to replace the product at no cost. If the warrantor or its representative is unable to repair or replace the product, then the warrantor must refund the purchase price. The warrantor may specify the duration of the full warranty. The act classifies all warranties that fall short of the coverage of full warranties as limited warranties and requires that the warrantors label them as such.

The Magnuson-Moss Warranty Act requires that all consumer-directed written warranties be stated in clear and unambiguous language. Consumers should know the following information after reading the written warranty: which parts and repairs are covered by the warranty, whether any expenses are excluded from coverage, how long the warranty lasts, the necessary steps in obtaining repairs, what the company will do if the product fails, whether the warranty covers consequential damages, and any conditions or limitations on the warranty. The act also includes some important requirements and prohibitions. It requires that consumers be apprised of their written warranty options before the sale, compels warrantors that want to limit or avoid consequential damages to include conspicuous language to that effect in the written warranty, and proscribes the use of warranty cards and other devices that may pose obstacles to purchasers unless the written warranty itself includes such requirements. The act also prohibits a warrantor that makes a written full or limited warranty from disclaiming any implied warranties.

DISPUTE RESOLUTION

To encourage the resolution of consumer warranty claims, the Magnuson-Moss Warranty Act requires all product warrantors to establish internal means of informal dispute resolution for these claims. Although the act does not require resort to informal resolution, it encourages consumers to use this method. If a consumer makes reasonable efforts to comply with the warrantor's wishes and if the warrantor is unable to remedy the consumer's claim adequately, then the consumer has the right, if he or she prevails in a later lawsuit against the warrantor, to recover from the warrantor the reasonable value of attorney fees and court costs arising from the litigation.

IMPACT ON CONSUMERS AND WARRANTORS

The Magnuson-Moss Warranty Act has had a varied but generally positive effect on consumer-directed warranty transactions. For example, the act's disclosure provisions appear to have had their intended effect of providing consumers with information so that they can make better purchasing decisions. After passage of the act, the federal government commissioned several studies to examine its effect. In general, the findings suggested that consumers were pleased with the warranty information required by Magnuson-Moss and used this information to make informed choices among comparable products.

Additional studies sought to determine whether and to what extent the act influenced potential warrantors. The findings suggested that product manufacturers and sellers were not more reluctant to make written warranties after the act. In fact, it appeared that many product marketers sought to use the act's requirements to their advantage by offering full warranties to consumers. The studies also suggested that warranties appearing after passage of the act were more readable and included more product information than did their predecessors. Finally, the studies revealed that virtually all warrantors were complying with the act's prohibition against implied warranty disclaimers but warrantors were more inclined to include conspicuous limitations of consequential damages in their written warranties.

The act's provision prohibiting warrantors from using their written warranties to disclaim implied warranties has had a significant influence on both warrantors and consumers. Perhaps the single most deceptive practice before the adoption of Magnuson-Moss was a warrantor's assertion of product quality through a written warranty coupled with an almost contradictory provision disclaiming the UCC's implied warranties of merchantability and fitness for a particular purpose. The written warranty would suggest to most reasonable consumers that the product was of good quality, would include language that often restricted the consumer's options in case the product was less than advertised, and then would eliminate resort to implied warranties, which provided the only other recourse should the written warranty fail for some reason.

Despite the act's attempt to simplify the dispute process, dispute resolution remained the biggest problem for consumers wishing to pursue warranty actions against product warrantors. Whether the product deviates from a written warranty or is of poor quality continued to be a key issue in warranty disputes. Although the Magnuson-Moss Warranty Act improved the dispute process and encouraged warrantors to cure the problem, the act did not, and likely could not, eliminate frivolous consumer claims, unreasonable warrantor reactions to legitimate claims, and high litigation costs for those cases in which both sides strongly support their positions and are therefore unwilling to resolve their dispute in an informal manner.

A final and largely unanswered question raised by the act concerns the effects of federal intervention in an area such as warranty law that historically had been governed by states' laws. This question becomes more important when examined within the context of congressional efforts to reform another area reserved to states' laws, product liability. Magnuson-Moss received wide support in Congress, but throughout the 1980's proposed product liability reform legislation did not succeed.

Nim Razook

SOURCES FOR FURTHER STUDY

Arthur Young & Company. *Warranties Rules Consumer Baseline Study.* Washington, D.C.: Government Printing Office, 1979.

Reitz, Curtis R. *Consumer Protection Under the Magnuson-Moss Warranty Act.* Philadelphia Pennsylvania: American Law Institute-American Bar Association Committee on Continuing Professional Education, 1978.

Schmitt, Jacqueline, Lawrence Kanter, and Rachel Miller. *Impact Report on the Magnuson-Moss Warranty Act.* Washington, D.C.: Government Printing Office, 1980.

U.S. Federal Trade Commission. *A Businessperson's Guide to Federal Warranty Law.* Washington, D.C.: Government Printing Office, 1987.

SEE ALSO: Child product safety laws (1970's); Child Protection and Toy Safety Act (1969); Consumer Product Safety Act (1972).

EARNED INCOME TAX CREDIT

DATE: February 18, 1975, as part of the Tax Reduction Act of 1975
U.S. STATUTES AT LARGE: 89 Stat. 26 (Tax Reduction Act)
PUBLIC LAW: 94-12 (Tax Reduction Act)
CATEGORIES: Tariffs and Taxation

The earned income tax credit, an attempt to use the tax system as a method of social policy, provided for government cash payments to lower-income families with children.

The earned income tax credit is traceable to the early attempts to reform the nation's welfare system. In 1969 President Richard M. Nixon proposed a guaranteed annual income as part of his Family Assistance Plan. Under this plan, the government was to establish a minimum income level, and Americans, whether employed or not, would have been eligible for coverage. No American family would have been permitted, under Nixon's proposal, to fall below a certain income level. Nixon's Family Assistance Plan was controversial and was opposed by both Democrats and Republicans. Although it was passed by the House of Representatives, it was defeated in the Senate. Nevertheless, the concept, in a much-revised format, became the earned income tax credit.

The earned income tax credit became part of American public policy in 1975, when Congress passed a new tax law. One component of this law provided for government cash payments to lower-income families with children. While not as far-reaching in scope as Nixon's plan, the earned income tax credit has become an important part of American social welfare policy. During the 1980's the administration of President Ronald Reagan supported increases in the program, and in 1993 the administration of President Bill Clinton supported an expansion of the program.

Michael E. Meagher

Sources for Further Study

Drake, Susan L. *The Tax Reduction Act of 1975 Public Law 94-12 (H.R. 2166): The Legislative Development of Each Provision, Including Those Items Not Adopted.* Washington, D.C.: Congressional Research Service, 1975.

Meyer, Bruce D., and Douglas Holtz-Eakin, eds. *Making Work Pay: The Earned Income Tax Credit and Its Impact on America's Families.* New York: Russell Sage, 2002.

See also: Economic Recovery Tax Act and Omnibus Budget Reconciliation Act (1981); Tax Reform Act of 1986 (1986).

CONVENTION ON INTERNATIONAL TRADE IN ENDANGERED SPECIES

DATE: July 1, 1975
CATEGORIES: Animals; Business, Commerce, and Trade; Environment and Conservation; Treaties and Agreements

The Convention on International Trade in Endangered Species resulted from an international conference on endangered species held in Washington, D.C., in 1973. The 144 signatories made legal commitments to conserve endangered animal and plant species.

Until the 1970's the international agreements that dealt with preservation of species did not include a binding legal commitment on the part of the countries signing them. They were ineffectual in protecting the species that they were written to protect. In 1969, however, the United States passed the Endangered Species Conservation Act (ESA), which contained a provision that gave the secretaries of interior and commerce until June 30, 1971, to call for an international conference on endangered species.

Although it went beyond the ESA's time limit, the international conference was held in Washington, D.C., in March, 1973, resulting in the Convention on International Trade in Endangered Species of Wild Fauna and Flora (CITES). The United States was the first country to ratify the convention, which entered into effect on July 1, 1975; more than 140 other countries have also ratified.

PROVISIONS OF THE AGREEMENT

CITES is intended to conserve species and does this by managing international trade in those species. It was the first international convention on the conservation of wildlife that constituted a legal commitment by the parties to the convention and also included a means of enforcing its provisions. This enforcement includes a system of trade sanctions and an international reporting network to stop trade in endangered species.

However, the system established by CITES does contain loopholes through which states with a special interest in a particular species can opt out of the global control for that species. The major aspect of CITES is its creation of three levels of vulnerability of species. Appendix I includes all species that are threatened with extinction and whose status may be affected by international trade. Appendix II includes species that are not yet threatened but might become endangered if trade in them is not regulated. It also includes other species that, if traded, might affect the vulnerability of the first group. Appendix III lists species that a signatory party identifies as subject to regulation in order to restrict exploitation of that species. The parties to the treaty agree not to allow any trade in the species on the three lists unless an exception is allowed in CITES.

The species listed in the appendices may be moved from one list to another as their vulnerability increases or decreases. According to the convention, states may implement stricter measures of conservation than those specified in the convention or may ban trade in species not included in the appendices. CITES also established a series of import and export trade permits within each of the categories. Each nation designates a management authority and a scientific authority to implement CITES. Exceptions to the ban on trade are made for scientific and museum specimens, exhibitions, and movement of a species under permit by a national management authority.

OBLIGATIONS OF THE SIGNATORIES

The parties to CITES maintain records of trade in specimens of species that are listed in the appendices and prepare periodic reports on their compliance with the convention. These reports are sent to the CITES secretariat in Switzerland, administered by the United Nations Environment Program (UNEP), which issues notifications to all parties of state actions and bans. The secretariat's functions are established by the convention and include interpreting the provisions of CITES and advising countries on implementing those provisions by providing assistance in writing their national legislation and organizing training seminars. The secretariat also studies the status of species being traded in order to assure that the exploitation of such species is within sustainable limits.

The CITES Conference of Parties meets every two or three years in order to review implementation of the convention. The meetings are also attended by nonparty states, intergovernmental agencies of the United Nations, and nongovernmental organizations considered "technically qualified in protection, conservation or management of wild fauna and flora." The meetings are held in different signatories' countries: The first took place in Berne, Switzerland, on November 2-6, 1976. At the conference, the parties may adopt amendments to the convention and make recommendations to improve the effectiveness of CITES.

CITES has been incorporated into Caring for the Earth: A Strategy for Sustainable Living. The strategy was launched in 1991 by UNEP, the International Union for the Conservation of Nature (IUCN), and the World Wildlife Fund (WWF). Other nongovernmental groups working to support CITES are Fauna and Flora International (FFI), Trade Records Analysis of Flora and Fauna in Commerce (TRAFFIC International), and the World Conservation Monitoring Centre (WCMC).

LATER AGREEMENTS

Some of the species protected by CITES have received additional protection under later agreements. In certain cases, however, states have allowed trade in listed species to continue for economic purposes or have refused to sign CITES because of the extent to which they trade in a species or species part, such as ivory. Others have signed because they needed help in stopping illegal trade and poaching of species within their borders. Whales have proven to be a difficult species to protect. Whales were given protection under CITES according to the status of the specific whale species. The moratorium on commercial whaling by the International Whaling Commission (IWC) was intended to strengthen the CITES protection by species, but the whaling states have disagreed on the numbers of whale populations, and some have withdrawn from the IWC and resumed their whaling activities.

Colleen M. Driscoll

SOURCES FOR FURTHER STUDY

Ehrlich, Paul, and Anne Ehrlich. *Extinction: The Causes and Consequences of the Disappearance of Species.* New York: Random House, 1981.

McNeely, Jeffrey A., et al. *Conserving the World's Biological Diversity.* Washington, D.C.: World Resources Institute, 1990.

SEE ALSO: Endangered Species Preservation Act (1966); Endangered Species Act (1973).

VOTING RIGHTS ACT OF 1975

DATE: August 6, 1975
U.S. STATUTES AT LARGE: 89 Stat. 402
PUBLIC LAW: 94-73
U.S. CODE: 42 § 1973
CATEGORIES: Asia or Asian Americans; Civil Rights and Liberties; Voting and Elections

The Voting Rights Act of 1975 formally ended use of literacy tests designed to deny voting rights to language minorities in the United States.

Civil rights became a central concern of American politics in the 1960's. Numerous civil rights acts were passed during that decade, and none was more important for the extension of voting rights in particular than the Voting Rights Act 1965. The 1975 extension of this act included a ban on literacy tests for minorities. Many consider these acts to be the most important extensions of rights ever granted by Congress. In American history, the only actions that surpass the 1965 and 1975 voting rights acts in importance for extending voting rights are the Fifteenth (1870) and Nineteenth (1920) amendments to the U.S. Constitution, respectively prohibiting denial of voting rights on the basis of race, color, or previous servitude and granting the vote to women.

TWENTY-FOURTH AMENDMENT

By the mid-1960's, the number of demonstrations by civil rights groups had increased considerably. Violence surrounding even the "peaceful" demonstrations had intensified their impact. President Lyndon B. Johnson had hoped that the states would address voting rights problems within their own borders. The federal government attempted to assist states by removing some of the obstacles to voting rights. One clear example was President Johnson's leadership in securing the passage of the Twenty-fourth Amendment in 1964, outlawing the use of poll taxes as a necessary prerequisite to voting in federal elections. This was a major step in encouraging minorities to exercise their voting rights.

Although the Twenty-fourth Amendment was a major electoral breakthrough, it had the same shortcoming as the civil rights acts Congress approved in 1957, 1960, and 1964: It left the federal government in a passive role in the crucial area of voter registration. The voting rights acts of 1965, 1970, and 1975 overcame this critical shortcoming.

VOTING RIGHTS ACT OF 1965

The history of the Voting Rights Act of 1965 is also the history of the Voting Rights Act of 1975, since the later action was an extension of the earlier act. The 1965 act largely was forced on President Johnson and others who hoped that the federal government could avoid direct intervention in what historically had been a local prerogative. Public opinion grew intolerant and impatient after a series of bloody demonstrations. By most accounts, the decisive event that led to congressional action in 1965 was the Freedom March from Selma to Montgomery, Alabama. The Reverend Martin Luther King, Jr., organized this march to protest the registration process in Dallas County. Like other marches during this period, it drew marchers from the entire nation. What distinguished this particular march was the violence that erupted when Governor George Wallace called out state troopers to stop the march. The clash between marchers and troopers resulted in the deaths of two marchers and severe injuries to scores of others.

This conflict produced an outburst of demonstrations and protest across the nation. The cries for an end to this violence forced President Johnson to introduce a comprehensive voting rights bill to the U.S. Congress. The final version of this bill, which Johnson signed into law on August 6, ended literacy tests in the states of Alabama, Georgia, Louisiana, Mississippi, South Carolina, and Virginia and in thirty-nine counties in North Carolina.

The other key provision of this law was the authorization of federal examiners to conduct registration and federal observers to oversee elections. The states and counties within the affected jurisdictions also had to submit any changes in their election laws and procedures to federal examiners for clearance. The literacy provision affected Southern states primarily, but the broader jurisdiction of the act affected states in every region of the nation.

VOTING RIGHTS ACT OF 1970

The voting rights act was due for renewal in 1970. In June of that year, Congress extended the act and made some significant changes. The major changes in the 1970 amendments were a ban on literacy tests in all states, prohibition of long-term residency requirements for voting in presidential elections, and establishment of eighteen as the legal age for voting in national elections. Like the 1965 act, this legislation had a five-year life.

The 1970 act created two distinct legal categories, general and special. The general provisions dealt with literacy tests, voting age, residency requirements, and penalties for interfering with voting rights. The general provisions were permanent laws that were applied nationally. The special provisions, like the 1965 act, were selectively applied to areas where such provisions were deemed necessary. States or counties were subjected to the special provisions if they had any test or device established as a prerequisite to either registration or voting and had less than half of the registered voters participate in the presidential elections of 1964 or 1968. The courts could also apply the special provisions to other electoral districts if the attorney general successfully brought suit against them for violating the Fifteenth Amendment.

Areas subjected to the special provisions were placed under additional federal controls. There was a provision for the suspension of literacy and other test devices beyond the ban. Federal examiners were assigned to these areas to conduct registration drives, and federal observers were sent into these areas to monitor elections. In addition, similar to the 1965 act, these areas had to submit any changes in voting laws or procedures to the federal government for clearance. The special provisions could be lifted from a state or county if it successfully filed suit in a three-judge federal district court in Washington, D.C. Such suits had to convince the court that the voter tests or devices in use were not discriminatory.

VOTING ACT OF 1975: PASSAGE THROUGH CONGRESS

Like the 1965 act, the 1970 amendments required reconsideration and renewal after five years. In preparation for this renewal, the U.S. Commission on Civil Rights prepared an extensive report for the president and Congress in January of 1975. The report, *The Voting Rights Act: Ten Years After,* set the tone for the congressional debate that was to follow. In general, the report found that minority participation in the electoral process had increased significantly since 1965. Discriminatory practices, however, were still hampering minority registration and voting. The report suggested a number of changes, the most controversial of which were its recommendation of a ten-year extension of the act and its call for greater attention to language minorities, or those who did not speak English.

In February, the House Judiciary Subcommittee on Civil and Constitutional Rights began hearings on extending the Voting Rights Act. Although many different bills were introduced in both the House and the Senate, the one that worked its way successfully through both chambers was H.R. 6219. After swift movement through the committee system, this bill passed the House of Representatives on June 4 by a 341-70 vote.

Efforts to stall this bill when it was sent to the Senate proved unsuccessful. Senator James O. Eastland, chair of the Senate Judiciary Committee and a strong opponent of the bill, put off action until mid-July. The tactics used by Senator Eastland proved unsuccessful when the Senate leadership under Mike Mansfield managed to bring the House bill directly to the Senate floor. When it appeared that the bill's opponents would stall it on the Senate floor. Majority Leader Mansfield and Majority Whip Robert Byrd skillfully passed two cloture motions (limiting debate) to get the bill passed. After considerable parliamentary maneuvering, the Senate leadership managed to get seventeen proposed amendments rejected or tabled. The one area where the bill's opponents succeeded was an amendment that limited the extension to seven years instead of ten. Once this issue was settled, the Senate passed the bill by a vote of 77 to 12.

The House quickly made some expedient rules changes that allowed it to accept the Senate version of the bill without going to a conference committee. The House then voted 346-56 to accept the Senate version and sent the bill to President Gerald Ford. President Ford signed the voting rights extension (PL 9473) on August 6.

PROVISIONS OF THE 1975 ACT

The passage of the Voting Rights Act of 1975 extended the rights secured by the initial 1965 act through August 6, 1982. This portion of the act, Title I, added little to the previous legislation. The most significant changes were the result of Titles II and III of the 1975 act. Title II of the new act expanded the basic protection of the old legislation to certain language minorities: persons of Spanish heritage, American Indians, Asian Americans, and Alaskan natives. Federal observers could be sent into areas if more than five percent of the voting-age population was identified by the Census Bureau as a single language minority, election material for the 1972 presidential election was printed in English only, or less than half of the voting-age citizens had voted in the 1974 presidential election.

As with the earlier acts, areas could be removed from Title II jurisdiction by appealing their case successfully to the federal district court in Washington, D.C. They had to prove that their election laws had posed no barrier to voting over the past ten years.

The provisions in Title III of the act required certain jurisdictions, those with at least five percent non-English-speaking populations, to conduct bilingual elections. The interesting twist to this provision was that areas could drop the bilingual elections if they could prove that the illiteracy rate among their language minority had dropped below the national illiteracy rate. States and their subdivisions could free themselves from these federal regulations by improving the educational opportunities of their language minorities.

IMPACT

Many people believe the 1975 Voting Rights Act to be the most significant expansion of suffrage rights outside the South since the passage of the Nineteenth Amendment. It was clearly the most significant ever for language minorities. The legislation gave access to the electoral process to a significant number of language minorities and expanded voting rights enforcement to numerous jurisdictions outside the South. The Justice Department identified 513 political jurisdictions in thirty states that provided bilingual elections in 1976. All of these bilingual elections were a direct result of the Voting Rights Act of 1975. The number of electoral districts required to seek clearance for changes in their election laws increased by 279 after this enactment.

Donald V. Weatherman

SOURCES FOR FURTHER STUDY
Congress and the Nation. "Voting Rights, Bilingual Elections." 12 (1977): 671-678.
Congressional Digest. "Controversy over Extension of the Federal Voting Rights Act." 54 (June/July, 1975): 163-192.
Grebler, Leo, Joan W. Moore, and Ralph Guzman. *The Mexican-American People.* New York: Free Press, 1970.
Hanus, Jerome J. *The Voting Rights Act of 1965, as Amended: History, Effects, and Alternatives.* Washington, D.C.: Government Printing Office, 1976.
Lawson, Steven. *Black Ballots: Voting Rights in the South, 1944-1969.* New York: Columbia University Press, 1976.
McCloskey, Clifton, and Bruce Merrill. "Mexican-American Political Behavior in Texas." *Social Science Quarterly* 53 (March, 1973): 785-798.
Matthews, Donald, and James W. Prothro. *Negroes and the New Southern Politics.* New York: Harcourt, Brace & World, 1966.
Pachon, Harry P. "Political Mobilization in the Mexican-American Community." In *Mexican-Americans in Comparative Perspective,* edited by Walker Conner. Washington, D.C.: Urban Institute Press, 1970.
Stanley, Harold W. *Voter Mobilization and the Politics of Race: The South and Universal Suffrage, 1952-1984.* New York: Praeger, 1987.
Thernstrom, Abigail M. *Whose Votes Count? Affirmative Action and Minority Voting Rights.* Cambridge, Mass.: Harvard University Press, 1987.
U.S. Commission on Civil Rights. *The Voting Rights Act: Ten Years After.* Washington, D.C.: Government Printing Office, 1975.

SEE ALSO: Fifteenth Amendment (1870); Civil Rights Act of 1957 (1957); Civil Rights Act of 1960 (1960); Twenty-fourth Amendment (1964); Voting Rights Act of 1965 (1965).

WOMEN IN ARMED SERVICES ACADEMIES ACT

DATE: October 7, 1975
U.S. STATUTES AT LARGE: 89 Stat. 538
PUBLIC LAW: 94-106
CATEGORIES: Education; Military and National Security; Women's Issues

The armed forces of the United States reflected the rapidly changing role of women in American society by allowing women to become professionally trained officers.

As the war in Vietnam came to an end with the withdrawal of United States forces and the Viet Cong take-over of that country in 1975, the nature of the armed forces of the United States also changed. During the war, the armed forces had utilized the draft to maintain a sufficient level of personnel, and to many people the draft had become a symbol of what was wrong and unfair about the war in Vietnam. Draft evaders and draft resisters numbered in the hundreds of thousands. Following the end of the war, the armed forces decided to depend on an all-volunteer force. This decision came at a time when the national economy was relatively weak and many young people were unable to find jobs. As a result, service in the armed forces looked attractive.

WOMEN ENLIST IN THE ARMED FORCES

The volunteer emphasis meant women could find careers in the services as well. By 1974, more than ninety thousand women were enlisted in the armed forces of the United States. Tradition and law directed many of these women into nursing, but an increasing number found their way into other non-combat roles. The Reserve Officers' Training Corps (ROTC) program on college campuses also trained female officers. These programs were glad to accept women because enrollment in the ROTC had declined drastically during the years of the Vietnam War. An increasing dependence on advanced technology in military affairs also meant that fewer military roles called for face-to-face, hand-to-hand confrontation with an enemy.

The movement of women into the armed forces was part of the overall movement of women out of the home during the postwar women's movement. It seemed logical for women to enroll in the service academies as well. As the defense appropriations bill for fiscal 1976 began to be debated, two of them, Representative Samuel Stratton of New York and Senator William Hathaway of Maine, sponsored amendments to the bill that would require the service academies to open enrollment to women.

THE U.S. SERVICE ACADEMIES

The U.S. Military Academy at West Point, New York, is the nation's oldest service academy, followed in age by the Naval Academy at Annapolis, Maryland, the Coast Guard Academy at New London, Connecticut, and the Air Force Academy at Colorado Springs, Colorado. Of these, the Coast Guard had already decided to admit women and so was exempt from the bill. The Merchant Marine Academy at Kings Point, New York, is not an armed service school, as it is operated by the Department of Transportation, but it too had admitted women voluntarily. In many ways the experience of the Merchant Marine Academy paved the way for the armed services. Fifteen women entered Kings Point in 1974 and ten completed the first year, taking the same classes and participating in the same physical activities as the men. The dropout rate in that class was the lowest in the history of the school. One school spokesperson expressed the theory that the male students were reluctant to quit while women were "sticking it out."

RESISTANCE, DEBATE, AND PASSAGE

Despite this positive model, there was a considerable amount of resistance to change on the part of some members of the military and from some women. The secretary of the Navy, J. William Middendorf, expressed a determination not to accept women at Annapolis voluntarily. He indicated that an acceptance of the ERA would change that policy but that he was opposed to any "unilateral" action. General William C. Westmoreland, former commander of United States forces in Vietnam, was more blunt in his views. During a Memorial Day celebration at Middle-town, Ohio, the general said it would be "silly" to permit women to enroll at West Point:

It's depriving young men of the limited places that are there. . . . The purpose of West Point is to train combat officers and women are not physically able to lead in combat. . . . Maybe you could find one woman in ten thousand who could lead in combat, but she would be a freak and we're not running the military academy for freaks. . . . I don't believe women can carry a pack, live in a foxhole or go a week without taking a bath.

Former commandant of West Point General Maxwell Taylor agreed with those sentiments by commenting on the limited space available in the schools and saying that a woman enrolled might take up the place of "another Grant or Lee, Pershing or MacArthur."

A letter from a woman published in *The New York Times* expressed the opinion that the "great colleges and universities" of the United States had diluted their moral and educational standards when they became coeducational. She feared the same would happen at the service academies. These views were challenged by other writers to the newspaper who saw such views as nothing more than traditional prejudices based on sex-role stereotypes. As one writer pointed out, the military leadership needed change, as the current group of leaders had produced only stalemates in Korea and Vietnam.

Debate in the Congress mirrored discussion in the society at large. The debate over Representative Stratton's amendment was especially raucous in the House of Representatives. One member of the House even raised the specter of female combat officers leaving their troops under fire so they could go to the rear to breastfeed babies. In the end, however, the House on May 21, 1975, voted 303 to 96 to allow women into the service academies. A few days later the Senate, with much less debate, unanimously passed the amendment sponsored by Senator Hathaway. President Gerald Ford signed the bill into law on October 8, 1975.

ADJUSTMENTS AT THE ACADEMIES

The major adjustment to be made at the academies was in their view that they existed to train combat leaders. Commander Robert Lewis of the Naval Academy feared that a two-track curriculum would have to be developed, one for combat and one for non-combat commanders. Colonel Nancy Hopfenspirger, the highest-ranking woman Army officer, agreed, saying she also viewed Army officers as leading combat troops. These arguments were undercut by the curricula of the academies, which emphasized not strategy and tactics but math, science, and engineering. The views of many were summed up by an exchange between an unnamed West Point cadet and Carol Barkalow, a member of the first West Point class to include women. At lunch during her pre-enrollment visit, a male cadet asked, "Excuse me, Miss, but why do you want to come here?" She replied, "Because I want to be the best Army officer I can be." He answered, "That's fine, but couldn't you do it someplace else?"

The first female cadets at all the academies began to enroll in the summer of 1976. They knew the eyes of America were on them. Sonya Nitibuls, one of the top high school female athletes in the nation, said of her enrollment at West Point, "If I can make it through this, I can make it through anything." Donna Smart may have voiced what many of these first female cadets in all the academies were thinking when she observed that one could either follow an established path or one could blaze a new trail.

At the service academies, certain physical changes had to be made. Toilet facilities had to be provided and other arrangements made to assure a degree of privacy. New uniforms had to be designed, especially formal dress uniforms. Since women would be sharing the same barracks as men, both sexes were required to wear robes to and from their separate bathrooms. Also, the women would be taught karate instead of boxing and would be issued modified rifles that were slightly shorter and lighter. A few of the physical drills would be modified to compensate for the lower upper-body strength of the women. The major factor at all the academies was the requirement, established by law, that women not be assigned to combat roles. This meant that certain kinds of training, such as for fighter pilots at the Air Force Academy, would not be offered to women.

Of all the service academies, the Air Force was the most enthusiastic about the presence of women. It was the only academy to recruit women and the only one to assign female officers to special duty at the academy. Thirteen special air training officers, all first and second lieutenants, were assigned to act as guidance counselors and role models for the female cadets. Despite this degree of preparation, there was some complaining that the basic training session had been weakened to accommodate women cadets, although the academy commander denied this was the case.

The female cadets faced similar first-year experiences. There was some overt harassment from male cadets who resented their presence and who believed women had no place in the armed forces.

Naturally, some problems of a sexual nature arose. The Naval Academy policy called for any cadet "responsible for a pregnancy" to resign. If a female cadet became pregnant the "responsibility" was obvious. At the Merchant Marine Academy a male and female cadet were found together in bed. The female was expelled, but the male was allowed to graduate. The Air Force Academy, the most accepting of women of all the academies, ruled that a cadet who became pregnant could take "excess leave" until after the child was born and then return to class to catch up on her work.

The women's dropout rate was about the same as or lower than that for men. Women won some West Point cadet leadership positions, and at Annapolis, midshipman Stephanie McManus was chosen to carry the flag for the honor company at graduation. The first women graduated from the academies in 1980. During the 1990-1991 Persian Gulf War, women proved their ability to make positive contributions to the military under wartime conditions.

Michael R. Bradley

Sources for Further Study

Ambrose, Stephen E., and James A. Barber, Jr. *The Military and American Society*. New York: Free Press, 1972.

Barkalow, Carol. *In the Men's House*. New York: Poseidon Press, 1990.

Galloway, K. Bruce, and Robert Bowie Johnson, Jr. *West Point: America's Power Fraternity*. New York: Simon & Schuster, 1973.

Janowitz, Morris, and Stephen D. Wesbrook. *The Political Education of Soldiers*. Beverly Hills, Calif.: Sage Publications, 1983.

Millis, Walter. *American Military Thought*. Indianapolis: Bobbs-Merrill, 1966.

See also: Title IX of the Education Amendments of 1972 (1972); Women's Educational Equity Act (1978).

AGE DISCRIMINATION ACT

DATE: November 28, 1975
U.S. STATUTES AT LARGE: 89 Stat. 728
PUBLIC LAW: 94-135
U.S. CODE: 42 § 6101
CATEGORIES: Aging Issues; Health and Welfare; Labor and Employment

> *Though limited in both scope and application, this law provided safeguards against bias-based abuse and served as a statutory foundation for antidiscrimination policies that followed.*

In its basic premises, the Age Discrimination Act of 1975 originated in the Civil Rights Act of 1964. Title VI, section 715 of this law mandated that the U.S. secretary of labor formulate a special report on the extent of age discrimination practices in employment. In 1965, the secretary's office completed the report, which documented widespread discrimination against senior citizens. The Age Discrimination in Employment Act of 1967 (ADEA) went so far as to prohibit discrimination in employment directed against workers aged from forty to seventy.

PROVISIONS AND EXEMPTIONS

Though the format of the Age Discrimination Act (ADA) of 1975 follows that of Title III to the Education Amendments of 1972 and section 504 of the Rehabilitation Act of 1973, without their respective prohibitions against discrimination based upon gender and disability, it is most closely modeled on the 1964 Civil Rights Act. The ADA itself is not a blanket prohibition against age-based discrimination but much more narrowly affects "programs or activities receiving Federal financial assistance"; it states that no one can be "excluded from participation, denied the benefits of, or be subjected to discrimination under" such programs.

The act's provisions are further limited by significant exceptions outlined in two subsections, 6103-b and 6103-c. The exemptive provisions apply to cases in which age is a factor necessary to "the normal operation or the achievement of any statutory objective"; in which "differentiation" occurs based on "reasonable factors other than age"; and in which programs provide benefits based upon age (such as Social Security and Medicare) or establish "criteria for participation in age-related terms." The ADEA is set apart as being outside the provisions of the ADA; with the exception of programs "receiving financial assistance under the Job Training Partnership Act," the ADA is denied the authority to extend the enforcement of its provisions to the private sector of the economy.

IMPLEMENTATION AND ENFORCEMENT

The lead time given for compliance was gradual; no provision of the act was to take effect until July 1, 1979. The Commission on Civil Rights was empowered to make a study determining the possible existence of instances of unreasonable age discrimination within the affected programs and agencies and to identify the alleged violators. The resulting report was to be submitted to the president and Congress no later than November 28, 1977.

The U.S. secretary of health and human services was then required, beginning in 1980, to make an annual report to Congress by March 31 describing the degree of compliance with the provisions of the act by the relevant agencies, departments, and programs. Enforcement methods include termination of federal assistance to violators and "any other means authorized by law."

Raymond Pierre Hylton

SOURCES FOR FURTHER STUDY

Gregory, Raymond F. *Age Discrimination in the American Workplace: Old at a Young Age.* New Brunswick, N.J.: Rutgers University Press, 2001.

Hushbeck, Judith C. *Old and Obsolete: Age Discrimination and the American Worker, 1860-1920.* New York: Garland, 1989.

Kalet, Joseph E. *Age Discrimination in Employment Law.* Washington, D.C.: BNA Books, 1990.

O'Meara, Daniel P. *Protecting the Growing Number of Older Workers: The Age Discrimination in Employment Act.* Philadelphia: University of Pennsylvania, Center for Human Resources, 1989.

Segrave, Kerry. *Age Discrimination by Employers.* Jefferson, N.C.: McFarland Press, 2002.

SEE ALSO: Executive Order 11141 (1964); Older Americans Act (1965); Age Discrimination in Employment Act (1967); Older Workers Benefit Protection Act (1990).

EDUCATION FOR ALL HANDICAPPED CHILDREN ACT

DATE: November 29, 1975
U.S. STATUTES AT LARGE: 89 Stat. 773
PUBLIC LAW: 94-142
U.S. CODE: 20 § 1400
CATEGORIES: Children's Issues; Disability Issues; Education

This legislation ensured all handicapped children in the United States access to "free appropriate public education" that would meet their individual needs.

Several years of congressional hearings revealed that the educational needs of millions of disabled children were not being met. Often families of students with special needs had to educate their children at their own expense. The Education for All Handicapped Children Act (EHA), which became effective in 1977, reshaped American education. All handicapped students were ensured an appropriate educational setting.

Specific learning disabilities and related services were clearly defined under the law. States were required to submit plans and procedures designed to meet the needs of handicapped persons between the ages of three and twenty-one. When necessary, the act allowed for the provision of services in private educational settings at public expense. It stated that students should receive special education and related services in the "least restrictive environment commensurate with their needs."

Safeguards were established to protect the rights of all concerned. These included provisions for assessment, detailed individualized education programs, and timetables for achievement of stated goals. Parental involvement in the educational process was strongly supported. Annual reviews of students' progress were mandated. A procedure for fair hearings was established to resolve disputes concerning educational placement. Failure to comply with the law would result in denial of federal funding.

Kathleen Schongar

SOURCES FOR FURTHER STUDY
Jones, Clarence, and Ted F. Rabold. *Public Law 94-142: A Guide for the Education for All Handicapped Children Act.* State College, Pa.: Penns Valley, 1978.
Turnbull, H. Rutherford, and Craig R. Fielder. *Judicial Interpretation of the Education for All Handicapped Children Act.* Arlington, Va.: Council for Exceptional Children, 1984.

SEE ALSO: Bilingual Education Act (1968); Juvenile Justice and Delinquency Prevention Act (1974); Indian Child Welfare Act (1978); Americans with Disabilities Act (1990); Child Care and Development Block Grant Act (1990).

ENERGY POLICY AND CONSERVATION ACT

DATE: December 22, 1975
U.S. STATUTES AT LARGE: 89 Stat. 871
PUBLIC LAW: 94-163
CATEGORIES: Energy

The Energy Act was aimed at reducing gasoline consumption and increasing domestic production by increasing gasoline prices.

Congress had been reexamining its energy policy since the 1973-1974 embargo imposed by the Organization of Petroleum Exporting Countries (OPEC) had dramatically raised prices for oil. OPEC states imposed the embargo after the United States supported Israel in the 1973 Arab-Israeli War (the Yom Kippur War). Imports provided more than one-third of the oil used in the United States. The embargo caused shortages throughout the country, and Congress responded by taking up legislation aimed at reducing American reliance on imported oil. After two years of debate Congress passed the Energy Policy and Conservation Act of 1976 and sent it to President Gerald Ford, who signed it into law.

PROVISIONS

The bill's major provisions gave the Federal Energy Administration (the FEA, which became the Department of Energy in 1978) authority to order major power plants to switch to using coal in place of oil or natural gas in the production of electricity. This would free more gasoline for automobile use. Another provision gave the president authority to control energy supplies in a number of ways. He could order refineries to increase production of fuel oil to meet increased demand, and he could order oil companies to maintain certain levels of oil and petroleum inventories in storage so that supplies would be available in case of another embargo. The president could also create a strategic petroleum reserve of one billion barrels of oil. This reserve would provide enough gasoline and fuel oil to last three months, another protection against any future boycott.

The chief executive also was given the power to mandate energy conservation measures (which were not spelled out) across the nation if another oil emergency struck, and he could even limit the amount of gas anyone could buy if the crisis continued. This rationing provision was strongly opposed by the oil industry but managed to win narrow approval in the House and Senate. For the first time, fuel economy standards for new automobiles were mandated for cars built after 1977. All cars were expected to reach an average fuel economy level of at least 26 miles per gallon by 1985—a great improvement, because the average in 1974 models had been only 14 miles per gallon. The automobile and oil industries fought bitterly against this measure, but it too passed by a slim margin. It was expected that this provision alone would save millions of gallons of gasoline a year.

The FEA was also empowered to establish an energy testing and labeling program for major consumer products, from refrigerators to television sets. Consumers would be able to tell which producers used the least energy and thus could buy the most efficient items if they so desired. Federal price controls on domestic oil were continued until 1979 so that the oil industry could not make excessive profits during the oil crisis. President Ford signed these provisions into law despite wide opposition from the petroleum industry.

Leslie V. Tischauser

SOURCE FOR FURTHER STUDY
United States. General Accounting Office. *GAO Work Involving Title V of the Energy Policy and Conservation Act of 1975: Report to the Congress.* Washington, D.C.: Author, 1978.

SEE ALSO: Clean Air Act Amendments of 1970 (1970); Department of Energy Organization Act (1977); Alternative Motor Fuels Act (1988).

TOXIC SUBSTANCES CONTROL ACT

DATE: October 11, 1976
U.S. STATUTES AT LARGE: 90 Stat. 2003
PUBLIC LAW: 94-469
U.S. CODE: 15 § 2601
CATEGORIES: Environment and Conservation; Health and Welfare

This act permitted the Environmental Protection Agency to regulate toxic chemicals that pose a threat to the environment or to human health.

There are seven million known chemical compounds, sixty thousand of which are used commercially. About one thousand new chemicals are put into production every year and introduced into the environment. The Toxic Substances Control Act (TSCA) was enacted in order to give the government the authority to regulate the use of a substance that can harm human health or the environment. The Environmental Protection Agency (EPA) was charged with reviewing risk information on all new chemicals before they are manufactured or imported and with deciding whether they should be admitted, controlled, or banned.

CARCINOGENS AND OTHER TOXIC CHEMICALS

In the 1970's, a considerable number of newspaper accounts reported that some commonly used chemicals were associated with such problems as cancer, birth defects, and sterility. A milestone in the regulation of environmental hazards was the passage of the Toxic Substances Control Act, which represented the federal response to a growing awareness of and concern over the existence of hazardous chemicals in the environment that were not subject to regulation or testing under any of the other environmental laws.

The act was preceded by the Clean Air Act and its amendments, which regulated discharges and emissions into the air and water; the Occupational Safety and Health Act, which established safety standards for the workplace; and the Consumer Product Safety Act, which authorized standards for consumer products. None of these laws had allowed the government to explore the potentially adverse effects of chemicals on health and the environment. The TSCA was enacted to fill the gap in the existing statutory framework by giving the EPA the authority to acquire information about the nature of the vast number of chemical substances before they were introduced into the marketplace, as well as the authority to regulate those found to be hazardous.

Enactment of the TSCA had been considered for several years by Congress, which recognized that the technological revolution in the chemical industry had led to a tremendous increase in the number and development of toxic chemicals. Congress responded to chemical pollution controversies, such as those regarding polychlorinated biphenyls (PCBs), vinyl chloride, and chlorofluorocarbons (CFCs), by establishing that the control of toxic chemicals was a priority health requirement. The Senate commerce report estimated that at the time the TSCA was passed between 60 and 90 percent of all human cancers were the result of exposure to environmental contaminants. Congress concluded that a preclearance regulatory system was necessary. Ideally, a safety system should be in place before the introduction of a proposed chemical into the commercial marketplace.

PROVISIONS AND IMPLEMENTATION

The TSCA gave the EPA four tools to use in regulating toxic chemicals: the authority to require that chemicals suspected of posing risks be tested; a procedure to screen all new chemicals for possible risks; a framework for gathering information on existing chemicals; and the authority to regulate those chemicals found to be hazardous. The TSCA regulated an estimated sixty thousand chemicals manufactured for commercial purposes and several million chemicals used in research and development. For the first time, the entire chemical industry was put under comprehensive regulation. The law applied to almost every facet of the industry, including product development, testing, manufacturing, distribution, use, and disposal. In addition, importers of chemical substances were treated the same as domestic manufacturers, which extended the EPA's control to certain aspects of international trade.

There were two parts to the TSCA. One part involved the gathering of information about chemicals, the other involved the control of chemicals. A large portion of the TSCA addressed the gathering of information to enable the EPA to decide whether certain substances should be controlled. Companies were required to keep records about the chemicals they used; some records were made available to the EPA when it conducted inspections, while other records needed to be reported to the EPA on a regular basis. The most stringent regulations designated by the TSCA were those that affected PCBs, which were singled out by Congress because of their high toxicity, widespread use, and longevity. One of the primary functions of the TSCA was to regulate the manufacture, use, and distribution of PCBs.

Section 7 of the TSCA granted the EPA the authority to use judicial means against an imminently hazardous substance or mixture. This provision could be used to require PCB and dioxin cleanups, although the EPA could also use the Comprehensive Environmental Response, Compensation, and Liability Act (CERCLA) of 1980, the Resource Conservation and Recovery Act (RCRA) of 1976, or the Clean Water Act to order such cleanups. The TSCA also gave the government the right to bring suits for noncompliance, and to pursue both civil and criminal penalties. Citizen suits were also made possible, cases in which private citizens can bring a civil action against someone who may be in violation of the TSCA; alternatively, a citizen could sue the EPA administrator to compel the performance of a nondiscretionary duty.

IMPLEMENTATION AND ENFORCEMENT

The first act of the EPA under the TSCA was to make an inventory of all chemicals manufactured, imported, or processed in the United States. The inventory was based on reports from manufacturers, importers, processors, and users of chemical substances, which they were required to submit to the agency. The TSCA defined a chemical substance as any organic or inorganic substance of a particular molecular identity, as well as any combination of such substances occurring in whole or in part as a result of a chemical reaction or in nature. The administrator of the EPA was obliged to compile and keep a current list of all such substances manufactured or imported in the United States. After the inventory was taken, the premanufacture provisions of the TSCA went into effect. Subject to certain exemptions and time requirements, no new chemical substances or significant new chemical use could be introduced without a notice of intention filed with the EPA at least ninety days before the intended manufacture or use. The notice included information on all known data on health or environmental effects. The notice requirement was essential because it provided the administrator with an opportunity to evaluate the information and determine whether the manufacture or use should be permitted, limited, or delayed.

The Toxic Substances Control Act was an enabling act. As such, it conferred authority from Congress to an administrative agency to regulate the manufacture, use, and disposal of toxic substances. Congress mandated comprehensive regulation of chemicals through the TSCA. Manufacturers and processors were made subject to regulation if they emitted chemicals into air, water, or land. The TSCA recognized that disposing of many human-made chemicals could involve risks to natural resources (such as groundwater, the source of much of the drinking water) and to humans. The TSCA gave the EPA broad powers to regulate the disposal of all toxic organic chemicals. The EPA had the authority to regulate certain chemicals from their development to manufacture and finally to disposal. The TSCA required the EPA to inventory the approximately fifty-five thousand chemicals involved in interstate commerce, and it required chemical manufacturers to notify the EPA of all new chemicals produced, so that the EPA could keep a current inventory. This requirement was called the Premanufacture Notice (PMN).

Once the EPA had all the information it needed about a toxic chemical that presented an unreasonable danger to people or the environment, it was authorized under the TSCA to stop the manufacture. This authority implied great regulatory power over the chemical industry, but it applied only to toxic chemicals.

CRITICISM

The Toxic Substances Control Act was a compromise between a rigid preclearance regulatory scheme, such as that contained in pesticide and drug laws, and a system of notice and selective interdiction.

As such, the act became the object of frequent criticism from proregulation environmental groups as well as from the chemical industry, which was opposed to government regulation. The industry complained about red tape, the cost of compliance, and the potential for losing trade secrets as a result of the reporting requirements. The environmental groups complained that the EPA was slow to regulate. By 1986, only five chemical classes had been regulated: PCBs, CFCs, phthalate esters, chlorinated benzenes, and chloromethane. Even the EPA complained about the TSCA. Most of the EPA's complaints were in response to delayed regulation as a result of a lack of staff and foot-dragging by private industry in supplying information on whether a chemical is toxic.

Amy Bloom

SOURCES FOR FURTHER STUDY

Freedman, Warren. *Federal Statutes of Environmental Protection.* New York: Quorum Books, 1987.

Grad, Frank. *Treatise on Environmental Law.* New York: Matthew Bender, 1994.

O'Leary, Rosemary. *Environmental Change: Federal Courts and the EPA.* Philadelphia: Temple University Press, 1993.

The Toxic Substances Control Act. Executive Legal Summary 98. Chesterland, Ohio: Business Laws, 1989.

Worobec, Mary Devine. *Toxic Substance Control Primer.* Washington, D.C.: BNA Books, 1984.

SEE ALSO: Hazardous Substances Labeling Act (1960); Federal Environmental Pesticide Control Act (1972); Hazardous Materials Transportation Act (1974).

COPYRIGHT ACT OF 1976

DATE: October 19, 1976
U.S. STATUTES AT LARGE: 90 Stat. 2541
PUBLIC LAW: 94-553
U.S. CODE: 17 § 101
CATEGORIES: Business, Commerce, and Trade; Copyrights, Patents, and Trademarks

These amendments to the 1909 act corrected imbalances between the competing rights of copyright owners and users that had developed as a result of technological changes.

Prior to enactment of the 1976 Copyright Act, which became effective on January 1, 1978, the last wholesale revision of U.S. copyright law had been made in 1909. In the intervening decades, technological advances in communications rendered many provisions of the 1909 act ineffective. A number of efforts to amend the copyright law in piecemeal fashion were introduced, but it was not until an appropriations act in 1955 provided funds for research by the Copyright Office of the Library of Congress that a more general effort to revise the copyright law was undertaken.

THE CHALLENGE OF CABLE TELEVISION

Congressional hearings on proposed revisions began on May 26, 1965, before the House Judiciary Subcommittee on Courts, Civil Liberties, and the Administration of Justice, which ultimately voted favorably on the proposed legislation. Prior to approving the bill, however, the subcommittee jettisoned an entire section devoted to copyright issues raised by cable television's secondary transmission of broadcast signals. This would prove to be the issue upon which the legislation would founder for some time. Senator John L. McClellan, chair of the Senate Judiciary Subcommittee on Patents, Trademarks, and Copyrights, which had begun its hearings on August 18, 1965, insisted that any copyright legislation that passed must address the status of the cable industry. His concern grew out of the Federal Communications Commission's failure to adopt a new cable regulatory scheme that would relax restrictions on the carriage of signals. It was only after the FCC approved such regulations in 1972 that McClellan resumed his efforts to push through a new copyright bill.

PASSAGE AND BASIC PROVISIONS

Active debate on the copyright bill resumed in 1974 with the Ninety-third Congress. The bill finally passed in the Senate on February 19, 1976, and in the House of Representatives on September 22, 1976. President Gerald R. Ford signed the bill into law on October 19, 1976.

The new copyright statute was divided into eight chapters. The first chapter defined the subject matter of copyright, stated what rights copyright affords, and outlined the limitations on those rights. Chapter 2 was concerned with the ownership and transfer of copyrights. The third chapter dealt with the duration of copyrights. Chapter 4 dealt with formalities such as the form and placement of copyright notice and the details of depositing and registering a copyrighted work. Chapter 5 addressed copyright infringement and its remedies. Chapter 6 concerned the manufacture, importation, and public distribution of copies. Chapter 7 dealt with the organization and responsibilities of the Copyright Office. Finally, chapter 8 established the Copyright Royalty Tribunal.

Perhaps the most conspicuous change in U.S. copyright law had to do with the utilization, in the 1976 act, of compulsory licenses—such as the annual fees levied on jukeboxes—to balance the competing interests of copyright owners and users. Analogously, several sections of the new act established statutory royalty rates, such as those connected with secondary transmission by cable television, the collection of which was to be overseen by the Copyright Royalty Tribunal, itself created by the 1976 act.

Less conspicuously, but more profoundly, the statute amended U.S. copyright law by making four major changes: abolishing common law copyright; changing the concept of copyright by clarifying what it protects; creating an electronic copyright to supplement the print copyright; and codifying the doctrine of fair use. In addition, the statute marked, as noted by Barbara Ringer, then the register of copyrights, a shift in the philosophical underpinnings of copyright, resolving a centuries-old debate whether copyright was a natural law property right or only a statutory grant of limited monopoly, in favor of the latter. Chapter 1 of the act opens with a proclamation of the exclusive rights of copyright owners, which are five: the right to reproduce a work; the right to prepare derivative works, such as abridgments; the right to distribute copies of a work to the public; the right to perform a work in public; and the right to display a work in public.

COMMON LAW COPYRIGHT ELIMINATED

Prior to the 1976 act, copyright had been governed by two systems of law: federal statutory copyright and common law copyright, which was largely the province of individual states. By decreeing that a work was copyrighted the moment it was fixed in a tangible medium of expression, the new statute did away with the concept of common law copyright, which previously had governed works prior to publication, when statutory law took over.

REDEFINING INTELLECTUAL PROPERTY

The elimination of common law copyright clarified the concept of copyright protection by making it clear that what was being protected was an original work of authorship, which must fall into one of three categories: an imaginative work, such as a novel; a derivative work, such as a film based on the novel; or a compilation of previously existing materials, such as an anthology. In the latter two cases, copyright now protected only the original aspects of the work: that is, in the case of a derivative work, only the new elements added to the underlying work, and in the case of a compilation, only the collection as a whole (although copying an individual short story in a collection, for example, might violate the copyright of that story). Thus, the impact of this reconceptualization of copyright protection was to do away with earlier confusion of the original work of authorship with the material object embodying it, such as a compilation or film. Under the 1976 act, the two must be merged in order for copyright protection to attach.

ELECTRONIC COPYRIGHT

Common law copyright lived on, however, in a new copyright created by the 1976 statute: the electronic copyright. The electronic copyright was meant to cover television and also apply to computers and software. It differed fundamentally from print copyright in that the subject matter consisted of works that are performed rather than published. These performances—for example, a live telecast of a National Football League game—may or may not be based on writing of some kind and may have no author per se. The statute gets around these requirements by making performance equivalent to publication if any fixation (even simultaneous transmission and recording) takes place and making the employer of those creating the work its "author." The electronic copyright is thus equivalent to common law copyright protection of an improvised stage performance.

FAIR USE DOCTRINE

The fourth, and potentially the most far-reaching, major change introduced by the 1976 act was the codification of what had always been a judicially determined doctrine limiting the powers of copyright holders, the doctrine of fair use. United States copyright law originated with the Constitution, which, in article I, section 8, clause 8, empowers Congress "to promote the progress of science and the useful arts, by securing for limited times to authors and inventors the exclusive right to their respective writings and discoveries." The original idea was to provide creators with the incentive of a limited monopoly while at the same time allowing those who followed to build on ideas that already had been formulated and disseminated. This is clearly a delicate balance to maintain, requiring constant adjustment. American law traditionally responded by allowing fair use to remain a rule of reason developed and applied by the judiciary. Even when codified, the fair use doctrine consisted of a number of significantly nonexclusive factors that are reconfigured with each new infringement case that arises.

Section 107, the fair use section of the 1976 act, was not intended to change previous judicial interpretations of the doctrine. Section 107 was loosely formulated, refraining from formally defining "fair use" and including a list of exemptions from the restrictions of copyright, such as criticism and research. The section also included a list of four factors to be considered by judges when weighing fair use defenses raised against claims of copyright infringement. First was the purpose and character of the use, including whether such use is of a commercial nature or is for nonprofit educational purposes. Second was the nature of the copyrighted work. Third was the amount and substantially of the portion used in relation to the copyrighted work as a whole. The fourth consideration was the effect of the use on the potential market for or value of the copyrighted work. The fact that a work is unpublished was not to bar a finding of fair use.

SUPREME COURT DECISIONS

The final proviso, indicating that even unpublished work is subject to fair use, was an addition to the act, adopted by Congress in 1992 largely in response to constriction of the fair use doctrine resulting from several Supreme Court decisions. *Harper & Row Publishers v. Nation Enterprises* (1985) revolved around the unauthorized publication by the magazine *The Nation* of excerpts, concerning the pardon of President Richard M. Nixon, from President Ford's forthcoming memoir. The most notorious of similar cases is *Salinger v. Random House* (1987).

In both the Nation and Salinger cases, the courts refused to acknowledge as fair use what might in an earlier time have been seen as minimal borrowing. One of the pivotal issues in both cases was the unpublished nature of the infringed works. As the Supreme Court reasoned in the Nation case, perhaps because the fair use doctrine was based on the author's implied consent to reasonable use of his or her work upon publication, fair use was not traditionally recognized as a defense to charges of copying works not yet released for public consumption.

Arguably, the fair use doctrine was intended to protect copyright owners from competitors, not consumers. In the Salinger case, however, fair use was pressed into service as a rationale for censorship. In this case, the writer J. D. Salinger brought suit seeking an injunction against publication of an unauthorized biography that included quotations and paraphrases from his correspondence with various persons who had deposited these letters with archives, seeking to protect personal interests. In view of the purpose of federal copyright laws, that type of deposit is a misuse of what is fundamentally a property right.

When the fair use proviso regarding unpublished works was proposed, largely in reaction to demands made by reporters, historians, biographers, and book publishers, it was vigorously opposed by the computer software industry, which feared that such a change in the copyright law would legitimize already rampant piracy of programs. These copyright owners argued that fair use of their products, unlike books, would of necessity involve extensive copying. The battle between these interest groups was reflected in congressional debate over the proviso, which raged for two years. Finally, a compromise was reached late in 1992, with the Senate adopting the seemingly restrictive language of the House bill but adding, in the legislative history attached to the bill, that its intent was "to clearly and indisputably reject the view that the unpublished nature of the work triggers a virtual per se ruling against a finding of fair use."

Lisa Paddock

SOURCES FOR FURTHER STUDY

Grossman, George S. *Omnibus Copyright Revision Legislative History*. Reprint. Buffalo, N.Y.: William S. Hein, 2001.

Miller, Jerome K. *U.S. Copyright Documents An Annotated Collection for Use by Educators and Librarians*. Littleton, Colo.: Libraries Unlimited, 1981.

Patterson, L. Ray, and Stanley W. Lindberg. *The Nature of Copyright: A Law of Users' Rights*. Athens: University of Georgia Press, 1991.

Strong, William S. *The Copyright Book: A Practical Guide*. 4th ed. Cambridge, Mass.: MIT Press, 1993.

White, Herbert S., ed. *The Copyright Dilemma*. Chicago: American Library Association, 1978.

SEE ALSO: Copyright Act of 1909 (1909); Trademark Law Revision Act (1988); North American Free Trade Agreement (1993); General Agreement on Tariffs and Trade of 1994 (1994); Digital Millennium Copyright Act (1998).

FEDERAL LAND POLICY AND MANAGEMENT ACT

DATE: October 21, 1976
U.S. STATUTES AT LARGE: 90 Stat. 2743
PUBLIC LAW: 94-579
U.S. CODE: 43 § 1701
CATEGORIES: Land Management; Natural Resources

The act declared the intent of Congress to retain permanently the re-maining public domain and legislatively established the Bureau of Land Management.

The Federal Land Policy and Management Act of 1976 (FLPMA) provided congressional recognition of the authority of the Bureau of Land Management (BLM) in managing the public lands. The law also officially established a policy of permanently retaining the remaining public domain lands. Passage of the act was marked by considerable negotiation between conservation, livestock grazing, and mining interest groups. Until the act passed, the BLM had rarely had the support or interest of conservation groups.

NEED FOR MODERNIZATION

Because of the circumstances of its creation from the ruins of the Grazing Service in 1946, the BLM lacked a strong legislative mandate. Over the years, Congress had passed more than thirty-five hundred individual laws dealing with the public lands, and there was no coherent management policy to guide the bureau. Early in the administration of John F. Kennedy, the BLM began to seek a series of laws that would modernize the agency's legislative mandates. The bureau began to draft laws to reform procedures for sale of nonmineral lands. In 1961, the Department of the Interior submitted a legislative proposal to Congress that would reform the land-sale laws, provide basic authority to the BLM to manage the public lands under a multiple-use and sustained-yield philosophy, reform rights-of-way policy, reform mineral policy, and repeal some of the many outdated public domain statutes still on the books.

Additional bills were contemplated, but the department's efforts were halted when it became apparent that Representative Wayne Aspinall's efforts to establish a comprehensive public-lands review commission were likely to succeed. Aspinall had begun to urge establishment of such a commission in the late 1950's, but his efforts were opposed by the Eisenhower and Kennedy administrations. In September, 1964, Congress passed the Public Land Law Review Commission Act, the Classification and Multiple Use Act, and the Public Land Sales Act. All three were temporary measures.

When the Public Land Law Review Commission (PLLRC) finished its work in 1970, it was apparent that there was little political support for many of its recommendations. Nevertheless, commission and House Interior and Insular Affairs Committee chairman Aspinall began the process of drafting a broad law that would enact the commission's recommendations and apply to all federal multiple-use lands. At the same time, the BLM began to draft an organic act for itself and submitted it to the Senate in 1971. It was not considered by the full Senate and was reintroduced in the ninety-third Congress. The Senate declined to consider the BLM's own bill and instead passed a similar bill introduced by Senator Henry Jackson. The House took no action on either bill.

CONTENTIOUS PASSAGE

Jackson's bill offered multiple-use, sustained-yield, and fair market-value pricing for commodities as a basis for management of the public lands. It also included language on advisory boards, law enforcement authority, reform of the 1920 mineral-leasing act, and development of a land management plan for BLM lands in the California desert. The Jackson bill passed the Senate by a large margin in February, 1976.

The House bill was quite different from the Senate version. Aspinall had been defeated in a primary challenge and Representative John Melcher of Montana had redrafted the House bill after an extensive series of hearings in the Western states. The Melcher bill also included language on grazing fees for BLM and U.S. Forest Service lands and the wild horse and burro issue. Representative John Seiberling also introduced a version of the bill that contained many provisions favored by conservation interests.

There were considerable differences within the House Subcommittee on Public Lands over grazing fees, law enforcement authority, and local government influence on federal-land planning. By late 1975, the House efforts had bogged down and passage of a bill by the full House appeared unlikely. Following passage of the Senate bill in 1976, the House Committee on Interior and Insular Affairs again took up the bill. The committee passed the bill twenty votes to sixteen votes, with seven members not voting, reflecting the deeply divided positions of the members and the conservation and development interests. Livestock interests supported the bill because it contained a favorable grazing fee formula, and environmentalists supported the bill because they believed they could later eliminate the fee language and preserve the other elements of the bill. The bill passed the full House by about twenty votes with weak support from the Department of the Interior and conservation interests.

In the conference committee, the House members were still divided over the bill, with representatives Morris Udall and John Seiberling favoring the Senate version. Four issues were the subject of critical compromises. Unlike other federal land-management agencies, the BLM had no authority to enforce federal laws on its own lands. In the remote deserts of the West, the bureau was forced to rely on county sheriffs who were often far from the scene of the violations. The compromise version of the FLPMA provided for full law enforcement authority for the BLM but also required maximum feasible reliance upon local law enforcement. In addition, the FLPMA authorized a uniformed desert ranger force for the California Desert Conservation Area.

Many provisions of the House bill pertained to the U.S. Forest Service as a result of Aspinall's views and the PLLRC report. Most provisions in the law pertaining to the Forest Service were deleted in the conference committee except for the grazing fee language. A third area of contention was congressional limitation on the executive branch to withdraw land for special purposes.

GRAZING DEBATES

The most contentious issues were related to grazing management, including the grazing fee formula, the length of grazing permits and leases, and the structure of grazing advisory boards. Senator Lee Metcalf of Montana offered a compromise, which included the elimination of the grazing fee formula, the establishment of a ten-year term for permits and leases, and the limitation of the functions of the advisory boards. The Senate conferees supported the compromise, but the House conferees split five votes to five votes. A majority of both sides is required to pass a bill. Many observers believed the bill was dead.

At the behest of the bureau, Senator Metcalf called the conferees back together and offered a one-year moratorium on grazing fee increases and a one-year-long comprehensive study of the grazing fee situation. The suggestion broke the deadlock. The final version of the FLPMA is more than fifty pages long and contains provisions for land-use planning, recording mineral claims, naming the director as a presidential appointee subject to Senate confirmation, law enforcement authority, grazing management, rights-of-way, creation of two national conservation areas, provisions for a wilderness review program, and the deletion of many outdated public land statutes. President Gerald Ford signed the bill on October 21, 1976.

A NEW ROLE FOR THE BLM: COMPETING CONSTITUENCIES
The contentious passage of the FLPMA indicates an important turn of events for the Bureau of Land Management. From the time that the Taylor Grazing Act passed in 1934 until the mid-1970's, the Grazing Service and its successor agency, the BLM, were forced to rely on commodity-oriented interest groups such as livestock producers and miners for their political support. As that support ebbed and flowed, the fortunes of the agency rose and fell.

It was not until the late 1960's and early 1970's that environmental interests devoted enough time and energy to influence effectively public policy regarding the BLM. With adoption of a multiple-use mandate, the BLM was subject to many of the same multidirectional pressures that affected the U.S. Forest Service. Conservation interest groups routinely criticize the bureau for its close ties to commodity interests, and the commodity interests often berate the agency because it has come to represent environmental interests. The BLM is no longer captured by a single interest group but it frequently finds itself in a struggle between conflicting interests and values.

Passage of the FLPMA coincided with the election of President Jimmy Carter and a philosophical change among administration officials who were openly supportive of environmental interests. Implementation of the new law fell to Frank Gregg, who became the bureau's director in 1977. Gregg had held staff positions in the Department of the Interior under Stewart Udall and with conservation groups such as the Izaak Walton League. He was familiar with the bureau's operations and the tension between commodity and amenity interests as they squared off over control of the public lands. Many in the bureau hoped that passage of the FLPMA would lead to a period of growth and stability for the agency. Instead, Gregg and the bureau were often the subject of much controversy. The increased influence of environmental interests as well as court challenges to existing mining, timber, and grazing programs polarized the bureau's constituencies.

THE SAGEBRUSH REBELLION

A lawsuit initiated by the Natural Resources Defense Council (NRDC) in October, 1973, had challenged the adequacy of a single, nationwide, BLM environmental impact statement (EIS) reviewing livestock grazing. In April, 1975, the bureau and the NRDC reached a court-supervised settlement in which the BLM agreed to prepare more than 200 (later reduced to 142) site-specific grazing impact statements. The impact of the court's ruling was immense. As the BLM tried to implement the requirements of the FLPMA, it was simultaneously forced to expand its grazing- and minerals-management planning capabilities.

Many in the BLM looked upon the problem of EIS production as an opportunity for making new decisions about allocating rangeland resources for multiple use under the FLPMA. The bureau rapidly set out to conduct intensive rangeland inventories and set livestock carrying capacities. As a result of the early EIS's, about one-half of the grazing allotments were scheduled for reductions, averaging about 10 percent from their current use levels. Politically astute grazing interests countered with court challenges, legislation limiting the levels of reductions, and scientific challenges to the bureau's use of single-year forage inventory rather than a rangeland monitoring approach to carrying capacity.

Western commodity interests were already angered by President Carter's list of water resource development projects targeted for deletion in the appropriations process. A prodevelopment backlash seemed inevitable. Eventually, three Nevada BLM grazing permittees who were also state legislators developed a legal strategy that asserted that the federal lands in the West ought to belong to the states as a matter of constitutional law. This Sagebrush Rebellion soon attracted political support throughout the region. It had many similarities to earlier antifederal land management movements during late 1940's and early 1950's.

With the election of Ronald Reagan in 1980 and an ensuing ideological shift in the Interior Department under Secretary James Watt, political opposition shifted from the commodity interests to the environmental interests. The wholesale changes advocated by Watt and other sagebrush rebels, however, were moderated by

Western governors and the balanced multiple-use mandate of the FLPMA itself. Eventually, the rebellion lost momentum and ended without significant structural changes in the law or in the relationship between the bureau and its constituency groups.

Donald W. Floyd

SOURCES FOR FURTHER STUDY
Dana, Samuel T., and Sally K. Fairfax. *Forest and Range Policy.* New York: McGraw-Hill, 1980.
Foss, Phillip O. *Politics and Grass.* Seattle: University of Washington Press, 1960.
Muhn, James, and Hanson R. Stuart. *Opportunity and Challenge: The Story of the BLM.* Washington, D.C.: U.S. Department of the Interior, Bureau of Land Management, 1988.
Peffer, E. Louise. *The Closing of the Public Domain.* Stanford, Calif.: Stanford University Press, 1951.
Senzel, Irving. "Genesis of a Law." *American Forests* 84 (January, 1978): 30-32, 62-64.
U.S. Department of the Interior. Bureau of Land Management. *Public Land Statistics—1992.* Washington, D.C.: Government Printing Office, 1993.

SEE ALSO: Mineral Leasing Act (1920); Taylor Grazing Act (1934); Multiple Use-Sustained Yield Act (1960); Mining and Minerals Policy Act (1970); Forest and Rangeland Renewable Resources Planning Act (1974); National Forest Management Act (1976).

RESOURCE CONSERVATION AND RECOVERY ACT

DATE: October 21, 1976
U.S. STATUTES AT LARGE: 90 Stat. 2796
PUBLIC LAW: 94-580
U.S. CODE: 42 § 6901
CATEGORIES: Environment and Conservation

This law provided for the "cradle-to-grave" management of hazard-ous wastes in the United States.

In 1976, the Ninety-fourth Congress enacted the Resource Conservation and Recovery Act (RCRA), which proved to be the benchmark piece of legislation for the management of hazardous wastes. In June of that year, the Senate enacted its version, after which the House held hearings on the legislation. The House version eventually integrated the Senate's version, and the bill passed by a vote of 367 to 8 and was signed by President Gerald R. Ford. The bill had a relatively short legislative history, and because of the limited time for debate and conference, the legislation was ambiguously formulated in many aspects. As a result, the bill would continue to be interpreted years after its passage.

AMENDMENTS
The first amendments to the RCRA—the Quiet Communities Act of 1978 and the Solid Waste Disposal Act of 1980—did little to interpret the myriad aspects of the complex legislation. The Hazardous and Solid Waste Amendments of 1984 added many provisions that directed the Environmental Protection Agency (EPA) to develop new rules. The EPA was directed to develop regulations for waste generators and transporters and for facilities for treatment, storage, and disposal (TSD) that managed less than 1,000 kilograms (kg) of hazardous waste per month. The 1984 amendments added approximately seventy major provisions, of which fifty required the EPA to undertake studies and take actions in 1985 and 1986. The result of the 1984 amendments was a substantially revamped and expanded version of the RCRA that provided for more effective management, tracking, and regulation of hazardous wastes in the United States.

Through required permitting, monitoring, and enforcement programs, the RCRA would affect an estimated 500,000 companies and individuals. The rate of hazardous waste generation in the United States has been estimated at several hundred million tons per year. The RCRA provided the basis for controlling these materials through its regulatory structure and through management requirements imposed upon companies and individuals that generate, transport, treat, store, and dispose of hazardous wastes. The act did not address the management of abandoned or closed facilities. Wastes at these sites were later made subject to the 1980 Comprehensive Environmental Response, Compensation, and Liability Act (CERCLA), better known as Superfund.

PROVISIONS

The RCRA, which is managed by the EPA, was originally divided into subtitles A through J. Subtitle C remained the most routinely cited and best known, since it provided guidance for the national hazardous waste management program. In subtitle C, the EPA was required to develop regulations for the identification of hazardous wastes either listing them specifically or by identifying them by their characteristics. A company that disagreed with the listing of its waste could submit a delisting petition to have the waste exempted from coverage by the RCRA; the EPA had to act on a delisting petition within two years of its submission.

A waste not listed by the EPA could still be covered by the RCRA if it exhibited one or more of the following characteristics: ignitability, corrosivity, reactivity, or toxicity. There were specific and detailed guidelines for determining the characteristics of a waste to ascertain whether it met any of the criteria. There were additional guidelines for mixed wastes and for those that were derived from hazardous wastes.

In addition to the inherent regulatory powers provided to the EPA by the RCRA, the act provided the administrator of the EPA with the power to bring suit to remedy hazardous waste situations that represented an imminent and substantial endangerment to health or the environment. Suit could be brought in district court against any person or company, and it could be brought for past infractions as well.

IMPACT AND EFFECTS

The RCRA, which provided for criminal penalties, fines, and imprisonment, was the mechanism by which many corporate officers and employees were prosecuted for improper management of hazardous wastes.

The record-keeping aspects of the RCRA were the basis for effective control of hazardous wastes in the United States. Since many disposal sites received wastes from all over the country, it was imperative that accurate records be maintained. The system called for in the act allowed hazardous wastes to be tracked from initial generation to disposal. Generators and transporters, as well as all TSD facilities, were required to keep records of every stage of the process.

One of the most beneficial aspects of the RCRA and its many amendments was the shift of focus on the part of industry away from hazardous waste production toward pollution prevention, waste minimization, and recycling. These efforts helped not only to preserve and protect the environment but also to reduce cost and enhance profitability. Incentives and other mechanisms to encourage efforts to minimize waste and prevent pollution appeared throughout the United States. Although levels of hazardous wastes continued to increase, the rate of increase was thought to slow.

SIGNIFICANCE

Until the RCRA, no federal legislation addressed hazardous waste management. As a result, billions of dollars needed to be spent for the cleanup of abandoned and historical hazardous waste problems. The focus of the RCRA was to avoid making this aspect of the problem even worse. To that end, waste minimization was thought to be the most desirable approach, since it reduced the amount of waste and therefore the associated risks. Many companies began to change their approach to manufacturing, production, and fabrication and actively sought alternatives to hazardous materials and to activities that led to the production of hazardous wastes. Choosing wisely among the options for minimizing wastes was imperative. This was particularly true because of the difficulty of finding sites for new, permitted facilities. Public opposition to new RCRA facilities proved high, a response called the not-in-my-backyard (NIMBY) syndrome. This response from the public was frequently accompanied by its political equivalent, not-in-my-term-of-office. The lack of disposal capacity led to large volumes of hazardous wastes being shipped long distances, which in turn led to expensive liability and risk issues. Thus the cost for transport and disposal, along with local opposition to hazardous waste production and disposal, played a significant role in developing the waste-minimization programs that many companies pursued to avoid RCRA fines.

The number of facilities available for managing hazardous wastes shrank steadily. Many facilities that no longer had the financial resources and technical means to ensure safe management, as mandated by law, had to close. Their closing was desirable from a health and environmental standpoint, but there was the danger that too many facilities might close and result in inadequate capacity for managing and disposing of hazardous wastes.

Although the EPA and the states would share the responsibility for regulating commercial hazardous wastes, the act did not address one of the major sources for hazardous wastes: the typical American household. Drain openers, oven cleaners, wood and metal polishes and cleaners, paint thinners, oil and fuel additives, herbicides, pesticides, adhesives, fungicides, wood preservatives, grease and rust solvents, and many other household items in common use were often sent to municipal landfills and other disposal facilities, with little control or monitoring.

The RCRA set the stage for managing large- and small-scale commercial sources of hazardous wastes. RCRA also made management of these wastes more costly and increased the liabilities associated with their production. By doing so, the act set in motion the shift seen in the late 1980's and early 1990's that moved industry toward innovative and alternative actions to minimize the volumes of hazardous wastes produced, stored, transported, treated, and disposed. The act also led to a significantly higher level of understanding and involvement of the American public in the debate about hazardous waste management.

Daniel T. Boatright

Sources for Further Study

Arbuckle, J. Gordon, et al. *Environmental Law Handbook.* 12th ed. Rockville, Md.: Government Institutes, 1993.

Environmental Progress and Challenges: EPA's Update. Washington, D.C.: U.S. Environmental Protection Agency, 1988.

Findlay, Roger W., and Daniel A. Farber. St. Paul, Minn.: *Environmental Law in a Nutshell.* St. Paul, Minn.: West Publishing, 1992.

See also: Hazardous Substances Labeling Act (1960); Solid Waste Disposal Act (1965); Water Pollution Control Act Amendments of 1972 (1972); Hazardous Materials Transportation Act (1974); Toxic Substances Control Act (1976); Surface Mining Control and Reclamation Act (1977); Low-Level Radioactive Waste Policy Act (1980); Superfund Act (1980); Nuclear Waste Policy Act (1983);

Emergency Planning and Community Right-to-Know Act (1986); Marine Plastic Pollution Research and Control Act (1987); Oil Pollution Act of 1990 (1990).

NATIONAL FOREST MANAGEMENT ACT

DATE: October 22, 1976
U.S. STATUTES AT LARGE: 90 Stat. 2949
PUBLIC LAW: 94-588
CATEGORIES: Agriculture; Environment and Conservation; Land Management; Natural Resources

An amendment to the 1974 Forest and Rangeland Renewable Resources Planning Act, this law further regulated national forest management.

After U.S. Department of Agriculture (USDA) Forest Service tradition and policy were formalized through the passage of the Multiple Use-Sustained Yield Act (MUSYA) in 1960, public debate continued over national forest management. Significant controversy circulated around clear-cutting in the Monongahela National Forest in West Virginia and the Bitterroot National Forest in Montana, and forest management became a much-publicized political issue. Arnold Bolle, the dean of forestry at the University of Montana, was asked by U.S. senator Lee Metcalf to investigate Forest Service practices. In 1970, Bolle issued a report stating that clear-cuts were too extensive and that other harvesting methods were more appropriate. Moreover, reforestation costs exceeded economic return, and given the abundance of land, timber removal without replanting was considered preferable to costly reforestation. Generally, the press and the public viewed the report as an indictment of clear-cutting, and the Forest Service fell under greater scrutiny.

CLEAR-CUTTING AND THE COURTS

In 1971, U.S. senator Frank Church of Idaho conducted hearings on clear-cutting policies in national forests, and testimony was given by forest scientists and concerned citizens. It was decided that no new legislation was required, but nonbinding recommendations concerning environmental protection and care in clearcut planning and applications—the Church guidelines—were agreed to be followed by the Forest Service.

In 1971, the Sierra Club published Nancy Wood's *Clearcut: The Deforestation of America*, which examined the Monongahela situation and proposed new forest management procedures. In 1973, the Izaak Walton League and the West Virginia Highlands Conservancy filed suit against Secretary of Agriculture Earl Butz to stop timber cutting in the Monongahela. The plaintiffs claimed that Forest Service practices exceeded the authority granted by the Organic Act of 1897, which allowed only marked and designated mature timber to be cut and removed from the forest. Because the judges found the Forest Service in violation of the Organic Act (the agency's harvesting agenda included immature and unmarked timber, which often was not removed from the forest), the court prohibited the Forest Service from further commercial harvesting until their management activities conformed to the law or Congress changed the law. The agency argued that a literal reading of the Organic Act was outdated and impractical and subsequently filed an appeal in the Fourth Circuit Court of Appeals. In 1975, the appeals court upheld the lower court's ruling and directed the Forest Service to halt clear-cutting in all states in the Fourth Circuit (West Virginia, Virginia, North Carolina, and South Carolina). The Monongahela decision influenced litigation elsewhere in the country; cases were presented in Alaska, Georgia, Oregon, South Carolina, Tennessee, and Texas, and injunctions prohibiting timber harvesting were issued in Texas and Alaska.

PASSAGE OF THE ACT

As a result, Congress was forced to reexamine national forest-management issues. U.S. senator Jennings Randolph of West Virginia proposed legislation limiting the authority of the Forest Service in national forest management. It was argued that the agency emphasized timber production, not multiple use as mandated. In contrast, Senator Hubert H. Humphrey of Minnesota, endorsed by the timber industry, presented a bill that advocated repeal of the Organic Act section upon which the Monongahela decision was founded, and he argued for the Forest Service's discretionary authority in national forest management. A variation of Humphrey's bill passed through Congress as the National Forest Management Act (NFMA) of 1976.

PREVIOUS LEGISLATION

The NFMA came about in an era of great environmental awareness among Americans fostered by the press and environmental activism and characterized by increased congressional environmental legislation. During the 1960's and 1970's, significant legislation that directly affected forest management and preceded NFMA included the National Environmental Policy Act of 1970, (NEPA) the Endangered Species Act (ESA) of 1973, and the Forest and Rangeland Renewable Resources Planning Act (RPA) of 1974. The NEPA established the Environmental Protection Agency (EPA) and required the research and design of an environmental impact statement (EIS) for all forest management plans. The EIS was to be prepared by implementing an interdisciplinary approach across the social and natural sciences, and remarks were to be solicited from people or organizations interested in or affected by the plan. The ESA was devoted to the conservation of threatened and endangered species and their habitats. This legislation was to have a far-reaching impact on national forest management because entire ecosystems would be affected.

In response to conflicts between the timber industry and conservation groups over national forest management, the Forest and Rangeland Renewable Resources Planning Act was signed by President Gerald Ford on August 17, 1974. This act mandated the preparation of national forest-management plans every ten years. The plans were to include an estimate of projected renewable resources supply-and-demand, a renewable resources inventory, an outline of Forest Service commitments and programs, and forest-management policies. Furthermore, the RPA directed the Forest Service to examine alternative ways for meeting U.S. forest-resource requirements.

Although the 1974 act directed the secretary of agriculture to formulate national forest-management plans, the act lacked guidelines on plan preparation and content. Moreover, the RPA was viewed as inadequate, especially given the Monongahela decision. The NFMA, which was amended to RPA, provided the direction the RPA lacked.

PROVISIONS OF NFMA

With intensive lobbying from the Forest Service, Congress, conservation groups, and timber interests, the NFMA developed as compromise legislation that blended the NEPA with Forest Service tradition, policy, and authority. The 1976 act revolved principally around regulating timber harvesting in national forests; however, the Forest Service also was affected by other NFMA requirements. For example, the agency was called to invite the public to participate in planning, and disciplines other than forestry and engineering were consulted for the development of natural resource management agendas.

Environmental issues such as clear-cutting, species diversity, marginal lands, rotation age, and nondeclining even flow were addressed. Congress authorized clear-cutting only in situations in which it was the optimal timber-harvesting method; however, the Forest Service maintained much discretionary authority in determining the suitability of clear-cutting. Concerning biodiversity, the agency was pressured to maintain feasible populations of native and desirable non-native vertebrate species, the diversity of tree species existent at the beginning of the management plan, the ecosystems necessary for the survival of endangered species, and biodiversity within managed areas. Marginal lands largely were determined unsuitable for timber production, and the past Forest Service policy of harvesting timber on every acre of land was considered to be not in the public's interest. The NFMA also called for the establishment of standards relating to rotation age, which ensured that generally mature stands of timber would be harvested. The agency, however, was allowed ample discretion to determine rotation age, and exceptions were permitted after the multiple uses of the forests were considered.

NONDECLINING EVEN FLOW (NDEF)

One of the most controversial issues addressed during the NFMA congressional debate related to NDEF. This concept refers to the basic forestry philosophy that annual yield is sustainable in perpetuity. Essentially, it was a regional issue restricted to forest management in the Rocky Mountains and the Pacific Northwest, where old growth stands of timber remained. The Forest Service and preservationists supported NDEF, whereas wood-products industry representatives and economists opposed it. In the end, Congress appeared to support the Forest Service position in maintaining NDEF. Salvage cuts and sanitation cuts were exempted from NDEF requirements, as was harvesting necessary to meet multiple-use goals. Moreover, variable amounts of timber could be harvested from year to year as long as the decennial average was maintained. Although the forest management guidelines became more explicit under the NFMA, and the legislation included directives that were notable departures from Forest Service practices, the Forest Service still maintained significant discretionary authority, and dispute over federal forest management continued.

DEFINING WILDERNESS

Significant controversy was ongoing concerning Forest Service efforts to determine wilderness areas—the Roadless Area Review and Evaluation (RARE) plans. The Sierra Club filed suit in San Francisco over the first RARE plan, which designated 56 million acres of wilderness, and the case was settled out of court in 1972, when the Forest Service consented to conform to the NEPA's guidelines before allowing development in roadless areas. In 1978, during the administration of Jimmy Carter, the second RARE study was completed, which designated 66 million acres of wilderness (10 million acres in addition to the land identified by RARE I). Five years later, the Ninth Circuit Court of Appeals determined that the Forest Service had not followed the EIS requirements established by the NEPA in the California RARE II study.

FROM TIMBER PRODUCTION TO ECOSYSTEM MANAGEMENT

Although the NFMA mandated stricter regulation of clear-cutting, the Forest Service continued to depend upon this method throughout the 1980's and spurred much public controversy. By 1992, clear-cutting had fallen into disfavor among many Forest Service foresters, and the agency adopted a policy of avoiding clear-cutting as a timber harvest method whenever possible. This exemplified a shift in the Forest Service mission—from timber production to ecosystem management—that also was characterized by the appointment during Bill Clinton's administration of wildlife biologist Jack Ward Thomas as forest service chief. Foresters became less dominant, and landscape architects, botanists, environmental planners, archaeologists, and environmental planners greatly diversified the agency.

In 1989, the Conservation Foundation and the Purdue University Department of Forestry performed an assessment of Forest Service planning. Although their report determined that some improvements were desirable—such as the implementation of plans, the agency's attitude toward public involvement, and appropriations and forest plans—it was largely favorable in its evaluation of the NFMA planning process. The report declared that the plans developed by the agency were the best ever developed and that "citizens' awareness of national forests is higher than ever before."

Michael S. DeVivo

SOURCES FOR FURTHER STUDY

Aplet, Gregory H., Nels Johnson, Jeffrey T. Olson, and V. Alaric Sample, eds. *Defining Sustainable Forestry.* Washington, D.C.: Island Press, 1993.

Bowes, Michael D., and John V. Krutilla. *Multiple-Use Management: The Economics of Public Forestlands.* Washington, D.C.: Resources for the Future, 1989.

Clawson, Marion. *The Economics of National Forest Management.* Washington, D.C.: Resources for the Future, 1976.

Cubbage, Frederick W., Jay O'Laughlin, and Charles S. Bullock. *Forest Resource Policy.* New York: John Wiley & Sons, 1993.

Dana, Samuel T., and Sally K. Fairfax. *Forest and Range Policy: Its Development in the United States.* New York: McGraw-Hill, 1980.

Ellefson, Paul V. *Forest Resources Policy: Process, Participants, and Programs.* New York: McGraw-Hill, 1992.

O'Toole, Randall. *Reforming the Forest Service.* Washington, D.C.: Island Press, 1988.

Robbins, William G. *American Forestry.* Lincoln: University of Nebraska Press, 1985.

Robinson, Gordon. *The Forest and the Trees.* Washington, D.C.: Island Press, 1988.

SEE ALSO: National Environmental Policy Act (1970); Endangered Species Act (1973); Forest and Rangeland Renewable Resources Planning Act (1974); Federal Land Policy and Management Act (1976).

SURFACE MINING CONTROL AND RECLAMATION ACT

DATE: August 3, 1977
U.S. STATUTES AT LARGE: 91 Stat. 447
PUBLIC LAW: 95-87
U.S. CODE: 30 § 1201
CATEGORIES: Environment and Conservation; Land Management; Natural Resources

This law regulates surface coal-mining operations and provides for the reclamation of contaminated surface coal-mining sites.

Surface coal-mining operations provide a valuable energy resource but can adversely impact commerce, public welfare, and the environment by destroying or diminishing the use of land for non-mining purposes; by causing erosion, groundwater and surface-water pollution, landslides, and land subsidence; by contributing to flood conditions; by destroying fish and wildlife habitats; and by marring the natural beauty of the land. The Surface Mining and Reclamation Act (SMCRA) was signed into law by President Jimmy Carter in 1977 in an effort to strike a balance between the United States' need for coal as an energy source and the protection of the environment.

Under SMCRA, land affected by surface coal-mining activities must be restored to beneficial use following mining. SMCRA establishes minimum federal standards for surface-mining operations and the surface effects of underground coal mining; under this law, states and Native American tribes may have "primacy"—that is, they may develop and implement their own surface-mining programs, provided they are consistent with SMCRA. Most of the major coal-producing states have achieved primacy. SMCRA requires permits for surface coal-mining operations and provides for public participation in the process of granting permits. Permit applicants must submit reclamation plans and bonds to guarantee that reclamation is properly conducted.

SMCRA establishes extensive environmental protection performance standards for the operation and reclamation of permitted mining operations. It regulates the aboveground effects of underground coal mines and authorizes citizen suits to enforce the act. Under SMCRA, some areas may be designated unsuitable for surface mining if it would irreparably damage the environment. SMCRA also provides for the identification and reclamation of abandoned mine sites. In exchange for the implementation of conservation and reclamation measures, owners of abandoned mine sites receive grants from the Abandoned Mine Reclamation Fund, created from a per-ton reclamation fee imposed on coal-mine operators. Correction of those conditions that threaten public health, safety, and the general welfare is given priority.

In addition, SMCRA includes provisions for university coal research laboratories and energy resource graduate fellowships to promote research and train professionals in surface mining. Provisions for State Mining and Mineral Resources and Research Institutes, originally part of SMCRA, became a separate law with the Mining and Mineral Institute Act of 1984. The Strategic and Critical Minerals Act of 1990 amended SMCRA to include the establishment of a Strategic Resources Mineral Technical Center.

The Office of Surface Mining Reclamation and Enforcement (OSM), a bureau of the United States Department of the Interior, was created by SMCRA to implement the requirements of the act. OSM publishes rules as necessary to carry out the purposes of SMCRA. Where state primacy programs are in effect, OSM provides oversight rather than direct regulation. OSM, in cooperation with the states and Native American tribes, is responsible for ensuring that coal-mining operations and subsequent reclamation are conducted in a manner that protects citizens and the environment and for ensuring that surface-mining operations abandoned before 1977 are reclaimed.

Karen Kähler

SOURCES FOR FURTHER STUDY

Caudill, Harry M. *Night Comes to the Cumberlands: A Biography of a Depressed Area.* Boston: Little, Brown, 1963.

Chilson, Peter. "Coal Miners' Story." *Audubon* 96 (March-April, 1994): 51-62, 118-119.

Desai, Uday, ed. *Moving the Earth: Cooperative Federalism and Implementation of the Surface Mining Act.* Westport, Conn.: Greenwood Press, 1993.

Plotkin, Steven E. "From Surface Mine to Cropland." *Environment* 28 (January/February, 1986): 17-43.
Vietor, Richard H. K. *Environmental Politics and the Coal Coalition.* College Station: Texas A&M Press, 1980.

SEE ALSO: General Mining Act (1872); Mineral Leasing Act (1920); Mining and Minerals Policy Act (1970).

DEPARTMENT OF ENERGY ORGANIZATION ACT

DATE: August 4, 1977
U.S. STATUTES AT LARGE: 91 Stat. 593
PUBLIC LAW: 95-91
U.S. CODE: 42 § 7101
CATEGORIES: Energy; Government Procedure and Organization

This act created the Federal Energy Regulatory Commission to administer the responsibilities formerly assigned to the Federal Power Commission.

In August of 1977, the Federal Energy Regulatory Commission was created by the Department of Energy Organization Act. Its mission was to regulate the electric power and natural gas industries. The agency was associated with the Department of Energy (DOE), which had been created to replace the Federal Power Commission (FPC). Where federal regulation of utilities did not apply, state regulatory commissions were created. The FERC began its operations on October 1, 1977.

FERC'S STRUCTURE AND FUNCTIONS
The Federal Energy Regulatory Commission (FERC), an independent five-member commission within the Department of Energy, was responsible for setting rates and charges for the transportation and sale of electricity and for the licensing of hydroelectric power projects. Members were to serve four-year terms and could be removed by the president only for inefficiency, neglect of duty, or

malfeasance in office. No more than three of the members could be of the same political party. The president appointed the members of the commission.

FERC was given most of the powers of the former Federal Power Commission. FERC was intended to be a separate entity within the Department of Energy and to retain a measure of autonomy. The specifics of the working relationship between the DOE and the FERC were left undefined; questions of authority on issues such as price regulations were left open.

The FERC was responsible for establishing limits on the rates and charges of natural-gas producers and gatherers; setting limits on rates and charges for the interstate transmission and sale of natural gas; issuing certificates for the abandonment and establishment of connections, for natural gas sales, for transportation of gas by pipeline, and for construction of natural gas pipelines and facilities; ruling on curtailment of natural gas service; limiting rates and charges for electric energy transmission and sale; issuing licenses and permits for hydroelectric plants; approving mergers between power and gas companies; supervising the issuance and acquisition of all regulated electric-power company securities; limiting interlocking directorates among electric-power industries; setting limits on oil-pipeline rates, charges, and valuations; and requiring a uniform system of accounts, accounting rules, and procedures for regulated industries. The commission also made the final decisions on DOE actions that required a formal hearing, and it reviewed DOE proposals.

The chair of the FERC was made responsible for the executive and administrative operation of the commission. The chair's duties included such functions as appointing administrative law judges; selecting, appointing, and fixing the compensation of personnel; and procuring the services of experts and consultants.

One of the main functions of the FERC was the regulation of the natural-gas industry, which consisted of producers, pipeline companies (which transport gas from producing areas to consuming markets), and local distribution companies (which sell gas to consumers). The FERC certified the status of gas wells and established, reviewed, and enforced rates and charges for the transportation and sale of natural gas by producers and local distribution companies. The commission also set the rates that interstate pipeline companies could charge for the transmission and sale of natural gas. (Local distribution companies that bought gas from pipeline facilities and sold it to homes and industries were generally regulated by state public utility commissions.) The FERC was also made responsible for the construction of interstate pipeline facilities. In acting on a proposal to build a major pipeline facility, the commission had to take a number of factors into account, including the market for the gas and the facility's safety, environmental impact, and financial viability. The FERC also approved the siting, construction, and operation of liquefied natural gas (LNG), as well as terminals to receive and regasify imported LNG.

IMPACT

In the 1970's, demand for natural gas exceeded supply in the interstate market, which caused pipeline companies to curtail deliveries of gas to some of their customers. The interstate natural gas supply improved greatly after the implementation of the 1978 Natural Gas Policy Act. By 1983, there were surpluses. The commission approved a number of programs for producers and pipelines that were aimed at lowering gas costs and increasing sales to industrial customers with fuel switching capabilities. FERC also reviewed proposals by interstate pipeline companies to provide service to new customers or to modify or abandon pipeline facilities.

Sales of electricity between utilities, or by a utility to a municipality, made up approximately 15 percent of the total amount of electricity sales in the United States in the 1970's. Retail sales of electricity, such as those to homeowners and businesses, were regulated by state public utility commissions. The commission ensured that rates for wholesale transactions in interstate commerce were fair and not unduly discriminatory. The commission also reviewed agreements for the interconnection of utility systems and the transfer of power between utilities, with the aim of achieving reliable service at reasonable rates.

During the fiscal year 1981, the commission adopted a new rule for the filing of changes in the electric rate schedules of public utilities under the Federal Power Act. Under the new rule, the commission could provide a full cost-of-service analysis to all parties involved in a dispute about rates. It was hoped that this would discourage trivial litigation and encourage more settlements. In addition to the review of rates and service standards, the FERC had authority over the mergers of regulated utilities, certain issuances of utility stock, and the existence of certain interlocking relationships between top officials in utilities and major firms doing business in utilities.

FERC was responsible for administering the Federal Power Act of 1920, which had established its predecessor, the Federal Power Commission, and had authorized it to grant preliminary licenses, study potential sites, and issue licenses for the development of hydroelectric power plants. This act subsequently became part of the Federal Power Act of 1935, which gave the FPC the added responsibility of regulating interstate transmission and wholesale sale of electric energy. The 1935 act also gave the commission authority to prescribe a system of accounts and to inspect the books and records of licensees and public utilities.

FERC became responsible for administering the Natural Gas Act of 1938, which had given the FPC jurisdiction over interstate transportation of natural gas, the wholesale price of natural gas in interstate commerce, and the accounting systems used by natural gas companies. FERC helped assist in administering compliance with the Clean Air Act and its amendments, which expanded federal responsibility for air pollution control.

FERC handled the National Environmental Policy Act, which established the Council on Environmental Quality (CEQ), and the Water Pollution Control Act Amendments of 1972, which set up a program of grants to states for construction of sewage treatment plants and established permit programs for industrial and municipal pollutant discharges.

DEREGULATION

The Federal Energy Regulatory Commission served for many years to help set the nation's energy policy, performing effectively under presidents Jimmy Carter, Ronald Reagan, George H. W. Bush, and Bill Clinton in setting policy, giving permits, and administering prices for more effective uses of the nation's natural resources.

During the 1990's, many states passed laws that deregulated their public utilites systems, and the public utilities industry underwent a restructuring and resultant economic stresses that were passed on to consumers. The most notorious case occurred in California, where deregulation in 1996 under Governor Pete Wilson was hampered by requirements placed on the industry to maintain certain rate charges, as well as a large bureaucracy that made capital improvements such as power stations extremely difficult and time-consuming for the state to approve.

In 2001, the role of the FERC became a matter of news when the agency refused to step in after energy brokers, such as Enron, allegedly manipulated the electric power market in California and other states for electric power. Under the Republican administration of George W. Bush, this foot-dragging on the part of FERC was seen by some as shirking its duties to guard the public interest. Nevertheless, the need for a strong agency to fill that role proved more apparent than ever in the wake of the utilities' deregulation.

Amy Bloom, updated by
Christina J. Moose

SOURCES FOR FURTHER STUDY
Crowley, Maureen. *Energy.* New York: Neal Schuman, 1980.
Ih-Fei Lie, Paul. *Energy and the Environment.* New York: Van Nostrand Reinhold, 1993.
U.S. Department of Energy. *Energy and Solid and Hazardous Waste.* Washington, D.C.: System Consultants, 1981.
Victor, Richard H. K. *Energy Policy in America Since 1945: A Study of Business-Government Regulations.* Cambridge, England: Cambridge University Press, 1984.
Witnah, Donald. *Government Agencies.* Westport, Conn.: Greenwood Press, 1983.

SEE ALSO: Federal Power Act (1920); Natural Gas Act (1938); Energy Policy and Conservation Act (1975); Public Utility Regulatory Policies Act (1978).

CLEAN AIR ACT AMENDMENTS OF 1977

DATE: August 7, 1977
U.S. STATUTES AT LARGE: 91 Stat. 685
PUBLIC LAW: 95-95
U.S. CODE: 42 § 7401
CATEGORIES: Environment and Conservation; Natural Resources

These amendments tightened regulatory controls to bring states into compliance with the standards set forth in the 1970 Clean Air Act.

The Clean Air Act Amendments of 1977 attempted to deal with increasingly complex and serious air pollution problems in the United States. At the time of its passage, the law was viewed as one of the most detailed, comprehensive, and complex environmental laws ever passed.

PREVIOUS LEGISLATION

The amendments were preceded by the Clean Air Act of 1963, which was designed to prevent and reduce air pollution but was a weak statute. Amendments were passed in 1965, when nationwide emissions standards for motor vehicles were established (including the required use of pollution-control devices), and in 1967, when air quality control regions were designated and quality control criteria were set forth.

The 1970 amendments established an enduring regulatory framework for air pollution control and became the basis for the changes made in the Clean Air Act Amendments of 1977. The 1970 act replaced state-set air quality standards with provisions for the establishment of national, uniform federal standards for air quality. While the law left the regulation of existing stationary pollution sources to the states, states were required to establish plans, called State Implementation Plans (SIPs), for each air quality region. These SIPs were subject to approval by the federal government. At the same time, the amendments also imposed stricter antipollution standards on automobile manufacturers.

PROBLEMS OF NONCOMPLIANCE

Evidence accumulated showing that the Clean Air Act was not functioning as it was originally envisioned. There were indications of widespread noncompliance with the SIPs, and many regions did not meet their air quality deadlines; the deadlines for meeting automobile tailpipe emission standards were extended on several occasions. In addition, while the Clean Air Act had provided for criminal penalties for noncompliance, the Environmental Protection Agency (EPA), the agency responsible for ensuring compliance with the Clean Air Act, almost always opted for less severe civil actions when it found violations.

Part of the problem with noncompliance was that most states initially were in no position to implement the federal regulations. States had neither the technological capacity nor the resources to deal with the large number of violations. States were also dealing from a weak position, because the hastily adopted SIPs from the early 1970's were widely regarded as technically flawed and overly ambitious. Furthermore, many states were reluctant to risk the political repercussions of closing down economically profitable plants in order to meet the federal mandates on clean air.

PROVISIONS OF THE 1977 AMENDMENTS

To deal with the states' lack of compliance with the law, the 1977 amendments were written to address several problems. The 1977 amendments specifically forbade the EPA to agree to compliance dates beyond 1982; in addition, any administrative orders inconsistent with a state's SIP had to be treated as an SIP revision and had to go through the extensive state and federal approval process. This made revisions much more difficult and forced states to comply with their original SIPs.

Another area addressed was the policy that centered on the prevention of deterioration of relatively clean air. Prior to the 1977 amendments, the EPA had divided clean-air regions into three categories based on how clean the air was in those particular areas. The 1977 amendments formalized these categories and established maximum allowable increases of air pollution for each category. The cleanest areas (national parks and national wilderness areas) were allowed variances of up to eighteen days a year. Areas that previously had not been able to meet the federal standards were given until the end of 1982 to meet those standards. Cities with severe ozone and carbon-monoxide problems were given an extension to 1987. All areas were required to demonstrate regular and consistent emission reductions until compliance was achieved.

Penalties for noncompliance by stationary sources were increased in an attempt to make the cost of noncompliance exceed the expenditures required to achieve compliance. For example, civil penalties of up to $25,000 a day were authorized for violation of the act, and criminal sanctions were imposed on those who knowingly violated the act. States were also required to collect permit fees from major stationary sources.

Finally, the 1977 Clean Air Act Amendments focused heavily on coal-burning power plants. While these plants contributed approximately half of all electrical power in the United States, they were also the major source of sulfur dioxide, one of the most substantial contributors to acid rain. The amendments required that all new coal-fired power plants utilize the best technological system of continuous emission reductions, essentially requiring the use of sophisticated pollution-reducing equipment on all new power plants that used coal for their primary source of fuel. This single requirement not only mandated what some scientists called the most costly of possible clean-air solutions, but also brought about a highly controversial and divisive debate that broke down along regional lines and lasted well into the following decade.

REQUIREMENTS FOR SCRUBBERS

The largest impact of the 1977 amendments centered on the requirement that all new coal-fired utilities had to install the best continuous emissions-reduction technology to reduce sulfur dioxide emissions. Flue gas desulfurization (FGD) systems, commonly called scrubbers, are considered to be the most effective means of reducing pollution—but also the most expensive. This ruling mandating the use of scrubbers set up a regional conflict between the states in the East and Midwest, which had the most high-sulfur coal and the greatest number of old, established utility plants, and states in the West, which had the most low-sulfur coal and the fewest old, established utility plants. Because the requirement for scrubbers was only for new plants, and because scrubbers were very expensive to install, the pollution-control costs were loaded disproportionately on new sources and, therefore, on geographic areas where the prospects for new investment in basic industries was strong. The older, less competitive power plants in the Eastern and Midwestern states benefited because their power systems were already in place; the Western states, which were experiencing tremendous population and industrial growth, had to pay the higher costs of installing scrubbers.

These new regulations mandated scrubbers on all new emitters of sulfur dioxide, regardless of whether they burned clean low-sulfur coal or dirty high-sulfur coal. This was a distinct advantage to the Eastern and Midwestern states, for two reasons. First, these requirements eliminated the incentive for utilities in the Midwest to import low-sulfur Western coal to comply with the new-source standards. Utilities instead could continue to use high-sulfur eastern coal, incurring no relative financial penalty for this inferior choice of pollution-control strategies. Second, prior to 1977, utilities in the West could use low-sulfur coal to minimize their emissions cheaply. The 1977 amendments, however, required these utilities to use scrubbers regardless of the sulfur content of the local coal. Essentially, eastern and midwestern states were put at a tremendous financial advantage because of the mandated scrubber rule of the 1977 Clean Air Act Amendments.

The results of this conflict between high- and low-sulfur coal interests were substantial. Senator Alan Simpson of Wyoming stated that people in the West would not forget the unfair treatment that they had received through the 1977 amendments. At the same time, Robert Byrd of West Virginia, the majority leader of the Senate, remained determined to protect the interests of his high-sulfur-coal state. Consequently, the Clean Air Act, which was supposed to be amended again in the early 1980's, became bogged down in a contentious and divisive debate along regional lines.

Leslie R. Alm

SOURCES FOR FURTHER STUDY

Ackerman, Bruce A., and William T. Hassler. *Clean Coal/Dirty Air.* New Haven, Conn.: Yale University Press, 1981.

Bryner, Gary C. *Blue Skies, Green Politics: The Clean Air Act of 1990.* Washington, D.C.: CQ Press, 1993.

Hamilton, Michael. *Regulatory Federalism, Natural Resources, and Environmental Management.* Washington, D.C.: American Association of Public Administration, 1990.

Landy, Marc K., Marc J. Roberts, and Stephen R. Thomas. *The Environmental Protection Agency: Asking the Wrong Questions.* New York: Oxford University Press, 1990.

Lave, Lester B., and Gilbert S. Omenn. *Clearing the Air: Reforming the Clean Air Act.* Washington, D.C.: Brookings Institution, 1981.

Marcus, Alfred A. *Promise and Performance: Choosing and Implementing an Environmental Policy.* Westport, Conn.: Greenwood Press, 1980.

Rosenbaum, Walter A. *Environmental Politics and Policy.* Washington, D.C.: CQ Press, 1985.

Schmandt, Jurgen, Judith Clarkson, and Hilliard Roderick. *Acid Rain and Friendly Neighbors: The Policy Dispute Between Canada and the United States.* Rev. ed. Durham, N.C.: Duke University Press, 1988.

Vig, Norman J., and Michael E. Kraft. *Environmental Policy in the 1980's.* Washington, D.C.: CQ Press, 1984.

SEE ALSO: Air Pollution Control Act (1955); Clean Air Act (1963); Motor Vehicle Air Pollution Control Act (1965); Clean Air Act Amendments of 1970 (1970); Convention on Long-Range Transboundary Air Pollution (1979); Clean Air Act Amendments of 1990 (1990).

PANAMA CANAL TREATIES

DATE: Senate ratified March 16-April 18, 1978
CATEGORIES: Business, Commerce, and Trade; Foreign Relations; Treaties and Agreements

After seventy-five years, the United States relinquished control of the Panama Canal.

The Senate's ratification of the Treaty Concerning the Permanent Neutrality and Operation of the Panama Canal and the Panama Canal Treaty in the spring of 1978 was the culmination of a long and often dramatic effort to achieve mutually satisfactory new agreements between the United States and the Republic of Panama. Opponents fought the treaties with conviction and determination, leaving the outcome in doubt until the day of the vote. The Panama Canal had became a major political issue, and the debate was charged with emotion and intensity.

THE PANAMA CANAL

U.S. interest in a transisthmian canal grew following the Spanish-American War of 1898, and specific plans were developed. Before buying out the French company's rights and resuming construction, the United States intended to ensure its complete control over the future canal. At the time, the Panamanian territory was a part of the Republic of Colombia, which was unwilling to make the kind of concessions sought by the United States. Thus, the United States saw its interests well served by assisting a Panamanian nationalist faction in forming the independent Republic of Panama in 1903. Two weeks after the independence proclamation, a treaty was signed between the new republic and the United States, granting the latter the use, occupation, and control of a ten-mile-wide strip of land across the isthmus in perpetuity. In return, Panama received ten million dollars and subsequent annual rent payments.

The building of the Panama Canal through the center of the Canal Zone required ten years, at a cost of more than $310 million and approximately four thousand lives, many of which were lost to sickness. It was formally opened to traffic on August 15, 1914. The construction of the canal was, and remains, one of the world's greatest engineering marvels. Through a series of locks, ships are raised or lowered for crossing from one ocean to the other. The canal has been immensely important for maritime transport and enormously beneficial to the Panamanian economy. Thousands of Panamanians have been employed in either the operation of or support services for the canal, or work for those living in the Canal Zone. The Republic of Panama, especially the cities of Cólon and Panama City, also has benefited from the presence of thousands of U.S. civilian and military personnel living in the Canal Zone. Cólon and Panama City are important centers of international banking and commerce.

TREATY NEGOTIATIONS

The fact that Panama did not control its major resource became a fundamental issue in the country. A growing nationalistic sentiment generated vehement resentment of the "neocolonial enclave." A bloody confrontation in January, 1964—precipitated by an attempt by Panamanian students to hoist their national flag in the Canal Zone and resulting in two dozen deaths and hundreds of injuries—convinced U.S. government leaders of the need to enter into negotiations with Panama for a new treaty. In 1967, after three years of deliberations, three treaties were drafted. They dealt with jurisdiction over the canal, defense and status of the military forces, and the possibility of a new sea-level canal. These tentative agreements subsequently were repudiated by Panama. The negotiations resumed in June, 1971, but remained intractable. Meanwhile, Panama succeeded in drawing worldwide attention to, and critical scrutiny of, the canal controversy. In March, 1973, the United Nations Security Council held a special meeting in Panama. A resolution calling for a just and equitable solution to the dispute and effective sovereignty for Panama over all its territory was introduced. The United States defeated the motion through the exercise of its veto power. Nevertheless, these actions gave Panama an important propaganda victory.

On February 7, 1974, Secretary of State Henry Kissinger and Foreign Minister Juan Antonio Tack of Panama met in Panama City and signed a joint statement of principle to serve as a framework for a new round of negotiations. The mutual goal was to arrive at a new treaty satisfying the basic concerns of both nations. This effort reached a successful conclusion on September 7, 1977, when the new Panama Canal Treaty and the Treaty Concerning the Permanent Neutrality and Operation of the Panama Canal were signed in Washington.

THE TREATIES' PROVISIONS
One treaty governed the operations and defense of the Panama Canal through December 31, 1999; the other guaranteed the permanent neutrality of the canal. The treaties provided for the orderly and complete transfer of jurisdiction over the canal and the Canal Zone from the United States to Panama by the year 2000. A major point in the treaties was the removal of U.S. military forces, leaving Panamanian military forces as the sole guardians of the canal. A new U.S. government agency, the Panama Canal Commission, was to operate the canal for the rest of the century. Its board of directors would comprise five U.S. directors and four Panamanians. The plans called for a U.S. director to be the administrator until 1990 and a Panamanian the deputy; thereafter, the roles would be reversed.

NEGOTIATIONS, AND RATIFICATION WITH RESERVATIONS
The new treaties encountered formidable opposition from conservative and rightist elements and required an intense public relations campaign, as well as vigorous lobbying, to ensure ratification by the United States Senate. President Jimmy Carter, Secretary of State Cyrus Vance, and other leading administration officials made every effort to persuade the country that the treaties were in the national interest. The agreements were presented as constituting a better

defense against possible sabotage and terrorist attacks, because they gave the Panamanian people a greater stake in keeping the canal open. Moreover, the treaties were designed to promote a constructive, positive relationship between the United States and the other nations of the Western Hemisphere; a failure to ratify them could be expected to lead to an increasingly hostile, anti-American atmosphere. President Carter talked of "fairness, not force" in U.S. dealings with other nations, positing such a policy not solely as a moral imperative but as an element of pragmatic foreign policy.

The Senate ratified the Neutrality Treaty on March 16, 1978, by a vote of 68 to 32. Two "reservations"—instead of amendments, which might have required a repetition of the ratification process in Panama—were added. The first reservation was introduced by Senator Dennis De Concini of Arizona, providing for U.S. armed intervention in Panama in the event the Panama Canal was closed. The second was introduced by Senator Sam Nunn of Georgia, allowing the United States and Panama to agree on stationing U.S. troops in Panama after 1999. Panamanian spokesmen indicated acceptance of these changes, but there was growing opposition in Panama to the Senate's efforts to alter the negotiated terms. The Panama Canal Treaty was ratified on April 18, 1978, again by a vote of 68 to 32. The added reservations included another by De Concini, allowing for U.S. troops to reopen the canal if operations were disrupted. Relieved that the long and intense process had finally come to an end, President Carter and Panamanian leader Omar Torrijos Herrera hailed the ratifications and predicted a new and amicable relationship between their countries. Both sides agreed to work toward making a smooth transition during the next two decades, allowing for Panama to work its way into running the canal and taking over the Canal Zone and the military installations.

The predictions of Carter and Torrijos were not immediately realized, as the political stability of Panama deteriorated with each passing year. Political corruption and the growing influence of criminals resulted in widespread poverty and high crime rates. By 1989, the situation had become so severe that it was believed that U.S. civilian and military personnel were endangered. In December, President George H. W. Bush launched Operation Just Cause, sending U.S. military forces to arrest Panamanian dictator Manuel Antonio Noriega, whose administration was involved in drug dealing, money laundering, and murder.

CANAL TRANSITION

By 1995, only five years before the final transfer of the canal, some questioned whether sufficient progress toward transition had been made. The United States had a timetable to turn over property so that by noon, December 31, 1999, it would all be under Panamanian control. There was hope of turning military bases into colleges, industrial parks, or tourist meccas. One of the first items turned over was the Panama Railroad, which had been in operation since 1855. By 1995, however, the railroad no longer operated. Depots were boarded up, engines sat rusting on the tracks, and the jungle had overtaken much of the track in the interior. Former railroad employees were without jobs, adding to unemployment rolls and street crime. One military installation had also been turned back to Panama, but squatters occupied it.

Nevertheless, plans moved forward: On January 25, 1995, Panamanian president Ernesto Pérez Balladares created the Transition Committee for the Canal transfer, and in 1996 President Bill Clinton signed the law that made the Panama Canal Commission a government corporation. In May of 1997, the Panama Canal Authority Organic Act was approved, and in December the new Panama Canal Authority was created. The new authority and the Panama Canal Commission met for the first time in June, 1998, and in September Alberto Alemán Zubieta was sworn in as the first Administrator of the Panama Canal Authority. The Canal Authority board of directors approves the regulations on procedures to revise Panama Canal toll rates and and measurement regulations. In June of 1999, the Panama Legislative Assembly approved the Panama Canal Authority's budget for fiscal year 2000, and the Authority began to make job offers to Canal employees. In August, the Panama Legislative Assembly approved new boundaries of the Panama Canal Watershed, and finally, in October, the Panama Canal Authority's contracting regulations were approved. On December 31, 1999, as agreed to in the 1978 treaties, the Panama Canal was transferred to the Republic of Panama.

Manfred Grote, updated by
Kay Hively and
Christina J. Moose

SOURCES FOR FURTHER STUDY
Buckley, Kevin. *Panama: The Whole Story.* New York: Simon & Schuster, 1991.
Crane, Philip M. *Surrender in Panama: The Case Against the Treaty.* New York: Dale Books, 1978.
Koster, R. M., and Guillermo Sanchez Borbon. *In the Time of the Tyrants: Panama, 1968-1990.* New York: Putnam, 1990.
Lefeber, Walter. *The Panama Canal.* New York: Oxford University Press, 1978.
McCullough, David. *The Path Between the Seas.* New York: Simon & Schuster, 1977.

SEE ALSO: Clayton-Bulwer Treaty (1850); Treaty of Paris (1898); Panama Canal Act (1912); Good Neighbor Policy (1933).

AMERICAN INDIAN RELIGIOUS FREEDOM ACT

DATE: August 11, 1978
U.S. STATUTES AT LARGE: 92 Stat. 469
PUBLIC LAW: 95-341
U.S. CODE: 42 § 1996
CATEGORIES: Civil Rights and Liberties; Native Americans; Religious Liberty

Congress recognized its obligation "to protect and preserve for American Indians their inherent right of freedom to believe, express, and exercise traditional religions."

Throughout most of U.S. history, the federal government has discouraged and abridged the free exercise of traditional American Indian religions. The federal government provided direct and indirect support to a variety of Christian denominations who sought to Christianize and "civilize" American Indians. In 1883, bowing to pressure from Christian churches, the federal government forbade "the savage and barbarous practices that are calculated to continue [American Indians] in savagery, no matter what exterior influ-

1333

ences are brought to bear on them." The Sun Dance, rites of purification, other religious ceremonies, and the practices of medicine men were forbidden. Violators could be prosecuted and receive ten days in jail if they continued their "heathenish practices." Such a law restricting freedom of religion was possible because tribes were regarded as distinct political units separate and apart from the United States, and so were not covered by the protections of the Constitution or the Bill of Rights.

JOHN COLLIER AND INDIAN RELIGIOUS FREEDOM

In the 1920's, there was a crusade for reform in federal American Indian policy, and there were outspoken concerns for the support of freedom of religion for American Indian peoples. In 1933, John Collier was appointed Commissioner of Indian Affairs under Franklin Roosevelt. On January 31, 1934, he circulated a pamphlet entitled *Indian Religious Freedom and Indian Culture* among employees of the Indian Service. This pamphlet, which stressed that "the fullest constitutional liberty, in all matters affecting religion, conscience, and culture" should be extended to all American Indians, established policies for Indian Service employees to follow. Collier directed unequivocally, "No interference with Indian religious life or ceremonial expression will hereafter be tolerated. The cultural liberty of Indians in all respects is to be considered equal to that of any non-Indian group." Two weeks later, Collier issued a second order, which dealt with religious services at government-operated schools. It had been common practice to require students in government schools to attend church services. This new policy statement, "Regulations for Religious Worship and Instruction," prohibited compulsory attendance at services, although it did allow religious denominations to use school facilities for services. Religious instruction was permitted one hour per week in the day schools; however, parents had to give written permission for their children to attend. This policy was especially controversial, because these regulations extended to representatives of native religions as well as to Christian missionaries.

These policy statements were not well received by missionaries who had been active on various reservations, and many regarded Collier's move to protect American Indian religious freedoms as a direct attack on the churches and Christianity. Collier was accused of being an atheist and of being antireligious. Criticism of Collier was especially strong among Protestant missionary societies and included attacks from Christian Indians who decried this return to the old ways as subverting American Indian progress. Nevertheless, Collier insisted that American Indians be granted complete constitutional liberty in all matters affecting religion, conscience, and culture, and he asserted that religious liberty extended to all people, not just Christians.

Most tribal governments endorsed Collier's policy of religious freedom, and, on many reservations, there was a revival of the older spiritual traditions. However, federal and state laws did not endorse or permitted freedom of religion for American Indians consistently. Certain state and federal laws and policies prevented the free exercise of religion for many American Indian people. A large area of concern was that many lands that were considered to be sacred by the tribes had passed from Indian control to state or federal jurisdiction. Access to such sacred sites often was limited or not permitted. The use of peyote in Native American Church ceremonies was a contentious issue, because peyote is a restricted substance because it has hallucinogenic properties. The use of eagle feathers in a variety of rituals was another source of friction with federal officials, because eagles were protected under endangered species laws. There also have been occasions of interference in religious ceremonies by government agents and curious onlookers. American Indian people had little recourse to remedy these situations, and tribal governments had no powers of prosecution or enforcement.

PASSAGE AND PROVISIONS

As a result of continuing problems with the free exercise of traditional American Indian religions, Congress passed a broad policy statement, Senate Joint Resolution 102, commonly known as the American Indian Religious Freedom Act (AIRFA), on August 11, 1978. After noting the U.S. right to freedom of religion and the inconsistent extension of that right to American Indian people, Congress acknowledged its obligation to "protect and preserve for American Indians their inherent right of freedom to believe, express, and exercise the traditional religions of the American Indian, Eskimo, Aleut, and Native Hawaiian, including but not limited to access to sites, use and possession of sacred objects, and the freedom to worship through ceremonial and traditional rites."

AIRFA also required all federal agencies to examine their regulations and practices for any inherent conflict with the practice of American Indian religions. These agencies were required to report back to Congress and recommend areas in which changes in policies and procedures were needed to ensure that American Indian religious freedoms were protected.

IMPACT

The American Indian Religious Freedom Act is a key element in self-determination and cultural freedom in the United States. However, even with passage of this act, Native Americans have continued to experience problems in access to sacred sites and the use of peyote. The right of Native Americans to use peyote is an unsettled issue in both federal and state courts. Although peyote is subject to control under the Comprehensive Drug Abuse Prevention and Control Act, a number of states exempt its use in Native American Church ceremonies. Some courts uphold the right of Native Americans who are church members to possess and use peyote; other courts do not. Likewise, American Indians are not guaranteed access to sacred sites that are located outside the bounds of Indian lands, even when these lands are under federal control.

COURT RULINGS

The Supreme Court has ruled that AIRFA is a policy statement only, and it does now allow American Indians to sue when federal agencies disregard native religious practices or when agencies pursue plans that will have an adverse impact on Native American religion or beliefs. In 1987, in *Lyng v. Northwest Indian Cemeteries Association*, the United States was granted the right to build a logging road through federal lands that were central to the traditional religions of the Yurok, Karuk, and Talowac tribes. In 1990, the United States Supreme Court ruled, in *Employment Division, Department of Human Resources of Oregon et al. v. Smith*, that the state of Oregon could prohibit a member of the Native American Church from using peyote, because that state regarded peyote as an illegal substance. These Supreme Court decisions made clear that if federal or state agencies fail to comply with the policies established in AIRFA, American Indian people had no legal recourse to sue or claim adverse impact on their religion. The extension of full religious freedom to Native American people is an evolving concept in

U.S. jurisprudence, and the American Indian Religious Freedom Act constitutes an important philosophical foundation toward ensuring the free exercise of religion and access to sacred areas.

Carole A. Barrett

Sources for Further Study

Deloria, Vine, Jr., ed. *American Indian Policy in the Twentieth Century.* Norman: University of Oklahoma Press, 1985.

Deloria, Vine, Jr., and Clifford Lytle. *The Nations Within: The Past and Future of American Indian Sovereignty.* New York: Pantheon Books, 1984.

Echo-Hawk, Walter E. "Loopholes in Religious Liberty. The Need for a Federal Law to Protect Freedom of Worship for Native American People." *NARF Legal Review* 14 (Summer, 1991): 7-14.

Josephy, Alvin M. *Now That the Buffalo's Gone: A Study of Today's American Indians.* Norman: University of Oklahoma Press, 1984.

Long, Carolyn N. *Religious Freedom and Indian Rights: The Case of Oregon v. Smith.* Lawrence: University Press of Kansas, 2000.

See also: Indian Offenses Act (1883); Indian Citizenship Act (1924); Indian Reorganization Act (1934); Indian Civil Rights Act (1968); Comprehensive Drug Abuse Prevention and Control Act (1970); Indian Self-Determination and Education Assistance Act (1975); Native American Graves Protection and Repatriation Act (1990).

Port and Tanker Safety Act

Date: October 17, 1978
U.S. Statutes at Large: 92 Stat. 1471
Public law: 95-474
U.S. Code: 33 § 1221
Categories: Environment and Conservation; Natural Resources

This act provided protections for the marine environment and public safety.

After World War I, the United States and other emerging industrialized nations witnessed a tremendous growth in both oil imports and domestic movements of refined petroleum products. Movement of oil remained comparatively unregulated until the 1930's, when a number of maritime casualties drew attention to some of the problems associated with maritime activities. Incidents involving loss of life, water pollution, and port safety prompted the government to enact the Tank Vessel Act of 1936, which addressed tank vessels carrying flammable or combustible liquid cargoes. This act concentrated on fire protection, safety equipment, standards for crews, and a general tightening of federal authority over the shipping industry. The legislation did not, however, address authority for pollution prevention within ports in the United States. Federal authority over port safety could be invoked only for considerations of national security.

The 1936 legislation remained essentially unchanged until it was extensively revised by the Port and Waterways Safety Act of 1972. This act contained the 1970 presidential proposal to expand the Coast Guard's jurisdiction over all vessels that use U.S. ports and provided the Coast Guard with the authority to protect inland waters and adjacent shore areas from environmental harm and structural damage. There were provisions in the law to establish and operate services for vessel traffic, to require certain navigational equipment, and to control vessel traffic and movement. Unfortunately, the Coast Guard was slow to implement these provisions, mostly because of budgetary constraints. In 1976, a series of major tanker accidents focused public and congressional attention on the continued problem of marine pollution. The tremendous growth in maritime traffic, commensurate with a massive increase in oil importation and the existence of generally larger vessels, led to increasing damage to the environment from accidental spills and from normal tanker operations. It also became clear to U.S. officials that a lack of control over foreign ships calling on U.S. ports was a serious problem.

Results from federal studies of marine pollution conducted in late 1976 and early 1977, including a study of the shortcomings of the 1972 act, prompted President Jimmy Carter to announce a number of proposals to Congress in March, 1977. These included recommendations for new tanker regulations, spill liability, and U.S. ratification of the 1973 International Conference for the Prevention of Pollution from Ships. More important perhaps, the president directed the State Department to begin diplomatic efforts to improve the international system of tanker inspection and certification through the International Maritime Consultative Organization (IMCO).

Continued tanker accidents, most notably the *Amoco Cadiz* in early 1978, coupled with diplomatic pressure from the United States, resulted in the early convening of IMCO's Council Conference on Tanker Safety and Pollution Prevention (TSPP). Given a climate of international concern over tanker pollution, the conference made recommendations to signatory nations to adopt provisions for tanker equipment, inspections, and certification.

PASSAGE IN CONGRESS

Early activity in the Ninety-fifth Congress included the introduction of approximately thirty bills to address tanker safety, port safety, and environmental protection from oil. It was during the bill consolidation process that some congressional members and government officials expressed concern, arguing that the initial Senate bill contained provisions that severely departed from harmonization with concurrent international standards being proposed by IMCO. It was believed by many in government that if the United States were to impose unilateral tanker requirements on the international shipping community, it would seriously jeopardize international relationships. The proposed U.S. legislation was seen by many to be hypocritical, illegal, and self-defeating, given the fact that the United States was already a signatory to the international agreements. Breaking away from international commitments (with subsequent loss of credibility among other maritime nations) was not viewed as a constructive way to bring about solutions to the worldwide oil pollution problem.

After much debate and committee work, an amended version of Senate Bill 682 was drafted from much of the language contained in a House version of the bill. The Senate eventually accepted the House changes to the bill and inserted its own minor alterations concerning offshore oil-drilling platforms and wider federal authority to impose stricter standards on domestic shipping than those being contemplated in the international TSPP conference. The amended Senate Bill 682—which ironically deleted the initial requirement for double-hulled tank vessels that the United States subsequently unilaterally mandated under OPA-90—passed both houses of Congress in October, 1978, and was signed into law by President Carter.

PROVISIONS

The law included provisions for mandatory state or federal pilots for every vessel calling on U.S. ports; expanded federal authority to investigate accidents and maintain ship and company performance databases; annual inspections of all tank vessels using U.S. ports; Coast Guard authority to deny entry or detain vessels that were not in compliance with the regulations; Coast Guard authority to issue regulations for domestic trade vessels that differed from regulations imposed by the multination agreement; federal authority to operate harbor traffic control systems (similar to those for aircraft); the requirement that certain tank vessels implement segregated ballast systems, crude-oil washing systems, and tank safety inert gas systems over a period of eight years; the requirement that tank vessels, except barges, carry electronic navigation and collision-avoidance equipment by 1982; implementation of new requirements for offshore lightering operations; prohibition of any ship docking in a U.S. port if it had dumped oil-tank washwater at sea; and authority for the secretary of transportation to assess stiffer civil and criminal penalties for noncompliance.

OIL SPILLS

Quantitative statistics vary dramatically as they relate to sources of oil in the sea. The National Academy of Sciences estimated in 1976, for example, that of the 6.1 million metric tons of oil that reached the sea each year, only 35 percent could be attributed to the commercial movement of oil. Of this, 18 percent was directly attributable to tanker operations and a mere 3 percent to collisions, groundings, and explosions. Different studies estimated that 85 percent of the oil spilled into the sea was the result of tank cleaning, whereas others put the figure at 26 percent from accidental spills and routine ship discharges. These conflicting figures were used by various special-interest lobbies, depending on their political and philosophical agendas. Regardless of the viewpoint, however, it was undisputed that while the lowest percentage of oil came from accidental discharges such as groundings and collisions, those discharges always gained the most media attention and caused great public outcry.

The various provisions of the Port and Tanker Safety Act of 1978 and those resulting from the international TSPP conference addressed issues that included prevention of accidental discharge through equipment, training, and traffic control; abatement of operational discharge through vessel design changes such as segregated ballast and crude-oil wash systems; and the use of terminal facilities to receive and recycle wastewater from washing out oil tanks (this was meant to discourage the practice of cleaning out huge oil tanks with water and pumping the liquid overboard).

The cleaning and segregated ballast systems eventually eliminated most of the routine oil pollution from tanker operations. These major equipment systems also caused the greatest financial burden on the maritime oil industry. Fitting an existing tanker in 1978 with a segregated ballast system cost approximately $2 million and reduced the vessel's carrying capability by 20-25 percent. Crude-oil wash and inert gas systems cost about $1 million for each vessel. These requirements forced most ship owners to build entirely new vessels and retire older tonnage. The resultant shipbuilding boom lasted until the worldwide oil shortages of the early 1980's.

COMPLIANCE DIFFICULTIES

For many operators, the cost of financing new vessels or retrofitting existing ones was prohibitively high and resulted in the replacement of competent operators with cheaper carriers who were willing to take chances. This rebound effect of regulation often contributed to yet more operational pollution and accidents. It was difficult to enforce laws on those who used the open sea. Yet while oil slicks from tank cleaning and bilge pumping were common throughout the world in the 1970's and early 1980's, the situation did improve as a result of the new regulations, and oil pollution in the sea from tanker operations was reduced.

Just how many catastrophic accidents were prevented as a result of better equipment and systems, stricter port movement regulations, and better crew and pilot training was not readily quantifiable. The fact that many accidents nevertheless continued to happens suggested that equipment-based regulation and political entreaties for international compliance to regulation may have overlooked other underlying causes.

Nevertheless, the 1978 Port and Tanker Safety Act and its influence on the international shipping community appeared to be instrumental in reducing worldwide pollution. The act forced a completely new operational doctrine for tanker operations into existence, along with technologically improved navigational safety measures. It also provided an inland vessel traffic control system designed to aid mariners at harbor entrance choke points, thereby avoiding growth of marine traffic congestion.

Paul Leyda

SOURCES FOR FURTHER STUDY

Barak, Joanne H. "Time Charters: Who Bears the Burden of Complying with Subsequent Legislation—The Port and Tanker Safety Act of 1978." *The George Washington Journal of International Law and Economics* 16, no. 2 (1982): 271-298.

Congressional Quarterly Almanac. "Tanker Safety." 34 (1978): 713-714.

Oil Companies International Marine Forum. *Tanker Safety and Pollution Prevention.* London: Author, 1976.

Peterson, Roger Andrew. *Maritime Oil Tanker Casualties (1964-1977): An Analysis of Safety and Policy Issues.* Knoxville, Tenn.: UMI, 1982.

U.S. Congress. House. *United States Code: Congressional and Administrative News.* St. Paul, Minn.: West Publishing, 1978.

Waters, W. G., II, T. D. Heaver, and T. Verrier. *Oil Pollution from Tanker Operations: Causes, Costs, Controls.* Vancouver: University of British Columbia, 1980.

SEE ALSO: Oil Pollution Act of 1924 (1924); Coastal Zone Management Act (1972); Marine Mammal Protection Act (1972); Convention on the Conservation of Migratory Species of Wild Animals (1979); Marine Plastic Pollution Research and Control Act (1987); Oil Pollution Act of 1990 (1990).

AIRLINE DEREGULATION ACT

DATE: October 24, 1978
U.S. STATUTES AT LARGE: 92 Stat. 1705
PUBLIC LAW: 95-504
U.S. CODE: 49 § 334
CATEGORIES: Business, Commerce, and Trade; Transportation

Although deregulation gave managers more flexibility to develop their business strategies, the subsequent shakeout in the airline industry underscored the need to avoid poorly planned rapid expansion.

BEFORE DEREGULATION: THE CIVIL AERONAUTICS BOARD

Prior to the Airline Deregulation Act, the Civil Aeronautics Board (CAB) strictly regulated airline routes, fares, and mergers. For example, before a trunk carrier (an airline that primarily served large cities and high-density routes) could provide service on a new route, it had to petition the CAB for approval. Approval was contingent upon the CAB's judgment regarding three issues: need for additional service on the route, which airline should be awarded the route, and whether the route tied into an airline's existing network. Incumbent airlines usually contended that the petitioned route could not support any additional service, so proceedings often dragged on for years.

The CAB also regulated airfares by establishing maximums, minimums, or both maximums and minimums. Each carrier was required to obtain permission before introducing a new fare. The CAB ruled on these fare changes to determine whether they were reasonable. Although the CAB designed the fare limits to provide a rate of return on investment equal to 12 percent, this target was rarely reached.

Mergers were a third area in which the CAB exercised control. The airlines used mergers to acquire the route networks and aircraft capacity of other carriers. This strategy was often more expedient than petitioning the CAB for individual routes because the acquiring carrier could receive many new routes simultaneously. The CAB generally approved a merger, however, only if it prevented a carrier from going bankrupt, with the result that a particular geographic area would lose air service.

The CAB regulations effectively prevented trunk carriers from competing on the basis of fares and routes. Although the airlines could offer different in-flight amenities, each aircraft had approximately the same level of comfort. Because their product was undifferentiated, airline managers realized that customers were more concerned with scheduling the most convenient flight than with maintaining brand loyalty. As a result, frequency of service became the most important determinant of market share. The CAB did not regulate flight frequency except to prevent de facto abandonment of routes.

THE ARGUMENT FOR DEREGULATION

Proponents of deregulation argued that the CAB regulations were responsible for increasing the cost of air transportation. Their argument was based on the premise that as the airlines scheduled more flights to increase market exposure, each flight carried fewer passengers. Costs, and thus fares, rose because the fixed cost of each flight was spread among fewer passengers. They argued that deregulation would permit the airlines to differentiate their product and provide a wider range of fares and services. One anticipated outcome was lower prices.

Advocates of deregulation also argued that the legislation would result in greater efficiency and flexibility. First, by increasing a carrier's flexibility to improve route structures and flight schedules, deregulation would permit better aircraft utilization. Second, assets would not be wasted simply to seek future route awards. Under regulations, some carriers had used artificially low fares to strengthen their bargaining position when seeking future routes. Third, carriers would have more leverage when dealing with labor unions because the U.S. government would not be obligated to aid an ailing airline.

ARGUMENTS AGAINST DEREGULATION

With the exception of United Air Lines, the trunk carriers either vehemently or tacitly opposed deregulation. They argued that the absence of entry restrictions on the more profitable routes would result in duplication and overcapacity. Because more planes would fly these routes, higher rather than lower fares would result. If increased competition resulted in excess capacity, then profitability would decline because each flight would carry more empty seats.

In addition, they argued that deregulation would diminish stable and reliable air service. In a deregulated environment, an airline could enter a market on weekends or holidays and carry full flights by offering reduced fares. During periods of reduced traffic demand, however, the carier could suspend its service. Finally, critics feared that rate wars would develop as airlines offered cut-rate fares to establish themselves in new markets. As incumbent airlines lowered their fares to remain competitive, profits would be reduced. As a result, carriers would have difficulty replacing their fleets.

Opponents of deregulation also argued that smaller cities would suffer reduced or suspended service because the trunk carriers would concentrate their equipment capacity on the lucrative long-haul routes between high-density population centers. This argument was similar to a cross-subsidy issue: The trunk airlines claimed that they used profits from their long-haul routes to negate losses on their shorter, less profitable routes. If deregulation eliminated these profits, then carriers would not be able to offset the losses from their shorter routes and might have to abandon them.

Flights over shorter distances are relatively more expensive in terms of cost per mile because fixed costs, such as passenger and luggage processing, are spread over fewer miles. In addition, slower average aircraft speeds cause higher labor costs per seat mile. Finally, fuel costs per seat mile are proportionately higher because the rate of fuel consumption is greater during takeoff and landing than it is during flight. Because other forms of transportation, such as the automobile, are relatively attractive at shorter distances, demand is highly elastic; that is, customers are very likely to choose a substitute form of transportation if prices go up. As a result, the higher costs of shorter flights cannot be offset by fares that reflect those costs and allow as much profit as earned on longer flights.

DEREGULATION AND ITS IMPACT

The Airline Deregulation Act of 1978 ended the government's regulation of the airlines and eliminated the CAB by the end of 1984. Airlines now were subject to market competition to "regulate" price, routes, and qualities of air travel. The effect was to reduce airfares significantly over the first decade of the law's existence.

The aftermath of airline deregulation underscored the need for managers to accurately evaluate corporate strategy. For many years, the airlines preferred to pay the costs of CAB regulation rather than face the uncertain environment that would exist without controls. Once the industry was deregulated, however, many carriers were lured by the freedom to expand and increase market share. The result was that many airlines overexpanded, faced overcapacity, and therefore had to sell their product at low prices, suffering declining profits as a result.

Prior to deregulation, managers were enamored of the concept of flight frequency. Because CAB regulations severely limited the trunk carriers' ability to compete on the basis of fares and routes, flight frequency became the most important determinant of market share. This led to the widespread practice of using long-term debt to finance large aircraft fleets that could provide frequent service. As a result, trunk carriers were highly leveraged, faced large interest charges, and were adversely affected by the 1980-1981 recession that reduced air traffic demand.

A brief description of the corporate strategies implemented by Delta Air Lines and Braniff Airways following deregulation illustrates these points. Delta and Braniff implemented strategies that resulted in good and poor performance, respectively. Both companies used a hub-and-spoke route network prior to deregulation, and both carriers flew the less popular routes to small and mid-sized cities. These flights were then aggregated at a hub city and efficiently scheduled to connect with the carrier's more profitable long-distance flights. This system minimized passenger inconvenience resulting from layovers and made the airlines less dependent on other carriers for their feeder traffic.

A major advantage of this type of network was that each airline was generally a monopoly carrier on its short-haul routes. Consequently, older planes could be used without worrying about flight frequency, competition, or price wars. As a result, these carriers entered the deregulated era in better financial shape than did the larger carriers. Delta had one of the industry's lowest debt ratios, whereas Braniff's leverage was commensurate with the industry average. These two carriers also tended to be more profitable than the larger carriers.

Following deregulation, Braniff changed its strategy and placed more emphasis on adding long-haul routes. In 1979, for example, Braniff added new routes to Europe and the Far East, even though it lacked marketing exposure in these areas. Braniff hoped that the new domestic and international routes would feed each other and

increase traffic flow through its domestic hub cities. It also expected that new traffic patterns would help smooth demand over
the entire system. This rapid expansion strategy was not compatible with the environment. Braniff tried to expand its operations
during a period of rising interest, fuel, and operating costs, but it
had to lower prices to remain competitive on existing routes and
offer promotional fares to increase its market exposure on the new
routes. Braniff ignored the importance of flight frequency and its
relationship to market share. In many cases, Braniff initiated only
one flight on its new routes, sometimes with an inconvenient arrival or departure time. As a result, Braniff was not able to schedule
its system as efficiently as it initially hoped. Braniff also shifted
capacity from markets in which it previously held a prominent position, with the result that competitors entered these cities and
gained market share.

In contrast to Braniff, Delta maintained its position as one of the
trunk industry's most profitable carriers. It did not deplete its resources in price wars on the more popular routes, and it added
routes only when it perceived a need for additional service. Delta
also added routes that could be profitable in the short term. As a
result, it initiated service to fast-growing regions in the Pacific
Northwest, California, and Texas. Delta did not sacrifice flight frequency in its traditional markets to provide service on these new
routes. When Eastern Airlines increased flight frequency to Atlanta, Delta's major hub, Delta countered by simultaneously adding more flights. To combat the tendency toward providing excess
capacity, Delta introduced flight complexes at its Atlanta hub.
Thirty or forty planes would converge on Atlanta at two-hour inter-
vals, exchange passengers, and fly to different spoke cities. The
strategy kept a greater percentage of passengers within the feeder
and connector system. Passenger layover was minimized through
efficient scheduling, which, in turn, reduced the chance that passengers would defect to another airline. Delta became one of the
dominant U.S. carriers, and Braniff filed for bankruptcy in 1982.

Along with lower fares, therefore, the hub-and-spoke strategy
was one of the major outcomes of deregulation. Passengers now
needed to travel from major hub to major hub, using connecting
flights or ground travel to reach the hubs, as fewer direct flights
were available. Other changes that passengers noticed were a
broader variation in the quality of service and amenities such as

meals ("no-frills" trips now could be offered to passengers wanting to minimize the cost of their tickets). The increase in competition—with the choice with the number of certified large-aircraft carriers doubling over the following three decades—provided passengers with more options in airlines and allowed them to benefit from discount pricing, frequent flyer programs, and cross-industry credit card promotions. Increasingly, however, passengers also saw overbooking, delayed schedules and missed connections, and longer overall travel times. Older passengers complained that the civility and graceful amenities of their earlier flying experience had been replaced with coach travel that resembled a bus trip.

Nevertheless, in 1999, the Brookings Institution estimated that deregulation had saved travelers more than $20 billion per year, and the increase in travelers seemed in line with that estimate: According to the Air Transport Association of America, in 1999 U.S. airlines 640 million passengers, more than two and one-half times the number of passengers traveling in 1977.

M. Mark Walker, updated by
Christina J. Moose

SOURCES FOR FURTHER STUDY

Dempsey, Paul Stephen, and Andrew R. Goetz. *Airline Deregulation and Laissez-Faire Mythology.* Westport Connecticut: Quorum Books, 1992.

Fruhan, William E., Jr. *The Fight for Competitive Advantage: A Study of the United States Trunk Air Carriers.* Boston: Division of Research, Graduate School of Business Administration, Harvard University, 1972.

Lewis, W. Davis, and Wesley P. Newton. *Delta: The History of an Airline.* Athens: University of Georgia Press, 1979. Comprehensive review of the history of Delta Air Lines from 1929 to 1979.

MacAvoy, Paul W., and John W. Snow, eds. *Regulation of Passenger Fares and Competition Among the Airlines.* Washington, D.C.: American Enterprise Institute for Public Research, 1977.

Saunders, Martha D. *Eastern's Armageddon: Labor Conflict and the Destruction of Eastern Airlines.* Westport, Conn.: Greenwood Press, 1992.

SEE ALSO: Air Commerce Act (1926); Aviation and Transportation Security Act (2001).

ETHICS IN GOVERNMENT ACT

DATE: October 26, 1978
U.S. STATUTES AT LARGE: 92 Stat. 1824-1867
PUBLIC LAW: 95-521
U.S. CODE: 28 § 591
CATEGORIES: Government Procedure and Organization

> *This law mandated that nominees for positions requiring Senate confirmation make financial disclosure reports; it also established the Office of Government Ethics to oversee the administration of ethics policies in the executive branch.*

The Ethics in Government Act was passed in the aftermath of the Watergate scandal during the Nixon administration to lessen the likelihood that presidential nominees for government positions would have conflicts of interest that might result in personal or financial gain. The law requires that presidential nominees for positions requiring Senate confirmation file financial disclosure reports. The required report lists sources of income, assets and liabilities, and affiliations with organizations that may lead to conflicts of interest. The act also created the Office of Government Ethics, which reviews the disclosure reports of presidential nominees and issues opinion letters concerning possible conflicts of interest.

POSSIBLE CONFLICTS OF INTEREST

The principal concerns that guide the reviews of financial disclosure reports are the potentials for officials to (1) participate in matters in which they have personal financial interests, (2) receive income from nongovernment sources for government service, (3) participate in outside activities that may involve the government, and (4) experience conflicts following their government employment because of restrictions on dealings with former agencies. The latter issue primarily affects former officials, but it is frequently a concern for officials entering government service because it can affect their future employment prospects.

THE REVIEW PROCESS

The Office of Counsel to the President typically solicits complete financial records to anticipate problems before nominations are announced and explains reporting requirements to potential nominees. The Office of Counsel provides forms to potential nominees and gives the completed reports to designated agency ethics officials and to the Office of Government Ethics. Agency heads are responsible for compliance with the ethics program, and they appoint the agency's ethics official. The financial disclosure reports are also reviewed by the employing agency's representative, and the agency's evaluation is included in the Office of Government Ethics' opinion letter. The opinion letters are reviewed by the president before the nomination is sent forward. The members of the Senate involved in the confirmation process review the letters and generally include their own assessment of possible conflicts of interest.

The identification of possible conflicts may result in nominees being asked to disqualify, or recuse, themselves from participation in decisions regarding firms or industries in which they may have personal or financial interests, divest themselves of financial interests in particular firms or industries which may cause conflicts of interest, or put their financial holdings into "blind trusts" so that they will have no knowledge of their financial interests in particular firms or industries. A waiver may also be granted if it is determined that a nominee's interests in a particular firm or industry are so slight or peripheral as to assure that any conflict of interest will be very minor.

RESTRICTIONS ON FUTURE EMPLOYMENT

President George H. W. Bush appointed a Commission on Federal Ethics Law Reform, which in 1989 recommended strengthening the provisions dealing with "influence peddling" as well as broadening the provisions dealing with conflicts of interest when officials may gain personally or financially. Subsequent amendment of the Ethics in Government Act expanded its scope to include influence peddling by former officials. The act restricts what former government officials may do upon leaving office, principally in terms of a two-year prohibition against representing private interests before their former agencies. These provisions were designed to lessen conflicts of interest that may arise during an official's tenure with an agency, when he or she may be anticipating future employment outside government, and to help stop the "revolving door" pattern of employment in which individuals move from government agencies to the industries they were responsible for regulating and vice versa. The provisions also include a one-year prohibition on former officials representing private interests before their former government employer when the individual had no responsibilities relating to his or her current employer.

IMPACT OF THE ACT

Critics of the Ethics in Government Act have charged that it makes it very difficult to recruit potential officials from the private sector. This criticism was expressed numerous times during the Reagan administration. At issue are whether the financial disclosure requirements themselves are impediments to recruitment because individuals do not want to make their finances public or whether other restrictions on employment discourage individuals from accepting nominations. In addition to financial disclosure and limitations on relationships with former and future employers, the act restricts the freedom of officials to manage their own financial affairs.

Supporters of the act argue that it focuses attention on the issue of ethics and, in particular, reinforces the principle that even the appearance of impropriety is to be avoided in public-sector employment. The Ethics in Government Act also reaffirms the principles that government officials should not use their positions for personal gain and that government business should be conducted "in the sunshine." Moreover, the act serves to protect appointing officials from inadvertently selecting someone who might be motivated to seek public employment for personal gain or who might later be charged with bias in making decisions.

The standards set in the Ethics in Government Act have had a broad impact in government. States and municipalities are increasingly requiring financial disclosure by political appointees and elected officials to lessen the potential for conflicts of interest. Conflicts that may arise because of dual employment, financial interests in businesses that deal with government agencies, and the use of public positions to benefit private interests are examined closely. Conflicts arising from the employment of law enforcement officers in private security during their off-duty hours are cases in point.

William L. Waugh, Jr.

SOURCES FOR FURTHER STUDY

Denhardt, Robert B. *Public Administration: An Action Orientation.* 2d ed. Belmont, Calif.: Wadsworth, 1995.

Richter, William L., Frances Burke, and Jameson Doig, eds. *Combating Corruption: Encouraging Ethics, a Sourcebook for Public Service Ethics.* 2d ed. Washington, D.C.: American Society for Public Administration, 1995.

SEE ALSO: Pendleton Act (1883); Hatch Act (1939); Securities Exchange Act (1934); Federal Election Campaign Act (1972); Twenty-seventh Amendment (1992); Bipartisan Campaign Reform Act (2002).

PREGNANCY DISCRIMINATION ACT

DATE: October 31, 1978
U.S. STATUTES AT LARGE: 92 Stat. 2076
PUBLIC LAW: 95-555
U.S. CODE: 42 § 2000e et seq.
CATEGORIES: Health and Welfare; Labor and Employment; Women's Issues

This act banned various forms of discrimination against pregnant employees.

When Congress banned employment discrimination on the basis of gender in Title VII of the Civil Rights Act of 1964, some employers refused to give reasonable accommodation to pregnant women and even fired pregnant employees or canceled their accumulated seniority when they went on unpaid maternity leave. Accordingly, Congress amended Title VII to provide that the terms in the statute "because of sex" or "on the basis of sex" should include "pregnancy, childbirth, or related medical conditions." Abortions, however, were covered only if necessary to protect the lives of mothers. Further protections were later extended under the Americans with Disabilities Act of 1990 and the Family and Medical Leave Act of

1993, including the opportunity under some conditions for men to go on leave to assist their pregnant wives and newborn children.

The nondiscrimination requirement does not place any affirmative requirements on employers, who are vaguely instructed to treat pregnancy and childbirth as they would all other medical conditions. In *Troupe v. May Department Stores*, the Seventh Circuit Court ruled in 1994 that the employer was justified in firing a pregnant woman who, as a result of "morning sickness," was repeatedly late to work.

Michael Haas

SOURCES FOR FURTHER STUDY

Eisenstein, Zillah. *The Female Body and the Law.* Berkeley: University of California Press, 1988.

Furnish, Hannah Arterian. "Prenatal Exposure to Fetally Toxic Work Environments: The Dilemma of the 1978 Amendments to Title VII of the Civil Rights Act of 1964." *Iowa Law Review* 66 (1980): 63-129.

Kenney, Sally J. *For Whose Protection? Reproductive Hazards and Exclusionary Politics in the United States and Britain.* Ann Arbor: University of Michigan Press, 1992.

Littleton, Christine A. "Reconstructing Sexual Equality." *California Law Review* 75 (1987): 1279-1337.

Vogel, Lise. *Mothers on the Job: Maternity Policy in the U.S. Workplace.* New Brunswick, N.J.: Rutgers University Press, 1993.

Williams, Wendy. "Equality's Riddle: Pregnancy and the Equal Treatment/Special Treatment Debate." *New York University Review of Law and Social Change* 13 (1984-1985): 325-380.

SEE ALSO: Equal Pay Act (1963); Title VII of the Civil Rights Act (1964); Family Planning Services and Population Research Act (1970); Family Support Act (1988); Women in Apprenticeship and Nontraditional Occupations Act (1992); Family and Medical Leave Act (1993).

WOMEN'S EDUCATIONAL EQUITY ACT

DATE: November 1, 1978
U.S. STATUTES AT LARGE: 92 Stat. 2298
PUBLIC LAW: 95-561
U.S. CODE: 20 § 7231 et seq.
CATEGORIES: Education; Women's Issues

This program was established by Congress to combat sexual discrimination and to develop a curriculum that does not perpetuate sex-role stereotyping in education, thereby recognizing that excellence in education cannot be achieved without gender equity.

The purpose of the Women's Educational Equity Act (WEEA) is to provide educational equity for women and girls in the United States and financial assistance to enable educational agencies and institutions to meet the requirements of Title IX of the Education Amendments of 1972. At first, the effort to purge sexism from curricular materials was enthusiastically embraced by educators and publishers. When President Ronald Reagan took office in 1981, however, the WEEA was immediately targeted for funding cuts. The program would continue to struggle against opponents.

The program funds programs to open mathematics, science, and technology courses and careers to girls and women; helps female students gain access to nontraditional vocational education; funds projects to eliminate bias against girls and women in school and the workplace; funds major programs to improve educational opportunities and career choices for women who do not earn incomes; and targets resources toward the educational needs of disabled women. It was again amended in 1994.

Netiva Caftori

SOURCE FOR FURTHER STUDY

Williams, Kathleen L., Beverly J. Parks, and Carmen J. Finley. *Measures of Educational Equity for Women*. Washington, D.C.: American Institutes for Research, 1977.

SEE ALSO: Title IX of the Education Amendments of 1972 (1972); Women in Armed Services Academies Act (1975).

INDIAN CHILD WELFARE ACT

DATE: November 8, 1978
U.S. STATUTES AT LARGE: 92 Stat. 3069
PUBLIC LAW: 95-608
U.S. CODE: 25 § 1901
CATEGORIES: Children's Issues; Native Americans

This act established minimum standards for placement of Indian children in foster or adoptive homes to prevent the breakup of Indian families.

The Indian Child Welfare Act, passed into law in 1978, establishes minimum federal standards for the removal of Indian children from their families and the placement of these children in foster or adoptive homes. In essence, the act restricts the placement of Indian children in non-Indian homes and gives jurisdiction to tribal courts in deciding matters of child welfare involving adoptive or foster placement. The law removes state jurisdiction in most Indian child welfare cases, even when problems occur off the reservation.

The law affirms the continued existence and the integrity of Indian tribes and was specifically designed to end discriminatory practices of state and county welfare agencies which disregarded Indian extended family arrangements and placed large numbers of Indian children in non-Indian homes. Senate hearings conducted in 1974 documented evidence that as many as 25 percent of Indian children were being systematically removed from their natural families. This in turn was causing the breakup of the Indian family and a high degree of social disruption in Indian communities.

The law provides that when foster care or adoption is necessary, the child's extended family has first priority to assume custody. If no extended family member is available, a member of the child's tribe or an Indian from another tribe has priority over non-Indians.

Carole A. Barrett

SOURCES FOR FURTHER STUDY

Johnson, Troy R., ed. *Indian Child Welfare Act: Unto the Seventh Generations Conference Proceedings.* Los Angeles: American Indian Studies Center, University of California, 1993.

Jones, Billy Joe. *Indian Child Welfare Act Handbook: A Legal Guide to the Custody and Adoption of Native American Children.* Chicago: Section of Family Law, American Bar Association, 1995.

Richardson, John G. *Indian Child Welfare Act: A Cultural and Legal Education Program.* Washington, D.C.: National Center for State Courts, 1997.

Thompson, Edward L. *Protecting Abused Children: A Judge's Perspective on Public Law, Deprived Child Proceedings, and the Impact of the Indian Child Welfare Acts.* New York: Garland, 1993.

SEE ALSO: Family Planning Services and Population Research Act (1970); Child Abuse Prevention and Treatment Act (1974); Indian Self-Determination and Education Assistance Act (1975); Education for All Handicapped Children Act (1975); Child Support Enforcement Amendments (1984); Family Support Act (1988); Child Care and Development Block Grant Act (1990).

PUBLIC UTILITY REGULATORY POLICIES ACT

DATE: November 9, 1978
U.S. STATUTES AT LARGE: 92 Stat. 3119
PUBLIC LAW: 95-617
U.S. CODE: 16 § 2601
CATEGORIES: Energy

Part of the National Energy Act, this law was designed to prevent energy crises and to encourage innovation in the production of electricity without the use of fossil fuels.

When President Jimmy Carter signed the Public Utilities Regulatory Policies Act (PURPA) into law in 1978, it was one of five pieces of legislation that together formed the National Energy Act. Drafted as a response to the so-called energy crisis, PURPA's provisions were meant to reduce dependence on foreign oil by encouraging the development of alternative energy. PURPA restructured the electric-utility industry by permitting the emergence of power producers who were not subject to the regulations that governed normal utility operations. In the ten years following enactment of the legislation, generation of electricity by independent nonutility producers more than doubled.

RESPONSE TO THE "ENERGY CRISIS"

As a former nuclear engineer, Carter had campaigned for office on a platform that promised to prevent any oil shortages similar to the one that had panicked the country in 1973. At that time, members of the Organization of Petroleum Exporting Countries (OPEC) had sharply curtailed sales of crude oil to the United States in what became a successful attempt to drive prices up. Although the United States was itself a major producer of petroleum, the OPEC oil embargo resulted in numerous shortages, higher prices, and impromptu rationing at gasoline service stations. The government responded to the crisis with a wide variety of new legislation designed either to relieve the existing shortages or to prevent future problems. The Federal Highway Administration, for example, lowered speed limits on federal interstate highways to 55 miles per hour after researchers determined that this was the most energy-efficient speed for motor vehicles.

OIL AND ELECTRICITY

Although many people think of petroleum products such as gasoline and fuel oil as being used primarily for transportation or home heating, fuel oil is also a major source of energy for the generation of electricity. The bulk of electricity produced in the United States in the 1970's came from power plants that generated electricity using steam boilers, and many of those boilers were fired with fuel oil refined from the crude petroleum imported from countries such as Saudi Arabia and Nigeria. Both elected officials and government analysts recognized the implications of an overdependence on foreign oil. Transporting crude oil in large tanker ships not only presented risks to the environment but also made the U.S. economy vulnerable in case of war.

Washington senator Henry Martin (Scoop) Jackson, for example, had long been critical of big oil companies. While serving as chairman of the Senate's Permanent Subcommittee on Investigations in 1974, Jackson rebuked U.S. executives of major oil companies regarding the high profits the oil companies enjoyed following the 1973 oil crisis. By the mid-1970's, when he became chairman of the Committee on Energy and Natural Resources, Jackson had amassed a solid record on defense, environmental, and energy issues. As a supporter of both the defense industries and environmental causes, Jackson could push for environmental legislation without alienating more conservative members of the Senate.

Jackson believed in achieving a balance between the environment and the economy. PURPA, which proposed reducing the use of fossil fuels, particularly foreign oil (despite the 1973 crisis, in 1977 the United States imported half the oil it consumed), while encouraging the development of alternative energy sources such as solar and wind power, seemed to strike such a balance. By encouraging entrepreneurs to enter the electrical power production industry, new technologies could be developed, using renewable resources. The National Energy Act provided for incentives such as tax breaks and government grants to new independent power producers.

EASING REGULATIONS, FUNDING ALTERNATIVE ENERGY
In addition, PURPA removed many of the existing restrictions on independent power producers while requiring utility companies to purchase electricity from those independents at a rate that made entry into the electrical-power market by entrepreneurs in alternative energy financially attractive. The legislation exempted small power producers and cogenerators of electricity from many of the regulations to which public utilities were subject. PURPA defined a small power producer as any independent producer whose facility generated less than eighty megawatts of electricity. (A megawatt is one million watts of electricity.) Cogeneration facilities are industrial plants, such as paper mills or other factories, that can generate electricity as a by-product of the waste heat their plants produce. Rather than being vented through a smokestack, the heat is captured and used to generate steam and electrical power. PURPA not only permitted such industries to sell any surplus power to the local public electrical utility but also mandated that the utility pay a

fair market rate for that surplus. In addition, PURPA required that utilities make electricity available to cogenerators as needed.

Officials in the Carter administration, legislators in Congress, and citizens concerned about both the environment and national security all hoped that PURPA would lead to the development of more alternative energy sources, such as small-scale hydroelectric plants, wind power, and geothermal sources. (Small-scale hydropower facilities are considered environmentally friendly, as they utilize the water from the run of a river without requiring construction of large dams.) By altering the regulatory structure, the electric-power industry would become more diversified, electric-utility companies would be able to meet increased consumer demand without having to build additional facilities, and consumers would benefit from lower rates for power. PURPA was designed to complement other pieces of the National Energy Act. While it focused on the utility industry and particularly on altering the regulations governing public utilities, other legislation within the framework of the National Energy Act provided for research funding in alternative energy.

For example, funds allocated to the Department of Energy (then under Secretary of Energy James Schlesinger) supported research projects in solar, wind, and small-scale hydropower as part of the administration's commitment to alternative energy. Thus, for a few brief years, the United States made a serious commitment to developing renewable resources for electrical-power generation.

With the support of Scoop Jackson in the Senate and Thomas P. (Tip) O'Neill in the House, the Carter administration passed a comprehensive National Energy Act. Of the five separate pieces of legislation that constituted the NEA, PURPA perhaps had the greatest impact.

THE REAGAN ADMINISTRATION

Following Ronald Reagan's election in 1980, many of the environmental initiatives of the Carter administration experienced reduced funding, revocation, or drastic revisions. Bipartisan support for environmental legislation dwindled during the economic recession the United States experienced as the 1970's ended. Many aspects of alternative-energy development suddenly appeared financially impractical or technically unattainable. Federal support for research into solar energy and wind power began to disappear. PURPA, however, because it dealt with regulations rather than with direct funding, initially remained relatively unaffected by the change in political administrations and societal conditions. Still, without active federal support for research into alternative sources of energy, the effects of PURPA inevitably were not what its supporters had envisioned.

UNINTENDED IMPACTS

PURPA had been intended to reduce the use of nonrenewable resources; that is, it was meant to discourage the use of fossil fuels such as oil. Because it forms over millions of years, oil is a finite resource. Although as-yet-unknown petroleum reserves may exist, those that have been untapped will last for only a limited period of time, and sooner or later all the earth's petroleum deposits will be exhausted. Sources of electrical energy such as solar or wind power, in contrast, theoretically are infinitely renewable. Rather than specifically stimulating the development of wind and solar power, however, the main effect of PURPA was simply to encourage the growth of independent power producers.

Until the passage of PURPA in 1978, most electricity for individual consumption in the United States was produced by public utility companies at central generating stations. The cost of electricity for the average ratepayer was based on what it cost the local utility to produce power at its own power plants, although there were exceptions. Smaller utilities, such as some municipal systems and rural electric cooperatives, did not always own their own generating facilities. These utilities purchased power from regional electric companies. In all cases, the states strictly regulated the rates the consumer, be it an individual household or a large manufacturing firm, paid for electricity. This regulation was meant to prevent the utilities from abusing their position as monopolies and overcharging consumers. Both the industry and state and federal government viewed regulation of electrical power production as being the prerogative of the states.

PURPA was an attempt to change that. It was the first entry of the federal government into public utility-rate regulation since the 1930's and the New Deal. From the viewpoint of advocates of alternative energy, however, PURPA contained a fatal flaw: While state public utility commissions were required to consider the use of energy-conservation methods, actual implementation of those energy-saving methods was strictly voluntary.

Large volume discounts, for example, formed one target for the Carter administration's energy-conservation policy. Under standard utility-system rate structures, the more electricity a business or industry consumed, the lower the rates it paid for power would become. Rather than rewarding consumers for attempting to conserve energy, the conventional rate structures imposed penalties. The lower an individual customer's consumption became, the more that individual consumer paid per kilowatt hour (the standard unit for measuring power consumption, representing the energy expended by 1,000 watts of electricity in one hour). Schlesinger and Carter both wanted to require the state utility commissions to force utility companies to discontinue large volume discounts. As part of the compromises that form an essential part of the legislative process, however, many of the energy-conservation provisions within PURPA were written as suggestions rather than as mandates. The utility commissions that reviewed the rate structures for the utility companies within each state thus might look at energy-conservation ideas but did not have to require that utilities actually employ them.

The practical effect of energy conservation being voluntary rather than mandatory was that, although PURPA did shake up the electric-utility industry, it did not result in the widespread substitution of alternative energy for fossil fuels. In his book *Technology and Transformation in the American Electric Utility Industry* (1989), historian Richard Hirsh documented the stagnation and conservative thinking that characterized electric public utilities in the early 1970's. The industry had experienced decades of expansion, ever-increasing consumer demand, greater technological efficiencies, falling costs, and minimal competition. The 1973 OPEC oil embargo found the utility companies complacent and sluggish. If the oil crisis woke up the utilities, PURPA helped to keep them awake.

Most significant, the act led to an upsurge in the generation of electricity by independent power producers. PURPA aimed to increase cogeneration and small power production through financial incentives and the removal of regulatory barriers. The number of both small power production facilities and cogeneration plants have indeed increased. Qualifying cogeneration facilities, however, were not required to employ alternative energy sources, so the development of cogeneration did not automatically lead to a reduction in fossil-fuel usage. Most cogeneration facilities are, in fact, fired with natural gas, a nonrenewable fuel source that is as finite as petroleum.

PURPA did require independent power producers to develop alternative energy sources, such as small-scale hydroelectricity and windmills. Since the curtailment of federal research funding for solar and wind, most of the growth of independent power production has occurred in areas where a proven technology existed, that is, in steam-power plants that burn renewable fuels such as wood or garbage and in hydroelectric plants. While these plants do reduce reliance on fossil fuels, their development often raises other environmental questions. It thus appears that PURPA failed to achieve most of its original objectives. Most telling, although it led to some diversification within the electric-power industry, it did not lead to the widespread adoption of alternative energy, nor did it provide consumers with lower rates. In fact, thirty years after the energy crisis of the 1970's, the United States remained dependent upon fossil fuels and foreign oil and actually imported a greater percentage of fuel than it had in 1973.

At the beginning of the twenty-first century, hope for the development of renewable fuels, although technologically feasible, had not advanced much further, despite some development of wind farms and the appearance on the market of a few automobiles using electricity and hydrogen fuel technology. During the 1990's, deregulation of public utilities by many states had coincided with the fraudulent business practices of power brokers such as Enron, and a brewing conflict in the Middle East after the terrorist attacks of September 11, 2001, both underscored the need for alternative enery and undermined steps toward it.

Nancy Farm Männikkö

SOURCES FOR FURTHER STUDY

Dickson, David. *The New Politics of Science.* Chicago: University of Chicago Press, 1988.

Hirsh, Richard F. *Technology and Transformation in the American Electric Utility Industry.* New York: Oxford University Press, 1989.

Joskow, Paul L., and Richard Schmanslee. *Markets for Power: An Analysis of Electric Utility Deregulation.* Cambridge, Mass.: MIT Press, 1983.

Navarro, Peter. *The Dimming of America: The Real Costs of Electric Utility Regulatory Failure.* Cambridge, Mass.: Ballinger, 1985.

Piasecki, Bruce, and Peter Asmus. *In Search of Environmental Excellence.* New York: Simon & Schuster, 1990.

Victor, Richard H. K. *Energy Policy in America Since 1945: A Study of Business-Government Regulations.* Cambridge, England: Cambridge University Press, 1984.

SEE ALSO: Federal Power Act (1920); Tennessee Valley Authority Act (1933); Natural Gas Act (1938); Atomic Energy Act of 1954 (1954); Energy Policy and Conservation Act (1975); Department of Energy Organization Act (1977); Alternative Motor Fuels Act (1988).

TAIWAN RELATIONS ACT

DATE: Passed April 10, 1979; retroactively effective January 1, 1979
U.S. STATUTES AT LARGE: 93 Stat. 14
PUBLIC LAW: 96-8
U.S. CODE: 22 § 3301
CATEGORIES: Asia or Asian Americans; Foreign Relations

Relations with China gained greater leverage for the United States in negotiations with the Soviet Union.

In 1949, guerrilla leader Mao Zedong completed his long struggle to overthrow the nationalist government of China. Mao consolidated his victory by establishing a communist government on the Chinese mainland. The nationalists, led by Chiang Kai-shek, fled to the island of Taiwan, where they established a rival Chinese government. Both Chiang and Mao claimed to represent all of China. The United States officially recognized Chiang's government in Taipei as the sole legitimate Chinese government.

As the Cold War intensified in subsequent years, the United States sought to isolate and weaken the communist Chinese government, just as Washington had sought to contain the power and influence of the Soviet Union. By the end of the 1950's, however, the nominal ideological affinity between the world's two largest communist countries, the People's Republic of China (PRC) and the Soviet Union, was unable to prevent a widening rift in their bilateral relations. In the 1960's, the growing Sino-Soviet split led policymakers in Washington, D.C., to consider improving relations with the PRC as a way of isolating the Soviet Union, which was seen as the larger threat to U.S. security. In 1971, the Foreign Relations Committee of the U.S. Senate held hearings on the possible establishment of official ties with the PRC, and on admitting it to the United Nations as the proper representative of China. The United Nations recognized the PRC that year, coincident with Taiwan's expulsion from that seat.

NIXON IN CHINA

A major breakthrough in U.S.-PRC relations came with President Richard Nixon's state visit to Beijing in 1972. As a champion of the realist school of foreign policy, Nixon believed that the PRC's ideological rhetoric and its disagreeable domestic behavior (including human rights abuses and intolerance of dissent) mattered less to U.S. interests than the PRC's foreign policy. By establishing contact with the PRC, Nixon sought to give the communist government a stake in friendly relations with the United States. Nixon's official visit opened the door to increased U.S.-PRC trade and a variety of military and security agreements. Nevertheless, the Nixon administration stopped short of granting the PRC full diplomatic recognition.

Ironically, it was President Jimmy Carter, noted for his self-professed commitment to human rights and morality in international affairs, who officially recognized the PRC. The political environment in which Carter found himself was fundamentally altered from the time of Nixon's visit to Beijing. Nixon had resigned the presidency in 1974 in disgrace as a result of the Watergate scandal. Mao had died in 1976. The leadership in the PRC came to be dominated by Deng Xiaoping, who promoted modernization, economic reform, and improved ties with the West. Although the PRC under Deng still was seen as a communist state guilty of continuing human rights abuses, it was considered to be an improvement over the Mao era. In addition, the PRC's improving economy presented enticing trade and business opportunities to the United States. U.S.-PRC relations were continually improving.

Washington made overtures to Beijing on the subject of establishing full diplomatic relations. Although formal recognition was attractive to the PRC, the communist leadership steadfastly demanded of the United States three conditions: the termination of official relations with Taiwan, the removal of U.S. troops from Taiwan, and the abrogation of the U.S.-Taiwan mutual defense treaty. These conditions would be difficult for the pro-Taiwanese and anticommunist groups who forcefully, and often successfully, lobbied Congress.

Nevertheless, the Carter administration was motivated to reach an agreement with Beijing. As a result of a number of factors, including renewed Soviet military involvement in Africa and stalled arms control talks, U.S.-Soviet relations were worsening. Playing the "China card" therefore became increasingly attractive to the Carter administration. Behind-the-scenes negotiations continually sought a compromise on the various issues. National Security Adviser Zbigniew Brzezinski held numerous and regular discussions with PRC officials in Washington, D.C.

U.S. CONCESSIONS TO CHINA

By the end of 1978, a breakthrough had occurred. On December 15, the White House announced that full diplomatic relations with China would be established on the first of the new year. It formally acknowledged "the Chinese position that there is but one China and Taiwan is part of China." It also recognized the People's Republic of China as "the sole legal Government of China." As a small concession to Taiwan, the United States proclaimed that "the people of the United States will maintain cultural, commercial, and other unofficial relations with the people of Taiwan." All this largely had been kept secret, and even much of the Congress had been kept in the dark.

Shortly thereafter, Deng Xiaoping was officially received in Washington, D.C. In their joint statements, the leaders of the United States and the PRC emphasized a shared anti-Soviet perspective. Despite scattered protests, most notably from Taiwan, the establishment of official ties between the United States and the PRC was widely applauded by governments around the world as a move that squared diplomacy with reality.

CARTER CRITICIZED

Within the United States itself, however, the Carter administration came under heavy criticism for "selling out" Taiwan. Making good on his promises to Beijing, Carter sought to replace the U.S.-Taiwan mutual defense treaty with a Taiwan Enabling Act, which did not guarantee Taiwan's security and which would replace the U.S. embassy in Taipei with an American Institute in Taiwan to represent U.S. interests. Senator Barry Goldwater challenged the president's right to terminate the mutual defense treaty without Senate approval. Although Goldwater failed in that effort, the final bill passed by the U.S. Congress in the spring of 1979, the Taiwan Relations Act, provided several concessions to Taiwan. It expressed an intent to ensure that Taiwan receive enough defensive arms to protect itself and guaranteed that the lack of formal diplomatic relations would not disqualify Taiwan from various aid programs.

SIGNIFICANCE OF THE AGREEMENT

The establishment of relations between Washington and Beijing consolidated the tripolar diplomacy that had been begun under Nixon. U.S.-PRC relations remained largely cooperative, although by no means was the PRC pulled into the United States' political orbit. In fact, when the Soviet Union and most other communist countries implemented radical reforms in the late 1980's and renounced communism altogether a short time later, China remained a committed communist state. Aside from a few anomalies like Cuba and Vietnam, in the mid-1990's the PRC was the only globally significant communist state in existence.

Despite continued human rights abuses, including the mass murder of student demonstrators at Tiananmen Square in 1989, U.S.-PRC relations have remained relatively steady, with Washington regularly granting Beijing "most favored nation" trade status.

Steve D. Boilard

SOURCES FOR FURTHER STUDY

Daley, John Charles, moderator. *The Future of Chinese-American Relations.* AEI Forum 29. Washington, D.C.: American Enterprise Institute for Public Policy Research, 1979.

Garrett, Banning N., and Bonnie S. Glaser. "From Nixon to Reagan: China's Changing Role in American Strategy." In *Eagle Re-*

surgent? The Reagan Era in American Foreign Policy, edited by Kenneth A. Oye, Robert J. Lieber, and Donald Rothchild. Boston: Little, Brown, 1987.

Garson, Robert. *The United States and China Since 1949: A Troubled Affair.* London: Pinter, 1994.

Gregor, A. James. *The China Connection: U.S. Policy and the People's Republic of China.* Stanford, Calif.: Hoover Institution Press, 1986.

Harding, Harry. *A Fragile Relationship: The United States and China Since 1972.* Washington, D.C.: Brookings Institution, 1992.

Starr, John Bryan, ed. *The Future of U.S.-China Relations.* New York: New York University Press, 1981.

SEE ALSO: Treaty of Wang Hiya (1844); Burlingame Treaty (1868); Formosa Resolution (1955).

SALT II Treaty

DATE: Signed June 18, 1979
CATEGORIES: Foreign Relations; Treaties and Agreements

This significant step in a long process toward arms reductions committed the United States and the Soviet Union to limitations in strategic weapons but failed to see ratification.

The SALT II treaty signed by Jimmy Carter and Leonid Brezhnev in Vienna on June 18, 1979, committed the United States and the Soviet Union to the first significant reduction in nuclear weapons since the beginning of the nuclear arms race after World War II. The treaty represented an attempt to mitigate the military buildup that characterized the Cold War.

SALT I
The Strategic Arms Limitations Talks (SALT) process started November 17, 1969, with negotiations between the United States and the Soviet Union and produced the first SALT agreement

(SALT I), signed in Moscow on May 26, 1972. SALT I comprised two separate agreements: an antiballistic missile treaty, prohibiting each country from building a nationwide defense against ballistic missiles; and an interim agreement establishing a five-year moratorium on the construction of strategic ballistic missile launchers. SALT I was intended to be the first of several arms control agreements to end the arms race in strategic weapons.

SALT II NEGOTIATIONS

Following ratification of the SALT I agreements by the United States in the summer of 1972, negotiations for SALT II began in November. Almost immediately, the two sides found themselves stalemated on a number of difficult issues. Each party wanted to legalize a strategic force structure that maximized its advantages against the other. Thus, a principal objective of the United States was to eliminate the Soviet numerical superiority by equalizing the number of launchers each side could possess. At the time of the moratorium, the Soviet Union possessed 1,618 intercontinental ballistic missiles (ICBMs) compared to 1,054 in the United States, and 740 submarine-launched ballistic missiles (SLBMs) compared to the United States' 656. This U.S. deficit was compensated for by the fact that the United States had the ability to deploy more than one warhead in a single missile. Technically, that capacity is referred to as a multiple independently targeted reentry vehicle (MIRV). Thus, at the time of SALT I, the United States could hit more targets with nuclear weapons than could the Soviet Union. However, it was only a matter of time before the Soviet Union would acquire MIRV ability for its missiles; then its total destructive capacity would exceed that of the United States.

The Soviets wanted to include in the total calculations weapons systems that were deployed in the European theater, which had not been included in the SALT I accord. These were known as forward-based systems (FBS) and consisted of tactical aircraft based in Europe or on aircraft carriers in waters around Europe. Because the United States considered FBS forces to be dedicated to the defense of Europe, it had refused to count them as strategic weapons.

The United States wanted to limit indirectly the anticipated Soviet deployment of MIRV'd missiles by mandating deep reductions in the total weight (called throwweight) of Soviet missiles. Soviet missiles were larger than U.S. missiles and had greater throwweight. Other difficult issues were what to do about cruise missiles (air-breathing guided missiles developed first by the United States); whether to require the Soviets to include their Backfire bomber in the totals permitted to them; and what kinds of modernization of weapons to permit.

Compounding the difficulty of the military-technical issues was a deteriorating political climate. In 1973, war in the Middle East had exacerbated tensions in U.S.-Soviet relations. In 1974, the Watergate trauma had eroded the political authority of the Nixon administration, undercutting both public and congressional support for the SALT process. The mood of détente produced by SALT I had deteriorated during the mid-1970's. A renewed effort to negotiate was undertaken by the Ford administration, which came into office in 1974. In December, Gerald Ford and Leonid Brezhnev met in the Soviet city of Vladivostok to sign an interim agreement. The Vladivostok agreement simply set a number of goals for a future SALT treaty: a maximum of 2,400 strategic nuclear vehicles for each side, with a subceiling of 1,320 that could be MIRV'd.

The SALT II negotiations were completed during the administration of Jimmy Carter, but only after a series of tense and acrimonious exchanges between the two sides. After a comprehensive review of the negotiations, President Carter's advisers came up with a comprehensive proposal to reduce strategic nuclear launchers well below the figures agreed to at Vladivostok. Presented to the Soviets in March, 1977, the new plan was harshly rejected by the Soviet leaders, who charged the United States with repudiating previously agreed-upon positions. That setback proved to be only temporary, however. In October, 1977, when the five-year period of the SALT I moratorium expired, both countries agreed to abide by its terms, although were not formally bound to do so. By May, 1979, the text of the SALT II treaty was completed, and Carter and Brezhnev journeyed to Vienna to sign the treaty in an elaborate ceremony.

TREATY PROVISIONS

The SALT II treaty was a lengthy and complex agreement, comprising four parts. The treaty itself contained numerical ceilings and subceilings on launchers and was to remain in force until 1985. SALT II set a limit of 2,400 for strategic launchers (ICBMs, SLBMs and strategic bombers), to decline to 2,250 by 1981. This provision would have required the Soviet Union to dismantle 250 launchers but would not have affected the United States' arsenal, which was then under the ceiling. A subceiling of 1,320 was established for MIRV'd systems; within that limit, a further subceiling of 1,200 applied to all ballistic missiles and a further subceiling of 820 was set for all ICBMs. Other provisions in the treaty placed qualitative restraints on the development of new weapons and prohibited mobile launchers for heavy missiles. To meet U.S. demands, limits were set for the number of warheads that could be placed in MIRV'd missiles; to satisfy the Soviets, limits were placed on the number of cruise missiles that could be deployed on an airplane. A protocol to the treaty provided for limitations that would apply for only two years. In a separate document, Leonid Brezhnev promised to build no more than thirty Backfire bombers per year. The final part of the treaty specified principles for future SALT negotiations.

FAILURE TO RATIFY

For all the effort that went into the negotiations, SALT II was never ratified. The single most important factor in derailing SALT II was the Soviet invasion of Afghanistan in December, 1979. In response to the invasion, President Carter withdrew the treaty from Senate consideration. Even before the Afghan crisis, opposition to the treaty had been building in the U.S. Congress and in the public at large. Support for arms control during the mid- to latter 1970's declined as a result of the collapse of détente in Soviet-United States relations. A major factor in the collapse was the spurt of Soviet activism in the Third World, particularly in Africa. Between 1975 and 1978, the Soviet Union and Cuba became active participants in the civil and regional wars in Angola and the Horn of Africa. Their involvement contributed to the strengthening of Marxist, anti-Western regimes in Angola and Ethiopia, which led to an intensification of anti-Soviet sentiment in the United States. In the face of that sentiment, the prospects for arms control declined.

There was still widespread agreement in Washington and Moscow that the substance of SALT II served the security interests of both countries well. As a result, both governments agreed that they would continue to observe its provisions, if the other side continued to do so. This observance continued even under the administration of Ronald Reagan, who, in his presidential campaign, called SALT II fatally flawed. The failure of SALT II's ratification was only a temporary setback in the long effort to reduce the nuclear arsenals of the two superpowers. U.S.-Soviet relations altered dramatically during the 1980's, following the accession to power of Mikhail Gorbachev in Moscow. In the 1980's and 1990's, treaties such as the INF (intermediate nuclear force) and START I and START II (strategic arms reduction talks) agreements brought about nuclear arms reduction unimaginable during the 1970's.

Joseph L. Nogee

SOURCES FOR FURTHER STUDY
Blacker, Coit D. "The Soviets and Arms Control: The SALT II Negotiations, November 1972-March 1976." In *The Other Side of the Table: The Soviet Approach to Arms Control,* edited by Michael Mandelbaum. New York: Council on Foreign Relations Press, 1990.
Blacker, Coit D., and Gloria Duffy, eds. *International Arms Control, Issues and Agreements.* 2d ed. Stanford, Calif.: Stanford University Press, 1984.
Bundy, McGeorge. *Danger and Survival: Choices About the Bomb in the First Fifty Years.* New York: Random House, 1988.
Flanagan, Stephen J. "SALT II." In *Superpower Arms Control: Setting the Record Straight,* edited by Albert Carnesale and Richard N. Haass. Cambridge, Mass.: Ballinger, 1987.
Talbott, Strobe. *Endgame: The Inside Story of SALT II.* New York: Harper & Row, 1979.
U.S. Arms Control and Disarmament Agency. *Arms Control and Disarmament Agreements: Texts and Histories of Negotiations.* Washington, D.C.: Author, 1982.

SEE ALSO: Nuclear Test Ban Treaty (1963); Nuclear Nonproliferation Treaty (1968); SALT I Treaty (1973); INF Treaty (1987); START II Treaty (1993); U.S.-Russia Arms Agreement (2002).

CONVENTION ON THE CONSERVATION OF MIGRATORY SPECIES OF WILD ANIMALS

DATE: Signed June 23, 1979
CATEGORIES: Animals; Environment and Conservation; Treaties and Agreements

This international treaty is designed to protect vulnerable species of wild animals that migrate across national boundaries.

On June 23, 1979, several sovereign nations and regional economic organizations signed the Convention on the Conservation of Migratory Species of Wild Animals in Bonn, Germany. After receiving the necessary fifteen ratifications, the treaty went into effect on November 1, 1983.

TREATY PROVISIONS

The signatories to the treaty agreed to protect any endangered species whose entire population (or a significant portion of the population) "cyclically and predictably cross one or more national jurisdictional boundaries." The term "endangered" was defined as meaning that "the migratory species is in danger of extinction throughout all or a significant portion of its range." In addition, the treaty obligated the signatories to take appropriate action to prevent unfavorable-status species from becoming endangered.

The treaty established a Conference of the Parties, which makes decisions concerning the obligations of the signatories. The conference determines its budget and formulates a scale for assessing the contribution of each party to the conference. The treaty also provided for a Secretariat, which is appointed by the executive director of the United Nations Environment Program (UNEP). The Secretariat has several executive functions, which include listing endangered species, arranging meetings of the conference, promoting liaisons between the parties, and performing duties entrusted to it by the conference. Finally, the treaty established a Scientific Council for the purpose of providing scientific recommendations to the conference.

Appendix I of the treaty lists those migratory species that are considered endangered, and the list is regularly updated and generally is increasing. Some of those listed include species of whales, birds, marine turtles, and the one remaining species of gorilla. In regard to such species, the parties to the treaty agreed to conserve and, where feasible, restore the habitats that were important "in removing the species from danger of extinction." The parties agreed to prohibit the taking of members of species on the list, with exceptions for scientific purposes and a few extraordinary circumstances.

Appendix II lists those migratory species that have an "unfavorable conservation status," as well as additional "conservation status" species that would benefit from an international agreement. In regard to the species of Appendix II, the parties agreed to endeavor to conclude agreements that would promote survival of the species, especially those in an unfavorable conservation status. The Secretariat is provided with a copy of each such agreement.

The convention of 1979 was primarily a declaration of principles, and it delegated almost no enforcement powers to the Conference of the Parties or to the Secretariat. Although sometimes referred to as an example of "soft law," the convention's importance is enhanced by other international agreements that deal with related problems, and it has the potential of making a significant impact on public opinion.

Thomas T. Lewis

Sources for Further Study

Ehrlich, Paul, and Anne Ehrlich. *Extinction: The Causes and Consequences of the Disappearance of Species.* New York: Random House, 1981.

Mann, Charles, and Mark Plummer. *Noah's Choice: The Future of Endangered Species,* 1995.

McNeely, Jeffrey A., et al. *Conserving the World's Biological Diversity.* Washington, D.C.: World Resources Institute, 1990.

Rodgers, William H. *Environmental Law.* 2d ed. St. Paul, Minn.: West Publishing, 1994.

Twiss, John R., Jr., and Randall R. Reeves, eds. *Conservation and Management of Marine Mammals.* Washington, D.C.: Smithsonian Institution Press, 1999.

SEE ALSO: Migratory Bird Act (1913); Migratory Bird Treaty Act (1918); Migratory Bird Hunting and Conservation Stamp Act (1934); Endangered Species Preservation Act (1966); Endangered Species Act (1973); Convention on International Trade in Endangered Species (1975).

CONVENTION ON LONG-RANGE TRANSBOUNDARY AIR POLLUTION

DATE: Signed November 13, 1979
CATEGORIES: Environment and Conservation; Treaties and Agreements

In 1979, thirty-two nations signed this agreement to limit air pollution, including pollution created in one country that affects the environment in another.

Until the 1970's most local, regional, and national regulations regarding industrial air pollution were concerned only with pollution generated in the immediate area. For example, regulations in a particular community might call for taller industrial smokestacks to carry pollution farther away, but there was little official concern about where that pollution might eventually return to earth. Similarly, local assessments and treatments of pollution tended not to consider pollution that might come to an area from distant generators. The only exceptions were a small number of treaties between two countries, such as the United States and Canada, or Germany and France.

A TRANSNATIONAL PROBLEM
In 1972 the United Nations Environmental Conference in Stockholm, Sweden, drew attention to the harmful effects of acid rain, including damage to forests, crops, surface water, and building and monuments, especially in Europe. Data revealed that while all European nations produced alarming levels of air pollution, several nations were receiving more pollution from beyond their borders than they were generating on their own. It became clear that pollu-

tion is both imported and exported, that sulfur and nitrogen compounds can travel through the air for thousands of miles, and that any serious attempt to deal with air pollution must reach beyond political boundaries. Two major studies of the long-range transport of air pollutants (LRTAP) were conducted under United Nations (U.N.) sponsorship in 1972 and 1977, conclusively proving that air pollution was an international—even a global—problem primarily caused by fossil fuel combustion. However, the pollution caused harm to both industrial and nonindustrial nations around the world.

In 1979 the United Nations Environment Program organized a convention in Geneva, Switzerland, for the thirty-four member countries of the United Nations Economic Commission for Europe (ECE), a group that includes all European nations, the United States, and Canada. Significantly, the gathering had the participation of Eastern European nations under the Soviet Union, marking the first time that these nations had collaborated with Western Europe to solve an international environmental problem. The Convention on Long-Range Transboundary Air Pollution was signed by thirty-two nations on November 13, 1979, and went into effect on March 16, 1983.

PROVISIONS AND RESPONSE

The agreement called upon signatory nations to limit and eventually reduce air pollution, in particular sulfur emissions, using the best and most economically feasible technology; share scientific and technical information regarding air pollution and its reduction; permit transboundary monitoring; and collaborate in developing new antipollution policies. Under the terms of the convention, an international panel would undertake a comprehensive review every four years to determine whether goals were being met, and an executive body would meet each year.

The convention did not include any specific plan for the reduction of air pollution; there was no language calling for particular amounts by which emissions would be reduced, nor was there a schedule by which the reductions would occur. Scandinavian nations, which were among the countries most affected by acid rain, urged the other participants to adopt these kinds of policies, but other countries, led by the United States, the United Kingdom, and West Germany, defeated the proposal.

In the years following the convention, however, several nations did make commitments to reduce emissions by specific amounts, although neither the United States nor the United Kingdom agreed to the 30 percent reductions, and neither country signed the 1985 protocol. The United Kingdom informally agreed to attempt to reduce emissions by 30 percent but was unwilling to commit the financial resources to guarantee it, especially since the benefits were uncertain. In fact, many scientists felt that 30 percent reductions would not be enough to yield significant improvement. The United States argued that it had already taken major steps to reduce its emissions prior to 1980, so using 1980 data as a baseline would subject the it to unrealistic and unfair demands for further reduction. This refusal to ratify the protocol caused tension between the United States and Canada, because much of the air pollution that affects Eastern Canada comes from the Great Lakes industrial belt in the United States.

Cynthia A. Bily

Sources for Further Study

Brunnée, Jutta. *Acid Rain and Ozone Layer Depletion: International Law and Regulation.* Dobbs Ferry, N.Y.: Transnational, 1988.

Elsom, Derek. *Atmospheric Pollution: A Global Problem.* 2d ed. Cambridge, Mass.: Blackwell, 1992.

Fishman, Jack, and Robert Kalish. *Global Alert: The Ozone Pollution Crisis.* New York: Plenum, 1990.

Long-Range Transboundary Air Pollution: Protocols Between the United States of America and Other Governments. Washington, D.C.: Government Printing Office, 1996.

Sand, Peter H. "Air Pollution in Europe: International Policy Responses." *Environment* (1987).

Wetstone, G. S., and Armin Rosencranz. *Acid Rain in Europe and North America: National Responses to an International Problem.* Washington, D.C.: Environmental Law Institute, 1983.

See also: Air Pollution Control Act (1955); Clean Air Act (1963); Motor Vehicle Air Pollution Control Act (1965); Clean Air Act Amendments of 1970 (1970); Clean Air Act Amendments of 1977 (1977); Clean Air Act Amendments of 1990 (1990); Montreal Protocol (1990); Pollution Prevention Act (1990).

MAINE INDIAN CLAIMS ACT

DATE: October 10, 1980
U.S. STATUTES AT LARGE: 94 Stat. 1785
PUBLIC LAW: 96-420
U.S. CODE: 25 § 1721
CATEGORIES: Land Management; Native Americans

Beginning in the 1960's, tribes in the eastern United States alleged that state governments had illegally taken their lands; the Maine Indian Claims Act prompted a number of eastern tribes to settle similar claims rather than go through the courts.

In 1964, the Passamaquoddy tribe, recognized by the state of Maine but not the federal government, sought protection from what it determined were illegal incursions on their lands. Both state and federal governments refused to assist the tribe. The Passamaquoddy, joined by the Penobscots, initiated a lawsuit in which they asserted protection under the Trade and Intercourse Act of 1790, which prevented tribes from selling lands unless approved by Congress. The basis of the lawsuit was that their land transfers never received such approval. The tribes won a series of lower court cases, and so the United States was obliged to bring suit against Maine for illegal purchase of Indian land. The court decisions left 1.25 million acres, two-thirds of Maine, under clouded land titles. The Maliseet tribe also joined the lawsuit. Maine agreed to settle out of court rather than face complicated, expensive legal negotiations. The settlement extinguished all Indian claims to land. In return, the United States provided $27 million in a trust fund for the tribes, and another $54.5 million was set aside for the tribes to purchase land. The tribes also received federal recognition.

Carole A. Barrett

SOURCES FOR FURTHER STUDY
Bourque, Bruce J. *Twelve Thousand Years: American Indians in Maine.* Lincoln: University of Nebraska Press, 2001.

Confederation of American Indians, comp. *Indian Reservations: A State and Federal Handbook.* Jefferson, N.C.: McFarland, 1986.
Deloria, Vine, Jr., and David E. Wilkins. *Tribes, Treaties, and Constitutional Tribulations.* Austin: University of Texas Press, 1999.

SEE ALSO: Trade and Intercourse Acts (1790-1834).

PRIVACY PROTECTION ACT

ALSO KNOWN AS: News Room Search Act
DATE: October 13, 1980
U.S. STATUTES AT LARGE: 94 Stat. 1879
PUBLIC LAW: 96-440
U.S. CODE: 42 § 2000aa
CATEGORIES: Civil Rights and Liberties; Communications and Media; Privacy

This federal law increased protections against unreasonable government searches of newsrooms by requiring officials to secure subpoenas.

The United States has never had a national shield law giving journalists special privileges to protect their news sources. The Privacy Protection Act of 1980 arose from incidents occurring during the 1970's that heightened congressional awareness of the need for greater protection of news gatherers.

In 1971, police searching for evidence in a criminal investigation rifled the offices of Stanford University's student newspaper. When the U.S. Supreme Court, in *Zurcher v. The Stanford Daily* (1978), upheld the power of government to conduct such searches armed only with court-issued warrants, the nation's press was outraged. President Jimmy Carter responded by proposing legislation to protect newspapers and others from such searches. Fresh incidents of government invasions of newsrooms around this same time moved Congress to pass legislation, which Carter signed into law in October, 1980. The Privacy Protection Act of 1980—also known as the News Room Search Act—went into effect for the federal government the following New Year's Day, and for state and local governments exactly one year later.

Avoiding a problem common to such legislation, the new law did not single out the press for protection. Instead, it offered protection to all persons preparing material for publication. The law specifically forbade government officials from either seeking or issuing warrants to search for, or to seize, any work owned by persons "reasonably believed to have a purpose to disseminate [it] to the public." Its protections covered documentary materials, including magnetically or electronically recorded cards, tapes, and computer media; and any work product materials, created for the purpose of disseminating information to the public. The law exempted cases in which there is "probable cause to believe" that the custodians of the work in question have committed, or are planning to commit, criminal acts to which the materials relate. Also exempted were instances in which seizure of material is necessary to save human life, or in which the custodians would not comply with a valid subpoena, or try to hide or destroy material if a search is not undertaken.

The act established guidelines for federal officers mandating that recognition be given to the personal privacy of those holding the materials sought and requiring that the least intrusive means be used to obtain materials needed by the government. That act further mandated that care be given not to impair confidential relationships, such as those between doctor and patient or attorney and client, and required that except in rare and genuine emergencies, only a government attorney can authorize search and seizure under one of the exceptions built into the act.

Violations of the act are not punishable under criminal law, but aggrieved persons can seek redress against offenders in the civil courts. Damages are limited to actual damages, but the act is weakened by language that says a "reasonable good faith belief in the lawfulness of his conduct" would excuse an officer who violated the terms of the act.

Dwight Wm. Jensen

SOURCES FOR FURTHER STUDY

Cranberg, Gilbert. *Malice in Wonderland: Intrusion in the Newsroom.* Iowa City: University of Iowa, 1992.

Franklin, Marc A. *Mass Media Law: Cases and Materials.* New York: Foundations Press, 2000.

Holsinger, Ralph L., and Jon Paul Dilts. *Media Law.* 4th ed. New York: McGraw-Hill, 1997.
Lively, Donald E. *Modern Communications Law.* New York: Praeger, 1991.

SEE ALSO: Ninth Amendment (1789); Freedom of Information Act (1966); Privacy Act (1974).

ALASKA NATIONAL INTEREST LANDS CONSERVATION ACT

ALSO KNOWN AS: Alaska Lands Act
DATE: December 2, 1980
U.S. STATUTES AT LARGE: 94 Stat. 2371
PUBLIC LAW: 96-487
U.S. CODE: 16 § 3101
CATEGORIES: Agriculture; Environment and Conservation; Land Management; Native Americans

This act added more than 100 million acres of pristine lands to existing parks, preserves, and refuges.

Under the 1958 Alaska Statehood Act, section 17(d)(2) authorized the secretary of the interior to set aside as much as 80 million acres of Alaskan land for addition to national parks, wildlife refuges, national forests, or the wild and scenic rivers systems. Section 17(d)(1) allowed the secretary to set aside other unreserved and unappropriated public lands for study and classification in order to protect the public's interest in such lands. Secretary of the Interior Rogers C. B. Morton signed both of these sections into law on March 15, 1972. Congress set the deadline for passage of an Alaska lands conservation law as midnight on December 16, 1978.

The "d-2" decision on Alaska represented many things to many people. It was a unique decision in America's history, serving as a commitment to protect national treasures for all times and all peoples. Selection of these lands pitted the idealistic conservation movement, centered in the eastern United States, against the pragmatic, development-oriented, individualistic Westerners. It was a decision made by all in an open, democratic fashion. It affected more than conservation issues in Alaska: This legislation influenced how the country acted on conservation decisions elsewhere.

A Battle in Congress

In 1972, various federal agencies—the National Park Service, the U.S. Fish and Wildlife Service, the Bureau of Outdoor Recreation, and the U.S. Forest Service—began studying Alaska national interest lands for d-2 selection. Some 125 million acres were proposed for selection by these different federal agencies.

The U.S. House of Representatives had voted in May, 1958, to set aside more than 116 million acres of federally owned lands and waters in Alaska, out of a total of about 375 million acres. The bill, authored by Morris K. Udall of Arizona in the House and Lee Metcalf of Montana in the Senate, would have placed all of these lands in the wilderness classification. President Jimmy Carter declared the Alaskan wildlands his administration's top environmental priority. Secretary Cecil D. Andrus proposed that more than 92 million acres be preserved with this legislation.

The House Subcommittee on General Oversight and Alaska Lands studied these proposals and held extensive hearings. The state of Alaska disputed some of the d-2 lands chosen for selection; compromise revised the Udall bill and reduced the d-2 lands' acreage.

In the Senate, Senator Ted Stevens of Alaska delayed action on the Senate bill, and it was badly weakened by state and development interests. Senator Mike Gravel killed the bill on the last day of the Ninety-fifth Congress with his filibuster at 2:00 A.M. The real issue was not the protection of lands but rather the preservation of the Alaskan lifestyle and freedom, especially in regard to mining and hunting activities. Compromises failed to extend the congressional deadline for acting on the d-2 legislation; its seven-year deadline was fast approaching. If the legislation did not pass by December 16, 1978, the d-2 lands under consideration for annexation to other protected federal areas would become available for state selection and development. The Carter administration had to act to save these lands.

In November, 1978, Andrus, by special order, closed 110 million acres of Alaska to development for three years to give Congress more time to act on the d-2 legislation. On December 1, 1978, Carter invoked the 1906 Antiquities Act and declared 56 million acres as seventeen national monuments and directed Secretary Andrus to protect another 39 million acres as national wildlife refuges. Secretary of Agriculture Bob Bergland closed mining on another 11 million acres in southeastern Alaska.

New d-2 legislation again passed the House in 1979, but Senate resistance to the legislation again stalled passage of any Alaska lands bill. A weakened compromise bill finally passed the Senate in August, 1980, surviving massive attacks from development interests and from those who believed that Alaska's individualistic lifestyle was being threatened by outside interests. As the Senate compromise bill went to the House for approval, little time remained for conservationists to restore many of the deleted lands to the bill. No action was taken on this lands bill until the lame duck session following the 1980 election. Threats of Senate filibusters by Alaska's Stevens and Gravel convinced congressional supporters that this compromise legislation was the best action that could be achieved. The unfavorable political climate for d-2 legislation forecast by the election of Ronald Reagan to the presidency and many conservatives to both houses of Congress stimulated acceptance of the Senate land bill. Consequently, the House passed the Senate bill on November 12, 1980, and Carter signed it into law on December 2, 1980.

PROVISIONS
Despite the compromise, the Alaska National Interest Lands Conservation Act, often known as the Alaska Lands Act, was one of the greatest conservation actions of the twentieth century. It doubled the acreage of the national park system with its 43.6 million acres, added 53.8 million acres to the national wildlife refuge system, and added 3.4 million acres to the national forest system, including two new national monuments on Forest Service land. It also designated the protection of twenty-six wild and scenic rivers or segments of rivers. It tripled the size of the national wilderness preservation system with its 56.4 million acres. This single legislative act, born of the Alaska Statehood Act and the Alaska Native Claims Settlement Act, set aside a total of 104.3 million acres.

IMPACT ON ALASKA

Alaska is in many ways considered to be the last frontier, but the passage of the Alaska National Interest Lands Conservation Act opened a new era in conservation history, in state and federal cooperation, and in the preservation of resources, cultural heritages, and lifestyles. Because of their importance to Alaskan natives, subsistence hunting, fishing, and gathering were allowed on some of the d-2 lands that were added to the National Park Service in Alaska. The cultural values and lifestyles of Alaska Natives were considered as important as the physical features of these new parks. Subsistence hunting rights for Alaskan natives is, however, a controversial issue and has not been successfully resolved between the state of Alaska and the federal government. Other federal legislation has recognized the needs of subsistence rights for Alaska Natives. The Marine Mammal Protection Act of 1972 allowed them to hunt sea mammals for subsistence. The Endangered Species Act of 1973 exempted Alaska's Indians, Eskimos, Aleuts, and non-native village residents from its provisions as long as these peoples were engaged in non-wasteful subsistence activities. Subsistence use of wildlife receives priority over sport hunting. Conflict over the state of Alaska's refusal to recognize these subsistence rights led the U.S. government to usurp the rights of wildlife management from the state of Alaska on all federal lands. Alaska's federally owned lands constitute about 256 million acres, more than one-third of the state's total area.

Recreational or sport hunting generates several million dollars for Alaskan businesses each year. Normally, no sport hunting is allowed on lands managed by the National Park Service. D-2 lands legislation, however, recognized the importance of this activity in Alaska and designated some 18.9 million acres of land to be added to the national park system as preserves rather than parks; sport hunting is allowed on these preserve lands in Alaska. National parks in Alaska where sport hunting is not allowed make up about 8 percent of Alaska's total area.

Subsistence activities are also allowed on the newly established national wildlife refuges under section 810 of the Alaska Lands Act. It requires federal land managers to assess the impacts of their management actions on the refuges in light of subsistence needs. Six regional councils were established to advise the secretary of the interior on the management of the refuge system as it related to subsistence needs of Native Americans.

Other sections of the Alaska Lands Act were proposed for special interests within the state. One section of this legislation provided an annual subsidy of $40 million to guarantee that timber production from the Tongass National Forest averaged 450 million board feet per year, even if the timber harvest lost money. The legislation also required the U.S. Forest Service to re-evaluate timber-sale prices every five years if these prices had declined; no recalculation was required if the timber prices rose during this time. A price increase added to the profits of the timber company holding the sale rights but did not increase the revenues gained by the Forest Service. This provision encouraged disastrous timber harvests in the Tongass National Forest and in 1990, was repealed.

THE REAGAN ADMINISTRATION

In the early 1980's, the Reagan administration selectively distorted, ignored, and violated the intent of the Alaska Lands Act; in many instances, the administration made it a development act. Secretary of the Interior James G. Watt led the attack on these lands in Alaska by controlling the budgets for their management. Without adequate funds to hire personnel to study the d-2 lands and to prepare scientifically sound management plans as required by the act, many lands were not adequately protected or managed. The remoteness and size of Alaska and its resources produce special problems for land management. Strong pressures for development of oil and gas areas, increased timber harvest, more mining, and consumptive use of wildlife resources continue on the d-2 lands of Alaska. Many of the lands that were excluded from d-2 land acquisitions are under federal control, particularly by the U.S. Bureau of Land Management. A lack of funding prevented the adequate study of these lands so that they could be added to federal preserves under the 17(d)(1) section of the Alaska Lands Act. In the early 1990's, adequate funding for the d-2 lands and those that should be studied under the d-1 section of this act still had not been provided.

QUESTIONS OF FUTURE DEVELOPMENT

Many of the d-2 lands include parcels owned by Alaska Natives through lands selected under the jurisdiction of the Alaska Native Claims Settlement Act. These lands represent potential development within otherwise undisturbed wilderness areas. Effective planning is needed to control development of these areas so that it does not destroy the unique qualities of the surrounding d-2 lands.

What has been preserved by congressional action is not always protected. Section 810 of the act requires that federal land managers assess the impacts of their decisions on subsistence users. The Supreme Court in 1987 heard the case of *Amoco Production Company v. the Village of Gambell.* The village sought to enjoin the secretary of the interior from leasing Outer Continental Shelf areas in Norton Sound and the Navarin Basin of the Bering Sea for oil and gas exploration. The native Alaskans argued that such exploration damaged their subsistence rights activities. The Court held that section 810 did not apply to these leases on the Outer Continental Shelf.

A key concept of the d-2 land selections was to include entire ecosystems so that the ecological integrity of these biological systems on wildlife refuges would be maintained in Alaska. Detailed plans were to be compiled for sixteen areas. The greatest conservation fight involving d-2 lands was expected to be related to the development of oil reserves within the boundaries of the Arctic National Wildlife Refuge. Enlarged by the addition of d-2 lands, the refuge lies east of the Prudhoe Bay oil field and may contain more oil and natural gas reserves than did Prudhoe Bay. Its 19.3 million acres also contain perhaps the most pristine wilderness in North America. A legacy of the Alaska National Interest Lands Conservation Act, it serves as a constant reminder that lands once preserved by Congress must continue to be protected and defended from development.

David L. Chesemore

SOURCES FOR FURTHER STUDY

National Geographic Society. *A Guide to Our Federal Lands.* Washington, D.C.: Author, 1984.
National Parks Magazine 55, no. 3 (1981).
Stock, Dennis. *Alaska.* New York: Harrison House, 1983.
Strohmeyer, John. *Extreme Conditions: Big Oil and the Transformation of Alaska.* New York: Simon & Schuster, 1993.
Wilderness 41, no. 164 (1984).

SEE ALSO: Wild and Scenic Rivers Act and National Trails System Act (1968); Alaska Native Claims Settlement Act (1971).

SUPERFUND ACT

ALSO KNOWN AS: Comprehensive Environmental Response, Compensation, and Liability Act
DATE: December 11, 1980
U.S. STATUTES AT LARGE: 94 Stat. 2767
PUBLIC LAW: 96-510
U.S. CODE: 42 § 9601 et seq.
CATEGORIES: Energy; Environment and Conservation

Known also by its acronym CERCLA, this act provided cleanup funding and assistance for hazardous waste sites.

More than six billion metric tons of solid waste are disposed of in the United States every year. These wastes include municipal garbage and industrial wastes that contain complex and sometimes hazardous substances. Solid wastes also include sewage, agricultural refuse, demolition wastes, and mining residues. Disposal of these wastes, especially those considered to be hazardous, is time-consuming. Waste presents serious environmental risks and requires complex measures to control its disposal. One of the most important environmental problems is the problem of hazardous waste disposal. Hazardous wastes are defined as wastes that cause or significantly contribute to an increase in mortality or pose a substantial present or potential hazard to human health or the environment when improperly treated, stored, transported, or disposed of or otherwise managed.

PASSAGE OF SUPERFUND

The U.S. Congress passed the Comprehensive Environmental Response, Compensation, and Liability Act (CERCLA), more commonly known as Superfund, in 1980 to allocate money for the cleanup of hazardous waste. The Environmental Protection Agency (EPA) had determined that by January of 1979 there were between 32,000 and 50,000 disposal sites in the United States that needed to be cleaned up. The Superfund Act required notification of any release into the environment of substances that might "present substantial danger to public health or welfare, or to the environment." The act imposed criminal sanctions for failure to give notice of such releases and imposed strict liability on owners and operators of facilities that released hazardous wastes or substances, as well as on transporters of hazardous wastes or substances. The Superfund law was also intended to provide compensation for damages caused by hazardous wastes and hazardous substances.

LOVE CANAL

Congress passed CERCLA mainly in response to several highly publicized incidents of improper disposal of hazardous wastes and toxic chemicals. One of the main incidents was the discovery of buried toxic wastes at Love Canal, an uncompleted, abandoned nineteenth-century waterway in Niagara Falls, New York. An industrial dump site since the 1930's, it had been purchased in 1947 by Hooker Chemical and Plastics Company as a site in which to dispose of its toxic chemical waste. Afterwards, the dump was covered and sold to the Niagara Falls Board of Education in 1953, which built an elementary school and a playing field on the site. Part of the site was also sold to a developer, who built several hundred houses on the periphery of the old canal. In 1976, after unusually heavy rains and snow, the chemicals began seeping into the basements of houses. The canal itself overflowed and chemicals that had leaked from the drums spilled out into the environment. In August, 1978, New York State's Department of Health declared the Love Canal area a "grave and imminent peril" to the health of those living nearby. Investigations into complaints about the abnormally high number of miscarriages, birth defects, cancer, and a variety of other illnesses found eleven different actual or suspected carcinogens, including dioxin, in the air, water, and soil. Air-monitoring equipment found pollution levels as high as five thousand times the maximum safe level. President Jimmy Carter eventually declared Love Canal a disaster area and made federal disaster relief available to the residents, who were relocated.

MANAGING HAZARDOUS WASTES

CERCLA was also enacted because of concerns that serious gaps existed in the regulatory scheme for management of hazardous wastes, particularly with respect to abandoned or dormant sites where hazardous substances had been disposed of in the past. These sites continued to present either immediate or long-term threats to public health and environmental quality. CERCLA was designed to bring order to the federal laws regulating the cleanup of hazardous substances and compensation, which were regarded as inadequate and redundant.

Two concerns motivated Congress in the drafting and passage of the Superfund act: CERCLA was intended to provide the federal government with the enforcement tools for responding promptly, adequately, and appropriately to releases of hazardous substances into the environment, and the act was to shift the costs of cleaning up hazardous substances to those who had created or otherwise contributed to the situation.

RESPONSES: REMEDIAL OR REMOVAL

CERCLA applied mainly to inactive or abandoned sites from which hazardous substances were being released. The act authorized two kinds of response to releases of hazardous substances: remedial response, which generally involved permanent actions to contain, treat, or dispose of hazardous substances, and removal actions involving relatively rapid action to control, contain, and clean up spills or other releases of hazardous substances. CERCLA allocated funds to the EPA and gave it the authority to direct and oversee cleanup of old and abandoned waste sites. The first phase of the effort was to make a nationwide inventory of the sites that contained hazardous wastes and to list them in order of priority. Once the sites were identified, the EPA could require owners of old or abandoned dumps to perform the cleanup work themselves; alternatively, the EPA or the states could step in and perform the cleanup.

FIVE MAJOR PROVISIONS

There were five major provisions of CERCLA. The first provided means for enforcement. Through agreements and other judicial procedures, owners of abandoned sites were directed to clean up the sites themselves; if the EPA had to step in, the owners could be charged as much as three times the cost of the cleanup. Second, CERCLA was designed to respond to emergencies. Where ownership of sites was difficult to determine or danger imminent, CERCLA authorized the EPA to take immediate steps to correct the problem; the state in which the site was located was required to pay at least 10 percent of the cleanup costs. Third, the act provided for remedial response, ensuring a series of actions to be taken by the cleanup team. The fourth provision in CERCLA established regulations for federal-state collaboration; in addition to sharing costs, the states participated in selecting the sites and in establishing priorities for cleanup. States also provided new sites to receive waste removed from old ones. Finally, the fifth CERCLA provision used a federal tax on chemical manufacturers, importers, and oil refiners, supplemented by federally appropriated funds, to create a fund of $1.6 billion for the cleanup of abandoned sites.

SLOW PROGRESS

Progress cleaning up the dump sites was slow. The EPA became embroiled in controversy, which resulted in the discharge of the head of the Office of Solid Waste and Emergency Response over alleged sweetheart deals with companies. In 1982, the EPA found 418 sites where federal funds could be used to pay for cleanup work. Nearly one-fourth of those sites were in Michigan and New Jersey, while Pennsylvania, New York, and Florida had at least twenty-five such sites. That same year, though, the EPA released a three-volume, five-million-dollar study that reported that Love Canal once again appeared to be a safe place to live.

Under new leadership the EPA in 1983 proposed that 133 additional sites be added to the list. New Jersey moved to the top of the expanded list, with eighty-five sites, including the worst site at the LiPari landfill in Pitman, where the EPA estimated that three million gallons of paint solvents, heavy metals, and various toxic organic compounds were stored. The EPA was expected to adopt more stringent standards for cleaning up those dumps and to require companies to pay 80 percent of the cleanup costs at a specific site before the EPA would negotiate for possible settlement of pollution charges.

One of the problems addressed by the Superfund act was the fair allocation of responsibility. Congress had charged the EPA with locating and supervising responsible parties in conducting cleanup operations. Cooperation by potentially responsible parties was mandated through administratively imposed fines. Often, parties were called upon to clean up dumps for which they denied responsibility. Enormous sums of money were spent by parties defending against actions they considered to be grossly unfair. This resulted in litigation that expended money and time, while the cleanup of dangerous sites remained postponed.

In 1984, spokespeople for industry noted that the EPA was not moving fast enough to clean up these sites. In the first three years, final cleanup had been certified in only three dumps. Some environmentalists and leaders from the chemical industry joined forces to form Clean Sites Inc., a company that tried to expedite the cleanup process and negotiate with the companies involved to share the costs of cleanup. It was hoped that these voluntary efforts would prove to be more cost efficient than the Superfund program.

IMPACT AND OUTLOOK

The Superfund program was hampered by the sheer number of the sites identified, as well as by the limits of technology for cleaning up toxic compounds. Perhaps most troublesome, there was no consensus on how clean a site had to become to conform to EPA standards. Usually, the EPA chose the strictest and most expensive standards, regardless of whether a site would be used as a factory or as a playground. As of 1994, only about 12 percent of the 1,300 sites listed on the National Priorities List (NPL) had been cleaned up. In the first fourteen years of the Superfund law, more than $18 billion was spent, at an average of between $25 and $30 million per site. Superfund litigation accounted for as much as 25 percent of total expenditures. Despite its problems, however, Superfund continues to make headway, and maintains a Web site listing current projects.

Amy Bloom

SOURCES FOR FURTHER STUDY

Freedman, Warren. *Federal Statutes of Environmental Protection.* New York: Quorum Books, 1987.

Grad, Frank. *Grad on Environmental Law.* New York: Matthew Bender, 1994.

Lake, Laura. *Environmental Protection.* New York: Praeger, 1982.

Lewis, Cynthia A., and James M. Thunder. *Federal Chemical Regulation: TSCA, EPCRA, and the Pollution Prevention Act.* Washington, D.C.: Bureau of National Affairs, 1997.

Stolaff, Neil. *Regulating the Environment.* Dobbs Ferry, N.Y.: Oceana, 1991.

Worobec, Mary Devine. *Toxic Substances Control Primer.* Washington, D.C.: BNA Books, 1984.

SEE ALSO: Solid Waste Disposal Act (1965); National Environmental Policy Act (1970); Federal Environmental Pesticide Control Act (1972); Hazardous Materials Transportation Act (1974); Toxic Substances Control Act (1976); Low-Level Radioactive Waste Policy Act (1980); Nuclear Waste Policy Act (1983); Emergency Planning and Community Right-to-Know Act (1986).

LOW-LEVEL RADIOACTIVE WASTE POLICY ACT

DATE: December 22, 1980
U.S. STATUTES AT LARGE: 94 Stat. 3347
PUBLIC LAW: 96-573
U.S. CODE: 42 § 2021
CATEGORIES: Energy; Environment and Conservation

This law provided a program for states to dispose of low-level radioactive wastes.

Different types of nuclear wastes present varying kinds of danger. High-level radioactive wastes are liquids that are generated when used nuclear reactor fuel is reprocessed. In the 1970's, Presidents Gerald Ford and Jimmy Carter both banned commercial reprocessing of such wastes on the grounds that the plutonium produced in the process could lead to the proliferation of nuclear weapons. The U.S. government continued, however, to reprocess fuel for military use. By 1979, about 75 million gallons of high-level waste had been generated, and it was stored at sites in Washington State, Idaho, South Carolina, and New York.

A second type of nuclear waste, uranium tailings, contain naturally occurring radioactive materials. Huge piles of these tailings, in the form of fine sand, were dumped at abandoned mills and mines in eleven states. A third type, spent nuclear fuel, while technically not classified as nuclear waste, contains minerals that can still be reused. Because of the ban on reprocessing, however, utilities had to store spent fuels in pools of water near their reactors, but the pools filled up rapidly. The Department of Energy (DOE) estimated that twenty-seven nuclear power plants would require additional nuclear storage before 1985.

"Low-Level" Nuclear Wastes

A fourth type of nuclear waste is low-level radioactive waste generated by all activities that involve radioactive materials; this includes contaminated paper, plastics, construction materials, tools, protective clothing, and industrial and medical wastes. The term "low-level" refers not to the degree of radioactivity but to the source; all wastes not produced in nuclear reactors or in the reprocessing of nuclear fuel are classified as low-level. Some experts complain that the name implies that low-level wastes are not dangerous when some are highly radioactive and dangerous.

Of the more than 100,000 cubic meters of low-level wastes buried each year in three commercial dumps in the United States, about 43 percent comes from nuclear power plants, 25 percent from hospitals, 24 percent from industry, and 8 percent from the federal government. The DOE buries another 50,000 cubic meters of low-level waste each year in its own dumps, which are adjacent to the commercial dumps. For twenty-five years, until 1970, a large amount of low-level waste was placed into metal barrels and dumped in fifty sites in the oceans. Officials from the Environmental Protection Agency (EPA) testified before Congress in 1980, when the bill was being debated, that as many as one-fourth of those barrels were leaking.

In the 1940's and 1950's, low-level wastes were either buried in shallow trenches at sites owned and operated by the federal government or packaged in steel drums and dumped at sea. The government-owned sites were developed primarily to serve defense and government nuclear research activities. Until the 1960's, the wastes were simply placed onto Navy ships and hauled out to sea. With the increase in waste caused by commercial nuclear power, it became more economical to replace ocean dumping with landfills, and to allow a shift from federal to private control. Commercial landfills were patterned after those at defense installations, where wastes were packaged in steel drums and dumped into trenches that were dumped into the earth once they were filled. These low-level waste dumps were created with almost no comprehensive planning or federal oversight. The first commercial dump opened near Beatty, Nevada, in 1962, and was followed in 1963 by dumps in Maxey Flats, Kentucky, and West Valley, New York. More dumps opened in Richland, Washington, in 1965; Sheffield, Illinois, in 1967; and Barnwell, South Carolina, in 1971. The West Valley dump closed in 1975, Maxey Flats in 1977, and Sheffield in 1978, because radioactive materials had migrated off the sites. Merely closing the sites did not end the problems at the sites. At Maxey Flats, the largest of the closed dumps, plutonium was detected more than one mile from the site. Groundwater contaminated with tritium was moving out of the Sheffield site at the rate of one-half mile per year. At West Valley, trenches were infiltrated with water, creating a bathtub effect that spilled tritium and strontium into nearby streams. As Marvin Resnikoff, the codirector of the Sierra Club Radioactive Waste Campaign put it, "Landfills act a lot like teabags: the water goes in, the flavor goes out." As a result of the closures and problems at other sites, the dump at South Carolina became the largest commercial dump in the country.

PILING THE PROBLEM ON A FEW STATES

As the amount of wastes accumulated, however, Congress became aware of the need to create a comprehensive nuclear waste policy to deal with nuclear wastes. The National Governors Association pushed for a low-level waste bill, asserting that the problem of dealing with low-level radioactive wastes was approaching crisis stage. The problem of low-level nuclear wastes was particularly crucial because of the vast amounts of waste being generated in every state throughout the United States; only three states—Washington, Nevada, and South Carolina—had dumps for these wastes, and they were threatening to stop taking it all. Washington voters had approved a ballot initiative on November 4, 1980, to close the disposal site of Hanford, Washington, to out-of-state nuclear garbage beginning in the summer of 1981. Nevada governor Robert List had promised to close his state's dump at Beatty, Nevada; and South Carolina's governor, Richard Riley, whose state accepted the majority of the low-level wastes from around the country, decided that his state would accept less in the future.

Congress was, however, unable to reach an agreement on a comprehensive plan. On December 10, 1980, Governor Riley let it be known that he was considering closing one dump to all out-of-state waste if Congress did not pass a bill that dealt with the problem. As a result, Butler Derrick, a Democrat from South Carolina, put together an unusually forceful effort to get at least a compromise bill passed in the Senate. This was finally accomplished on December 13, 1980, and the Low-Level Radioactive Waste Act was signed by President Jimmy Carter on December 22, 1980.

PROVISIONS OF THE 1980 ACT AND 1985 AMENDMENTS
The Low-Level Radioactive Waste Act encouraged individual states where low-level radioactive waste was dumped to enter into clubs, agreements, or regional "compacts" with neighboring states to create new regional disposal sites. As of 1986, it was decided that individual states would be allowed to restrict access to their disposal sites and to accept only waste generated within their region. At the time, it was anticipated that some six or seven compact sites would be established. By 1985, however, progress had been so slow that the January 1, 1986, deadline was declared to be unmanageable. Congress realized that the law had provided no incentives to meet the deadline. As a result, under President Ronald Reagan, Congress in 1985 passed an updated version of the Low-Level Radioactive Waste Policy Act; this act revised the timetable and allowed continued access, on a limited basis, to the three existing sites until January 1, 1993.

With the 1985 act, the DOE became responsible for facilitating the compact arrangement between states, for coordinating the national program on low-level radioactive waste disposal, and for reporting on progress to Congress. Penalties and surcharges were to be paid to the DOE escrow account, which was established to ensure compliance by the states with the conditions and the timetable of the 1985 act.

The revisions of the 1985 Low-Level Radioactive Policy Act resulted in the states becoming responsible for their own radioactive wastes. The revised law ordered the states to create more low-level nuclear-waste sites, however, not fewer, and to speed up the process rather than focus on better waste management.

CRITICISMS
There were various criticisms of the 1985 amendments. Instead of having the three original low-level radioactive waste sites, which were located in remote areas geographically suitable for radiation contaminants, the act called for twelve or more waste sites, some of

them in more populated and geographically unsuitable areas. As a result of the mandated timetables, states were discouraged from using more innovative techniques to dispose of low-level nuclear waste.

Scientific debate continued on how much radiation was harmful. Some authorities, including those setting federal exposure standards, believed that the effects of exposure below a certain level of radiation were imperceptible, while others argued that exposure to radiation of any amount could cause damage. Different substances could have different effects. Some radioactive substances decayed to the point of harmlessness in less than one day; others emitted energy and remained hazardous for thousands of years. Some radioactive substances posed a threat to humans through mere external exposure, while others presented a danger only if the substance was inhaled or swallowed.

The disposal of low-level radioactive waste remained problematic. It was difficult to define or to determine who should be responsible for it or where it should be discarded. Although several studies recommended that the low-level radioactive burial sites be returned to federal jurisdiction, the 1985 act returned the problem to the states. It called on them to form interstate compacts and construct burial sites to handle each region's wastes. The compacts then applied to Congress for ratification. Putting the Low-Level Radioactive Waste Policy Act into effect was not easy. Some states formed compacts, particularly those that already had dump sites, but others delayed. In some areas, negotiations broke down, as states negotiated with several different regions looking for the best deal. The situation in the Northeast, which generated 37 percent of the volume and 57 percent of the activity, was the worst. The situation gradually improved, however, and more cooperation was seen as the dangers of exposure to radioactive wastes through touching, breathing, or drinking became better understood.

Amy Bloom

SOURCES FOR FURTHER STUDY

Davis, Charles E., and James P. Lester, eds. *Dimensions of Hazardous Waste Politics and Policy.* Westport, Conn.: Greenwood Press, 1988.
Long, Robert Emmet. *The Problem of Waste Disposal.* New York: H. W. Wilson, 1988.

McCuen, Gary. *Nuclear Waste: The Biggest Clean-up in History.* Hudson, Wis.: G.E.M., 1990.

Murray, Raymond L. *Understanding Radioactive Waste.* Columbus, Ohio: Battelle Press, 1982.

Slesser, Malcolm. *Dictionary of Energy.* New York: Schocken Books, 1983.

SEE ALSO: Hazardous Materials Transportation Act (1974); Superfund Act (1980); Nuclear Waste Policy Act (1983).

PARENTAL KIDNAPPING PREVENTION ACT

DATE: December 28, 1980
U.S. STATUTES AT LARGE: 94 Stat. 3566
PUBLIC LAW: 96-611
CATEGORIES: Children's Issues; Crimes and Criminal Procedure; Women's Issues

This law is designed to discourage drawn-out interstate custody battles and prevent parents from fleeing with their children to states with more sympathetic custody laws than their states of residence.

According to the U.S. Department of Justice, approximately 350,000 children are abducted by family members each year in custody disputes. Revenge is often the motive, and nearly half of these cases involve concealment of the children, transportation of the children out of state, or the intention of keeping the children permanently.

Before 1968 noncustodial parents were able to take children out of state and get a new custody order, even if the children were wrongfully kept after visitation. Courts viewed custody orders as subject to modification, and the presence of the children in a different state, even if briefly, gave new courts jurisdiction. The Uniform Child Custody Jurisdiction Act (UCCJA) was drafted in 1968 to remedy the problem of conflicting state custody laws.

By 1980 only forty-three states had enacted the UCCJA, prompting Congress to institute a federal law. The PKPA applies to all interstate child-custody cases, requires all states to honor and enforce other states' custody and visitation decrees, and prevents other states from modifying already existing custody and visitation orders except under very limited circumstances.

P. S. Ramsey

SOURCE FOR FURTHER STUDY

Greif, Geoffrey L., and Rebecca L. Hegar. *When Parents Kidnap: The Families Behind the Headlines.* New York: Maxwell Macmillian, 1993.

SEE ALSO: Child Abuse Prevention and Treatment Act (1974); Child Support Enforcement Amendments (1984); Family Violence Prevention and Services Act (1984); Missing Children's Assistance Act (1984); Megan's Law (1996).

ECONOMIC RECOVERY TAX ACT AND OMNIBUS BUDGET RECONCILIATION ACT

DATE: August 13, 1981
U.S. STATUTES AT LARGE: 95 Stat. 170 (ERTA); 97-35 (OBRA)
PUBLIC LAW: 97-34 (ERA); 95 Stat. 357 (OBRA)
U.S. CODE: 42 § 9801
CATEGORIES: Tariffs and Taxation

These bills epitomized Reaganomics by cutting both government spending and taxes.

During the 1980 election campaign, Republican candidate Ronald Reagan taunted President Jimmy Carter by asking voters: "Are you better off than you were four years ago?" Carter had struggled with declining productivity rates, double-digit inflation, 20 percent interest rates, nearly eight million people unemployed, and a 5 percent drop in real hourly wages over the previous five years.

SUPPLY-SIDE ECONOMICS

Reagan defeated Carter in November, 1980, largely by promising new solutions to economic problems. Reagan championed free-market, supply-side economic theory rather than the use of governmental power to fine-tune the economy. Government regulations weighed down the natural tendency of a capitalist economy to grow, Reagan asserted: Government was the problem, not the solution. Reagan's economic policies over the next several years would come to be known as Reaganomics.

When Reagan took office in January, 1981, he subordinated all issues to economic recovery. David Stockman, director of the Office of Management and Budget, became the lead figure in formulating Reagan's program. Stockman, bright and hardworking, used his knowledge of budgetary details to dominate economic policy making in 1981.

While Reagan left the details to his economic experts, he established the basic elements of the programs: a massive tax cut, a huge increase in military spending, reduced nondefense spending, and a balanced budget by 1984. He believed that lower taxes would lead to economic growth and that that growth, along with cuts in nondefense programs, would allow a balanced budget. However, when Reagan succumbed to political pressure and ruled that there would be no cuts in Social Security or other major entitlement programs, Stockman's reductions could only come from a small part of the budget. Stockman's final figures projected a balanced budget in 1984 only by using overly optimistic forecasts of revenue gains and economic growth.

A FOUR-PART RECOVERY PROGRAM

On February 18, 1981, Reagan presented his program to a joint session of Congress. He proposed a four-part program: cutting government spending, reducing taxes, eliminating unnecessary and unproductive economic regulations, and encouraging a consistent anti-inflationary monetary policy. Reagan labeled government as the main source of the nation's economic problems and promised that his program would return government to its proper province, while restoring to the people the right to decide how to dispose of their earnings. He predicted that his recovery plan would create thirteen million new jobs and control inflation, while achieving a balanced budget by 1984. He asked Congress to cut $41.4 billion from eighty-three programs, without cutting Social Security, Medicare, or veterans' pensions. He increased defense spending, the president said, because even in its straitened economic condition, the United States had to respond to the Soviet military buildup. Reagan proposed 10 percent reductions in individual income taxes in each of the next three years and an increase in tax depreciation allowances for business.

BUDGET CUTS, TAX CUTS

After Reagan made his initial proposals, the hard political work began. Reagan met ninety-six times with senators and representatives and spent hours with them on the telephone, using charm, intimidation, and artful deal-making. After Reagan promised protection for the sugar industry, one important Louisiana Democrat admitted that while he could not be bought, he could be rented. The first step toward a Reagan victory came when Congress decided to use the relatively new budget reconciliation process, by which appropriations were packaged into one omnibus bill rather than voted on as separate items. The Democratic-dominated House Budget Committee had formulated its own budget, which made less than half the spending cuts that the president wanted, but Reagan's work paid off on May 7, when sixty-three Democrats revolted against party leaders and joined the Republicans to support the administration bill. On July 31, Congress agreed to the most widespread package of budget cuts in its history.

The final bill cut nearly $35.2 billion from a spending level of $740 billion projected by the Congressional Budget Office for fiscal year 1982, and it trimmed $130.6 billion of expected outlays for fiscal years 1981-1984. The bill tightened eligibility for food stamps and public assistance, cut funds for subsidized housing programs, reduced school lunch subsidies, instituted a "needs test" for student loans, limited pay raises for federal employees, and made hundreds of other changes.

The battle over Reagan's tax legislation was even more hard-fought than that over the budget bill. Reagan said government was a kind of organism with an insatiable appetite for money and a tendency to grow forever, unless he could starve it by reducing its food—tax revenue. In his February 18 message, Reagan asked for a 10 percent reduction in individual income taxes on July 1, 1981, followed by two additional 10 percent cuts in 1982 and 1983. He also called for more liberal depreciation allowances for business.

Two days before the vote, the outcome was still considered too close to call, but Reagan's skillful deal-making again brought him crucial Democratic support. Congress gave him most of what he wanted. The final bill reduced all individual income tax rates by 5 percent on October 1, 1981, 10 percent on July 1, 1982, and an additional 10 percent on July 1, 1983. The bill liberalized depreciation allowances for business; reduced the top rate on investment income from 70 percent to 50 percent; and indexed individual tax brackets to inflation, preventing inflation from pushing people into higher brackets. On August 13, 1981, Reagan signed the Economic Recovery Act of 1981 and the Omnibus Budget Reconciliation Act of 1981. He told reporters that over the next three years, the budget bill represented $130 billion in savings and the tax bill $750 billion in tax cuts.

IMPACT

Reagan's economic program had mixed results. In late 1981, the economy entered a severe recession, with the unemployment rate peaking at 10.3 percent in early 1983. The recession was followed by the longest period of sustained economic growth in U.S. history, but half the millions of new jobs created paid less than poverty-level wages. Reagan's most important economic success came through working with the Federal Reserve Board to bring inflation under control. His greatest failure was the exploding national debt. Although he had projected a balanced budget by 1984, deficits rose to record heights. From George Washington through Jimmy Carter's administration, the United States had accumulated $1.1 trillion in national debt; under Reagan the United States added $1.8 trillion to its debt. Reagan's legacy placed several constraints on his successors, which resulted in the need to allocate more than 10 percent of the nation's yearly budgets required to pay the interest on the debt, rather than being available to be reinvested in the country's social and economic infrastructure.

William E. Pemberton

SOURCES FOR FURTHER STUDY

Boskin, Michael J. *Reagan and the Economy: The Successes, Failures, and Unfinished Agenda.* San Francisco: Institute for Contemporary Studies Press, 1987.

Campagna, Anthony S. *The Economy in the Reagan Years: The Economic Consequences of the Reagan Administrations.* Westport, Conn.: Greenwood Press, 1994.

Friedman, Benjamin M. *Day of Reckoning: The Consequences of American Economic Policy Under Reagan and After.* New York: Random House, 1988.

Stockman, David A. *The Triumph of Politics: How the Reagan Revolution Failed.* New York: Harper & Row, 1986.

Wilber, Charles K., and Kenneth P. Jameson. *Beyond Reaganomics: A Further Inquiry into the Poverty of Economics.* Notre Dame, Ind.: University of Notre Dame Press, 1990.

SEE ALSO: Tax Reform Act of 1986 (1986).

INTELLIGENCE IDENTITIES PROTECTION ACT

DATE: June 23, 1982
U.S. STATUTES AT LARGE: 96 Stat. 122
PUBLIC LAW: 97-200
U.S. CODE: 50 § 421
CATEGORIES: Crimes and Criminal Procedure; Military and National Security

This federal law made it a crime to publish the names of Central Intelligence Agency (CIA) agents.

Congress's passage of the Intelligence Identities Protection Act (IIPA) in 1982 outlawed publication of the names of covert government agents. The law was drafted as a response to former CIA employee Philip Agee's publication of *Dirty Work: The CIA in*

Western Europe (1978) and *Dirty Work Two: The CIA in Africa* (1980), books that revealed the names of more than a thousand alleged CIA officers. Congress was also reacting to the work of Louis Wolf, co-editor of the *Covert Action Information Bulletin*, a magazine containing a section devoted to identifying CIA operatives. According to the congressional report accompanying the IIPA, Agee's practice of "naming names" had led directly to the assassination of CIA station chief Richard Welch in Athens, Greece, in 1975, and to other violent attacks on persons Agee identified as CIA officers.

The IIPA made it a crime intentionally to disclose the identities of CIA agents, establishing various penalties based on the accused's degree of access to classified information. The harshest penalties were reserved for "insiders"—persons holding authorized access to classified information. Any person with access to information identifying CIA agents who purposely disclosed an agent's identity could be jailed for up to ten years and fined as much as fifty thousand dollars. Any person who intentionally revealed the identity of a CIA agent after having had access to classified information in general could face up to five years in jail and a fine of twenty-five thousand dollars. Those penalties applied primarily to current and former government employees.

"Outsiders"—persons who did not have authorized access to classified information—were to be treated differently. Any such person who intentionally disclosed an agent's identity while knowing that such disclosure might harm U.S. foreign intelligence operations could be imprisoned for up to three years and fined up to fifteen thousand dollars.

A survey of news stories written before the IIPA was passed in 1982 turned up more than eighty major books and news articles whose authors could arguably have been indicted under the law. A representative sample would include revelations that former CIA agents were involved in the Watergate break-in, accounts of illegal domestic spying by the CIA, and disclosures that a CIA employee tried to infiltrate the House and Senate intelligence committees in 1980 at the direction of the Soviet State Security Committee (KGB).

Juliet Dee

SOURCE FOR FURTHER STUDY

Mello, Tara Baukus, and Arthur M. Schlesinger, eds. *The Central Intelligence Agency.* Broomall, Pa.: Chelsea House, 2000.

SEE ALSO: Freedom of Information Act (1966); Privacy Protection Act (1980).

LAW OF THE SEA TREATY

DATE: Signed December 10, 1982; effective November 24, 1994
CATEGORIES: Environment and Conservation; Foreign Relations; Treaties and Agreements

The treaty was designed to help ensure and maintain the peaceful use of the seas for all nations; its signatories hoped to accomplish this goal by standardizing and regulating areas of potential conflict between nations, including ship safety, mineral exploration and exploitation, and environmental protection.

The phrase "law of the sea" implies that activities at sea, like those on land, are subject to the rule of law and that compliance with the law is mandatory and enforced. In fact, the "law of the sea" is not a law but an agreement among nations. This agreement sets standards and regulations on all activities at sea and establishes clear lines of national jurisdiction. Compliance is voluntary, and there is no provision in the 1982 agreement for its enforcement. Despite the apparent weaknesses of such an agreement, compliance on most points has been excellent. The reason is that the "law of the sea" is based on a fundamental principle on which all nations can agree: the freedom of the seas.

EARLY CONCEPTS

As long as there have been ships, there has been some concept of freedom of the seas. While there were no written rules, a spirit of cooperation among mariners existed during times of peace. By the seventeenth century the Dutch had begun global maritime trade, and their economy was very much dependent on free access to the seas. In 1609 Hugo Grotius, a Dutch lawyer, was asked to codify the concept of freedom of the seas. Grotius produced a large treatise on the law of the seas entitled *Mare Liberum* (1609). This work established the "freedom of the seas" as a concept based on law. The conclusion of Grotius was that all nations could use the oceans provided they did not interfere with one another's use. This first attempt at a law of the sea recognized three divisions of the seas: internal waters, territorial seas, and the high seas. Grotius maintained that a nation had sovereignty over internal and territorial seas but that the high seas were open to all. This concept of the law of the sea survived into the twentieth century.

THE TRUMAN PROCLAMATION
In 1947 President Harry S. Truman of the United States was advised by geologists of the potential of large oil reserves on the continental shelf. To protect these resources, Truman declared that all resources of the continental shelf belonged exclusively to the United States. This became known as the Truman Proclamation. It had broad international implications, with many nations issuing similar decrees regarding the continental shelf.

THE GENEVA CONFERENCES
Because of increased economic and military activity at sea, it became apparent that some formal agreement regarding the use of the oceans was needed to ensure peace. In 1958 and again in 1960, conferences on the law of the sea were convened in Geneva. A treaty was drafted and ratified; it included many basic issues on which there was wide agreement. Two points included in the treaty were particularly important. The depth limit of the continental shelf was limited by treaty to 200 meters. This depth limit included an "exploitability clause," however, whereby a nation could exploit ocean resources below 200 meters on adjacent seafloor if it had the technology to do so. Such a concept was favorable to the industrial nations and placed less developed nations at a disadvantage.

After 1960 many formerly colonial countries received independence; these were primarily nonindustrial states. They feared that the ocean's resources would be exploited by the industrial nations. So great was the fear that in 1967 the nation of Malta proposed to the United Nations that a treaty be developed that would reserve the economic resources of the seafloor. The Maltese ambassador, Arvid Pardo, further declared that the ocean floor should be reserved for peaceful uses alone and that the ocean resources were the "common heritage of all mankind."

THE THIRD LAW OF THE SEA CONFERENCE

The Third Law of the Sea Conference was begun in 1973 and continued meeting until 1982. The major result of this conference was the Law of the Sea Treaty dealing with boundary issues, economic rights of nations, rights of passage through straits, the freedom of scientific research, and the exploitation of ocean-floor resources.

The Law of the Sea Treaty established the width of the territorial sea at 12 nautical miles. This could be modified to allow passage of ships through narrow straits critical to international commerce. The territorial sea is under the direct jurisdiction of the adjacent nation, and that nation may enforce its laws and regulate the passage of ships through it. Beyond the territorial limit, a coastal nation or any inhabitable land can also declare an exclusive economic zone (EEZ) of 200 nautical miles. The EEZ is open to ships of all nations, but the resources within it can be exploited only by the nation declaring the EEZ.

The Law of the Sea Treaty established regulations on scientific research in the oceans. While the freedom of scientific research in the open ocean is universally recognized, investigations in a nation's territorial seas and EEZ require the permission of that nation. The treaty also governs the mining of deep sea mineral resources. In certain locations on the deep seafloor, there are nodules of manganese, cobalt, nickel, and copper. Exploitation of these resources requires a highly advanced and expensive technology. Such requirements place less developed nations at a disadvantage. The Law of the Sea Treaty attempts to address this problem. Any group wishing to mine the deep seafloor must declare its intent to do so and state the geographic location of the mining operation. An international authority will grant permission to mine. All revenues from a successful mining operation on the deep seafloor must be shared among the nations of the world. Further, the technology used to mine the deep seafloor must be shared with all nations.

The Law of the Sea Treaty left many issues unresolved and others open to multiple interpretations. Despite areas of disagreement, however, most maritime nations adhere to the majority of the provisions of the Law of the Sea Treaty.

Richard H. Fluegeman, Jr.

SOURCES FOR FURTHER STUDY

Borgese, E. M. "The Law of the Sea." *Scientific American* 247, no. 3 (1982).

Ross, David A., and J. A. Knauss. "How the Law of the Sea Treaty Will Affect U.S. Marine Science." *Science* 217 (September 10, 1982).

Zuleta, B. "The Law of the Sea: Myths and Realities." *Oceanus* 25, no. 3 (1982).

SEE ALSO: Outer Space Treaty (1967); Seabed Treaty (1972).

NUCLEAR WASTE POLICY ACT

DATE: January 7, 1983
U.S. STATUTES AT LARGE: 96 Stat. 2202
PUBLIC LAW: 97-425
U.S. CODE: 42 § 10101
CATEGORIES: Energy; Environment and Conservation

This legislation mandated the Department of Energy to locate and develop a permanent repository for high-level nuclear wastes.

After a long process of negotiations, both the Senate and the House of Representatives on December 21, 1982, gave final passage to the Nuclear Waste Policy Act (NWPA), and President Ronald Reagan signed the bill into law on January 7, 1983. The NWPA was designed to deal with the controversial issue of spent fuel rods from nuclear power plants. Such rods contained high-level nuclear wastes that were intensely radioactive and lethal and were expected to remain so for thousands of years. By 1982, about ten thousand tons of spent fuel were in temporary storage tanks next to power plants, and it was projected that, by the end of the century, the figure would be 41,500 tons. While small in volume compared with other industrial wastes, this high-level waste was deadly to humans and could render land or water unusable.

PROVISIONS

The NWPA authorized the Department of Energy (DOE) to choose potential sites for both permanent and long-term storage. There were to be two permanent sites, thousands of feet under the ground, in basalt or granite caverns. The DOE was to recommend from three to five satisfactory sites to the Congress by 1985, and the president was to make the final choices in consultation with the states involved. Before making its selection, the DOE was required to make a comprehensive environmental impact statement, and the Nuclear Regulatory Commission (NRC) was to provide an independent supervision of the DOE's activities. The president was to choose the first permanent site in a Western state before 1987, and he was to select the second in the East or Midwest by 1989. The law stipulated that the first repository would begin accepting wastes for permanent storage by 1998.

The long-term repositories were also called "monitored, retrievable storage" (MRS) facilities because they were expected to hold, for one hundred years, spent fuel which would be available for reprocessing, a complex job of separating useful uranium and plutonium from wastes. This provision of the law was based on hopes for future technological innovations that would make reprocessing truly feasible, thereby reducing the volume of storage. Many critics of nuclear power disliked the idea of MRS facilities, because the facilities could simply become a cheaper, less secure alternative for dealing with wastes.

The NWPA required the nuclear power plants to continue to store their spent fuel rods in temporary storage pools until such time as the repositories were constructed. The financing of the future repositories would be accomplished through a federal surcharge on nuclear plants and the charges would be passed on to consumers. An amendment to the act gave states the power to veto any proposed site. The veto required a vote in both houses of Congress to override the veto. Another amendment allowed high-level military wastes (about 10 percent of the total volume) to be stored with the civilian wastes.

BACKGROUND

In its early years, the Atomic Energy Commission (AEC) had placed a low priority on the question of nuclear wastes. In part, this was because officials had assumed that much of the waste could be dealt with in reprocessing plants. By the late 1960's, however, the nuclear power plants were beginning to run out of storage capacity for spent fuel, and in a comprehensive study in 1969, AEC scientists concluded that spent fuel should be converted to solid form and sent to federally controlled repositories. The AEC recommended and publicized that a salt mine in Lyons, Kansas, was a suitable location, but agency personnel were embarrassed when non-AEC scientists discovered serious leakage problems in 1970.

When Jimmy Carter became president in 1977, the issue of nuclear wastes was of widespread concern. Private industry appeared to be abandoning the hope that reprocessing could be profitable, and in any case, the Carter administration concluded that reprocessing plants posed a threat to the policy of controlling the proliferation of plutonium used in nuclear weapons. Carter did appoint an interagency review group to suggest policy options; the group's report in 1979 expressed urgency about the problem of spent fuel rods and recommended consideration of deep geologic storage. With Carter's endorsement of the report, both houses of Congress passed different bills in 1980, but the two houses were unable to agree on the question of a veto for potential host states.

When Ronald Reagan became president in 1981, all concerned parties were anxious for a law dealing with high-level wastes. Reagan, long a supporter of nuclear power, was hopeful that private enterprise could make reprocessing profitable, but he did not disagree with most of Carter's recommendations on storage sites. By 1982, ninety-five orders for nuclear reactors had been canceled, and with all of the negative publicity associated with nuclear power plants, industrial leaders hoped that waste-disposal legislation would help their public-relations image. Environmental lobbyists also wanted to see legislation enacted, but they were not going to allow the nuclear industry to claim prematurely that the waste-disposal problem had been solved.

PASSAGE THROUGH CONGRESS

In this context in 1981, Senator James McClure, the Republican chairman of the Energy Committee, introduced the McClure bill, which resembled the earlier recommendations of the Carter administration. In the debates, senators from sparsely populated states tended to be in favor of many regional repositories, but states with larger populations had the votes to reject this idea. Senator Alan Simpson added a controversial amendment to combine military and civilian wastes in the same repository. After a number of adjustments, the McClure bill easily passed the Senate in April, 1982.

Approval in the House of Representatives, with its Democratic majority, was more difficult. Representative Morris Udall, the chairman of the House Interior Committee, and other Democrats managed to write a bill that was more sensitive to the views of the host states, and the bill passed the House by a voice vote on December 2. House and Senate leaders met to work out their differences on December 14. Just as they believed they had worked out a compromise, Senator William Proxmire of Wisconsin threatened a filibuster unless the bill required both chambers to override a state's veto. When Senator McClure agreed to Proxmire's amendment, McClure and Udall put together the final bill and sent it to the lame-duck session of Congress, where it passed easily on December 20, just hours before Congress was to adjourn. In signing the bill in January, 1983, Reagan stated that the bill "should demonstrate to the public that the challenge of coping with nuclear wastes can and will be met."

THE NIMBY RESPONSE

In 1982, the progress heralded by enactment of the NWPA was overshadowed by frustrations in locating an appropriate site for high-level wastes. When hearings were held in potential host states, angry crowds turned out in huge numbers with the cry of NIMBY (not in my backyard). The Department of Energy found it impossible to meet the earliest deadlines for site selection. In 1984, moreover, Getty Oil Company announced that it was abandoning its attempt to reprocess spent fuel at the Barnwell plant; since no other serious efforts were being made to reprocess spent fuel, it appeared that the reprocessing business was financially unfeasible. This meant that the storing of high-level nuclear wastes would be more difficult than had been anticipated.

In 1986, the secretary of the interior announced that its list of three candidates for the first permanent repository included the states of Texas, Nevada, and Washington. The secretary also announced that an attempt to find a second site in the East or Midwest had been postponed indefinitely because of public opposition and political realities. The next year, the DOE announced that Yucca Mountain, Nevada, had been chosen as the site for the repository. In Nevada, the opposition to high-level wastes was not as great as elsewhere, although the governor and others expressed concern about a negative influence on tourism. Although Yucca Mountain appeared to be ideal in many ways, some scientists expressed concerns about climatic change and possible volcanic activity.

THE 1987 AMENDMENTS

On December 22, 1987, Congress, as part of a deficit reconciliation bill, passed important amendments to the NWPA. The major provision designated Yucca Mountain, Nevada, as the only candidate site eligible for consideration as a permanent repository. In the event that the DOE were to decide that the site were unsatisfactory, the department would be required to notify Congress, to take steps to reclaim the site, and to recommend further action for permanent disposal.

The NWPA amendments also authorized the DOE to designate, construct, and operate a long-term, retrievable-storage facility, and to recommend to Congress whether such a facility should be a part of the nuclear-waste management system. Another provision created the Nuclear Waste Technical Review Board as an independent agency to evaluate the DOE's activities in nuclear-waste management. Finally, the amendments established a nuclear-waste negotiator, appointed by the president, to reach agreements with states or Indian tribes about the hosting of long-term or permanent repositories. Such an agreement, however, would require statutory approval by Congress.

After the passage of the 1987 amendments, frustrations and unforeseen problems complicated the efforts to deal with high-level nuclear wastes. Few observers were surprised in November, 1989, when the Department of Energy announced that it was moving the target date for opening a storage site to the year 2010 at the earliest. New temporary storage pools would be constructed to house the increasing number of spent fuel rods. In effect, the search for a satisfactory resolution to the problem of disposal of high-level nuclear wastes was postponed until the twenty-first century.

YUCCA MOUNTAIN

As of 2002, nuclear materials were stored in 131 aboveground facilities in thirty-nine states, with 161 million Americans residing within 75 miles of those sites. The terrorist attacks of September 11, 2001, on the World Trade Center towers and the Pentagon made fullfilment of the NWPA mandate more compelling than ever, and the consensus of the administration of George W. Bush was that a central site offered more protection for high-level nuclear wastes than did the existing 131 sites.

On February 14, 2002, Secretary of Energy Spencer Abraham recommended approval of the Yucca Mountain site to President George W. Bush. President Bush accepted the recommendation and forwarded it to Congress the next day. Both the House and the Senate approved the selection of the site on July 9, 2002. President Bush issued the following statement through his press secretary:

> Finding a safe and central repository is not only mandated by law, but it is in America's national security and homeland security interests. . . . Since the Congress passed a law requiring a repository in 1982, this has been a serious issue for the American people. The President recognizes that the law now gives Nevada the opportunity to disapprove the recommendation and, if they do, then the Congress will have an opportunity to act. After two decades, the time has come to resolve this issue once and for all.

Thomas T. Lewis, updated by
Christina J. Moose

SOURCES FOR FURTHER STUDY

Barlett, Donald, and James Steele. *Forevermore: Nuclear Wastes in America.* New York: W. W. Norton, 1985.

Campbell, John. *Collapse of an Industry: Nuclear Power and the Contradictions of U.S. Policy.* Ithaca, N.Y.: Cornell University Press, 1988.

Carter, Luther J. *Nuclear Imperatives and the Public Trust: Dealing with Radioactive Wastes.* Washington, D.C.: Resources for the Future, 1987.

Cohen, Bernard. *Before It's Too Late: A Scientist's Case for Nuclear Energy.* New York: Plenum Press, 1982.
Hare, Tony. *Nuclear Waste Disposal.* New York: Gloucester Press, 1991.
Krukschke, Earl. *Nuclear Energy Policy: A Reference Handbook.* Santa Barbara, Calif.: ABC-CLIO, 1990.

SEE ALSO: Atomic Energy Act of 1954 (1954); Price-Anderson Act (1957); Seabed Treaty (1972); Hazardous Materials Transportation Act (1974); Superfund Act (1980); Low-Level Radioactive Waste Policy Act (1980); Nuclear Waste Policy Act (1983); Emergency Planning and Community Right-to-Know Act (1986).

EQUAL ACCESS ACT

DATE: August 11, 1984
U.S. STATUTES AT LARGE: 98 Stat. 1302
PUBLIC LAW: 98-377
U.S. CODE: 20 § 4071
CATEGORIES: Civil Rights and Liberties; Speech and Expression

This federal law requires public secondary schools receiving federal financial assistance not to deny students opportunities to conduct meetings on their premises solely on the basis of the content of the speech at such meetings.

In a 1981 case entitled *Widmar v. Vincent,* the Supreme Court ruled that a student religious group at the University of Missouri should be allowed to use campus facilities for its meetings. The state-supported public institution had previously allowed only non-religious student groups access to its facilities. When it was approached by members of a student religious group, the university denied the group use of its facilities in order not to violate the establishment clause of the First Amendment to the U.S. Constitution. In deciding in favor of these students, the Court ruled that allowing only nonreligious groups to use the same facilities violated the religious groups' rights to freedom of speech.

PROVISIONS OF THE LAW

Following the *Widmar* decision Congress passed the Equal Access Act in 1984. This act effectively extended the Supreme Court's *Widmar* decision to include all pubic secondary schools that receive federal funds. The act required all such secondary schools that create limited open forums for noncurriculum-related student groups to meet during noninstructional times not to deny similar access to other student groups solely on the basis of the religious, political, philosophical, or other content of their meetings. Thus, any public secondary school that allowed at least one voluntary student-initiated and nonschool-sponsored club or group unrelated to specific classes to meet on school premises outside of normal classroom instructional settings, must allow any other student groups to conduct their meetings at school in a similar fashion.

Although broadly worded, the legislation limited the scope of access in certain situations. For example, school administrators were permitted to deny access to any student group whose meetings had the potential to interfere with the orderly conduct of educational activities within the school. Otherwise eligible student groups were also restricted in certain other ways; for example, nonschool persons could not direct, control, or regularly attend group activities. Also, if a student group were to embrace a religious orientation, school personnel could be present at its meetings only in a nonparticipatory capacity. Along these same lines, student groups would lose their eligibility under the act if they were sponsored by the school, its agents, or its employees. However, the act also provided that schools and their employees had the authority to maintain order and discipline, to protect the well-being of students and faculty, and to ensure that student involvement in group activities would be strictly voluntary.

The law gave public secondary schools the option of avoiding its requirements by simply declining to create limited open forums. Schools could accomplish this by denying the use of their facilities to all noncurriculum-related student groups, while restricting access only to groups directly connected to existing school curricula. For example, the existence of a student-initiated Spanish club in a high school that provides Spanish-language instruction would not fall under the act's jurisdiction. By contrast, groups such as a scuba club or student service club closely related to nonschool organizations probably would trigger the act, thereby opening the door for other noncurriculum-related groups to request access to school facilities. It should also be noted that any school district that would normally be subject to the Equal Access Act that forgoes federal funding is not affected by the act.

COURT RULINGS

In 1990 the U.S. Supreme Court was asked to consider the constitutionality of the Equal Access Act and whether the establishment clause of the First Amendment prohibited a secondary school with a limited open forum from denying access to a student religious group. In *Board of Education of the Westside Community Schools v. Mergens* (1990) the Court ruled that the act was constitutional. The Court concluded that Congress had not implied an endorsement of religion when it acknowledged the presumed maturity of secondary school students in schools with limited open forums voluntarily to form religious or other types of clubs.

In reaching this decision, the Court confronted Congress's failure to define several key terms and concepts within its act. For example, since "noncurriculum-related student group" was not defined, the Court had to develop its own interpretation of what Congress meant by the term. The Court held that any student club involving subject matter comparable to that in a class that was being taught—or that would soon be taught—in a regularly scheduled course would not trigger the act. Similarly, the act would not be triggered if the group's subject matter concerned a body of courses taken as a whole (such as student government), or in cases in which group participation is either required or results in the awarding of academic credit (such as school band or choir).

After the *Mergens* case was decided in 1990 at least one court ruled on the question of the durational length of a secondary school limited open forum. In *Pope v. East Brunswick Board of Education* (1993), the U.S. Third Circuit Court of Appeals held that although a school district had created a limited open forum at a high school when it recognized a noncurriculum-related student group, the district retained authority to eliminate all its noncurriculum-related student groups and totally close its forum.

As the Equal Access Act has been interpreted by the Supreme Court, public secondary schools that create limited open forums by allowing noncurriculum-related student clubs to meet on their premises during noninstructional hours may not arbitrarily discriminate against other student groups solely on the basis of their religious, philosophical, or political content or orientations. As the act's title implies, Congress supports the notion that all students wishing to meet for legal and nondisruptive purposes must have the same access to public facilities that is afforded to other noncurricular student clubs or groups. Whenever the act has been triggered, it has generally prevented public school authorities from unilaterally abridging the rights of secondary school students to gather and discuss topics and issues of common interest on school grounds during noninstructional time.

Fred Hartmeister

SOURCES FOR FURTHER STUDY

Hartmeister, Fred. *Surviving as a Teacher: The Legal Dimension.* Chicago: Precept Press, 1995.

McCarthy, Martha M., and Nelda H. Cambron-McCabe. *Public School Law.* 3d ed. Boseon, Mass.: Allyn and Bacon, 1992.

Morris, Arval A. "The Equal Access Act After Mergens." *West's Education Law Reporter* 61, no. 4 (1990).

Rossow, Lawrence F., and Mark G. Rice. "The Constitutionality of the Equal Access Act: *Board of Education of Westside Community School District v. Mergens.*" *West's Education Law Reporter* 64, no. 3 (1991).

SEE ALSO: First Amendment (1789).

CHILD SUPPORT ENFORCEMENT AMENDMENTS

DATE: August 16, 1984
U.S. STATUTES AT LARGE: 98 Stat. 1305
PUBLIC LAW: 98-378
U.S. CODE: 42 § 651
CATEGORIES: Children's Issues; Women's Issues

Congress set a goal of establishing an efficient system to find absent parents, establish paternity, obtain support orders, and collect back support.

Following a sharp increase in divorce and out-of-wedlock births in the early 1970's, the federal government established the Child Support Enforcement Program to collect money from fathers whose children received welfare. At that time, the collections reimbursed the government and did not go directly to the affected children.

The Child Support Enforcement Amendments of 1984 extended this program to all noncustodial parents and required that each state establish one set of guidelines for determining and modifying child support. These guidelines must take into account all earnings and income of noncustodial parents, define the dollar amounts of support obligations, and provide for the children's health care needs. Courts may deviate from these guidelines in limited circumstances—for example, when the guideline amount would be unjust or inappropriate in particular cases. Individual states vary between judicial and administrative processes, but all must ensure that payments are made to custodial parents. Above all, each state's criteria must take into the consideration the best interests of the children.

P. S. Ramsey

SOURCE FOR FURTHER STUDY
Garfinkel, Irwin, et al., eds. *Fathers Under Fire: The Revolution in Child Support Enforcement.* New York: Russell Sage Foundation, 1998.

SEE ALSO: Parental Kidnapping Prevention Act (1980); Family Violence Prevention and Services Act (1984); Family Support Act (1988); Child Care and Development Block Grant Act (1990).

FAMILY VIOLENCE PREVENTION AND SERVICES ACT

DATE: October 9, 1984
U.S. STATUTES AT LARGE: 98 Stat. 1757
PUBLIC LAW: 98-457
U.S. CODE: 42 § 10401
CATEGORIES: Children's Issues; Crimes and Criminal Procedure; Women's Issues

The act was the first comprehensive federal measure to address the problem of domestic violence.

The Family Violence Prevention and Services Act of 1984, Title III of the Child Abuse Amendments of 1984, provided $65 million to states to fund shelters for abused women and for research into domestic violence. It authorized, among other things, state demonstration grants to provide shelter and related services. It also established a National Clearinghouse on Family Violence.

The programs established by the act were intended to emphasize support for effective community-based projects operated by nonprofit organizations, particularly those whose primary purpose is to operate shelters for victims of family violence and their dependents and those which provide counseling, treatment for alcohol and drug abuse, and self-help services to victims and abusers. The federal government distributed funds under the act according to states' population size, although each state was guaranteed a minimum of $50,000. Sixty percent of this money had to be spent on immediate shelter and related assistance to victims of family violence. In 1994 the act was amended to include provisions making interstate domestic violence a crime. In general, the new provisions make it a crime to cross a state line and commit domestic violence or to cause spouses or intimate partners to cross a state line and then commit domestic violence against them.

Timothy L. Hall

SOURCES FOR FURTHER STUDY
Dalton, Clare, and Elizabeth M. Schneider. *Battered Women and the Law.* New York: Foundation Press, 2001.

Schneider, Elizabeth M. *Battered Women and Feminist Lawmaking.* New Haven, Conn.: Yale University Press, 2000.

SEE ALSO: Parental Kidnapping Prevention Act (1980); Child Support Enforcement Amendments (1984); Family Support Act (1988); Child Care and Development Block Grant Act (1990).

COMPREHENSIVE CRIME CONTROL ACT

DATE: October 12, 1984
U.S. STATUTES AT LARGE: 98 Stat. 1837
PUBLIC LAW: 98-473
CATEGORIES: Crimes and Criminal Procedure

A selective but fundamental overhaul of the federal criminal code, this act expanded the government's law-enforcement power and emphasized the rights of the public over those of the criminal or accused criminal.

Work on this legislation began in the 1970's in a Democratic-controlled Senate. Passage of the bill (by a vote of 94 to 1) reflected close cooperation between Democrat Edward Kennedy and Republican Strom Thurmond. Democrats in the House of Representatives were less cooperative because they wanted a more piecemeal approach to the revision of the federal criminal code than the major recodification supported in the Senate. Thus a collection of procedural and substantive crime proposals were made instead of a systematic overhaul.

Fearing that the Democratic House leadership would block passage of the proposals, Republican Dan Lungren moved to add the crime proposals to an unrelated resolution on continuing appropriations, which would require urgent consideration on the House floor in order to keep the government in operation. Facing reelection in November, 1984, congressional Democrats voted in favor of law and order rather than explain a recorded "no" vote to their constituents. When the joint appropriations resolution emerged from the House, it had tacked to it a Title XI: the Comprehensive Crime Control Act of 1984.

PROVISIONS

For the first time federal judges could detain repeat offenders in preventive detention, without bail, before trial. They could also detain individuals accused of certain major crimes if they were deemed dangerous to the community. In the past, bail was granted unless there was reason to believe the defendant would flee. Moreover, if the detained defendant were later acquitted or the charges dismissed, no recompense would be given for the time spent in jail awaiting trial.

Under the act, federal judges follow a system of guidelines in imposing sentences. The guidelines, established by a presidentially appointed sentencing commission, eliminate disparities in sentences for the same crimes and dismantle the early-release parole system. Under the guidelines, federal prosecutors are able to select charges that carry the likelihood of the longest sentence. Judges are required to explain in writing any departure from the guidelines, while both prosecutors and defendants are entitled to appeal sentences that depart from the standard.

The act also restricts the use of insanity as a defense to individuals who are unable to understand the nature and wrongfulness of their acts. The law prevents expert testimony on the ultimate issue of whether the defendant has a particular mental state or condition. It shifts the burden of proof from the prosecutor, who formerly had to prove that the defendant was not insane, to the defendant, who must prove that he or she is. This change in the insanity defense was a direct response to the John Hinckley case. Hinckley's lawyer proved that Hinckley was psychotic and depressed. The jury found him not guilty because of insanity in the attempted assassination of President Ronald Reagan on March 30, 1981.

Finally, the legislation allows the government to seize profits and assets, including real estate, that are used in organized crime enterprises such as drug trafficking.

Bill Manikas

SOURCES FOR FURTHER STUDY

Abrams, Norman, and Sara Sun Beale. *Federal Criminal Law and Its Enforcement.* 3d ed. Eagan, Minn.: West Group, 2000.

Strazzella, James A., ed. *Federal Role in Criminal Law.* Philadelphia, Pa.: American Academy of Political and Social Science, 1996.

SEE ALSO: Insanity Defense Reform Act (1984); Missing Children's Assistance Act (1984); National Narcotics Act (1984); Victims of Crime Act (1984); Violent Crime Control and Law Enforcement Act (1994).

INSANITY DEFENSE REFORM ACT

DATE: October 12, 1984
U.S. STATUTES AT LARGE: 98 Stat. 2057
PUBLIC LAW: 98-473
U.S. CODE: 18 § 4241
CATEGORIES: Crimes and Criminal Procedure; Health and Welfare

This act was the first federal law to establish a uniform definition of criminal insanity and require mandatory incarceration of the criminally insane; it significantly narrowed the opportunities for mounting a successful insanity defense.

After the 1982 acquittal of John Hinckley, an allegedly insane defendant who had tried to assassinate President Ronald Reagan, public outcry spurred the Congress to place new restrictions on the use of the insanity defense. Previously, insanity as a defense generally was defined in federal courts as lacking the capacity to understand the criminality of one's conduct (the "cognitive" test), or lacking the ability to conform one's behavior to the requirements of law (the "volitional" test).

The Insanity Defense Reform Act limited the definition of insanity to the cognitive test. It also required that the defendant prove insanity with "clear and convincing evidence." Prior to the act, no uniform requirements had been established for the disposition of defendants found to be criminally insane. The act required that all such defendants be committed to a mental hospital and made them ineligible for release until after they could demonstrate that they pose no substantial risk to others.

Steve D. Boilard

SOURCES FOR FURTHER STUDY

Robinson, Daniel N. *Wild Beasts and Idle Humours: The Insanity Defense from Antiquity to the Present.* Cambridge, Mass.: Harvard University Press, 1996.

Simon, Rita James, and David E. Aaronson. *The Insanity Defense: A Critical Assessment of Law and Policy in the Post-Hinckley Era.* New York: Praeger, 1988.

Wrightsman, Lawrence S., et al. *Psychology and the Legal System.* 5th ed. Belmont, Calif.: Wadsworth/Thomson Learning, 2002.

SEE ALSO: Comprehensive Crime Control Act (1984); Victims of Crime Act (1984).

MISSING CHILDREN'S ASSISTANCE ACT

DATE: October 12, 1984
U.S. STATUTES AT LARGE: 98 Stat. 2107
PUBLIC LAW: 98-473
U.S. CODE: 42 § 5771
CATEGORIES: Children's Issues; Crimes and Criminal Procedure; Health and Welfare

This act focused national attention on the approximately one million cases of missing, abducted, and runaway children in the United States.

On October 12, 1984, Congress passed the Missing Children's Assistance Act, leading to establishment of the National Center for Missing and Exploited Children (NCMEC) in Arlington, Virginia. The center was established under the auspices of the Justice Department. A 1982 bill known as the Missing Children's Act had been sponsored by Representative Paul Simon, a Democrat from Illinois, and Senator Paul Hawkins, a Republican from Florida. This bill mandated the entry of data on missing children into the national crime computer maintained by the Federal Bureau of Investigation (FBI). The 1984 law focused further attention on a serious national problem: the growing population of missing, abducted, runaway, and exploited children. According to a somewhat conservative estimate, some one million children fall within this definition.

While media attention has focused on high-profile cases of abduction, sexual molestation, and murder, such as the Adam Walsh case in Florida and the Polly Klaas case in California, the majority of cases that fall under the jurisdiction of the Missing Children's Assistance Act of 1984 involve abductions by family members, particularly in child-custody battles; short-term abduction by strangers, often involving sexual abuse and violence; runaways; and lost or missing children who may have been injured.

The NCMEC is aided by the FBI's crime computer and by other technological advances, including age-progression computer programs that can create images of missing children as they might look many months or years after their initial disappearance. Other techniques, such as infant footprinting, are also invaluable in tracking abducted children. Ongoing school and community-based programs aimed at educating children and parents about the dangers of abduction have contributed to greater social awareness of the problem of missing children, while enthusiastic support from private and corporate donors, including IBM and Intel, have helped safeguard children and youths.

Jo Manning

SOURCE FOR FURTHER STUDY
Forst, Martin Lyle. *Missing Children: The Law Enforcement Response.* Springfield, Ill.: Charles C. Thomas, 1990.

SEE ALSO: Child Abuse Prevention and Treatment Act (1974); Parental Kidnapping Prevention Act (1980); Megan's Law (1996).

NATIONAL NARCOTICS ACT

DATE: October 12, 1984
U.S. STATUTES AT LARGE: 98 Stat. 2168
PUBLIC LAW: 98-473
U.S. CODE: 21 § 1201
CATEGORIES: Crimes and Criminal Procedure; Food and Drugs

This law, chapter 13 of the Comprehensive Crime Control Act of 1984, created the National Drug Enforcement Policy Board as a high-level interagency council to coordinate federal drug-enforcement activities.

The National Narcotics Act was part of an omnibus crime package that had been eleven years in the making. Congress passed this package, the most extensive revision of the federal criminal code since 1968, after President Ronald Reagan made it a high priority. The narcotics act proclaimed that the flow of illegal narcotics into the United States fed drug use that had reached epidemic proportions. Drug trafficking was an eighty-billion-dollar-per-year industry, and government agencies were able to interdict only 5 to 15 percent of the illegal product crossing American borders. The law created the National Drug Enforcement Policy Board (NDEPB) as a high-level board to coordinate drug interdiction activities. The attorney general chaired the board, which included the secretaries of state, defense, treasury, and health and human services along with other officials. It authorized the board to develop and coordinate all U.S. efforts to halt national and international drug trafficking.

William E. Pemberton

SOURCES FOR FURTHER STUDY

Bewley-Taylor, David R. *The United States and International Drug Control, 1909-1997.* New York: Pinter, 1999.

Musto, David F. *The American Disease: Origins of Narcotic Control.* 3d ed. New York: Oxford University Press, 1999.

_____, ed. *Drugs in America: A Documentary History.* New York: New York University Press, 2002.

SEE ALSO: Organized Crime Control Act (1970); Comprehensive Drug Abuse Prevention and Control Act (1970); Comprehensive Crime Control Act (1984); Violent Crime Control and Law Enforcement Act (1994).

VICTIMS OF CRIME ACT

DATE: October 12, 1984
U.S. STATUTES AT LARGE: 98 Stat. 2170
PUBLIC LAW: 98-473
U.S. CODE: 42 § 10601
CATEGORIES: Health and Welfare

This legislation established a Crime Victims Fund to help finance state compensation programs as well as assist victims of federal crimes. Demonstrating the federal commitment to assist crime victims, the Victims of Crime Act quickly became a key component in the funding of programs throughout the nation.

In the early 1980's, many groups worked for the right of crime victims to receive fair treatment. In 1981, President Ronald Reagan, a supporter of the movement, proclaimed an annual National Victims of Crime Week. In April, 1982, Reagan established the President's Task Force on Victims of Crime, which made sixty-eight recommendations to help victims. On October 18, 1982, he signed the Victim and Witness Protection Act, which increased penalties on those who tried to intimidate victims or witnesses, mandated restitution to victims from offenders, and required the consideration of victim impact statements at sentencing in federal criminal trials.

The Victims of Crime Act of 1984 (VOCA) established the Crime Victims Fund, which at first had a cap of $100 million a year. Each state was to receive at least $100,000, and 5 percent of the fund would go to victims of federal crimes. Rather than coming from the taxpayer, revenues for the fund are obtained from fines, penalty fees, forfeitures of bail bonds, and literary profits from convicted offenders. By 1988, the fund was supporting fifteen hundred programs a year, and its maximum was increased to $150 million. VOCA was well received by the public, and it encouraged states to do more to assist victims.

Thomas T. Lewis

SOURCE FOR FURTHER STUDY
Adams, Aileen, ed. *Victims of Crime Act of 1984 as Amended: A Report to the President and the Congress.* Collingdale, Pa.: DIANE, 1998.

SEE ALSO: Family Violence Prevention and Services Act (1984); Comprehensive Crime Control Act (1984); Insanity Defense Reform Act (1984); Missing Children's Assistance Act (1984); Violence Against Women Act (1994).

MOTOR VEHICLE THEFT LAW ENFORCEMENT ACT

DATE: October 25, 1984
U.S. STATUTES AT LARGE: 98 Stat. 2754
PUBLIC LAW: 98-547
CATEGORIES: Crimes and Criminal Procedure

This law established criminal penalties for trafficking in stolen vehicles and their parts. To facilitate prosecutions, it required automobile manufacturers to mark fourteen major car parts with a vehicle identification number (VIN).

Pressure for legislation to combat vehicle theft stemmed from a dramatic increase in the number of stolen automobiles. Organized crime controlled networks of "chop shops" that dismantled stolen cars and sold their parts, costing the nation five billion dollars annually. The law required manufacturers to place vehicle identification number (VIN) marks on major parts of automobile models that were subject to higher than average theft rates. In response to company complaints that the proposal added to car costs, the final act signed by President Ronald Reagan limited the number of marked parts to fourteen and required each manufacturer to mark no more than fourteen of its models. It established penalties for altering VIN marks (a fine of up to five thousand dollars and/or a maximum of five years in prison) and for trafficking in stolen vehicles and their parts (up to twenty-five thousand dollars and/or ten years in prison). The secretary of transportation selected the parts and models to be marked.

William E. Pemberton

SOURCES FOR FURTHER STUDY

Stewart, M. G., et al. *Evaluation of Methods and Costs to Mark Vehicle Parts for Theft Prevention.* Washington, D.C.: National Highway Traffic Safety Adminstration, 1988.

United States. *Motor Vehicle Theft Law Enforcement Act of 1984.* Washington, D.C.: Government Printing Office, 1984.

SEE ALSO: Motor Vehicle Theft Act (1919).

FOOD SECURITY ACT

ALSO KNOWN AS: Farm Act of 1985
DATE: December 23, 1985
U.S. STATUTES AT LARGE: 99 Stat. 1535
PUBLIC LAW: 99-198
CATEGORIES: Agriculture; Environment and Conservation; Food and Drugs

This law contained conservation provisions to reduce soil erosion, to prevent an overabundance of grain crops, and to protect wetlands.

The Food Security Act (FSA) created the largest change in farm-subsidy programs since the middle of the twentieth century. Prior to the act, the U.S. Department of Agriculture (USDA) estimated that 3.1 billion tons of soil were eroding annually on approximately 420 million acres of cropland, and 3.7 million acres of land were being converted annually from pasture and wetlands to cropland. Under the FSA, agricultural producers could be denied farm benefits for implementing improper land-use practices on cropland and non-cropland. Objectives of the 1985 FSA were to reduce the increasing problems of sedimentation and water and wind erosion, to enhance water quality and habitat for fish and wildlife populations, to protect the long-term ability to produce food and fiber resources, to reduce the supply of grain crops, and to provide income to farmers.

THE SWAMPBUSTER PROVISION

The Swampbuster provision was established to discourage the conversion of wetlands to agricultural land. This provision was considered an essential component of the legislation, since more than one-half of the wetlands that existed when the United States was first settled had been eliminated by the mid-1980's. Protecting wetlands would have significant implications in controlling floodwaters and providing recreational opportunities. Under the Swampbuster provision, farmers who produced agricultural crops on wetlands converted after December 23, 1985, would be ineligible for farm benefits, including commodity loans and purchases, subsidies, and crop insurance. In addition, benefits would be lost not only on converted land but also on all lands farmers wanted to enroll into the program.

THE SODBUSTER PROVISION

The Sodbuster provision was similar to Swampbuster but focused on the conversion of highly erodible land to agricultural production. This provision applied to highly erodible land that was not planted to annually tilled crops during the period between 1981 and 1985. For land to be considered highly erodible, potential erosion had to be estimated at more than eight times the rate at which soil could maintain continued productivity. Farmers who produced commodities on previously uncultivated land with highly erodible soils after December 23, 1985, were ineligible for federal farm programs unless the owner farmed under a conservation plan approved by the local soil and water conservation district. Natural-resource managers estimated that implementing the Sodbuster and Swampbuster programs would prevent the conversion of more than 225 million acres of grasslands, forests, and wetlands to croplands.

THE CONSERVATION COMPLIANCE PROVISION

The Conservation Compliance provision was developed to discourage the production of crops on highly erodible cropland where land was not protected from erosion. Under this provision, if landowners produced crops on fields with highly erodible soils without an approved conservation plan, they could lose their eligibility for specific USDA benefits. Conservation Compliance applied to land where annually tilled crops were grown at least once between 1981 and 1985; the provision was to apply to all highly erodible land in annual crop production by 1990.

THE CONSERVATION RESERVE PROGRAM

The Agricultural Stabilization and Conservation Service (ASCS) administered the CRP provision of the Farm Bill with the intention of converting up to 45 million acres of highly erodible farmland to permanent cover. Federal officials hoped that this program would reduce soil erosion by 760 million tons, stream sedimentation by in excess of 200 million tons, pesticide use by 61 million pounds, and fertilizer use by approximately 1.4 million tons annually. Specific objectives of the CRP, were to assist in controlling soil erosion, reduce surplus crop production, improve water quality, and provide wildlife habitat.

Under the CRP, landowners would submit bids through the ASCS to establish ten-year contracts with the USDA. While under contract, landowners received annual rental payments for converting highly erodible cropland to permanent vegetative cover for the duration of the contracts. Participants in the program were required to establish permanent vegetative cover (grasses, legumes, forest plantations, field windbreaks, shallow-water areas, or a combination of these practices) as quickly as possible. Approximately one-half the cost was shared by the USDA. In some states, additional funds were available to farmers for developing selected permanent cover on CRP lands for wildlife species.

IMPACT

By implementing the conservation provisions of the 1985 FSA, the USDA was able to provide economic benefits to landowners and to conserve natural resources on agricultural lands. These programs would produce large-scale changes in the composition of agricultural landscapes in the United States by the early 1990's.

In the first year under the 1985 FSA, from March, 1986, through the fourth sign-up in February, 1987, nearly 18 million acres were enrolled in the CRP alone. One year later, more than 25 million acres had been enrolled.

Henry Campa III

Sources for Further Study

Berner, Alfred. "The 1985 Farm Act and Its Implications for Wildlife." In *Audubon Wildlife Reports 1988/1989*, edited by T. Chandler and L. Labate. New York: Audubon Society and Academic Press, 1989.

Bjerke, Keith. "An Overview of the Agricultural Resources Conservation Program." In *The Conservation Reserve—Yesterday, Today, and Tomorrow*, edited by Linda Joyce, John Mitchell, and Melvin Skold. Fort Collins, Colo.: U.S. Department of Agriculture, 1991.

Burger, Loren, Jr., Eric Kurzejeski, Thomas Dailey, and Mark Ryan. "Structural Characteristics of Vegetation in CRP Fields in Northern Missouri and Their Suitability as Bobwhite Habitat." *Transactions of the 55th North American Wildlife and Natural Resources Conference* 55 (March, 1990): 74-83.

Chapman, E. Wayne. "Rationale and Legislation for the Creation of the Conservation Reserve Program." In *Impacts of the Conservation Reserve Program in the Great Plains*, edited by John Mitchell. Fort Collins, Colo.: U.S. Department of Agriculture, 1988.

Hayden, F. Gregory. "Wetlands Provisions in the 1985 and 1990 Farm Bills." *Journal of Economic Issues* 24 (June, 1990): 575-587.

Isaacs, Barry, and David Howell. "Opportunities for Enhancing Wildlife Benefits Through the Conservation Reserve Program." *Transactions of the 53rd North American Wildlife and Natural Resources Conference* 53 (March, 1988): 222-231.

Kurzejeski, Eric, Loren Burger, Jr., M. Monson, and Robert Lenkner. "Wildlife Conservation Attitudes and Land Use Intentions of Conservation Reserve Program Participants in Missouri." *Wildlife Society Bulletin* 20 (Fall, 1992): 253-259.

Payne, Neil, and Fred Bryant. *Techniques for Wildlife Habitat Management of Uplands*. San Francisco: McGraw-Hill, 1994.

Schenck, Eric, and Lonnie Williamson. "Conservation Reserve Program Effects on Wildlife and Recreation." In *The Conservation Reserve—Yesterday, Today, and Tomorrow*, edited by Linda Joyce, John Mitchell, and Melvin Skold. Fort Collins, Colo.: U.S. Department of Agriculture, 1991.

See also: Reclamation Act (1902); Pure Food and Drugs Act (1906); Agricultural Marketing Act (1929): Taylor Grazing Act (1934); Multiple Use-Sustained Yield Act (1960).

EMERGENCY PLANNING AND COMMUNITY RIGHT-TO-KNOW ACT

ALSO KNOWN AS: Title III of Superfund Amendments Reauthorization Act
DATE: October 17, 1986
U.S. STATUTES AT LARGE: 100 Stat. 1741
PUBLIC LAW: 99-499
U.S. CODE: 42 § 11001 et seq.
CATEGORIES: Environment and Conservation; Health and Welfare

This law required federal, state, and local governments and industry to work together to keep the public informed about toxic chemicals and to develop plans to deal with emergencies.

Enacted in 1986 as part of the Superfund Reauthorization Act, the Emergency Planning and Community Right-to-Know Act (EPCRA) was passed to increase public awareness of the nature and extent of hazardous and toxic substances in communities and to require governmental emergency planning and notification. The law was enacted after the accidental release of chemicals at a Union Carbide plant in Bhopal, India, claimed thousands of lives in 1985.

PROVISIONS

Congress decided that legislation was needed to prevent similar accidents in the United States. As a first step toward establishing an inventory of all the toxic chemicals used, stored, and disposed of in the United States, EPCRA made it mandatory for every owner and operator of a facility containing hazardous substances to register the information officially. Each state governor was required to establish a state emergency response commission (SERC), which was in turn responsible for designating emergency planning districts and appointing local emergency planning committees (LEPC) for each district; local governments were made responsible for the preparation and implementation of emergency plans. The state committees, whose members were required to have technical experience in emergency response, were to supervise and coordinate the local communities. Under EPCRA, the state committees were also responsible for establishing procedures for receiving and processing requests for information and for designating an official information coordinator.

EPCRA stipulated that the state committees designate the local districts within nine months of the law's passage. Each local committee was to reflect, as far as possible, those segments of the community with an interest in emergency planning. Each was to have representatives from local environmental and community groups; transportation, law enforcement, civil defense, and firefighting agencies; health departments and hospitals; broadcast and print media; and owners and operators of facilities using hazardous substances. Finally, each local committee was required to prepare an emergency plan (to be reviewed annually), establish provisions for public notification of committee activities, and hold public meetings to discuss the emergency plan. EPCRA permitted state committees to revise their designations and appointments, and local citizens could petition the state committees to modify the membership of local committees. The law also identified the conditions under which facilities were to notify the local committee and the state commission in the event that a toxic substance had been released in an amount exceeding the threshold quantity established for that substance.

LOCAL EMERGENCY PLANS

The local emergency planning committee was required under EPCRA to complete an emergency plan; evaluate the need for resources to develop, implement, and exercise the plan; and determine if additional resources were necessary. The local committee was made responsible for identifying the facilities that were subject to EPCRA, the routes used to transport hazardous substances, and any additional facilities that might pose risks because of their proximity to facilities with hazardous substances. The plan was to contain the methods and procedures that facility owners and operators and local emergency and medical personnel were to follow in responding to releases of toxic substances. A community emergency coordinator and facility emergency coordinators were to be appointed to implement the plan. The plan was also to include the methods for determining when a release occurred, the area and population affected by such a release, the community's available emergency equipment and facilities, and the names of people responsible for operating the equipment and facilities. Training programs for local emergency response and medical personnel were also called for, as well as methods and schedules for exercising the emergency plan.

Once the plan had been completed by the local district, the local planning committee was to submit it to the state emergency response commission for review. The commission could make further recommendations. A regional response team established under EPCRA could also review the plan, but the law specified that reviews were not to delay implementation of a plan.

NOTIFICATION OF CHEMICAL RELEASES

All owners of facilities subject to EPCRA requirements were required to notify the state emergency response commission for the state in which each facility was located. Notification of a release or anticipation of a release of an extremely hazardous substance was to be made to the local emergency planning committee. Notification would include the chemical name or identity of the substance to be released and identify whether the material was an extremely hazardous substance. Notification also had to include indication of any health effects that were anticipated from the release and, if appropriate, medical advice for exposed individuals, as well as what precautions were required as a result of the release. Facilities could also be required to provide information to health professionals upon request.

OTHER PROVISIONS

EPCRA also provided appropriations for training and authorized federal officials who were already carrying out existing federal programs for emergency training when EPCRA was enacted to provide education programs for federal, state, and local employees in hazard mitigation, emergency preparedness, fire prevention and control, disaster response, long-term disaster recovery, national security, technological and natural hazards, and emergency processes.

Finally, EPCRA required that owners and operators of plants and facilities that had to provide a material data safety sheet for a hazardous chemical under the 1970 Occupational Safety and Health Act to submit a copy of the sheet for each hazardous chemical to the appropriate local emergency planning committee, state emergency response commission, and fire department with jurisdiction over the facility. The inventories were also to be made available to the general public.

RESPONSE AND CONSEQUENCES

Industry officials objected strongly to the act's requirements that companies submit information on the chemicals they use. Often, the identity of these chemicals was considered to be a trade secret. Industry officials argued that if information submitted to government agencies was made available to the general public, the government should not be permitted to require the submission of information that qualified as a trade secret. As a consequence, EPCRA included a provision that facilities could withhold information upon demonstrating that it constituted a trade secret.

EPCRA provided for both criminal and civil penalties for individuals and organizations found to be in violation of the law. The EPA could assess administrative penalties as high as $25,000 per day per violation for the first incident, and up to $75,000 per day for subsequent violations. EPCRA also authorized the use of citizen suits, which, for example, allowed victims of toxic dumping to bring lawsuits against those proven to be responsible. Civil actions could be brought by state or local authorities against a facility owner or operator for failing to submit a material data safety sheet, a followup emergency notice, or an inventory form, or for failing to comply with any of the regulations.

Amy Bloom

SOURCES FOR FURTHER STUDY

Arbuckle, J. Gordon, Timothy A. Vanderver, Jr., and Paul A. J. Wilson. *SARA Title III Law and Regulations.* Rockville, Md.: Government Institutes, 1989.

Berger, Donald A., and Christopher Harris. *A Guide to Emergency Preparedness and Community Right-to-Know.* New York: Executive Enterprises, 1988.

Grad, Frank. *Grad on Environmental Law.* New York: Matthew Bender, 1994.

Lowry, George, and Robert Lowry. *Right-to-Know and Emergency Planning.* Chelsea, Mich.: Lewis, 1985.

Stoloff, Neil. *Regulating the Environment: An Overview of Environmental Law.* Dobbs, Ferry, N.Y.: Oceana, 1991.

SEE ALSO: Resource Conservation and Recovery Act (1976); Low-Level Radioactive Waste Policy Act (1980); Superfund Act (1980); Nuclear Waste Policy Act (1983).

TAX REFORM ACT OF 1986

DATE: October 22, 1986
U.S. STATUTES AT LARGE: 100 Stat. 2085
PUBLIC LAW: 99-514
CATEGORIES: Tariffs and Taxation

The most sweeping reform of the federal income tax law since World War II, this law reduced top marginal income tax rates substantially and eliminated or reduced several popular deductions.

The purposes of the Tax Reform Act of 1986 were to reduce tax rates and to broaden the tax base. The basic rate of corporate tax was reduced from 46 percent to 34 percent, and the marginal rate of individual income tax at higher levels of income fell from 50 percent to 28 percent. The Tax Reform Act also eliminated investment tax credits, slowed depreciation schedules, and scrapped several other deductions for corporations. On the individual side, it eliminated sales tax deduction, scrapped preferential treatment of capital gains, and imposed limits on passive losses and deductibility of individual retirement account (IRA) contributions.

The Tax Reform Act enjoyed broad bipartisan congressional support. Critics argued that it would reduce nonresident investment, the gross national product (GNP), and the competitiveness of U.S. business. Supporters argued that it would remove distortions from the economy and improve fairness. Nonresident investment proved to be stable, and savings increased marginally in the 1987-1989 period. Fairness in the tax system, however, did not improve. The Congress repealed parts of the act in 1990; the top tax rate increased to 31 percent, payroll taxes increased, and itemized deductions were limited.

Srinivasan Ragothaman

SOURCES FOR FURTHER STUDY

Joint Commission of Taxation. *General Explanation of Tax Reform Act 1986.* Washington, D.C.: Government Printing Office, 1987.

Prentice-Hall Staff. *Complete Guide to the Tax Reform Act of 1986, as Passed by the Congress and Sent to the President: Explanation, Code Sections as Amended, Committee Reports, Index.* Paramus, N.J.: Prentice-Hall Information Services, 1986.

Reams, Bernard D., Jr., and Margaret H. McDermott. *Tax Reform 1986: A Legislative History of the Tax Reform Act of 1986. The Law, Reports, Hearings, Debates, and Documents.* Buffalo, N.Y.: William S. Hein, 1987.

Slemrod, Joel, ed. *Do Taxes Matter? The Impact of the Tax Reform Act of 1986.* Cambridge, Mass.: MIT Press, 1991.

Tax Reform Act of 1986: Quick Reference Guide. Chicago: Dearborn Financial Publishing, 1986.

SEE ALSO: Sixteenth Amendment (1913); Earned Income Tax Credit (1975); Economic Recovery Tax Act and Omnibus Budget Reconciliation Act (1981).

IMMIGRATION REFORM AND CONTROL ACT OF 1986

DATE: November 6, 1986
U.S. STATUTES AT LARGE: 100 Stat. 3359
PUBLIC LAW: 99-603
CATEGORIES: Immigration; Latinos

This law provided for the legalization of illegal aliens and established sanctions against employers who hire undocumented workers.

The Immigration Reform and Control Act (IRCA) was signed into law by President Ronald Reagan on November 6, 1986. The act amended the Immigration and Nationality Act of 1965 and was based in part on the findings and recommendations of the Select Commission on Immigration and Refugee Policy (1978-1981). In its 1981 report to Congress, this commission had proposed that the United States continue to accept large numbers of immigrants and enact a program of amnesty for undocumented aliens already in the United States. To deter further migration of undocumented aliens to the United States, the commission also proposed to make the employment of illegal aliens a punishable offense.

DEVELOPMENT OF THE BILL

These proposals were incorporated into the Simpson-Mazzoli bill, a first version of which was introduced in 1982. In the five years between its introduction and its enactment, the bill ran into opposition from a variety of quarters. Agricultural interests, especially growers of perishable commodities, were concerned that the proposed employer sanctions would jeopardize their labor supply. Mexican American advocacy groups also opposed employer sanctions, while organized labor and restrictionists who were concerned about the massive influx of foreign workers favored employer sanctions. Many liberals and humanitarians supported the notion of legalizing the status of undocumented aliens and expressed concerns over potential discrimination against them.

In the 1980's, the bill repeatedly was pronounced dead only to be revived again as various lawmakers, notably Representatives Leon Panetta, Charles Schumer, and Peter Rodino, introduced compromises and amendments to respond to their constituencies or to overcome opposition by congressional factions. Differences also developed between the House Democratic leadership and the Republican White House over funding the legalization program. On October 15, 1986, the House at last approved the bill, by a vote of 238 to 173; the Senate approved the bill on October 17, by a vote of 63 to 24.

PROVISIONS

The major components of the Immigration Control and Reform Act provided for the control of illegal immigration (Title I), the legalization of undocumented aliens (Title II), and the reform of legal immigration (Title III). Other sections of the act provided for reports to Congress (Title IV), state assistance for the incarceration costs of illegal aliens and certain Cuban nationals (Title V), the creation of a commission for the study of international migration and cooperative economic development (Title VI), and federal responsibility for deportable and excludable aliens convicted of crimes (Title VII).

A major objective of the IRCA, the control of illegal immigration, was to be achieved by imposing sanctions on employers. The IRCA made it unlawful for any person knowingly to hire, recruit, or refer for a fee any alien not authorized to work in the United States. Before hiring new employees, employers would be required to examine certain specified documents to verify a job applicant's identity and authority to work.

PENALTIES TO NONCOMPLIANT EMPLOYERS

The act established civil and criminal penalties, and employers could be fined up to two thousand dollars per unauthorized alien, even for a first offense. Employers who demonstrated a pattern of knowingly hiring undocumented aliens could face felony penalties of up to six months' imprisonment and/or a three-thousand-dollar fine per violation. Employers also were required to keep appropriate records. Failure to do so could result in a civil fine of up to one thousand dollars. In order to allow time for a public education campaign to become effective, penalties against employers for hiring undocumented aliens were not phased in until June, 1987.

LEGALIZATION OF UNDOCUMENT ALIENS

The second major objective of the IRCA, the legalization of undocumented aliens, was to be realized by granting temporary residence status to aliens who had entered the United States illegally prior to January 1, 1982, and who had resided in the United States continuously since then. They could be granted permanent residence status after eighteen months if they could demonstrate a minimal understanding of English and some knowledge of the history and government of the United States. After a five-year period of permanent residence, they would become eligible for citizenship.

The act also permitted the attorney general to grant legal status to aliens who could show that they had entered the United States prior to January, 1972, and lived in the country since then. Newly legalized aliens were barred from most forms of public assistance for five years, although exceptions could be made for emergency medical care, aid to the blind or disabled, or other assistance deemed to be in the interest of public health.

SUPPORT FROM FARMERS

To assure passage of the bill, support of the growers in the West and Southwest was essential. After protracted negotiations, the growers succeeded in getting the kind of legislation that assured them of a continued supply of temporary agricultural workers. The new program differed from earlier bracero programs by providing for the legalization of special agricultural workers who could work anywhere and who could become eligible for permanent resident status or for citizenship. The IRCA granted temporary residence status to aliens who had performed field labor in perishable agricultural commodities in the United States for at least ninety days during the twelve-month period ending May 1, 1986, as well as to persons who could demonstrate to the Immigration and Naturalization Service that they had performed appropriate agricultural field labor for ninety days in three successive previous years while residing in the United States for six months in each year.

EXPANDING THE H-2 PROGRAM

The act also revised and expanded an existing temporary foreign worker program known as H-2. In case of a shortage of seasonal farmworkers, employers could apply to the secretary of labor no more than sixty days in advance of needing workers. The employer also was required to try to recruit domestic workers for the jobs. H-2 also provided that during fiscal years 1990-1993, additional special agricultural workers could be admitted to temporary residence status as "replenishment workers." Their admission was contingent upon certification of the need for such workers by the secretaries of labor and of agriculture. Replenishment workers who performed ninety days of field work in perishable agricultural commodities in each of the first three years would be eligible for permanent resident status. They were, however, disqualified from public assistance. In order to become eligible for citizenship, they would have to perform seasonal agricultural services for ninety days during five separate years.

CUBAN AND HAITIAN IMMIGRANTS

The IRCA also provided permanent resident status for one hundred thousand specified Cubans and Haitians who entered the United States prior to January 1, 1982. The law increased quotas from former colonies and dependencies from five hundred to six thousand and provided for the admission of five thousand immigrants annually for two years, to be chosen from nationals of thirty-six countries with low rates of immigration. Altogether, the Immigration Reform and Control Act led to the legalization of the status of three million aliens; however, IRCA was not as successful in curbing illegal immigration as had been anticipated.

Mindful of the potential for discrimination, Congress established an Office of Special Counsel in the Department of Justice to investigate and prosecute charges of discrimination connected with unlawful immigration practices. The act also required states to verify the status of noncitizens applying for public aid and provided that states be reimbursed for the implementation costs of this provision. To reimburse states for the public assistance, health, and education costs resulting from legalizing aliens, the act provided for the appropriation of one billion dollars in each of the four fiscal years following its enactment.

Helmut J. Schmeller

SOURCES FOR FURTHER STUDY

Bean, Frank D., Georges Vernez, and Charles B. Keely. *Opening and Closing the Doors: Evaluating Immigration Reform and Control.* Washington, D.C.: Rand Corporation and the Urban Institute, 1989.

Daniels, Roger. "The 1980's and Beyond." In *Coming to America: A History of Immigration and Ethnicity in American Life.* New York: HarperCollins, 1990.

Fuchs, Lawrence H. *The American Kaleidoscope: Race, Ethnicity, and the Civic Culture.* Hannover, N.H.: University Press of New England, 1990.

Ueda, Reed. *Postwar Immigrant America: A Social History.* Boston: St. Martin's Press, 1994.

Zolberg, Aristide R. "Reforming the Back Door: The Immigration Reform and Control Act of 1986 in Historical Perspective." In *Immigration Reconsidered: History, Sociology, and Politics,* edited by Virginia Yans-McLaughlin. New York: Oxford University Press, 1990.

SEE ALSO: Immigration and Nationality Act of 1952 (1952); Refugee Relief Act (1953); Immigration and Nationality Act Amendments of 1965 (1965); Amerasian Homecoming Act (1987); Immigration Act of 1990 (1990).

McKinney Homeless Assistance Act

Date: July 22, 1987
U.S. Statutes at Large: 101 Stat. 482
Public law: 100-77
Categories: Health and Welfare

This act provided a substantial increase in federal funds for emergency support to shelter programs for the homeless.

The passage of the Stewart McKinney Homeless Assistance Act in the summer of 1987 represented the culmination of a decade of debate about homelessness, its causes, and the federal government's responsibility to respond to the problem. The prominence of the issue in 1980's was the result of the visibility of homeless people on the streets of America cities.

The "New Homeless"

The homeless of the 1980's were a different group both in size and in demographics from those who had traditionally occupied the skid rows of large cities. The "new homeless," although also plagued with alcohol and drug problems, were more likely to be younger and to be members of ethnic or racial minorities. Further, they were more likely to be completely lacking in shelter and employment of any kind. Finally, there were many more women and children among the new homeless.

Call for Action

A 1987 report by the United States Conference of Mayors found that there had been a 25 percent increase in the number of families with children seeking shelter. In 1986, New York City provided shelter in welfare hotels for an average of thirty-five hundred families every month. During the 1980's, families were the fastest-growing segment of the homeless population and, by the end of the decade, constituted approximately 30 percent of the homeless. The visibility and changed nature of the homeless population were largely responsible for the pressure placed on the federal government to respond to the problem.

During the 1986-1987 winter, several events helped motivate Congress to act on emergency housing assistance. A U.S. Conference of Mayors study released the week before Christmas announced a marked increase in the number of people seeking emergency shelter. The study found that a quarter of the demand was not satisfied with the existing provision of shelter and food by private charity groups. It called for Congress to provide federal aid to the overtaxed services of local governments and private groups. The National Coalition for the Homeless released a similar report that winter, demonstrating that families with children were the fastest growing group among the homeless. To encourage support for legislation, Mitch Snyder and actor Martin Sheen organized a "Grate American Sleep Out," encouraging members of Congress to spend the night on the streets of Washington, D.C. Some did, including Stewart B. McKinney, the ranking minority member of the House Subcommittee on Housing and Community Development and an active supporter of aid to the homeless.

GOVERNMENT RESPONSE

Prior to this period, Congress had allocated some increased aid, through existing housing programs, to the homeless, and in 1982 the Housing and Community Development Subcommittee of the House Committee on Banking, Finance, and Urban Affairs held a series of hearings on the problems of the homeless.

However, in 1986 the Reagan administration and Congress argued over the number of homeless and whether that number warranted increased federal aid. Many congressional Democrats also argued that the increasing number of homeless was the result of 70 percent cuts in federal housing programs and tightened eligibility requirements for welfare, which had moved members of the working poor to the ranks of the homeless. In its final report on the McKinney bill, the House subcommittee argued: "In a nation so blessed with natural resources and material wealth, as in the United States, there is no justifiable reason for the Federal Government to abdicate an appropriate role to assist these most needy citizens."

When the emergency aid package was first introduced in January of 1987, President Reagan threatened to veto the package as unnecessary and fiscally irresponsible. The bill nevertheless passed with broad bipartisan support in both houses of Congress (65-8 in the Senate and 301-115 in the House) and was signed into law by the president on July 22, 1987. The bill was named after Stewart B. McKinney, who had died on May 7, 1987, of AIDS, complicated by pneumonia that had resulted from his participation in the "Grate American Sleep Out" in March.

PROVISIONS AND IMPACT

The McKinney Act appropriated $442 million for homeless assistance in fiscal year 1987 and promised $616 million for 1988. The funds were to be channeled through a number of existing housing programs and provided housing assistance, subsidies for existing private and public shelter programs, funds for rehabilitation of abandoned buildings to provide increased shelter, and help for programs of health care, mental health, and assistance to the handicapped serving the homeless. It also created an Interagency Commission on the Homeless, made up of representatives of various federal agencies, with oversight responsibilities for programs assisting the homeless.

Passage of the McKinney Act was important because it acknowledged the extent to which the needs of the homeless in the United States had reached emergency proportions and admitted a federal responsibility to respond to that emergency. In the short term, it certainly helped ease the burden of care that small private shelters throughout the country were experiencing in trying to meet the increased demands for aid. Even its short-term effect, however, was less than its supporters had hoped, because the money authorized in the bill was never fully allocated, a pattern that continued in later years. Spiraling federal budget deficits through the 1980's made the intentions of the bill increasingly difficult to fulfill.

With its focus on the provision of emergency assistance, the McKinney Act did little to provide any long-term solutions to the problems underlying homelessness. Its emphasis on shelter support meant that there was less attention to addressing the root causes of homelessness or to the provision of larger quantities of stable low-income housing. The problem of homelessness did not disappear as a result of the McKinney Act, but the prominence of the issue of homelessness diminished. A study by the United States

Conference of Mayors in 1990 found declining public concern about and support for aiding the homeless. The public had become weary of the issue and demonstrated a marked lack of sympathy for the plight of homeless people. As Congress and the president struggled with a burgeoning federal deficit that made increased funding for any social programs unlikely, the issue faded from the public agenda.

Katy Jean Harriger

SOURCES FOR FURTHER STUDY

Belcher, John R., and Frederick A. DiBlasio. *Helping the Homeless: Where Do We Go from Here?* Lexington, Mass.: Lexington Books, 1990.

Bingham, Richard D., Roy E. Green, and Sammis B. White, eds. *The Homeless in Contemporary Society.* Newbury Park, Calif.: Sage Publications, 1987.

Hollyman, Stephenie. *We the Homeless: Portraits of America's Displaced People.* Text by Victoria Irwin. New York: Philosophical Library, 1988.

Hombs, Mary Ellen, and Mitch Snyder. *Homelessness in America: A Forced March to Nowhere.* Washington, D.C.: Community for Creative Non-Violence, 1982.

Kozol, Jonathan. *Rachel and Her Children: Homeless Families in America.* New York: Fawcett Columbine, 1988.

Rossi, Peter. *Without Shelter: Homelessness in the 1980's.* New York: Priority Press Publications, 1989.

SEE ALSO: Social Security Act (1935); Aid to Families with Dependent Children (1935); Refugee Relief Act (1953); Mental Retardation Facilities and Community Mental Health Centers Construction Act (1963); Medicare and Medicaid Amendments (1965); Juvenile Justice and Delinquency Prevention Act (1974); Americans with Disabilities Act (1990); Personal Responsibility and Work Opportunity Reconciliation Act (1996).

INF TREATY

DATE: Signed December 8, 1987
CATEGORIES: Foreign Relations; Treaties and Agreements

This nuclear arms control agreement eliminated an entire class of American and Soviet missiles in the European theater.

In the late 1950's and early 1960's, at the height of the Cold War, the Soviet Union deployed nuclear missiles, SS-4's and SS-5's, capable of reaching Western European countries. U.S. nuclear missiles capable of reaching Soviet targets were deployed in small numbers in the United Kingdom, Italy, and Turkey in the early 1960's. These missiles were removed after Soviet missiles in Cuba were withdrawn in the wake of the 1962 Cuban Missile Crisis. Thereafter, there were no land-based intermediate-range missiles in Europe until 1983.

RENEWED NUCLEAR THREATS

Beginning in the late 1970's and early 1980's, the Soviet Union began to deploy new and modernized intermediate-range missiles, SS-20's. Coupled with the simultaneous deployment of the new Backfire bomber, these nuclear forces roused concerns in Western Europe about security and the nuclear deterrence capability of the North Atlantic Treaty Organization (NATO). Led by West German chancellor Helmut Schmidt, NATO leaders concluded that the increased threat posed to Europe by the mobile and highly accurate SS-20 missiles, each capable of carrying three independently targetable nuclear warheads, needed a strong NATO response. In December, 1979, NATO foreign and defense ministries adopted a dual-track strategy of deploying U.S. intermediate-range ballistic and cruise missiles with a total of 572 nuclear warheads, while negotiating with the Soviets on arms control treaties to reduce the overall nuclear threat as well as the SS-20 threat. Pershing II and ground-launched cruise missiles (GLCM) were to be deployed in Belgium, the Netherlands, the Federal Republic of Germany, the United Kingdom, and Italy. The first deployment of these missiles began in late 1983.

NEGOTIATING A COMPROMISE

The negotiations on an intermediate-range nuclear forces (INF) treaty began in November, 1980, at the end of Jimmy Carter's presidency. With the election of Ronald Reagan as U.S. president, these talks proceeded fitfully. In November, 1981, Reagan presented his new zero-option proposal in the INF talks, offering to cancel planned deployment of the Pershing II and GLCMs if the Soviets would dismantle their SS-20, SS-4, and SS-5 missiles. In response, Soviet president Leonid Brezhnev sought a moratorium on the deployment of new intermediate-range launchers in Europe.

Faced with U.S. and Soviet negotiating positions unacceptable to both sides, chief U.S. and Soviet negotiators in Geneva, Paul Nitze and Yuli Kvitsinskiy, devised a compromise formula. It called for a two-thirds reduction in the SS-20's directed at Western Europe in exchange for the elimination of Pershing II deployments, but not the GLCMs. The compromise formula was rejected by both Moscow and Washington, D.C. When, in November, 1983, the German Bundestag voted in favor of the deployments of the Pershing II and cruise missiles, the Soviet Union walked out of the INF talks, thus ending the first phase of these negotiations.

The INF talks did not resume until March, 1985, by which time two significant developments had occurred. Mikhail Gorbachev had assumed leadership of the Soviet Union and, over the period of the next several years, made a series of concessions that eliminated the major differences in positions in the INF talks between the United States and the Soviet Union. On the U.S. side, there was mounting popular pressure to pursue serious arms control negotiations with the Soviet Union, and Reagan, during his second term in office, gave this issue priority. The INF negotiations were complex and featured prominently in the Reagan-Gorbachev summits in Geneva in November, 1985, and Reykjavik in October, 1986. In April, 1987, Gorbachev proposed an INF treaty that would eliminate both long-range and shorter-range intermediate missiles in Europe, a proposal expanded later to include such missiles globally—in effect, a global zero-option. With U.S. and German acceptance of the global zero option and Soviet acquiescence to on-site verification, the last stumbling blocks to the treaty were removed.

PROVISIONS AND RATIFICATION

This second phase ended with the signing of the INF Treaty by President Reagan and General Secretary Gorbachev on December 8, 1987, at a summit meeting in Washington, D.C. The treaty consisted of seventeen articles, supplemented by two protocols and a memorandum of understanding (MOU). The first protocol defined the elimination procedures. The second protocol spelled out the purpose, rules, and procedures for conducting on-site inspections regarding treaty compliance. The MOU provided for an accounting by each party of the number and location of missiles and other systems and facilities covered in the treaty.

The treaty called for elimination of all ground-launched missiles, of which there were approximately twenty-seven hundred with ranges between five hundred and five thousand kilometers (approximately three hundred to thirty-three hundred miles). On the U.S. side, the intermediate long-range missiles slated for elimination were the Pershing II and the BGM-109 GLCM; the intermediate shorter-range missiles included the Pershing IA. On the Soviet side, the intermediate long-range missiles were the SS-20, SS-4, SS-5, and SSC-X-4; the intermediate shorter-range missiles were the SS-23 and SS-12. All U.S. and Soviet INF missile systems had to be eliminated by the third treaty year.

The INF Treaty was ratified by the U.S. Senate on May 27, 1988, and was ratified by the Presidium of the Supreme Soviet of the U.S.S.R. the following day. At the Moscow summit on June 1, 1988, Reagan and Gorbachev exchanged the instruments of ratification, and the INF Treaty entered into force.

INSPECTION AND VERIFICATION

In order to assist the mission of on-site inspections and escort responsibilities under the provisions of the INF Treaty, on January 18, 1988, Reagan instructed Secretary of Defense Frank Carlucci to establish the On-Site Inspection Agency. Its first director, Major General Roland Lajoie of the U.S. Army, was appointed on February 1, 1988. Together with their counterparts from the Soviet Union, Lajoie's staff adhered to the meticulous timetable for elimination of the affected intermediate-range missiles. All such missiles were eliminated by the target year of 1991.

The INF Treaty represented a significant milestone in the history of U.S.-Soviet arms control talks. It eliminated, for the first time, an entire class of missiles; more important, it set a precedent for intensive on-site inspections to monitor treaty compliance. The treaty required or permitted the United States and the Soviet Union to conduct several hundred such inspections at operational missile sites, repair facilities, storage depots, training sites, and former missile production or assembly facilities. Soviet INF sites in the Soviet Union, Czechoslovakia, and East Germany, and United States INF sites in West Germany, Belgium, the Netherlands, Italy, Great Britain, and the United States were targeted for inspections.

The INF Treaty set in motion the U.S.-Soviet arms control agenda for the future and was an important precursor to the Strategic Arms Reduction Treaty I (START I), which was signed in 1991; the Conventional Forces in Europe (CFE) Treaty of 1992; and START II in 1993. Together, these treaties laid the groundwork for significant reductions in Soviet and U.S. nuclear arsenals.

Vidya Nadkarni

SOURCES FOR FURTHER STUDY

Brady, Linda P. *The Politics of Negotiation: America's Dealing with Allies, Adversaries, and Friends.* Chapel Hill: University of North Carolina Press, 1991.

Bunn, George. *Arms Control by Committee: Managing Negotiations with the Russians.* Stanford, Calif.: Stanford University Press, 1992.

Dewitt, David, and Hans Rattinger, eds. *East-West Arms Control: Challenges for the Western Alliance.* London: Routledge, 1992.

Mayers, Teena Karsa. *Understanding Weapons and Arms Control: A Guide to the Issues.* Rev. 6th ed. McLean, Va.: Brassey's, 1991.

Rueckert, George L. *Global Double Zero: The INF Treaty from Its Origins to Implementation.* Contributions in Military Studies 135. Westport, Conn.: Greenwood Press, 1993.

SEE ALSO: SALT I Treaty (1972); SALT II Treaty (1979); START II Treaty (1993); U.S.-Russia Arms Agreement (2002).

AMERASIAN HOMECOMING ACT

DATE: December 22, 1987
U.S. STATUTES AT LARGE: 101 Stat. 1329
PUBLIC LAW: 100-202
CATEGORIES: Asia or Asian Americans; Immigration

This law authorized appropriations for the U.S. Department of State to extend its program of admitting Amerasian children to the United States.

When the United States withdrew all personnel from Vietnam in 1975, many Vietnamese wives of American citizens and their Amerasian children remained. The Amerasian children were excluded from the mainstream of Vietnamese society, and their mothers were unable to secure employment with the Vietnamese government or in government enterprises. The children were often placed in orphanages, awaiting adoption by unknown fathers in the United States.

In 1984, the U.S. State Department informed Vietnam that all Amerasian children and their qualifying family members would be admitted as refugees by the end of 1987 under the Orderly Departure Program (ODP) of the United Nations High Commissioner for Refugees. However, on January 1, 1986, Vietnam ceased cooperating with the program because of differences with the United States on other issues. When Vietnam resumed processing ODP applicants on October 19, 1987, the three-year deadline was running out. Accordingly, on December 22, 1987, Congress passed the Amerasian Homecoming Act as a part of legislation authorizing appropriations for the U.S. Department of State to establish the program on a more permanent basis.

Michael Haas

SOURCES FOR FURTHER STUDY

Bass, Thomas A. *Vietnamerica: The War Comes Home*. New York: Soho Press, 1996.
McKelvey, Robert S. *The Dust of Life: America's Children Abandoned in Vietnam*. Seattle: University of Washington Press, 1999.

SEE ALSO: United States recognition of Vietnam (1995).

MARINE PLASTIC POLLUTION RESEARCH AND CONTROL ACT

DATE: December 29, 1987
U.S. STATUTES AT LARGE: 101 Stat. 1460
PUBLIC LAW: 100-220
U.S. CODE: 33 § 1901
CATEGORIES: Environment and Conservation

This legislation prohibited dumping of plastics into the sea and required shoreside reception facilities for plastics.

By the mid-1980's, the world's oceans had become a dumping ground for all types of garbage and pollution. Beaches, estuaries, and marshes were becoming clogged with garbage rising with the tide. Animals large and small were killed year after year by garbage dumped into the sea. Much of this garbage and waste decomposed after being dumped into the sea, but some types of debris, such as plastic and styrofoam, could not decompose in seawater.

The international community had banded together in 1973 to pass the International Convention for the Prevention of Pollution from Ships. This convention, commonly called the MARPOL (for "Marine Pollution") convention, was amended in 1978. This international protocol was adopted by virtually all maritime nations. The MARPOL convention has five different annexes that address oil, sewage, garbage, and plastics. Each of the annexes not only highlights a prohibited commodity but also indicates where garbage may not be dumped and designates controlled amounts and allowable concentrations of these commodities.

It was necessary for these protocols to be incorporated in U.S. law in order for them to be enforceable in the United States. Thus, legislation was needed to commit U.S. government support to these conventions and to their enforcement. U.S. jurisdiction included U.S. waters and U.S.-registered ships anywhere in the world. There were also a number of issues that dealt with the oceans and the environment that needed to be addressed. Thus, U.S. legislation in support of the MARPOL convention, ultimately named the Marine Plastic Pollution Research and Control Act, included other environmental topics, not simply ocean pollution by plastics.

PROVISIONS: FIVE TITLES

Each of the five components of the Marine Plastic Pollution Research and Control Act addressed a specific problem, area of the ocean, or ocean research. Taken alone, none of the topics was significant enough to generate its own legislation. Titles I and IV of the legislation dealt with fishing.

Title I was the recognition of the U.S.-Japan Fishing Agreement. This agreement allowed control over Japanese vessels fishing in the U.S. Exclusive Economic Zone (EEZ). The EEZ extends two hundred miles from the coast of the United States. This agreement was a component of the 1982 Law of the Sea convention. The number of vessels, types of fishing, areas of fishing, and amount of each type of fish caught were all covered in this agreement. (The United States has similar agreements with other nations as well.)

Title II of the act addressed the issue of plastics and attempted not only to limit the disposal of plastic at sea from ship dumping but also to address shoreside disposal sites for shipboard plastics. The issues of violations, penalties, and enforcement monitoring were also contained in this title. One specific area south of Long Island and east of the coast of New Jersey, called the New York Bight, was singled out for cleanup and restoration.

Title III of the legislation addressed research and development. This component renewed the Sea Grant College Program. This program authorizes the funding of various studies of the sea and its environment through funding by a number of different colleges, universities, and facilities in the United States. As with the fishing agreement, this legislation is renewable in its appropriation. In this title, the legislation also addressed the issue of the Great Lakes shoreline mapping; these shorelines had not been mapped for a number of years. Resources and environmental concerns also were addressed in the act.

Title IV was controversial in that it addressed drift nets, extremely large fishing nets that are placed in the open ocean. They float at or near the surface but may extend hundreds of feet down into the sea. Because they are miles long and drift with the current, they may trap and kill a variety of fish and animals regardless of the type of catch desired. This type of fishing was relatively new at the time the act was passed and was very effective in catching large volumes of fish. Drift nets were producing an adverse impact on the environment, killing unwanted fish and animals unnecessarily.

Title V of this legislation was introduced by Representative Walter Jones, whose district in North Carolina had been experiencing a bloom of plankton commonly called red tide. Red tides had had a disastrous effect on the local fishing and tourist industries. The legislation provided for assistance to this region.

IMPLEMENTATION AND ENFORCEMENT
The Coast Guard was charged with enforcing the elimination of plastic pollution, not only from U.S.-registered ships but also from ships from other nations operating in U.S. territorial waters. Fines and punishments were set in the regulations, and vessels could be inspected either at the dock or while under way to determine if they are in compliance with regulations.

The Environmental Protection Agency (EPA) was charged with the inspection and licensing of the required shoreside reception facilities for shipboard-generated waste. Ports and other facilities are certifiable by the EPA as acceptable sites for disposal. Further, the EPA was mandated to study the use of plastics and the effects of the legislation on the marine environment and also to report its findings to Congress.

The National Oceanic and Atmospheric Administration (NOAA) was required by the act to generate a public-service program to educate Americans about the hazards that plastic objects pose to animals in the marine environment, the proper use and disposal of plastics in the marine environment, and the use of alternative, environmentally friendly products.

IMPACT
Passage of the 1987 Marine Plastic Pollution Research and Control Act has had a dramatic impact on a variety of fronts. The funding of the National College Sea Grant Program continues to benefit the marine environment through research and development programs. The reduction in the use of large-scale drift-net fishing operations has had a positive effect on the ability of many species of fish and other marine organisms to survive and reproduce in the open ocean. The use of plastic packaging aboard ships has decreased dramatically, while the availability of alternative packaging increased. The availability of shoreside reception sites for waste has also increased.

Robert J. Stewart

SOURCES FOR FURTHER STUDY

Gourlay, K. A. *Poisoners of the Seas.* London: Zed Books International, 1988.

Ketchum, Bostwick, H., et al. *Nearshore Waste Disposal.* Vol. 6 in *Wastes in the Ocean.* New York: John Wiley & Sons, 1985.

O'Hara, Kathryn. *A Citizen's Guide to Plastics in the Ocean.* 2d ed. Washington, D.C.: Center for Environmental Education, 1988.

Talan, Maria. *Ocean Pollution.* San Diego: Lucent Books, 1991.

Wild, R. *The Earth Care Annual.* Emmaus, Pa.: Rodale Press, 1990.

SEE ALSO: Oil Pollution Act of 1924 (1924); Solid Waste Disposal Act (1965); Seabed Treaty (1972); Marine Mammal Protection Act (1972); Port and Tanker Safety Act (1978); Oil Pollution Act of 1990 (1990).

CIVIL RIGHTS RESTORATION ACT

DATE: March 22, 1988
U.S. STATUTES AT LARGE: 102 Stat. 28
PUBLIC LAW: 100-259
CATEGORIES: Civil Rights and Liberties; Education

Schools receiving federal financial assistance were obligated by non-discriminatory requirements in all respects, not merely in activity aided by federal funds.

Title VI of the Civil Rights Act of 1964 mandated that federal funds could not be used to support segregation or discrimination based on race, color, or national origin. The law did not affect a number of other civil rights problems, however. At Cornell University's School of Agriculture, for example, women could not gain admission unless their entrance exam scores were 30 to 40 percent higher than those of male applicants. Epileptics were often barred from employment, and persons in wheelchairs had difficulty gaining access to libraries and schools. Persons in their fifties were often told that they were qualified for a job but too old.

RECTIFYING CIVIL RIGHTS LOOPHOLES

To rectify these problems, Congress extended the scope of unlawful discrimination in federally assisted schools in Title IX of the Education Amendments Act of 1972 to cover gender, the Rehabilitation Act of 1973 to cover the disabled, and the Age Discrimination Act of 1975 to cover older persons.

Enforcement of the statute regarding education was initially assigned to the Office for Civil Rights (OCR) of the U.S. Department of Health, Education, and Welfare, which later became the U.S. Department of Education. OCR ruled that the statute outlawed not only discrimination in the particular program supported by federal funds but also discrimination in programs supported by nonfederal funds. All recipients of federal financial assistance were asked to sign an agreement with OCR, known as the "Assurance of Compliance with Title IX of the Education Amendments of 1972 and the Regulation Issued by the Department of Health, Education, and Welfare in Implementation Thereof," as a condition of receiving a federal grant.

THE GROVE CITY COLLEGE CASE

From 1974 to 1984, Grove City College, located in western Pennsylvania, received $1.8 million in tuition grants and guaranteed student loans but was the only such recipient to refuse to sign an assurance of compliance. The college argued that the funds were for students, not the college, but OCR insisted that the financial aid was administered as a part of the college's financial aid program, so the college must pledge as a whole not to discriminate on the basis of race, color, national origin, or gender. OCR instituted enforcement proceedings against Grove City College, and an administrative law judge ruled in 1978 that the college could no longer receive federal student loan monies.

Grove City College and four students desiring financial aid (Marianne Sickafuse, Kenneth J. Hockenberry, Jennifer S. Smith, and Victor E. Vouga) then sued. The original defendant was Patricia Roberts Harris, secretary of health, education, and welfare. In 1980, when the case was first tried, the federal district court ruled in favor of Grove City College on the grounds that no sex discrimination had actually occurred. On appeal, the court of appeals reversed the lower court's decision, and the matter was taken up by the Supreme Court of the United States, this time with Terrel H.

Bell, head of the newly created federal Department of Education, as the defendant.

In *Grove City College v. Bell* (1984), Justice Byron R. White delivered the majority opinion of the court, which held that OCR did not have sufficient congressional authority to withhold funds from Grove City College for failure to sign the assurance of compliance. Moreover, according to the court, violations of Title VI could occur only in the specific program or activity supported directly with federal funds, a judgment that went beyond the question raised by the case. Justices William J. Brennan, Jr., and Thurgood Marshall dissented, arguing that the Court's ruling gutted Title VI.

CONFLICTS IN CONGRESS

Shortly after the Supreme Court ruling, OCR dropped some seven hundred pending enforcement actions, resulting in an outcry from civil rights groups over the decision. Representative Augustus F. Hawkins then authored the Civil Rights Restoration Act in the House, and Senator Edward M. Kennedy sponsored the bill in the Senate. Their aim was to amend all the affected statutes—Title VI of the Civil Rights Act of 1964, Title IX of the Education Amendments of 1972 Act, the Rehabilitation Act of 1973, and the Age Discrimination Act of 1975. According to the bill, any agency or private firm that wanted to receive federal financial assistance would have to comply with the nondiscrimination requirement as a whole, even if the aid went to only one subunit of that agency or firm.

The road toward passage of the proposed statute was full of potholes, however. Although Hawkins's version quickly passed in the House of Representatives, the measure was caught up in the politics of abortion, and the bill died in the Senate. Opponents advanced more than one thousand amendments over a period of four years, and representatives of the administration of President Ronald Reagan testified against passage of the law. A group known as the Moral Majority broadcast the fear that the bill would protect alcoholics, drug addicts, and homosexuals from discrimination, although there were no such provisions in the proposal.

More crucially, the Catholic Conference of Bishops, which was traditionally aligned with the Civil Rights movement, wanted two amendments to the bill. One proposed amendment, which was unsuccessful, would have exempted institutions affiliated with religious institutions from complying with the law if religious views would be compromised thereby. The other proposed amendment, which was opposed by the National Organization for Women, was an assurance that no federal funds would be spent on abortion. With two parts of the Civil Rights movement at loggerheads, Congress delayed finding a compromise.

In 1987, leaving out references to abortion, Congress finally adopted the Civil Rights Restoration Act, which then went to President Ronald Reagan for his signature to become law. Reagan, however, became the first president to veto a civil rights bill since Andrew Johnson. Instead, he sent a substitute bill to Congress, which would have exempted farmers, grocery stores, ranchers, and religious institutions.

OVERRIDING A PRESIDENTIAL VETO

Supporters of the act next sought to gain sufficient votes to override the presidential veto, and the act had sufficient support. With the gallery filled with persons in wheelchairs, opponents in the Senate tried to destroy the bill by various amendments in debate on the floor of the Senate on January 28, 1988. An amendment by Senator Orrin G. Hatch, for example, would have legislatively exempted organizations closely identified with the tenets of a religious organization, although the bill enabled such groups to obtain exemptions from OCR. He also sought to restrict coverage to the specific affected statutes. Both efforts were defeated. Senators Thomas R. Harkin and Gordon J. Humphrey gained support for an amendment that permitted employers to discriminate against persons with an infection or contagious disease whose presence on the job might threaten the health or safety of others or could not otherwise perform the duties of the job. This reflected contemporary concerns about acquired immunodeficiency syndrome (AIDS).

Senator John C. Danforth proposed an amendment that would disallow federal payments for abortion. This amendment passed, providing that neither Title VI nor Title IX was intended to require an abortion or payment for an abortion. With the passage of the act by the Senate on March 22, 1988, Congress overrode Reagan's veto, and the law went into effect immediately. The law restored civil rights enforcement to where it was before the *Grove* case.

Michael Haas

SOURCES FOR FURTHER STUDY

Blow, Richard. "Don't Look NOW." *New Republic* 198 (April 11, 1988): 11-12.

Gillespie, Veronica M., and Gregory L. McClinton. "The Civil Rights Restoration Act of 1987: A Defeat for Judicial Conservatism." *National Black Law Journal* 12 (Spring, 1990): 61-72.

Robinson, Robert K., Billie Morgan Allen, and Geralyn McClure Franklin. "The Civil Rights Restoration Act of 1987: Broadening the Scope of Civil Rights Legislation." *Labor Law Journal* 40 (January, 1989): 45-49.

Schultz, Jon S., comp. *Legislative History and Analysis of the Civil Rights Restoration Act.* Littleton, Colo.: F. B. Rothman, 1989.

Watson, Robert. "Effects of the Civil Rights Restoration Act of 1987 upon Private Organizations and Religious Institutions." *Capital University Law Review* 18 (Spring, 1989): 93-118.

Willen, Mark. "Congress Overrides Reagan's Grove City Veto." *Congressional Quarterly Weekly Review* 46 (March 26, 1988): 774-776.

SEE ALSO: Civil Rights Act of 1964 (1964); Architectural Barriers Act (1968); Title IX of the Education Amendments of 1972 (1972); Age Discrimination Act (1975); Americans with Disabilities Act (1990); Civil Rights Act of 1991 (1991).

CIVIL LIBERTIES ACT

DATE: August 10, 1988
U.S. STATUTES AT LARGE: 102 Stat. 903
PUBLIC LAW: 100-383
CATEGORIES: Asia or Asian Americans; Civil Rights and Liberties

This act mandated monetary damages as reparations to U.S. residents of Japanese ancestry, as well as relocated Aleuts, who were interned during World War II.

During World War II, Japanese residents on the West Coast and Aleuts in Alaska were interned by the U.S. military. In effect, American citizens—merely because they shared a national or ethnic heritage with the Japanese enemy—were imprisoned and forced to live under bleak conditions in isolated camps for the duration of the war. Although after the war the Evacuation Claims Act of 1948 provided some compensation, the amounts were not enough for those displaced to recover the resulting wartime losses. Pressure from the affected groups prompted Congress on August 10, 1988, to pass the Civil Liberties Act, which authorized the attorney general of the United States to pay $20,000 in damages to each interned Japanese or his or her immediate family heirs, with a ceiling of $1.25 billion.

The law also provided payments of $12,000 to each Aleut who was similarly relocated (up to a ceiling of $5 million); $1.4 million for wartime damage to Aleut church property; $15 million for the loss of Aleut lands that resulted from designating part of Attu Island as part of the National Wilderness Preservation System; and $5 million to aid elderly, disabled, and seriously ill Aleuts, to provide scholarships for Aleuts, to improve Aleut community centers, and to provide for Aleut cultural preservation. No funds were appropriated until November 21, 1989. The first letters of apology were sent out October 9, 1990. Recipients, in turn, gave up all claims for future recovery of damages.

Michael Haas

SOURCE FOR FURTHER STUDY
Hatamiya, Leslie T. *Righting a Wrong: Japanese Americans and the Passage of the Civil Liberties Act of 1988.* Palo Alto, Calif.: Stanford University Press, 1994.

SEE ALSO: Gentlemen's Agreement (1907); Alien land laws (1913); Immigration Act of 1921 (1921); Immigration Act of 1943 (1943); War Brides Act (1945).

FAMILY SUPPORT ACT

DATE: October 13, 1988
U.S. STATUTES AT LARGE: 102 Stat. 2343
PUBLIC LAW: 100-485
CATEGORIES: Children's Issues; Health and Welfare; Women's Issues

The first overhaul of the welfare system in more than half a century, the act cemented a link between welfare and work.

After years of debate, Congress cleared welfare reform legislation on September 30, 1988, and on October 13, President Ronald Reagan signed the Family Support Act of 1988 (FSA) into law. The new law affirmed an evolving vision of the responsibilities of parents and government for the well-being of poor adults and their dependent children.

PROVISIONS

FSA left intact the basic entitlement nature of the federal-state Aid to Families with Dependent Children (AFDC) program and even expanded it by requiring states to extend coverage to certain two-parent families. The anchoring principle of FSA was that parents should be the primary supports of their children and that, for many people, public assistance should be coupled with encouragement, support, and requirements to aid them in moving from welfare to self-support. FSA placed a responsibility both on welfare recipients to take jobs and participate in employment services, and on government to provide the incentives and services to help welfare recipients find employment. For noncustodial parents, usually absent fathers, this was reflected in greater enforcement of child support collections. For custodial parents, usually mothers, this meant new obligations to cooperate in child support collection efforts, as well as new opportunities for publicly supported child care, education, training, and employment services, coupled with obligations to take a job or cooperate with the program.

THIRD ATTEMPT AT WELFARE REFORM

FSA was Congress's third attempt in twenty years to overhaul the welfare system. Two previous efforts, in 1969 and 1977, had foundered over many of the same philosophical differences and technical issues about how best to reduce welfare dependency that threatened to defeat the new law. Most elusive was how to maintain an economic safety net for government-assisted poor parents and their children, while discouraging nonsubsidized working-poor parents from becoming welfare-dependent and preventing the underwriting of low-wage labor. President Reagan's vow in his 1986 state of the union message to make welfare reform a priority buoyed advocates of the law. A commitment by the nation's governors to overhaul welfare also encouraged reformers.

WORK VS. WELFARE
A consensus emerged around the idea that work was better than welfare, but it proved fragile in 1987 when the White House proposed that states should experiment with existing programs without benefit of new federal funds, while House Democrats pushed through a bill that expanded benefits and cost more than $7 billion. Senators Daniel P. Moynihan (Democrat, New York) and Lloyd Bentson (Democrat, Texas), chairman of the Senate Finance Committee, steered a more modest $2.8 billion plan through the Senate on June 16, 1988. To gain White House and Republican support, Moynihan and Bentson accepted work and participation requirements added by Senate Minority Leader Robert Dole (Republican, Kansas) and Senator William L. Armstrong (Republican, Colorado). Liberal Democrats recoiled at the thought of work requirements, and many governors worried about increased costs associated with meeting job training and other requirements.

JOBS PROGRAM
FSA established the Job Opportunities and Basic Skills (JOBS) training program to assure that needy families with children would obtain the education, training, and employment necessary to help them avoid long-term welfare dependency. The JOBS program replaced several other work-incentive programs, such as the Work Incentive (WIN) and WIN DEMO projects of the 1980's. Child care and supportive services were provided to enable individuals to accept employment or receive training.

State JOBS programs were required to include appropriate educational activities, such as high school or equivalent education, combined with training as needed; basic and remedial education to achieve functional literacy, and education for individuals with limited English proficiency; job skills training; job readiness activities; and job development and placement. State programs also included, but were not limited to, two of the four following services: group and individual job search; on-the-job training, during which the recipient would be placed in a paid job for which the employer provided training and wages and, in return, would be paid a supplement for the employee's wages by the state Social Security Act Title IV-A (AFDC) agency; work supplementation, in which the employed recipient's AFDC grant could be diverted to an employer to cover part of the cost of the wages paid to the recipient; and community work experience programs or other Department of Health and Human Services-approved work programs, which generally provided short-term work experience in public projects.

The JOBS program also amended the unemployed-parent component of AFDC to provide that at least one parent in a family must participate for a minimum of sixteen hours a week in a work program specified by the state. If a parent was less than twenty-five years of age and had not completed high school, the state could require the parent to participate in educational activities directed at attaining a high school diploma or in another basic education program. The second parent could be required to participate at state option, unless he or she met another exemption criteria. At the outset, many AFDC parents were excluded from participation in JOBS, and the legislation called for gradually increasing the participation rates throughout the 1990's from 5 to 20 percent.

Early critics of FSA's design and implementation noted that many JOBS requirements did not apply to AFDC recipients in two-parent families. Where they did, fathers were placed mainly in on-the-job training or "workplace" programs and provided with far fewer services than were available to mothers. A possible reason for this differential treatment is that work training and placement experiments with men receiving AFDC have resulted, at best, in only marginal, if at all measurable, gains when experimental groups are compared with controls. Another criticism has been that funding for JOBS is a "capped" entitlement: The federal government matches expenditures by each state up to a fixed amount. Congressional appropriations for this part of FSA cannot legally exceed the cap, regardless of state need or demand.

CHILD-SUPPORT ENFORCEMENT

The other major provision of FSA concerned child-support enforcement. FSA required automatic withholding of child support from an absent parent's paycheck for all new and modified support orders, commencing two years after enactment, regardless of whether the payments were in arrears, as had been specified in 1984 legislation. Initially this provision applied only to all cases being enforced by the state child-support agency, but after January 1, 1994, it covered all orders, regardless of whether a parent had sought assistance from the state child-support agency. FSA also required states, beginning in fiscal 1992, to meet federal standards in establishing paternity for children born out of wedlock. States must either establish paternity for half of all children born out of wedlock who were receiving state child-support services (with some exceptions for good cause); equal or exceed the average paternity-establishment percentage for all states; or have increased their paternity-establishment percentage by three percentage points or more from fiscal 1988-1991 or in any year thereafter.

Groups representing divorced fathers complained that automatic wage withholding could lead to their losing jobs, and that actually handing over the monthly support check was the only leverage they had to ensure that mothers obeyed visitation orders. Congress overruled such objections in the light of evidence showing that 52 percent of all women with children less than twenty-one years of age did not receive part or all of the child support legally due to them, and that nearly 40 percent of households with children in need of support did not have court orders or legal support agreements.

Richard K. Caputo

SOURCES FOR FURTHER STUDY

Berry, Mary Frances. *The Politics of Parenthood: Child Care, Women's Rights, and the Myth of the Good Mother.* New York: Viking Press, 1993.

Caputo, Richard K. "Limits of Welfare Reform." *Social Casework* 70, no. 2 (February, 1989): 85-95.

Chilman, Catherine S. "Welfare Reform or Revision? The Family Support Act of 1988." *Social Service Review* 66, no. 3 (September, 1992): 349-377.

Congressional Quarterly Almanac 1988. Vol. 44, pp. 349-364. Washington, D.C.: Congressional Quarterly Inc., 1988.

Gueron, Judith M., and Edward Pauly. *From Welfare to Work.* New York: Russell Sage Foundation, 1991.

Handler, Joel, and Yeheskel Hasenfeld. *The Moral Construction of Poverty: Welfare Reform in America.* Newbury Park, Calif.: Sage Publications, 1991.

SEE ALSO: Aid to Families with Dependent Children (1935); Child Support Enforcement Amendments (1984); Personal Responsibility and Work Opportunity Reconciliation Act (1996).

ALTERNATIVE MOTOR FUELS ACT

DATE: October 14, 1988
U.S. STATUTES AT LARGE: 102 Stat. 2441
PUBLIC LAW: 100-494
U.S. CODE: 42 § 6374
CATEGORIES: Energy; Environment and Conservation

> *The Alternative Motor Fuels Act encouraged automobile manufacturers to design and build cars that could burn alternative fuels such as methanol and ethanol.*

The Alternative Motor Fuels Act of 1988 was passed both to reduce American dependence on foreign oil and to address automobile makers' lack of interest in designing cars for nonexistent fuel—as well as fuel companies' unwillingness to produce fuel for nonexistent cars. The legislation was intended to resolve the problem by giving incentives to automobile makers and by requiring that a part of the federal fleet use alternative fuels.

PROVISIONS

The act required that a percentage of government vehicles use alternative fuels and established a timetable that enforced government purchase of vehicles capable of using alternative fuels. This provided an immediate market for the fuel, although a limited one. The act also allowed federal fleet operators to exceed their operational gasoline allowances by counting only the actual amount of gasoline in a gallon of fuel, rather than the total amount of fuel, against their allotment. Because the alternative fuels then contained approximately 15 percent gasoline, fleet operators could use more fuel and do more business. This provision provided an incentive to the private sector to develop and use alternative-fueled vehicles.

Because the technology was so new, little information was available on the performance of alternative-fueled vehicles. To solve this problem, an Alternative Fuels Council was established and charged with gathering information and filing the reports required by the act. The law required a methanol study: Data would be collected on the use of methanol as an alternative fuel, methanol's operating characteristics, and the ecological effect of using the fuel. The act also required a study of the safety of alternative fuel, mandated because some oxygenated fuels release harmful elements when transferred from storage tanks to individual automobiles. Another report required by the act was an independent environmental study to analyze air quality and make comparisons of the air quality of cities where alternative fuels were used and those where it was not. The act also called for an extended reasonable forecast on the impact of alternative fuels on the economy.

A significant provision of the act was to establish a national bus-testing program, wherein mass transit buses were to be developed that could use either compressed natural gas or other alternative fuels. Funding was established and guidelines were set to conduct tests in several cities using buses designed to run on alternative fuels and comparing their operating characteristics and maintenance records with those of diesel-fueled buses.

An equally important aspect of the new legislation was to amend existing laws to take into consideration the differences between alterative-fueled and petroleum-fueled vehicles. The laws that were in effect prior to the passage of the Alternative Motor Fuels Act of 1988 would have created economic obstacles to development of the technologies needed to make alternative-fueled vehicles a reality.

The act established the Interagency Commission on Alternative Motor Fuels, responsible for ensuring that all agencies within the government work together in implementing the law.

IMPACT

With the incentives offered by this act, it was hoped that alternative fuels and the vehicles to use them would be developed and that dependence on foreign oil and the overall dependence on nonrenewable resources would be relieved. It was thought that the United States would be able to maintain its standard of living and at the same time exert a less harmful impact on the environment.

The immediate impact of the legislation was to encourage development of the necessary technology. The Interagency Commission on Alternative Motor Fuels reported that a significant market for alternative-fueled vehicles developed within government and commercial fleets within three years of the passage of the Alternative Motor Fuels Act. The commission also noted in its final report, however, that additional amendments were necessary to ensure that alternative-fueled vehicles would be available.

Carl A. Thames

SOURCES FOR FURTHER STUDY

Lincoln, John Ware. *Methanol and Other Ways Around the Gas Pump.* Charlotte, Vt.: Garden Way, 1976.

Nadis, Steve, and James J. MacKenzie. *Car Trouble.* Boston: Beacon Press, 1993.

Pack, Janet. *Fueling the Future.* Chicago: Children's Press, 1992.

Solar Energy Research Institute. *Fuel from Farms: A Guide to Small-Scale Ethanol Production.* Washington, D.C.: Government Printing Office, 1980.

U.S. Congress. Office of Technology Assessment. *Gasohol: A Technical Memorandum.* Washington, D.C.: Government Printing Office, 1979.

SEE ALSO: Clean Air Act (1963); Motor Vehicle Air Pollution Control Act (1965); Clean Air Act Amendments of 1970 (1970); Clean Air Act Amendments of 1977 (1977); Convention on Long-Range Transboundary Air Pollution (1979); Clean Air Act Amendments of 1990 (1990); Montreal Protocol (1990); Pollution Prevention Act (1990).

INDIAN GAMING REGULATORY ACT

DATE: October 17, 1988
U.S. STATUTES AT LARGE: 102 Stat. 2467
PUBLIC LAW: 100-497
U.S. CODE: 25 § 2701
CATEGORIES: Native Americans

Congress regulated gaming on Indian lands by dividing it into three classes and authorizing compacts between tribes and states.

The Indian Gaming Regulatory Act (IGRA), signed into law on October 17, 1988, by President George H. W. Bush, represents an amalgamation of ideas presented in various bills introduced in Congress from 1983 through 1987 and provides a system to permit and regulate gaming on American Indian lands.

PROVISIONS

The IGRA divides gaming into three classes. Class I gaming includes social games of minimal value, as well as traditional games played as a part of tribal ceremonies or celebrations. Class I gaming is exclusively regulated by the tribes. Class II gaming includes bingo, and if played within the same location, pull tabs, lotto, tip jars, instant bingo, games similar to bingo, and certain card games. A tribe may engage in Class II games if the state in which the tribe is located permits such gaming for any purpose by any person, organization, or entity. Class III gaming includes all forms of gaming other than Class I or II, for example, banking card games like blackjack, baccarat and chemin de fer, slot machines, craps, parimutuel horse racing, and dog racing. Class III gaming is prohibited unless authorized by a tribal-state compact.

In addition to classifying games, the IGRA established a three-member National Indian Gaming Commission within the Department of the Interior. The commission chairman is appointed by the president of the United States with Senate approval; the other two members are appointed by the secretary of the interior. At least two members must be enrolled members of an American Indian tribe. The commission has the power to approve all tribal gaming ordinances and resolutions, shut down gaming activities, levy and collect fines, and approve gaming management contracts for Class II and III gaming. The commission has broad power to monitor Class II gaming by inspecting gaming permits, conducting background investigations of personnel, and inspecting and auditing books and records. Regulation and jurisdiction of Class III gaming is more complicated. Class III gaming is lawful when it is authorized by a tribal ordinance, approved by the chairman of the commission, located in a state that permits such gaming (whether for charitable, commercial, or government purposes), and conducted in compliance with a tribal-state compact that is approved by the secretary of the interior.

A tribe seeking to conduct Class III gaming must request that the state in which its lands are located negotiate a tribal-state compact governing the conduct of gaming activities. The compact may include provisions concerning the application of tribal or state criminal and civil laws directly related to gaming, the allocation of jurisdiction between the state and tribe, state assessments to defray the costs of regulation, standards for operation and maintenance of the gaming facility, and other subjects related to the gaming activity. The state is not authorized to impose a tax or assessment upon a tribe unless the tribe agrees. The state cannot refuse to negotiate a compact based on its inability to impose a tax, fee, or other assessment.

SOVEREIGNTY AND ECONOMY

The question of gaming on American Indian reservations is one that involves both sovereignty and economic issues for tribes and states alike. The IGRA grants U.S. district courts jurisdiction over actions by tribes. Reasons for such action include failure of a state to negotiate with a tribe seeking to enter a compact; failure of the state to negotiate in good faith; or any violation of the tribal-state compact. The IGRA provides that a federal district court may order a tribe and state to reach a compact if the state fails to meet its burden of proving that it negotiated in good faith. If no compact is forthcoming, a court may appoint a mediator to recommend a compact. In March, 1996, the United States Supreme Court ruled in *Seminole Tribe of Indians v. Florida* that Congress cannot force states into federal court to settle disputes over gambling on reservations. Federal law, through the IGRA, still permits tribes to seek help from the secretary of the interior when state officials balk at tribal plans for gaming operations.

The IGRA requires that all gaming facilities be tribally owned and that revenue from gaming operations be directed for specific tribal programs, such as education, elderly programs, or housing. Restriction of gaming to tribal governments ensures that American Indian gaming remains a government function rather than a personal endeavor.

The most controversial aspect of the IGRA involves the tribal-state compacting required for Class III gaming. Tribal sovereignty is diminished by the IGRA, because it forces states and tribes into an agreement. Most laws recognize that tribes have a government-to-government relationship with the federal government and are not under state jurisdiction unless there is prior agreement (as in Public Law 280 states). The IGRA specifically requires negotiations between tribes and states, a relationship they do not normally have.

IMPACT

States objected to the tribal-state compacting on the grounds that it violated their sovereignty under the Eleventh Amendment of the Constitution, which protects states from being sued in federal court against their will. In a 1996 Supreme Court decision, it was ruled that Congress cannot attempt to resolve stalled negotiations between states and tribes over on-reservation gambling by making states and their officials targets of federal lawsuits. The Eleventh Amendment rights of states were upheld.

The IGRA has been embraced by many tribes in the United States as a way to bolster reservation economies. Some of the most poverty-stricken areas in the United States are American Indian reservations, and gaming revenues give tribes income to reinvest in other business ventures. The need to generate widespread support for ballot initiatives such as California's Propositions 5 (1998) and 1A (2000), the California Indian Self-Reliance Initiative, helped Native American tribes develop more powerful political lobbies, with influence beyond issues of gambling. However, the compacting process can result in conflict of interest for some states that rely heavily on gaming revenues. In addition, the issue of untaxed revenues resulting from American Indian gaming operations is a factor in establishing compacts, and states in need of such revenue cannot act dispassionately with tribes when they negotiate those compacts. Gaming on American Indian reservations is fraught with issues of competing interests for both tribes and states.

Carole A. Barrett

Sources for Further Study

Canby, William C. *American Indian Law in a Nutshell.* Minneapolis: West, 1981.

Eisler, Kim Isaac. *The Revenge of the Pequots: How a Small Native American Tribe Created the World's Most Profitable Casino.* Lincoln: University of Nebraska Press, 2002.

MacFarlan, Allan A. *Book of American Indian Games.* New York: Associated Press, 1958.

Pommersheim, Frank. "Economic Development in Indian Country: What Are the Questions?" *American Indian Law Review* 12 (1987): 195-217.

Santoni, Roland J. "The Indian Gaming Regulatory Act: How Did We Get Here? Where Are We Going?" *Creighton Law Review* 26 (1993): 387-447.

Turner, Allen C. "Evolution, Assimilation, and State Control of Gambling in Indian Country: Is *Cabazon v. California* an Assimilationist Wolf in Preemptive Clothing?" *Idaho Law Review* 24, no. 2 (1987-1988): 317-338.

Wilkinson, Charles F. *American Indians, Time, and the Law: Native Societies in a Modern Constitutional Democracy.* New Haven, Conn.: Yale University Press, 1987.

Wunder, John R. *"Retained by the People": A History of American Indians and the Bill of Rights.* New York: Oxford University Press, 1994.

See also: Public Law 280 (1953); Indian Self-Determination and Education Assistance Act (1975).

TRADEMARK LAW REVISION ACT

ALSO KNOWN AS: Trademark Act
DATE: November 16, 1988
U.S. STATUTES AT LARGE: 102 Stat. 3943
PUBLIC LAW: 100-667
U.S. CODE: 15 § 1051-1127
CATEGORIES: Business, Commerce, and Trade; Copyrights, Patents, and Trademarks

A response to global marketing, this act was the most sweeping revision of trademark law since the 1946 Lanham Act.

Trademarks have had a long history but have not had a great deal of protection for commercial products in the United States. Congress enacted the first trademark law in 1870, primarily to protect product identity. Manufacturers were concerned that the law did not go far enough for protection and at times was too vague. In 1900 the Congress reviewed a blue ribbon commission report that recommended that commercial names, patents, and other marks be included for protection, which became the basis of the Trade-Mark Act of 1905. The United States, fifteen years later, modified the 1905 act with an updated version that implemented international commitment for the general protection of industrial property and the Trade-Mark Act of 1920 was established.

LANHAM ACT AND OTHER PRIOR LEGISLATION

In 1945 the postwar economy was producing an enormous growth in both communications systems and new technology. The expansion brought about a vast amount of trademark and patent registration. Congressman Fritz Lanham from Texas introduced a bill in Congress that sought registration and protection for unfair competition in the marketplace. The bill defined what a trademark was and how it could be distinguished from other marks or symbols. After a year and a half of debate and discussion, the bill was passed by the Congress and signed into law by President Truman on July 5, 1946. The Lanham Act, as it came to be known, was enacted under its constitutional grant of authority to regulate interstate and international commerce.

With the continued growth in new ideas and inventions, fraud became a legal problem. Trademark and patent counterfeiting became a cottage industry, and vast quantities of inferior or bogus products were sold to unsuspecting customers. Because of this problem, the Congress passed the Trademark Counterfeiting Act of 1984, which amended the Lanham Act (1946) by allowing several new types of civil actions to be established with mandatory financial awards for damages and lawyers' fees.

During the same year, Congress also established the Trademark Clarification Act, which nullified the efforts of the Ninth Circuit's decision in *Anti-Monopoly, Inc. v. General Mills Fun Group, Inc.* In this case, the court held that in determining if a trademark was or was not generic, the buyer's reason for purchasing the product was the crucial test.

THE 1988 PROVISIONS

The Trademark Law Revision Act of 1988 was the most far-reaching of the Lanham Act's amendments. The legislative change was brought about because of the ever-increasing expansion of global marketing. The act made many minor as well as technical changes in the Lanham Act, but what is considered the most significant element of the amendment was the creation of an "intent-to-use" system that required that a mark or symbol must be used in commerce before it could be registered. What this means is that an organization can file a registration application with the Patents and Trademark Office that will allow the mark to become officially recognized before it is used in the marketplace.

The establishment of the intent-to-use system had an enormous change in U.S. trademark protection. The change itself conforms to trademark laws by almost all other nations in the world. The adoption was a major step forward for U.S. membership in the international filing pact that is part of the Trademark Registration Treaty of 1980.

Earl R. Andresen

SOURCES FOR FURTHER STUDY

Pember, Don R., and Michelle Johnson. *Mass Media Law: 2003 Edition.* New York: McGraw-Hill, 2002.

Teeter, Dwight L., Don R. Le Duc, and Bill Loving. *Law of Mass Communications.* New York: Foundation Press, 2001.

SEE ALSO: Copyright Act of 1909 (1909); Copyright Act of 1976 (1976); North American Free Trade Agreement (1993); General Agreement on Tariffs and Trade of 1994 (1994); Digital Millennium Copyright Act (1998).

HATE CRIME STATISTICS ACT

DATE: Passed April 23, 1990; reauthorized September 13, 1994
U.S. STATUTES AT LARGE: 102 Stat. 4469
PUBLIC LAW: 100-690
U.S. CODE: 28 § 534
CATEGORIES: Crimes and Criminal Procedure

> *This law required the U.S. attorney general to collect data annually on crimes that "manifest evidence of prejudice based on race, religion, disability, sexual orientation, or ethnicity."*

The responsibility to collect data on crimes of discrimination, mandated by this law, was assigned by the attorney general to the Federal Bureau of Investigation (FBI). The data enable the government and other agencies to conduct accurate research and perform statistical analysis on these types of crimes. Until passage of this law, there was no way to identify crimes that were committed as a result of hate. This was a concern both in the law enforcement community and among civil rights organizations that represented affected constituencies.

The FBI wanted to make sure that the various police agencies across the nation used sufficiently objective criteria, as described in a set of guidelines that the FBI distributed, to assess hate accurately as a motivation for a particular offense. Most jurisdictions found it necessary to create legislation to address hate crimes to facilitate the counting of these offenses. These cases were eventually litigated to the Supreme Court on First Amendment issues. The cases of *R.A.V. v. City of St. Paul* (1992) and *Wisconsin v. Mitchell* (1993) settled the constitutional questions surrounding this act and related local and state legislation.

Michael L. Barrett

SOURCES FOR FURTHER STUDY

Altschiller, Donald. *Hate Crimes*. Santa Barbara, Calif.: ABC-CLIO, 1999.

Association of State Uniform Crime Reporting Programs and the Center for Applied Social Research, Northeastern University, comp. *Hate Crime Statistics: A Resource Book*. Collingdale, Pa.: DIANE, 1994.

U.S. Congress. Senate. Committee on the Judiciary. *Reauthorization of the Hate Crimes Statistics Act*. 104th Congress, 2d session. Washington, D.C.: Government Printing Office, 1997.

SEE ALSO: First Amendment (1789).

MONTREAL PROTOCOL

DATE: June 29, 1990
CATEGORIES: Environment and Conservation; Treaties and Agreements

The members of the United Nations met to ratify an agreement initially fashioned in Montreal to phase out the use of substances known to be damaging the stratosphere's vitally important ozone layer.

Representatives of many nations met at Montreal Protocol sessions in Canada in 1987 in the hope that the governments of all nations of the world would eventually ratify the document that was fashioned there. Some governments were eager to do so, but others balked because of the possible expenses and hardships that would be entailed following the protocol's recommendations, which included phasing out the use of chlorofluorocarbons (CFCs) and converting to harmless substitutes. It had been scientifically demonstrated that CFCs (used widely in aerosol propellants, refrigerators, and air conditioners) were damaging the earth's protective atmospheric ozone layer, and the impact on skin cancers and global warming had led to the meeting. Representatives of twenty-four nations, mostly the developed, industrialized nations of the world, signed the agreement in Montreal on September 16, 1987.

The Third World countries that had balked at ratifying the protocol were eventually persuaded to do so by the creation of the Montreal Protocol Multilateral Fund. The developed nations had created most of the ozone depletion problem with heavy commercial use of destructive chemicals. Their representatives thought it appropriate that developed nations bear the cost because they were the nations that had created the problem. On June 29, 1990, representatives of ninety-three nations agreed in London to ban production of most ozone-destroying chemicals by the end of the twentieth century.

In November, 1992, delegates from all over the world met in Copenhagen, Denmark, to discuss further revisions of the protocol because of alarming new discoveries about the damage being done to the ozone layer. It was agreed to phase out production of CFCs and carbon tetrachloride by January 1, 1996; to ban the production of halons by 1994; to ban production of methyl chloroform by 1996; to control the use of hydrochlorofluorocarbons (HCFSs) and eliminate them completely by 2030; and to increase the Montreal Protocol Multilateral Fund in order to make it possible for developing nations to accelerate the changeover from machinery and consumer products using ozone-destroying gases to harmless alternatives.

Bill Delaney

SOURCES FOR FURTHER STUDY

Benedick, R. E. *Ozone Diplomacy: New Directions in Safeguarding the Planet.* Washington, D.C.: World Wildlife Fund, 1991.

Clark, S. L. *Protecting the Ozone Layer—What You Can Do: A Citizen's Guide to Reducing the Use of Ozone-Depleting Chemicals.* New York: Environmental Information Exchange, Environmental Defense Fund, 1988.

Firor, John. *The Changing Atmosphere: A Global Challenge.* New Haven, Conn.: Yale University Press, 1990.

Gliedman, John. "Is the Pact Too Little, Too Late?" *The Nation,* October 10, 1987, 376-380.

Gore, Albert. *Earth in the Balance: Ecology and the Human Spirit.* Boston: Houghton Mifflin, 1992.

Gribbin, John R. *The Hole in the Sky: Man's Threat to the Ozone Layer.* New York: Bantam Books, 1988.

Klingeman, Henry. "The Twilight Ozone: D. Hodel's Alleged Remarks Concerning the International Protocol on Ozone." *National Review,* August 14, 1987, 40-41.

Lemonick, Michael D. "The Ozone Vanishes." *Time,* February 17, 1992, 60-68.

Molina, M. J., and F. S. Rowland. "Stratospheric Sink for Chlorofluoromethanes: Chlorine Atom-Catalyzed Destruction of Ozone." *Nature* 249 (1974): 810-812.

Van Dusen, Lisa. "Fresh Hope in the Sky." *Maclean's,* September 28, 1987, 56-57.

SEE ALSO: Foreign Agents Registration Act (1938); Air Pollution Control Act (1955); Clean Air Act (1963); Clean Air Act Amendments of 1970 (1970); Clean Air Act Amendments of 1977 (1977); Convention on Long-Range Transboundary Air Pollution (1979); Clean Air Act Amendments of 1990 (1990).

AMERICANS WITH DISABILITIES ACT

DATE: July 26, 1990
U.S. STATUTES AT LARGE: 104 Stat. 327
PUBLIC LAW: 101-336
U.S. CODE: 42 § 12101-12213
CATEGORIES: Civil Rights and Liberties; Disability Issues; Health and Welfare

This law guaranteed equal opportunity for people with disabilities by mandating access in public accommodations, transportation, state and local government services, and telecommunications. It also prohibited employment discrimination.

The Americans with Disabilities Act (ADA) prohibits discrimination on the basis of disability in employment, programs, and services provided by state and local governments, private companies, and commercial facilities. It also mandates establishment of telecommunications devices for deaf persons. The employment provision covers all companies that employ fifteen or more people. American Indian tribes, tax-exempt private-membership clubs (not including labor unions), and the federal government are not covered by the ADA. However, the federal government is covered by the Rehabilitation Act of 1973, which prevents the federal government, federal contractors, and educational programs receiving federal funds from discriminating against disabled persons. Religious organizations are governed by the ADA but may give employment preference to people of their own religion or religious organization.

QUALIFIED INDIVIDUALS UNDER THE ADA

Only individuals who are qualified under the ADA may claim discrimination under the act. The act establishes three categories of criteria for such qualification. To qualify as a disabled individual, a person must have a physical or mental impairment that substantially limits one or more major life activities, have a record of such an impairment, or be regarded as having such an impairment. Persons discriminated against because they have a known association or relationship with a disabled individual are also protected by the act.

The first category includes disabilities such as impairments in seeing, hearing, speaking, walking, breathing, performing manual tasks, learning, caring for oneself, and working. It does not include minor, nonchronic conditions of short duration such as sprains, influenza, and broken limbs. However, an individual with a broken limb that does not heal within a few months or that fails to heal properly may be considered disabled; determining whether a condition is a disability under the ADA is done on a case-by-case basis.

The second category covers people who have recovered from cancer, heart disease, mental illness, or other debilitating illness. It also includes individuals who were misdiagnosed with such illnesses if the misdiagnosis leads to discrimination. The third category protects individuals who are regarded as having a substantially limiting impairment, even though they may not. This would include individuals with controlled high blood pressure, individuals rumored to be infected with the human immunodeficiency virus (HIV), and individuals with observable deformities such as severe facial disfigurement.

Characteristics that are not considered disabilities under the ADA include current illegal drug use (although rehabilitated drug abusers may be covered), homosexuality, bisexuality, various sexual disorders (including pedophilia, exhibitionism, and voyeurism), certain behavioral disorders (such as compulsive gambling, kleptomania, and pyromania), and such personality traits as poor judgment, a quick temper, or irresponsible behavior. Environmental, cultural, and economic disadvantages, such as lack of education or a prison record, are not covered by the ADA.

Title I: Employment

The ADA prohibits discrimination against qualified individuals in all employment practices, including job application procedures, hiring, firing, advancement, compensation, and training. A qualified individual is a person who meets legitimate skill, experience, education, or other requirements of an employment position and who can perform the essential functions of the position with or without reasonable accommodation. A written job description can provide evidence of the essential functions of a position but is not necessarily definitive. Whether an activity is an essential function must be determined on a case-by-case basis. Reasonable accommodations are those that would not impose an undue hardship on the operation of the employer's business; an undue hardship is an action that requires difficulty or expense when considered in the light of the size, resources, nature, and structure of the employer's operation. Reasonable accommodations may include remodeling existing facilities to make them readily accessible and usable by an individual with a disability, restructuring a job or work schedule, providing qualified readers or interpreters, or modifying examination or training to allow a disabled individual to demonstrate the knowledge or skills actually required for the position.

An employer may not ask or require a job applicant to have a medical examination before making a job offer but may condition a job offer on the satisfactory result of a postoffer medical examination or medical inquiry if such an examination or inquiry is required of all entering employees in the same job category. Information from all medical examinations and inquiries must be kept apart from general personnel files as a separate, confidential medical record. Drug testing is not a medical examination under the ADA. An employer cannot make any preemployment inquiry about the nature or severity of a disability but can ask about an applicant's ability to perform specific job functions and may ask for a reasonable demonstration of the required ability.

Employers may refuse to hire or may terminate the employment of disabled individuals if such individuals would pose a direct threat to the health and safety of themselves or others. This type of discrimination is allowed only if there is significant risk of substantial harm. The direct threat must be based on valid medical analyses or other objective evidence, not on speculation by the employer. The employer must attempt to eliminate the threat or reduce it to acceptable levels with reasonable accommodations. If elimination or reduction is not possible, the employer may refuse to hire or may terminate the employment of a disabled person. For example, an employer at a day care center might refuse to hire an individual with an active tuberculosis infection if no reasonable accommodation could be made to reduce the risk of infection to others.

TITLE II: PUBLIC SERVICES

Under the ADA's provisions, state and local government facilities, the National Railroad Passenger Corporation, and public transportation systems cannot deny services to people with disabilities. This prohibition extends to publicly owned buildings and vehicles and also affirmatively requires state and local governments to provide access to programs offered to the public. The ADA also covers effective communication with people with disabilities that may restrict or prevent their access to such programs. The act does not require that state and local governments provide all documents in Braille if workers are present to read documents to persons with vision or reading disabilities, nor does it require that sign-language interpreters be available if communication can be accomplished via note-writing.

However, the act does require reasonable modifications of policies and practices that may be discriminatory. For example, if a town council were to meet on the second floor of a building with no elevator, it would discriminate against disabled persons with mobility problems who could not walk to the second floor. Such an act would violate the ADA's provisions. However, if the town council were to meet without a sign-language interpreter, it would not discriminate against a deaf person who chooses to attend the meeting alone.

TITLE III: PUBLIC ACCOMMODATIONS

The ADA requires that construction of and modifications to structures that house entities providing goods or services to the public must be accessible to the disabled. Organizations that provide goods or services to the public, regardless of their size or number of employees, are considered to be public accommodations; these include stores, banks, libraries, hotels, restaurants, nursing homes, and privately owned transportation systems such as taxis and cruise ships. Residential facilities, independent-living centers, and retirement communities are covered by Title III if they provide a significant enough level of social services such as medical care, assistance with daily-living activities, provision of meals, transportation, counseling, and organized recreational activities.

The ADA also contains requirements for improving access to existing facilities. The act requires public accommodations to remove architectural barriers in existing facilities when such alteration is readily achievable without much difficulty or expense. Examples of readily achievable alterations include the ramping of one or a few steps, the installation of a bathroom grab bar, the lowering of towel dispensers, the rearranging of furniture, the installation of offset hinges to widen a doorway, and the painting of new lines to create an accessible parking space.

TITLES IV AND V: TELECOMMUNICATIONS AND OTHER PROVISIONS
The ADA mandates establishment of TDD/telephone relay systems and prohibits telecommunications companies from substituting a seven-number emergency line for the 911 emergency line for hearing-impaired individuals. The ADA prohibits coercing, threatening, or retaliating against disabled persons when those persons assert their rights under the act. Further, it prohibits threats or retaliation against individuals who attempt to aid disabled persons in asserting their rights under the ADA.

Complaints concerning violations of the ADA may be filed with the Equal Employment Opportunity Commission or with designated state human rights agencies. Available remedies include hiring, reinstatement, promotion, back pay, restored benefits, reasonable accommodation, attorneys' fees, expert witness fees, and court costs as well as real and punitive damages.

Lisa M. Sardinia

SOURCES FOR FURTHER STUDY

Anderson, Robert C. *A Look Back: The Birth of the Americans with Disabilities Act.* Binghamton, N.Y.: Haworth Press, 1997.

Congressional Quarterly Almanac. "Sweeping Law for Rights of Disabled: Private Discrimination Barred; Access Mandated." 46 (1990): 447-461.

Gostin, Lawrence O., and Henry A. Beyer, eds. *Implementing the Americans with Disabilities Act: Rights and Responsibilities of All Americans.* Baltimore: P. H. Brookes, 1993.

Johnson, William G. *The Americans with Disabilities Act: Social Contract or Special Privilege?* Thousand Oaks, Calif.: Sage Publications, 1996.

Perritt, Henry H. *Americans with Disabilities Act Handbook.* New York: John Wiley & Sons, 1990.

Reams, Bernard D., Jr., Peter J. McGovern, and Jon S. Schultz. *Disability Law in the United States: A Legislative History of the Americans with Disabilities Act of 1990, Public Law 101-336.* 6 vols. Buffalo, N.Y.: William S. Hein, 1992.

Shapiro, Joseph P. *No Pity: People with Disabilities Forging a New Civil Rights Movement.* New York: Times Books, 1993.

U.S. Equal Employment Opportunity Commission Staff. *Americans with Disabilities Act with Resource Directory.* Indianapolis: JIST Works, 1992.

West, Jane, ed. *The Americans with Disabilities Act: From Policy to Practice.* New York: Mill Bank Memorial Fund, 1991.

SEE ALSO: Mental Retardation Facilities and Community Mental Health Centers Construction Act (1963); Architectural Barriers Act (1968); Family Planning Services and Population Research Act (1970); Equal Employment Opportunity Act (1972); Child Abuse Prevention and Treatment Act (1974); Age Discrimination Act (1975); Education for All Handicapped Children Act (1975); Pregnancy Discrimination Act (1978); McKinney Homeless Assistance Act (1987); Family and Medical Leave Act (1993).

OIL POLLUTION ACT OF 1990

DATE: August 18, 1990
U.S. STATUTES AT LARGE: 104 Stat. 486
PUBLIC LAW: 101-380
U.S. CODE: 33 § 2701
CATEGORIES: Environment and Conservation

> *Congress passed comprehensive environmental legislation, the Oil Pollution Act of 1990, in response to the grounding of the Exxon Valdez.*

Congress turned its attention to legislation regulating oil spills following the grounding of the oil tanker *Exxon Valdez* in Prince William Sound, Alaska. The oil spill and accompanying damage to the wildlife and its ecosystem were the subject of broadcast news for weeks following the accident and rallied public pressure for action.

PREVIOUS LEGISLATION

To be effective, oil spill legislation had to be at the federal level, because state and local governments could legislate only those terminals and facilities within their jurisdictions. Comprehensive federal legislation had to address not only pollution cleanup problems but also the entire transport system. A number of laws already existed that addressed some of the problems. The earliest of these, the Federal Water Pollution Control Act of 1970, concerned oil spilled into the navigable waters of the United States. The Deepwater Ports Act of 1974 covered spillage in the territorial sea, which extends twelve miles from the U.S. coasts, and the Outer Continental Shelf Lands Act of 1978 covered oil spilled into the waters of the Exclusive Economic Zone. In 1980, Congress had passed the Comprehensive Environmental Response, Compensation, and Liability Act, which created the first "superfund." The fund was designed to provide the resources needed to clean up an oil spill if a cargo or ship owner was unwilling or unable to pay for it.

PROVISIONS

The Oil Pollution Act addressed not only the prevention of oil pollution but also oil pollution response and cleanup. It set standards for crew certification, work hours, and vessel traffic systems. Further, the legislation set new design and life-span requirements for tank vessels and addressed the question of liability for the cleanup of spills and accidents involving tank vessels. Finally, the bill continued provisions for the superfund established by the 1980 act.

The bill had eight sections, each of which added something to the existing body of law. In the first two, Congress significantly increased the liability of the "polluter" and added third-party liability, as well as addressing the new law's relationship with already existing regulations and allowing states to override the federal standards with stricter legislation of their own. The third section addressed the international aspects covered by the act, and the fourth set higher standards for the industry. Issues specifically related to the Prince William Sound situation were covered in the fifth section, in which provisions were made for a technical committee, better oversight of the tanker terminal, and modifications to the navigation aids in that area. The act went on to address miscellaneous issues such as administrative appropriations and a ban on drilling off the North Carolina coast; oil pollution research and development programs, which included recommendations for the types of equipment required to track and contain oil spills; and liability and pollution issues associated with oil transported by pipeline.

IMPACT

The Oil Pollution Act of 1990 was a far-reaching piece of legislation. Almost immediately, the act had a dramatic impact, not only on the operation of tanker fleets in the United States but also on the operation of international tanker fleets that called at American ports. The act mandated new standards that required both short-term and long-term adaptation on the part of the maritime industry.

The legislation also had a significant impact on the government because it required that a number of agencies, including the Department of Energy, institute the new policies and programs and cooperate in implementing the stricter standards. The U.S. Coast Guard, for example, was made responsible for issues such as crew licensing, vessel inspection, and plans to deal with oil spills and oil transfers.

The act also generated the need for new agencies, such as the Marine Spill Response Corporation, to support oil spill recovery procedures. Vessels specially designed, equipped, and staffed to handle oil spills were stationed around the country, their crews permanently on call to respond to emergencies.

The act affected owners and operators of U.S.-flag tank vessels as well as their crews, who were subject to a new set of certification and licensing standards. The Coast Guard began checking the driving records of all applicants, and periodic renewal became mandatory for a number of endorsements, or jobs, for which crew members were certified. Daily ship operations were also affected by the legislation. To cut down on shipboard fatigue, which often underlies human error, the act limited work hours to no more than twelve per day. That in turn usually required vessels, in order to operate competitively, to hire additional crew.

The act also addressed the issue of vessel obsolescence by requiring that all vessels calling in U.S. ports be double-hulled by the year 2015. Shipyards and ship repair facilities worldwide had to develop plans to meet the new construction standard. Ship terminals, too, were affected by the legislation, which required that they develop and maintain oil spill contingency plans and provide terminal operations manuals to shipboard and shoreside personnel during oil transfers. The law has also had an effect on nonmaritime businesses such as banking and insurance: The act called for minimum insurance coverage and strengthened the government's power to enforce oil pollution liability.

Robert J. Stewart

Sources for Further Study

Alaska Oil Spill Commission. *Spill, Wreck of the Exxon Valdez.* Juneau, Alaska: Author, 1990.

National Research Council, Marine Board, Commission on Engineering and Technical Systems. *Using Oil Spill Dispersants on the Sea.* Washington, D.C.: National Academy Press, 1989.

Smith, Zachary A. *The Environmental Paradox.* Englewood Cliffs, N.J.: Prentice Hall, 1992.

Wardley-Smith, J. *The Control of Oil Pollution.* London: Graham & Trotman, 1983.

White, Harris H. *Concepts in Marine Pollution.* College Park: University of Maryland Press, 1984.

SEE ALSO: Oil Pollution Act of 1924 (1924); Clean Water Act and Amendments (1965); Marine Mammal Protection Act (1972); Coastal Zone Management Act (1972); Hazardous Materials Transportation Act (1974); Port and Tanker Safety Act (1978); Superfund Act (1980); Marine Plastic Pollution Research and Control Act (1987).

PERKINS ACT

ALSO KNOWN AS: Vocational and Applied Technology Education Act
DATE: September 25, 1990
U.S. STATUTES AT LARGE: 104 Stat. 753
PUBLIC LAW: 101-392
CATEGORIES: Education

Designed to make the United States more competitive by developing the academic and occupational skills of all segments of the population, the Perkins Act addressed state and local vocational education programs and services.

A reauthorization of the Perkins Act of 1984, the 1990 act shifted responsibility for the design and implementation of vocational programs from the federal government to states and localities. It required participation in planning by those most concerned, including students and parents. While giving state and local educational agencies more flexibility in the design of programs, it also required them to address accountability at the state and local level.

Based on the projection that members of certain groups—including those who are educationally and economically disadvantaged, disabled, or limited in English proficiency; and those who are in correctional institutions—will make up an increasingly large segment of the American labor pool in the twenty-first century, this act addressed diversity of the workforce and student body, the skills needed to keep the United States competitive, the role that vocational education plays in restructuring schools, professional development, and the accountability of vocational programs. It can be seen as a step toward achieving civil rights for individuals who face barriers to education and employment.

Rebecca Lovell Scott

SOURCES FOR FURTHER STUDY

Felder, Henry, and Sarah L. Glavin, eds. *Vocational Education: Changes at High School Level After Amendments to Perkins Act.* Collingdale, Pa.: DIANE, 1997.

Plawin, Paul. *Official Guide to the Perkins Act of 1998.* Alexandria, Va.: Association for Career and Technical Education, 1998.

SEE ALSO: Morrill Land Grant Act of 1862 (1862); Morrill Land Grant Act of 1890 (1890); G.I. Bill (1944); National Defense Education Act (1958); Economic Opportunity Act (1964); Equal Employment Opportunity Act (1972); Comprehensive Employment Training Act (1973).

OLDER WORKERS BENEFIT PROTECTION ACT

DATE: October 16, 1990
U.S. STATUTES AT LARGE: 104 Stat. 978
PUBLIC LAW: 101-433
CATEGORIES: Aging Issues; Labor and Employment

This act ensures that older workers cannot be tricked by employers into losing retirement benefits.

The Age Discrimination in Employment Act of 1967 was designed to deter employers from discriminating against workers over the age of forty. Unscrupulous employers, however, decided to offer early retirement incentives to older workers—often threatening to lay off older workers just before they became eligible for a pension—provided that the workers waived their ADEA rights.

When one of these schemes was challenged, the U.S. Supreme Court ruled, in *Ohio v. Betts* (1989), that such waivers were perfectly legal. Congress then passed the Older Workers Benefit Protection Act (OWBPA) in 1990 to establish procedural safeguards so that such waivers could not be signed in haste and so employers could not target older workers in staff-cutting programs.

The OWBPA established the following requirements: The waiver must be written in a manner that can be understood by the average employee; the waiver cannot relinquish non-ADEA rights; the waiver cannot refer to rights subsequently established by an amended ADEA; the employee must be advised in writing to consult an attorney before signing a waiver; the employee can take at least three weeks before signing the waiver; and the waiver can be revoked within one week after signing.

The OWBPA provides that the burden of proof about the legality of a waiver falls on the employer. When an employer challenged the OWBPA, the Supreme Court, in *Oubre v. Entergy* (1998), affirmed that an employee has the right to sue under ADEA if an employer's waiver agreement fails to comply with these six procedural requirements. Moreover, an employee suing for a violation of the OWBPA need not return the severance pay provided in the waiver.

Michael Haas

SOURCES FOR FURTHER STUDY

Crown, William H., ed. *Handbook on Employment and the Elderly.* Westport, Conn.: Greenwood Press, 1996.

Gregory, Raymond F. *Age Discrimination in the American Workplace: Old at a Young Age.* New Brunswick, N.J.: Rutgers University Press, 2001.

Handa, Jagdish. *Discrimination, Retirement, and Pensions.* Brookfield, Vt.: Avebury, 1994.

Player, Mack A. *Federal Law of Employment Discrimination in a Nutshell.* St. Paul, Minn.: West Group, 1999.

Segrave, Kerry. *Age Discrimination by Employers.* Jefferson, N.C.: McFarland Press, 2002.

SEE ALSO: Executive Order 11141 (1964); Medicare and Medicaid Amendments (1965); Older Americans Act (1965); Age Discrimination in Employment Act (1967); Employee Retirement Income Security Act (1974); Age Discrimination Act (1975).

CHILD CARE AND DEVELOPMENT BLOCK GRANT ACT

DATE: November 5, 1990
U.S. STATUTES AT LARGE: 104 Stat. 1388
PUBLIC LAW: 97-35; 101-508
U.S. CODE: 42 § 9858
CATEGORIES: Children's Issues; Health and Welfare

The purpose of this act was to improve child-care options for low-income families.

Many factors influenced the Child Care and Development Block Grant Act of 1990. One of the most important factors was that by 1990 more than 50 percent of U.S. mothers of infants worked outside the home. Another was that during the 1980's criminal charges were filed against child-care workers in various parts of the United States, alleging that they were guilty of child abuse and neglect. The Child Care and Development Block Grant Act attempted to provide child-care assistance for those working mothers while establishing programs and guidelines to train and monitor child-care workers.

This act was an effort on the part of the federal government to provide support to states to improve child-care options for low-income workers. The act provides funds to low-income families to assist them in paying for child care, to increase the number of community child-care centers in the United States, and to pay professionals to train licensed caregivers and to allow such caregivers to attend training classes. Through a series of modest block grants, states receive money so that they can license and monitor child-care facilities. In general, the act has made more child-care options available to working mothers and has contributed to the public scrutiny of those who work in child-care facilities.

Annita Marie Ward

SOURCE FOR FURTHER STUDY
Hayes, Cheryl D., John L. Palmer, and Martha J. Zaslow, eds. *Who Cares for America's Children?: Child Care Policy for the 1990s.* Washington, D.C.: National Academy Press, 1990.

SEE ALSO: Sheppard-Towner Act (1921); Aid to Families with Dependent Children (1935); Family Planning Services and Population Research Act (1970); Education for All Handicapped Children Act (1975); Indian Child Welfare Act (1978); Pregnancy Discrimination Act (1978); Family Support Act (1988); Family and Medical Leave Act (1993).

POLLUTION PREVENTION ACT

DATE: November 5, 1990
U.S. STATUTES AT LARGE: 104 Stat. 1388-321
PUBLIC LAW: 101-508
U.S. CODE: 42 § 13101
CATEGORIES: Environment and Conservation

This act renewed an old approach to environmental management based on reduction of pollution at the source.

Until 1990, with the notable exception of the National Environmental Policy Act (1970), the federal government's approach to environmental management was remedial and medium-specific (that is, specifically limited to air, water, or land pollution problems) rather than preventive and comprehensive. This approach failed to address several critical issues in environmental management. First, pollutants do not remain in a single medium, such as air or water; second, there are many thousands of pollutants, with more being created each year; and finally, dealing with pollution at the point of its release to the environment often created new problems. That was the case with efforts to restrict pollutant discharges into surface water, which led to groundwater pollution as generators turned to on-site storage of liquid wastes in unlined ponds. It gradually became clear that a successful approach must attempt to prevent pollutants from being created in the first place, recycle those that are created, and look at the environment in which pollution takes place as an interdependent ecological unit. The result was the major policy shift reflected in the Pollution Prevention Act of 1990.

PROVISIONS

That Pollution Prevention Act (PPA) established pollution prevention as a "national objective" and declared that pollution can be prevented or reduced at the point of its creation. The law emphasized that the source-reduction approach to pollution management was "fundamentally different and more desirable" than the approach of the preceding federal laws and regulations, which had focused on the treatment and disposal of pollutants rather than on reduction at the source of their production.

The PPA specified a hierarchical approach to the reduction and prevention of pollution that enters the environment through recycling, treatment, disposal, or unintended escape. The act defined the most desirable approach as reduction at the source, that is, reducing the amounts of hazardous substances before they enter the environment; reduction should occur in such a way as to reduce the health and environmental hazards associated with release. Pollutants that cannot be eliminated at the source should be recycled in an environmentally safe manner. If recycling cannot eliminate all pollutants, those remaining should be treated. Attempts at disposal or other releases of pollutants into the environment should be regarded only as a last resort.

THREE PROGRAMS

The act mandated three specific programs. The first was the establishment of an Office of Pollution Prevention within the Environmental Protection Agency (EPA) but independent of its "single-medium" programs. The office was made responsible for the development and implementation of a strategy to promote source-reduction and reduce hazardous wastes. It was charged with encouraging businesses and other federal agencies to adopt source-reduction techniques, establishing standard methods for measuring source reduction, reviewing regulations to determine their effect on source reduction, determining instances in which the federal procurement process can be used to encourage source reduction, improving public access to data collected under federal environmental laws, and developing a source-reduction clearing-house, model procedures for auditing source reduction, a training program on opportunities for source reduction, and an annual awards program. This last requirement resulted in EPA's developing several videos, a speakers bureau, a newsletter, brochures, conferences, courses, and a resource guide to training programs. The EPA also established the Pollution Prevention Information Clearinghouse (PPIC), which offers a telephone hotline for pollution-prevention questions, an electronic bulletin board, several computerized databases, a reference library, and a document ordering system.

In the second program, the act, in order to encourage businesses to practice source reduction, authorized an $8 million, one- to three-year grant program, with funds allocated to those states that match the federal money. Individual states are responsible for developing their own source-reduction programs.

The third important program established by the act involves facilities that fall under the reporting provisions of the Toxic Release Inventory established by Title III of the Superfund Amendment and Reauthorization Act, or SARA. Commonly known as the Community Right-to-Know Act, Title III of SARA requires many businesses and industries to report the amounts of toxic substances released to the air, water, and land each year. These facilities were now additionally required to report their source-reduction practices and changes in production for each facility and each toxic chemical used, including the quantities of each toxic substance emitted, quantities recycled, and the percentage change in these figures from the previous year. The act also required that the EPA report to Congress every other year on the actions needed to implement the source-reduction strategy and that it provide an assessment of the grant and clearinghouse programs.

IMPACT

Since its inception, the PPIC responded to tens of thousands of requests for information. Data from the Toxics Release Inventory showed a 35 percent decline in the total amount of toxic chemicals released to the nation's environment between 1988 and 1992 and a 6 percent decline from 1991 to 1992. In the first four years of the grant program, more than $30 million was awarded to more than one hundred regional, state, and tribal organizations for pollution-prevention activities.

The major policy shift legislated with the Pollution Prevention Act was based on the approach taken in the National Environmental Policy Act (NEPA), which mandated consideration of the cumulative environmental effects of certain activities. NEPA, one of the most successful U.S. environmental laws, radically improved the way these activities were planned, and it withstood many court challenges and was never substantially amended. After NEPA, however, and until the passage of the 1990 Pollution Prevention Act, federal environmental management had taken a very different course. Most of those laws were repeatedly amended, and although billions of dollars were spent, it is questionable whether environmental quality improved during that time. The greatest significance of the Pollution Prevention Act of 1990 may lie not in its substantive programs but in its indication of a return to the environmental approach of NEPA.

Many of the specific programs defined by the Pollution Prevention Act already existed before 1990. Between the beginning of fiscal year 1988 and May, 1990, the EPA had awarded nearly $10.9 million in multimedia pollution-prevention grants to states; in 1989, the agency published a guidance document for industry to use in its efforts to minimize the generation of hazardous waste; and the Office of Pollution Prevention had been established several years before the act's passage. By legislatively sanctioning and strengthening these programs, Congress tried to ensure that their preventive, comprehensive focus would continue to shape federal environmental policy.

In the wake of the Pollution Prevention Act's passage, a number of state offices of pollution prevention were established, most of which received grant funding from the act for special projects. In fact, state involvement and response to industry needs generally increased in response to the act; states adopted their own pollution-prevention acts and regulations, and some began to require that companies convicted of violating state laws be environmentally audited. Such increased state activity in turn led to increased industrial compliance.

Local governments also became active in pollution prevention, as reflected in such activities as using waste-disposal companies that offer recycling and sponsorship of household hazardous waste pickups and educational seminars on waste minimization and conservation. To what extent these changes can be attributed directly to the Pollution Prevention Act is unclear, but the federal government's policy shift toward prevention was undoubtedly an important factor.

Elise M. Bright

SOURCES FOR FURTHER STUDY

Bergeson, Lynn L. "Pollution Prevention Act of 1990." *Pollution Engineering* 23 (February, 1991): 25-26.

Change Management Center. *Applying Industrial Ecology.* Oakland, Calif.: Author, 1993.

McGraw, J. "The Denver Airport: Pollution Prevention by Design." *Pollution Engineering,* January 1, 1993, 2-12.

Scerbo, Dominic. "The Pollution Prevention Act of 1990 and the Revised Toxic Chemical Release Inventory Reporting." *Wire Journal International* 26 (March, 1993): 70-77.

U.S. Environmental Protection Agency. "Notice of Availability of Pollution Prevention Grants." *Federal Register* 59 (February 23, 1994): 8613-8615.

_____. *Pollution Prevention Incentives for States.* Washington, D.C.: Author, 1993.

_____. "TRI Releases Decline by 6.6% in 1992." *Pollution Prevention News,* March-May, 1994, 1.

SEE ALSO: National Environmental Policy Act (1970); Convention on Long-Range Transboundary Air Pollution (1979); Superfund Act (1980); Emergency Planning and Community Right-to-Know Act (1986); Oil Pollution Act of 1990 (1990); Clean Air Act Amendments of 1990 (1990); Montreal Protocol (1990).

CLEAN AIR ACT AMENDMENTS OF 1990

DATE: November 15, 1990
U.S. STATUTES AT LARGE: 104 Stat. 2399
PUBLIC LAW: 101-549
U.S. CODE: 42 § 7401
CATEGORIES: Environment and Conservation; Natural Resources

The 1990 Clean Air Act Amendments provided comprehensive regulations dealing with some of the nation's worst air pollution problems, including hazardous air pollutants and acid deposition.

On November 15, 1990, President George H. W. Bush signed into law the Clean Air Act Amendments of 1990. These amendments were designed to improve and strengthen the regulations already established by the 1970 Clean Air Act and its 1977 amendments, which had given the federal government authority to set national standards to protect human health and welfare.

CONDITIONS FOR PASSAGE

A series of events prompted passage of legislation. After years of political obstacles to such an act, the political conditions were right: President Bush supported legislation, and Representative John Dingell (Democrat, Michigan), who had previously opposed similar legislation given his state's connection with the automobile industry, was more open to the law after a compromise on motor vehicle emissions. There was also a new majority leader in the Senate, George Mitchell, who replaced Robert Byrd, a previous opponent. Mitchell supported clean air legislation. The president's chief of staff, John Sununu, former governor of New Hampshire, who had worked for air pollution controls in the past, and William Reilly, head of the Environmental Protection Agency (EPA), known to have a strong environmental background, were also on board. These changes, all occurring between 1989 and 1990, appear to have been instrumental in the final passage of acid rain legislation.

One last influence must be mentioned: Canada. A scientific report released in 1979 confirmed what Canadians had been publicly stating for a long time: that U.S. sources contributed five times as much transboundary pollution in Canada as did Canadian sources. This concern spurred Canadians to use a multifaceted foreign policy approach in hopes of gaining U.S. reductions in emissions. Canada attempted to influence U.S. clean air policy through quiet diplomacy (formal diplomatic avenues), interventionist public diplomacy (agreements and conferences), personal diplomacy (interactions between the prime minister and the president), and by strengthening its own domestic environmental programs.

PROVISIONS

The 1990 Clean Air Act Amendments were divided into four main categories: attainment and maintenance of air quality standards (smog); motor vehicles and alternative fuels; toxic air pollutants; and acid deposition (acid rain). Furthermore, the acid rain provision created a new market system allowing the trading of air pollution allowances. Businesses that pollute below established standards may earn air pollution credits which may then be sold to companies that pollute more than the federally mandated standards allow.

The provisions on ambient air quality (smog) directly affect ozone, carbon monoxide, and particulate matter. Cities that failed to meet standards for human health were allowed six years to come under compliance. An exception was made for Los Angeles, the most highly polluted city in the United States, which was given approximately twenty years to attain the new standards.

States were required to initiate or upgrade inspection and maintenance programs, install vapor recovery at gas stations, and otherwise reduce hydrocarbon and nitrogen oxide emissions from both small and major stationary sources. States were also mandated to adopt transportation controls that would offset the rapid growth in vehicle miles traveled. In addition, the new act strengthened the ability of the EPA and the states to enforce standards by requiring individual sources of pollution to meet their obligations within a single five-year operating permit. The states were given three years to develop permit programs and submit them to the EPA. Sources were required to pay permit fees covering the costs of operating the programs.

The provisions on motor vehicles centered on vehicle emissions, alternative fuels, and the production of "clean" cars. Manufacturers of 1994-model-year cars were required to reduce tailpipe emissions of hydrocarbons, carbon monoxide, and nitrogen oxides and to maintain these standards over a longer vehicle life. Requirements were put in place to ensure that reformulated gasolines would be used in cities with severe ozone problems and that gasoline blended with alcohol (oxyfuels) would be sold during winter months in those cities having the worst carbon monoxide problems. California was instructed to implement tighter emission limits through a combination of vehicle technology and clean fuels—substitutes for gasoline or blends of substitutes with gasoline.

In a departure from the 1970 law, Congress required emission limits for all major sources of hazardous or toxic air pollutants. Furthermore, Congress did not leave the determination of "toxic" and "hazardous" to the EPA but instead specifically listed 189 chemicals to be regulated. Congress required the EPA to list the categories of industrial processes in chemical plants, oil refineries, steel plants, and other facilities that emit these pollutants; to issue standards for each of the source categories by the deadlines specified; and to use as a basis the minimum regulatory standards provided in Title III of the law. Moreover, Congress required risk management plans for accidental release of air toxics and established the independent Chemical Safety Board to investigate chemical accidents to determine their causes.

Title IV of the 1990 Clean Air Act Amendments centered on reducing the major precursors of acid rain—sulfur dioxide and nitrogen oxide. A two-phase, market-based system was established to reduce sulfur dioxide emissions from power plants by more than half. Plants are issued allowances based on fixed emission rates set in the law and on their previous fossil fuel use. They pay penalties if emissions exceed the allowances they hold. Allowances can be banked or traded. In phase 1, large high-emission plants located in eastern and midwestern states were mandated to achieve reductions by 1995. In phase 2, commencing on January 1, 2000, emission limits were imposed on smaller, cleaner plants and tightened on phase 1 plants. All sources were required to install continuous emission monitors to ensure compliance. Emissions of nitrogen oxides were to be reduced by two million tons a year from the 1980 levels.

The new act phased out production of chlorofluorocarbons (CFCs), carbon tetrachloride, and methyl chloride by the year

2000 and methyl chloroform by the year 2002. Companies servicing air conditioning for cars are required to purchase certified recycling equipment and to train employees to use this equipment. The EPA is directed to develop regulations requiring reduced emissions from all other refrigeration sectors to their lowest achievable levels. By November, 1992, use of CFCs in nonessential applications was prohibited. Finally, the act mandated warning labels on all containers and products (refrigerators, foam insulation) that enclose CFCs and other ozone-depleting chemicals.

IMPACT

The 1990 Clean Air Act Amendments were a notable achievement on several accounts. They are considered the most comprehensive set of regulations ever developed to reduce air pollution. In this regard, the amendments set up controls for three major pollution problems (CFCs, air toxics, and acid rain) that were not covered by the Clean Air Act of 1970 or the 1977 amendments. They clearly limited administrative discretion by specifying the requirements and deadlines for the EPA, states, and regulated industries to come under compliance, and they provided marketlike incentives to encourage compliance.

Leslie R. Alm

SOURCES FOR FURTHER STUDY

Bryner, Gary C. *Blue Skies, Green Politics: The Clean Air Act of 1990.* Washington, D.C.: CQ Press, 1993.

Cohen, Richard E. *Washington at Work: Back Rooms and Clean Air.* New York: Macmillan, 1992.

Environmental Law 21, no. 4 (1991). Special issue on the Clean Air Act Amendments of 1990.

Hollander, Jack M. *The Energy-Environment Connection.* Washington, D.C.: Island Press, 1992.

Library of Congress. Congressional Research Service. *Environment and Natural Resources Policy Division. A Legislative History of the Clean Air Act Amendments of 1990.* Buffalo, N.Y.: William S. Hein, 1998.

Rosenbaum, Walter A. *Environmental Politics and Policy.* 2d ed. Washington, D.C.: CQ Press, 1991.

Schmandt, Jurgen, Judith Clarkson, and Hilliard Roderick. *Acid Rain and Friendly Neighbors: The Policy Dispute Between Canada and the United States.* Rev. ed. Durham, N.C.: Duke University Press, 1988.

Switzer, Jacqueline Vaughn. *Environmental Politics: Domestic and Global Dimensions.* New York: St. Martin's Press, 1994.

Vig, Norman J., and Michael E. Kraft. *Environmental Policy in the 1990's.* Washington, D.C.: CQ Press, 1990.

SEE ALSO: Air Pollution Control Act (1955); Clean Air Act (1963); Motor Vehicle Air Pollution Control Act (1965); Clean Air Act Amendments of 1970 (1970); National Environmental Policy Act (1970); Clean Air Act Amendments of 1977 (1977); Convention on Long-Range Transboundary Air Pollution (1979); Alternative Motor Fuels Act (1988); Montreal Protocol (1990); Pollution Prevention Act (1990).

NATIVE AMERICAN GRAVES PROTECTION AND REPATRIATION ACT

DATE: November 16, 1990
U.S. STATUTES AT LARGE: 104 Stat. 3042
PUBLIC LAW: 101-601
U.S. CODE: 25 § 3001-3013
CATEGORIES: Native Americans; Religious Liberty

This act changed the relationship between American Indians and mainstream museums and academic institutions by insisting that rights of scientific inquiry do not supersede basic human rights to respect the dead.

By the middle of the nineteenth century, Americans were fascinated with the science of phrenology, a process of measuring skulls to determine intelligence. The so-called science operated on the premise that racial minority groups, including American Indians, were inferior to Europeans, and that this inferiority was detectable in their physical appearance. Indian graves were looted to provide skulls for study. Later in the nineteenth century, the U.S. surgeon general allowed Indian remains to be collected from battlefields and other areas, and these were shipped to the Army Medical Museum in Washington, D.C., for study. Eventually, the remains were transferred to the Smithsonian Institution for exhibit and study. By the 1880's, Indians were considered a vanishing race and there was a rush to collect Indian remains and artifacts. Many graves were looted to build museum collections. In 1906, Congress passed the Antiquities Act, which made it illegal to excavate Indian grave sites on public lands without a permit. However, Indian remains and funeral objects were categorized as "natural resources," and universities and museums readily obtained permits. In the 1930's, Indian artifacts became popular art collectibles and looting burial sites became a major way of supplying the market.

In the 1960's and 1970's, Indian activists began to seek return of remains and artifacts, but their requests were ignored. In the mid-1980's, Indian people sought congressional support to draft legislation for return of skeletal remains and funeral objects. In Indian belief, the remains of the dead should be returned to Mother Earth to complete their journey into the spirit world. However, the museum and scientific communities opposed return of any remains or grave items, stating these were necessary objects for study. Indians countered that all other Americans were protected against grave robbing and human remains were not property to be taken and studied at will.

In 1990, Indian groups and the scientific and museum communities worked to craft compromise legislation known as the Native American Graves Protection and Repatriation Act (NAGPRA). This law states that all agencies who receive federal funds must notify tribes of all human remains, funeral artifacts, and sacred objects in their collections, including objects of cultural patrimony, or objects that have ongoing importance to the tribe. Indian graves on federal lands are protected, and the sale of human remains and funeral objects is forbidden. NAGPRA permits tribes to negotiate for return of artifacts. Human remains are to be returned to the proper tribe for burial. A review committee appointed by the secretary of the interior mediates disputes; however, dissatisfied parties can go to court. The Smithsonian Institution is exempt from NAGPRA regulations, but the national museum does work closely with tribes on return of human remains. NAGPRA, though it has some loopholes, is an important piece of legislation, because it recognizes the sanctity of tribal religious teachings and honors the rights of American Indians to oversee and maintain cultural continuity from generation to generation.

Carole A. Barrett

SOURCES FOR FURTHER STUDY

Bray, Tamara L., ed. *The Future of the Past: Archaeologists, Native Americans and Repatriation.* New York: Garland Publishing, 2001.

Mihesuah, Devon A., ed. *Repatriation Reader: Who Owns American Indian Remains?* Lincoln: University of Nebraska Press, 2000.

Swindler, Nina, et al., eds. *Native Americans and Archaeologists: Stepping Stones to Common Ground.* Walnut Creek, Calif.: AltaMira Press, 1997.

SEE ALSO: American Indian Religious Freedom Act (1978); Alaska National Interest Lands Conservation Act (1980).

IMMIGRATION ACT OF 1990

DATE: November 29, 1990
U.S. STATUTES AT LARGE: 104 Stat. 4978
PUBLIC LAW: 101-649
CATEGORIES: Immigration

This law set numerical limits for immigrants to the United States and established a system of preferences to determine which of the many applicants for admission should be accepted.

This law was passed in response to a widespread belief among legislators and the general public that many of the economic and social ills of the United States are caused by large populations of poor, non-English-speaking immigrants and in response to a growing need for skilled workers in technical fields in an increasingly international marketplace. The act, one of a number of immigration laws passed since the Immigration Act of 1891, set numerical limits for immigrants to the United States and established a system of preferences to determine which of the many applicants for admission should be accepted. Under the terms of the 1990 act, only 675,000 immigrants, not including political refugees, were to be admitted to the United States each year. These immigrants were eligible for preferential admission consideration if they fell into one of three groups: immigrants who had family members already legally in the country; employment-based immigrants who were able to prove that they had exceptional ability in certain professions with a high demand; and those from designated underrepresented nations, who were labeled "diversity immigrants."

Because the new law nearly tripled the annual allotment of employment-based immigrants from 54,000 to 140,000, business and industry leaders heralded their increased opportunity to compete internationally for experienced and talented engineers, technicians, and multinational executives. Others believed that the preference for certain kinds of workers masked a preference for whites over nonwhites, and wealthier immigrants over poorer. Divisions over the law between racial and political groups intensified when successful lobbying led to refinements in the law making it easier for fashion models and musicians, especially from Europe, to gain visas, while efforts to gain admittance for more women fleeing abuse in African and Muslim nations failed.

The act made it easier for certain people—contract workers, musicians and other artists, researchers and educators participating in exchange programs—to perform skilled work in the United States on a temporary basis, with no intention of seeking citizenship. At the same time, the new law made it more difficult for unskilled workers, such as domestic workers and laborers, to obtain immigrant visas.

Finally, the Immigration Act of 1990 attempted to correct criticism of the 1986 Immigration Reform and Control Act by increasing that act's antidiscrimination provisions and increasing the penalties for discrimination. In a significant change in U.S. immigration law, the act revised the reasons a person might be refused immigrant status or be deported. After 1952, for example, communists were denied permission to enter the country on nonimmigrant work visas and were subject to deportation if identified, and potential political refugees from nations friendly to the United States were turned away as a matter of foreign policy. Under the new law, a wider range of political and ideological beliefs became acceptable.

Cynthia A. Bily

SOURCES FOR FURTHER STUDY

Kavass, Igor I., and Bernard D. Reams, eds. *Legislative History of the Immigration Act of 1990. Public Law 101-649.* Buffalo, N.Y.: William S. Hein, 1997.

National Immigration Project. *Immigration Act of 1990 Handbook: The Complete Guide to the 1990 Act.* New York: Clark Boardman Callaghan, 1994-1995.

SEE ALSO: Immigration Act of 1917 (1917); Immigration Act of 1921 (1921); Immigration Act of 1924 (1924); Immigration Act of 1943 (1943); Immigration and Nationality Act of 1952 (1952); Refugee Relief Act (1953); Communist Control Act (1954); Immigration and Nationality Act Amendments of 1965 (1965); Immigration Reform and Control Act of 1986 (1986); Amerasian Homecoming Act (1987).

CIVIL RIGHTS ACT OF 1991

DATE: November 21, 1991
U.S. STATUTES AT LARGE: 105 Stat. 1071
PUBLIC LAW: 102-166
CATEGORIES: Civil Rights and Liberties

This act restored equal-opportunity law to its status before 1989, the year in which several Supreme Court decisions weakened two decades of legal precedents.

The Civil Rights Act of 1991 has been described as among the most sweeping civil rights laws to be passed by Congress. In response to several adverse decisions by the Supreme Court, Senators Edward M. Kennedy and John C. Danforth jointly sponsored the Civil Rights Act of 1991, which was drafted with the objective of overturning these decisions. President George H. W. Bush, who had vetoed a similar bill in 1990, signed the bill into law in 1991.

REVERSING SUPREME COURT RULINGS

Through congressional hearings, Congress concluded that additional remedies under federal law were needed to deter unlawful harassment and intentional discrimination in the workplace; decisions of the Supreme Court had weakened the effectiveness of federal civil rights protection; and legislation was necessary to provide additional protection against unlawful discrimination in employment. The expressed purpose of the Civil Rights Act of 1991 was to restore the state of discrimination law to what it had been before 1989, the year in which a conservative Supreme Court issued several decisions that seriously threatened the enforceability of equal opportunity laws. The act further expanded the scope of coverage of relevant civil rights statutes to include individuals or plaintiffs who sued under the Age Discrimination Act (ADA) or the Rehabilitation Act of 1973, and granted coverage to federal employees of Congress and employees of U.S. companies located in foreign countries.

TITLE VII

Title VII of the Civil Rights Act of 1964 had made it unlawful to discriminate in employment because of race, ethnicity, color, sex, or religion. The primary issue facing judicial bodies empowered to adjudicate claims of discrimination was to define what employment practices violated Title VII and other antidiscrimination laws. Traditionally, employers screened potential employees by the use of general intelligence and aptitude tests, word-of-mouth recruiting, and other subjective criteria that disproportionately excluded or disparately impacted minorities from employment and promotion. In *Griggs v. Duke Power Company* (1971), which is considered the most important decision in the evolution of equal employment opportunity law, the Supreme Court had articulated the major principle that invalidated general intelligence tests and other criteria that had the effect of excluding minorities, regardless of the intent of the employer. The Court stated that if any criteria had a disparate impact upon the protected group, the criteria were unlawful and could be sustained only if they were related to the job and necessary for business. The burden of proof to rebut the claim shifted to the employer once the possibility of discrimination had been shown through statistical or other evidence.

In 1989, the Supreme Court issued several decisions that reversed the *Griggs* burden-of-proof standard and several other major legal principles governing unlawful discrimination. In *Wards Cove Packing Company v. Atonio*, the Supreme Court changed the *Griggs* standard by holding that employees not only must show that they were disparately and discriminatorily impacted but also must prove that the employer could have employed alternate ways with less disparate impact. In *Price Waterhouse v. Hopkins*, the Court held that even after the employer has been found guilty of unlawful discrimination, it could still escape liability by showing that the employee would have been dismissed or treated differently for another nondiscriminatory reason. These changes made it significantly more difficult for plaintiffs to prevail in suits.

The Civil Rights Act of 1991 restored the *Griggs* principle. It also reversed the *Price Waterhouse* decision, stipulating that an unlawful practice is established when the complaining party demonstrates that race, color, religion, or national origin was a motivating factor for any employment practice, even though other factors also motivated the decision.

Civil Rights Act of 1866

In *Paterson v. McLean Credit Union* (1989) the Supreme Court severely limited section 1981 of the Civil Rights Act of 1866 when it held that the act covered only unlawful discrimination with regard to race and national origin at the time of hiring. Acts of discrimination that occurred after hiring were no longer illegal under the Civil Rights Act of 1866. The Civil Rights Act of 1991 reversed this decision by prohibiting pre- and post-employment discrimination.

In *Lorance v. AT&T Technologies* (1989) the Supreme Court upheld the dismissal of discrimination charges by female employees who charged that the implementation of a new seniority system discriminated against them. This decision established the principle that although women had been adversely affected by a new seniority policy, their complaint was barred because the statute of limitations had expired. The Supreme Court ruled that the timing began at the time of the policy change and not when the women became aware of the discriminatory effects of the policy. This reasoning was criticized on the grounds that an individual often may not know the discriminatory impact of the policy change until long after the statute of limitations for filing has passed. The Civil Rights Act of 1991 restored the legal principle that the statute of limitations began when the individual becomes aware of the discrimination.

CONSENT DECREES

Many municipalities have entered into consent decrees that grant relief to minority employees to avoid lengthy and costly litigations. Such consent decrees may adversely affect the interests of white male employees. However, all parties affected by the decree are notified and given an opportunity to intervene to protect the interests of their members. Once the consent decree has been approved by the court, it cannot be challenged in the future. In *Martin v. Wilks* (1989) the Supreme Court established a new principle. It allowed new white firefighters who were not a party to the original consent decree and judgment to reopen the decision. Had this new principle been allowed to stand, it would have threatened the validity of hundreds of consent decrees in the United States. The Civil Rights Act of 1991 reversed this decision. The act precluded any later challenge by a present employee, former employee, or applicant to a consent decree granting affirmative rights to minority employees.

REMEDIES TO PLAINTIFFS

Several major differences existed between section 1981 of the Civil Rights Act of 1866 and other equal opportunity laws with respect to remedies available to plaintiffs. Whereas a plaintiff had a right to a jury trial and compensatory and punitive damages under section 1981 of the 1866 act, plaintiffs who sued under Title VII, the ADA, and the Rehabilitation Act had no right to a jury trial and could only seek compensatory damages. The Civil Rights Acts of 1991 expanded these rights accorded to plaintiffs under section 1981 to plaintiffs who were subjected to intentional discrimination under Title VII, the ADA, and the Rehabilitation Act.

FEDERAL EMPLOYEES

Another notable limitation in the equal opportunity law was the absence of protection from discrimination for federal employees and U.S. citizens working in U.S. firms overseas. The Civil Rights Act of 1991 extended the right to sue to federal employees in the legislative and executive branches under Title VII, ADA, and the Rehabilitation Act. One exception was made to the definition of unlawful practices: that party affiliation and political compatibility may not be attacked as unfair employment practices. Furthermore, the act extended coverage to U.S. employees employed in foreign lands by U.S. firms.

Civil service examinations are required for most jobs and promotions in the public sector. Applicants are supposed to be chosen based on competitive scores earned. It has been charged, however, that these tests are biased in favor of white men in particular and white applicants and employees in general. Generally, a higher proportion of whites will score higher than members of minority groups. To ensure that a larger number of minorities will be hired and promoted, the scores are adjusted for minorities such that some minorities with lower scores occasionally may be selected over whites with higher scores. This adjustment of test scores, which is referred to as race norming, emerged as a contentious issue in the United States. The Civil Rights Act of 1991 expressly prohibits compensatory adjustments to test scores in employment based upon race or other protected characteristics.

Richard Hudson

SOURCES FOR FURTHER STUDY

Cathcart, David A., et al. *The Civil Rights Act of 1991.* Philadelphia: American Law Institute, 1993.

Kmiec, D. W., et al. "The Civil Rights Act of 1991: Theory and Practice—A Symposium." *Notre Dame Law Review* 68 (1993): 911-1164.

McDowell, Douglas, S., ed. *Civil Rights Act of 1991: Legislative History.* Washington, D.C.: Employment Policy Foundation, 1992.

Practising Law Institute. *The Civil Rights Act of 1991: Its Impact on Employment Discrimination Litigation.* New York: Author, 1992.

Reams, Bernard D, and Faye Couture, eds. *The Civil Rights Act of*

1991: A Legislative History of Public Law 102-166. 7 vols. Buffalo, N.Y.: William S. Hein, 1994.

Rutgers Law Review 45, no. 4 (Summer, 1993): 887-1087.

U.S. Commission on Civil Rights. *Affirmative Action in 1980's: Dismantling the Process of Discrimination: A Statement of the United States Commission on Civil Rights.* Washington, D.C.: Author, 1981.

U.S. Equal Employment Opportunity Commission. *EEOC Compliance Manual.* Chicago: Commerce Clearing House, 1995.

SEE ALSO: Thirteenth Amendment (1865); Civil Rights Act of 1866 (1866); Fourteenth Amendment (1868); Fifteenth Amendment (1870); Civil Rights Act of 1957 (1957); Civil Rights Act of 1960 (1960); Civil Rights Act of 1964 (1964); Title VII of the Civil Rights Act of 1964 (1964); Twenty-fourth Amendment (1964); Voting Rights Act of 1965 (1965); Civil Rights Act of 1968 (1968); Fair Housing Act (1968); Voting Rights Act of 1975 (1975).

TWENTY-SEVENTH AMENDMENT

ALSO KNOWN AS: Madison Amendment
DATE: Ratified May 7, 1992; proclaimed May 19, 1992
U.S. STATUTES AT LARGE: 1 Stat. 97
CATEGORIES: Constitutional Law; Government Procedure and Organization

Although it has had little practical effect, the overwhelming public support for this amendment, which places controls on pay raises for politicians, signaled public dissatisfaction with the way in which its representatives were conducting themselves.

On September 25, 1789, in response to public pressure, Congress submitted twelve proposed amendments to the state legislatures. These had been introduced by James Madison of Virginia. The first two of these dealt with the formula for congressional representation and with congressional pay. The first would have fixed the ratio of one representative for every thirty thousand people. The other required that an intervening election take place before any change in congressional salaries could take effect. The first proposal, had it been ratified and continued, would require that the House of Representatives consist of approximately nine thousand members in the year 2000. In December, 1791, the third through twelfth of the 1789 proposals were ratified and became the Bill of Rights. The first two proposals were ratified by only six states—not reaching the three-quarters required for approval by the Constitution. For years afterward they seemed to have no more than academic or historical significance.

REVIVING MADISON'S PAY RAISE AMENDMENT

In March, 1982, a student at the University of Texas discovered this bit of history and decided to promote a ratification movement for Madison's congressional pay raise amendment. This seemed possible because the Madison Amendment did not contain the seven-year time limit on ratification that had been used ever since Congress passed the Eighteenth Amendment (Prohibition) on to the states in 1917.

Fueled by public disdain for politicians and the government, the ratification movement gained momentum. Although an earlier decision of the Supreme Court suggests that the ratification process must be "sufficiently contemporaneous . . . to reflect the will of the people," Congress voted to accept the amendment after Michigan became the thirty-eighth state to ratify it on May 7, 1992. The congressional vote also finally laid to rest a few other amendments that had been proposed but never ratified. These included the Child Labor Amendment of 1924 and the very first of Madison's group of twelve. Thus, the first of Madison's proposals became part of the Constitution as the Twenty-seventh Amendment after 202 years.

PROVISIONS

The amendment provides that "No law, varying the compensation of the senators and representatives, shall take effect, until an election of Representatives shall have intervened." Its purpose is to permit the public to vote out of office any members of Congress who have voted large pay raises for themselves. Although it has little practical effect, the overwhelming public support it received served as an indicator that the public was dissatisfied with the way in which its representatives were conducting themselves. It spoke to generalized contempt for "politicians." It may be that this same attitude contributed to bringing about the change from Democratic to Republican control only two years after the ratification of the Twenty-seventh Amendment.

Robert Jacobs

SOURCES FOR FURTHER STUDY
Farber, Daniel A., and Suzanna Sherry. *History of the American Constitution*. Belmont, Calif.: Wadsworth, 1999.
Peltason, J. W. *Corwin & Peltason's Understanding the Constitution*. 14th ed. New York: Harcourt Brace, 1997.
Vile, John R. *Encyclopedia of Constitutional Amendments, Proposed Amendments, and Amending Issues, 1789-1995*. Santa Barbara, Calif: ABC-CLIO, 1996.

SEE ALSO: Pendleton Act (1883); Hatch Act (1939); Federal Election Campaign Act (1972); Ethics in Government Act (1978); Bipartisan Campaign Reform Act (2002).

WOMEN IN APPRENTICESHIP AND NONTRADITIONAL OCCUPATIONS ACT

DATE: October 27, 1992
U.S. STATUTES AT LARGE: 106 Stat. 3468
PUBLIC LAW: 102-530
CATEGORIES: Labor and Employment; Women's Issues

This law recognized and attempted to remedy the exclusion of women from skilled trades, particularly those in which apprenticeship is required.

After the passage of the Equal Pay Act of 1963 and other federal civil rights laws that were designed to equalize women's position in the labor market many inequalities remained. Women were still not to be found in many occupations, especially in such skilled occupations as machinist, plumber, electrician, carpenter, or mason. In most of these skilled trades, apprenticeship programs are required for entry. Few women attempted to enter these occupations, largely because they had been traditionally filled by men.

In response, Congress passed the Women in Apprenticeship and Nontraditional Occupations Act in 1992. Congress recognized that two of every three new entrants to the labor market would be women and that significant barriers to women's employment in the skilled trades continued to exist. The law encourages women to enter nontraditional and apprenticeable occupations by establishing two new functions in the Department of Labor. First, employers and labor unions are to be informed of the availability of technical assistance to assist them in preparing for the employment of women in nontraditional occupations. Second, a program of grants to community organizations was established to provide technical assistance to employers and skills training for women.

By 1995, some progress had been made toward achieving the goals of the act, although there had not yet been any large-scale entry of women into nontraditional occupations. The program continued, however, and was expected to bring about more significant changes in the long run.

Robert Jacobs

SOURCES FOR FURTHER STUDY

Kerka, Sandra. *Has Nontraditional Training Worked for Women?* Columbus: Ohio State University, 1999.

United States. *Nontraditional Employment for Women Act.* Washington, D.C.: Government Printing Office, 1991.

United States Department of Labor. *Get the Skills That Pay the Bills: Secretary's Initiative to Support Women and Minorities in the Skilled Trades.* Washington, D.C.: Department of Labor, 1992.

SEE ALSO: Equal Pay Act (1963); Pregnancy Discrimination Act (1978).

START II TREATY

DATE: January 3, 1993
CATEGORIES: Foreign Relations; Treaties and Agreements

The United States and the Soviet Union agreed to deep reductions in their nuclear arsenals in an attempt to inaugurate a post-Cold War environment of reduced threats from superpowers.

For decades after the end of World War II, the United States and the Soviet Union amassed ever-increasing numbers of weapons. For most of that time, arms control agreements were elusive. The continuous improvement in East-West relations in the late 1980's paved the way for unprecedented agreements to reverse the arms race in Europe, including the treaty to eliminate intermediate-range nuclear forces (INF) in 1987 and to significantly cut conventional forces in Europe (CFE) in 1990. A year later, culminating almost a decade of arms control talks initiated by U.S. President Ronald Reagan, the United States and the Soviet Union signed an agreement to reduce strategic nuclear weapons, which by definition threatened the territory of the superpowers themselves. Only months after the Strategic Arms Reductions Treaty, or START, was signed, however, the Soviet Union dissolved into fifteen sovereign countries.

POST-COLD WAR WORLD

The United States and the former Soviet republics—particularly Russia—set about to restructure their relationships in the post-Soviet, post-Cold War world. In terms of nuclear arms, two issues were paramount. First, how could START be implemented when one of its signatories no longer existed? It was agreed at a meeting in Lisbon, Portugal, on May 23, 1992, that all the former Soviet republics would be bound by the treaty, that Russia would possess the remaining, permitted nuclear weapons, and that the other former Soviet republics would commit to forgo the acquisition of any nuclear arms. The second issue was how the nuclear reductions called for in START could be extended, acknowledging that the Cold War's nuclear legacy posed an unacceptable threat that must be reduced even more severely. Accordingly, the United States and Russia began work on a START II treaty.

NEGOTIATIONS

The president of the Russian Federation, Boris Yeltsin, was absorbed by numerous issues during his country's first year as a sovereign state. Russia was threatened by ethnic and national tensions, economic collapse, burgeoning crime, societal instability, tense relations with its newly independent neighbors, and a variety of other problems. Yeltsin, like Soviet President Mikhail Gorbachev before him, sought above all else to stabilize relations with the West, particularly the United States. Western cooperation, technical assistance, and financial aid would be critical to Yeltsin's efforts to address his country's problems. The United States, as the world's sole superpower, clearly approached the START II talks from a position of strength.

In a Washington, D.C., summit on June 17, 1992, scarcely six months after the collapse of the Soviet Union, the United States and Russia signed a joint understanding to reduce their strategic nuclear arsenals by two-thirds. In Moscow, six months later, on January 3, 1993, Yeltsin and President George H. W. Bush signed the Treaty Between the United States of America and the Russian Federation on Further Reduction and Limitation of Strategic Offensive Arms (START II).

TREATY PROVISIONS

One of the key features of START II was that it called for the complete elimination of heavy intercontinental ballistic missiles (ICBMs) and all ICBMs with multiple warheads. These land-based ICBMs are considered particularly threatening to international stability because they are effective offensive weapons and are relatively vulnerable to destruction by a preemptive strike. As a result, logic compels leaders in charge of these weapons to favor using them in a time of heightened international tensions. Therefore, eliminating these weapons can be expected to enhance stability in crisis situations. Because the Soviet Union, and thus Russia, traditionally had placed a large proportion of their nuclear warheads on heavy ICBMs, this provision of START II was seen to be of greater benefit to the United States.

Although START II was to eliminate the most destabilizing ICBMs, single-warhead ICBMs were still permitted. So were nuclear weapons deployed on aircraft and on submarines. The Central Limits provision of START II placed ceilings on the total number of strategic nuclear weapons, irrespective of deployment. The first phase of this provision, to be completed seven years after implementation of the first START treaty (now known as START I), required that Russia and the United States reduce their number of deployed strategic warheads to 3,800 and 4,250, respectively. (START I had set a limit of 6,000 for each country.) The second phase of START II, which was to be concluded by January 1, 2003, requires a further reduction to 3,000 for Russia and 3,500 for the United States. By this date, all heavy and multiwarhead ICBMs must be eliminated. Unlike its predecessor, START II required that certain classes of decommissioned missiles be destroyed. In general, START I allowed undeployed, decommissioned missiles to be stored or converted.

START II could not be implemented until START I was ratified by the respective legislatures and entered into force. In many ways, START II built upon and complemented START I. Specific sublimits placed on submarine- and plane-deployed warheads by START I remain in effect under START II. START I's ceiling of sixteen hundred total strategic nuclear delivery vehicles (such as missiles and bombers, as opposed to the warheads deployed on them) also remains in effect. START II did, however, change the way that bombers are counted. Under START I, each bomber would count toward the country's nuclear ceilings as one warhead, regardless of how many warheads were actually on board. START II counts the actual number of warheads on board.

Compliance with the provisions of START II was to be ensured by a series of highly intrusive verification measures. U.S. and Russian representatives would be permitted to observe the removal, conversion, and destruction of missiles. Heavy bombers could be inspected to confirm weapon loads. Various other remaining weapons systems must be exhibited to confirm their compliance with the treaty's provisions. The verification regime of START II built substantially upon that of START I.

RATIFICATION

Although START II was signed by the Russian and U.S. presidents, ratification of the treaty was not assured. Several factors interacted to complicate the situation. The first START treaty, a precondition for START II, had not gone into force at the time START II was signed. In addition, the Republican Bush administration was replaced by the Democratic administration of Bill Clinton only weeks after the Moscow summit. Although Yeltsin remained president of Russia, his policies and international agreements, including START II, were seen as too hasty and pro-Western by the new, independent Russian Parliament—a far cry from the compliant Soviet-era legislature. Finally, the legal questions arising from the disintegration of the Soviet Union complicated the question of precisely who was bound by START. For these reasons, the Clinton administration withdrew the treaty from Senate consideration until a more opportune political environment could be achieved. The December, 1998, bombing of Iraq by the United States and the Kosovo conflict in March, 1999, played a large part in the delay.

START I finally went into force on December 5, 1994. Controlled by the new Republican majority, Senate hearings on START II resumed in early 1995, and in January the Senate ratified the treaty. The Russian parliament also was considering the treaty, and on April 14, 2000, the Duma, the lower house, ratified START II, opening the door to negotiations on START III, which was designed to make even greater arms reductions.

Steve D. Boilard, updated by
Christina J. Moose

Sources for Further Study

Arbotov, Alexei. "START II, Red Ink, and Boris Yeltsin." *Bulletin of the Atomic Scientists* 49, no. 3 (April, 1993): 16-21.

Arms Control Today. "START II: Treaty Between the United States of America and the Russian Federation on the Further Reduction and Limitation of Strategic Offense Arms." 23, no. 1 (January/February, 1990): S5-S8.

Mendelsohn, Jack. "Next Steps in Nuclear Arms Control." *Issues in Science and Technology* 9, no. 3 (Spring, 1993): 28-34.

Quester, George H., and Victor A. Utgoff. "Toward an International Nuclear Security Policy." *Washington Quarterly* 17, no. 4 (Autumn, 1994): 5-19.

U.S. Department of State Dispatch. "START II Treaty Approval Urged." 4, no. 20 (May 17, 1993): 345-347.

Winkler, Allan M. "Keep Pressing for Arms Control." *The Chronicle of Higher Education* 39, no. 37 (May 19, 1993): B1-B4.

See also: Nuclear Nonproliferation Treaty (1968); SALT I Treaty (1973); SALT II Treaty (1979); INF Treaty (1987); U.S.-Russia Arms Agreement (2002).

FAMILY AND MEDICAL LEAVE ACT

DATE: February 5, 1993
U.S. STATUTES AT LARGE: 107 Stat. 6
PUBLIC LAW: 103-3
U.S. CODE: 29 § 2601
CATEGORIES: Children's Issues; Health and Welfare; Women's Issues

This law was the first federal act to protect employment status for workers who need to take leave in order to care for a sick relative or newborn child.

On February 3, 1993, Congress passed the Family and Medical Leave Act of 1993, a comprehensive plan to ensure job security and leave opportunities for U.S. employees in times of family and medical need or crisis. President Bill Clinton signed the act into law on February 5, and it took full effect on August 6, 1993.

CHANGING SOCIAL CONDITIONS
Through much of the twentieth century, the paradigm for families in North America was clearly defined: Husbands worked in the marketplace and provided financial support, and wives stayed home managing domestic life and child care. Women looked after children or ailing family members. Husbands tended to be "company men," so employers were not likely to accommodate family crises. Extended families were concentrated; there was often a grandparent, cousin, or other relative nearby who could help with family caretaking.

Shifts in lifestyles, demographics, and work patterns had rendered this paradigm virtually meaningless by the 1980's. The number of women in the workforce increased dramatically during the wartime 1940's, declined temporarily after the war's end, but then grew again. Economic realities engendered double-income families, and the women's movement encouraged women to establish their own careers. Only 19 percent of women in the United States worked outside the home in 1900, but by the early 1990's, that figure was as high as 74 percent. With increased rates of divorce and unmarried parenthood, single-parent families became common, especially in inner-city, impoverished, and minority communities. In 1988, 27 percent of families had a single parent, twice the percentage of 1970.

Another change was the increase in life expectancies as a result of advances in medical technology, both in general and in the treatment of serious illnesses. People lived longer, and the U.S. population as a whole had aged dramatically. In 1993, the thirty-two million citizens over the age of sixty-five constituted 12 percent of the populace and was its fastest-growing segment. Home care of the elderly often was viewed as preferable to institutionalization, and many serious illnesses could be treated without hospitalization. According to the National Council on Aging, at least 20 percent of the workforce had some caregiving responsibilities.

As a result of these factors, a vast majority of U.S. workers potentially faced difficult choices between work and family. A 1990 study by the Southport Institute for Policy Analysis estimated that 11 percent of caregivers were forced to quit their jobs to care for relatives. The U.S. Small Business Administration estimated that 150,000 workers were losing their jobs annually because they could not take medical leave. Others found their jobs less than secure upon returning from leave. In the absence of a national policy, even sympathetic employers could change policy without notice. The employee had little true protection.

The Civil Rights Act of 1964 and the Pregnancy Discrimination Act of 1978 provided certain guarantees, but comprehensive federal legislation was needed. Prior to the Family and Medical Leave Act of 1993, the United States was the only industrialized nation in the world without such a law; Japan provided twelve weeks of pregnancy leave with partial pay, and Canadian women were given forty-one weeks. Sweden offered eighteen months of family leave for use at the time of birth and when a child entered school. Norway, Austria, France, England, and Luxembourg had laws that provided leave for the care of an elderly parent.

PASSAGE AND PROVISIONS

Family and medical leave legislation was proposed several times during the 1980's, only to meet congressional gridlock and presidential vetoes. Earlier versions of the act were very strong, offering up to twenty-six weeks of leave. Conservatives of both parties feared that such legislation would weigh heavily on businesses and strongly opposed any federally mandated employee policies. President George H. W. Bush vetoed a watered-down 1992 bill, offering instead his own plan based on refundable tax credits for employers. Even the 1993 measure was almost blocked by Senate Republicans with an extraneous amendment reaffirming the ban on homosexuals in the military. However, in the opening weeks of the Clinton administration, the 1993 act was passed by bipartisan margins in both houses.

The Family and Medical Leave Act required U.S. employers to offer limited unpaid leave in four circumstances: upon the birth of an employee's child; upon the arrival of an adopted child; in cases in which the employee is needed to provide care for a spouse, child, or parent with a serious health condition; or in cases in which the employee is afflicted with a debilitating health condition. The act also provided definitions and restrictions to balance employers' and employees' interests. It ensured that employees returning from leave be given the same or a comparable position and salary with full benefits reinstated. The act exempted businesses with fewer than fifty employees, which could be seriously impaired by the loss of essential employees, and established employee eligibility according to length of employment. It also dealt with issues such as the substitution of available paid leave, advance notification of leave-taking, and formal certification of debilitating health conditions. The act established a bipartisan, sixteen-member Commission on Leave and gave the secretary of labor investigative authority for enforcement. It also opened the door for employees to initiate civil actions to remedy alleged violations.

RESPONSE AND IMPACT

The act was viewed by many as a halfway measure that achieved more by its mere existence than by its specific guarantees. The national policy stopped short of numerous state laws and countless corporate policies already in effect. Conversely, an estimated 50 percent of U.S. workers did not work enough hours or for large enough companies to be covered. The cost to the employee of unpaid time off remained too high for many workers to afford to leave to take care of family problems.

In 1992, the Family and Work Institute released a three-year study of a thousand companies in Rhode Island, Oregon, Minnesota, and Wisconsin regarding compliance with state leave laws. Ninety-one percent reported no trouble adapting to state rules; 94 percent of leave takers had returned to their positions; and 75 percent of supervisors reported a positive effect on company business. It was estimated to be two to five times as expensive to replace an employee permanently as to grant temporary leave. A large number of companies with established leave policies, including such giants as DuPont, AT&T, and Aetna, reported limited problems and favorable results—including cost-effectiveness—from their family leave programs.

The Family and Medical Leave Act of 1993 established important guarantees without a major overall effect on either the nation's economic health or its business practices. It helped to standardize those practices and relieve family leave policy making of the pressures of business competitiveness. Since the act has taken effect, hundreds of lawsuits and complaints have been brought to the courts and the Department of Labor. In 1995, new rules were issued to clarify the situations covered by the act and the procedures required of both employees and employers in requesting and granting leave.

Barry Mann

SOURCES FOR FURTHER STUDY

Bauer, Gary L. "Leaving Families Out." *National Review* 45, no. 6 (March 29, 1993): 58-60.

Congressional Digest. "Family and Medical Leave Legislation." 72, no. 1 (January, 1993): 2-32.

Maynard, Roberta. "Meet the New Law on Family Leave." *Nation's Business* 81, no. 4 (April, 1993): 26.

Murray, Marjorie. "Family Leave: Read This Before You Take (or Give) It." *Working Woman* 20, no. 5 (May, 1995): 15.

Saltzman, Amy. "Time Off Without Pain." *U.S. News & World Report* 115, no. 5 (August 2, 1993): 52-55.

Wilcox, Brian L., and Janet E. O'Keefe. "Families, Policy, and Family Support Policies." *Prevention in Human Services* 9, no. 1 (1990): 109-125.

Wisenale, Steven K., and Michael D. Allinson. "Family Leave Legislation: State and Federal Initiatives." *Family Relations* 38, no. 2 (1989): 182-189.

Zuckman, Jill. "Provisions: Family Leave Law." *Congressional Quarterly Weekly Report* 51, no. 7 (February 13, 1993): 335.

_____. "Top Priority Given Family Leave Bill." *Congressional Quarterly Weekly Report* 51, no. 2 (January 9, 1993): 79.

SEE ALSO: Age Discrimination Act (1975); Pregnancy Discrimination Act (1978); Family Support Act (1988); Americans with Disabilities Act (1990); Child Care and Development Block Grant Act (1990).

NATIONAL AND COMMUNITY SERVICE TRUST ACT

DATE: September 21, 1993
U.S. STATUTES AT LARGE: 107 Stat. 883
PUBLIC LAW: 103-82
CATEGORIES: Health and Welfare

This act was designed to coordinate and increase national service programs, establishing, among others, the AmeriCorps program.

The National and Community Service Trust Act of 1993 was drafted by the Clinton administration and a bipartisan group of legislators. Earlier national service programs include the Civilian Conservation Corps (CCC), established by President Franklin D. Roosevelt to enable young people to restore and conserve public lands; the Peace Corps, established in 1961 to provide service opportunities for young people in less developed counties; and Volunteers in Service to America (VISTA), established in 1964 as part of President Lyndon Johnson's War on Poverty.

Those promoting the 1993 bill believed that it would encourage civic engagement among young people and would address pressing social problems found among the poor and disadvantaged in the United States. The bill also represents part of the "reinventing government" movement, which supports innovative means, such as private-public partnerships, for solving public problems.

The 1993 legislation both built upon and amended the National and Community Service Act of 1990. Signed by President George H. W. Bush, the 1990 legislation created the Points of Light Foundation, which was a private and nonprofit corporation, and established the Commission on National and Community Service. The commission directed model service programs and educational programs for students in elementary and secondary schools. The 1993 act eliminated the Commission on National and Community Service and established a public corporation, the Corporation for National and Community Service (CNCS), to oversee and network federal service programs. A board of directors consisting of private citizens governs the CNCS. The act also established two programs to be overseen by the CNCS, AmeriCorps and Learn and Serve America. VISTA was made a part of AmeriCorps.

AMERICORPS

AmeriCorps is the best-known program established by the 1993 act. Through this program, young people between the ages of eighteen and twenty-four work in poor and disadvantaged communities to help health and educational needs. In addition to a small stipend, participants receive financial support for college education. In its first year, 20,000 young people participated. At the end of 2001, more than 250,000 had served under the auspices of the program. Participants in AmeriCorps-VISTA work in existing agencies, mostly state agencies and some national nonprofit organizations, which have sought additional support. Participants in AmeriCorps-National Civilian Community Corps work for ten months and are based in five regional campuses; they work in teams of ten to fifteen on public safety and public health projects.

SENIOR CORPS

The CNCS also supports Senior Corps, a program that provides opportunities for Americans over fifty-five years of age. Senior Corps directs three programs: Retired and Senior Volunteer Program

(RSVP), a program that engages engages people over fifty-five in a variety of programs; Foster Grandparents, a program that provides those over sixty with limited incomes an opportunity to serve young people with exceptional needs; and Senior Companions, provides opportunities for those over sixty to help adult clients with living needs.

Such programs continued after the Clinton administration: President George W. Bush, a strong advocate of community service, created the USA Freedom Corps through an executive order and supported legislation that would increase funding for the CNCS.

Michael L. Coulter

SOURCES FOR FURTHER STUDY

Lenkowsky, Leslie, and James L. Perry. "Reinventing Government: The Case of National Service." *Public Administration Review* 60, no. 4 (July, 2000).

Waldman, Steven. *The Bill: How the Adventures of Clinton's National Service Bill Reveal What Is Corrupt, Comic, Cynical, and Noble About Washington.* New York: Viking, 1995.

SEE ALSO: Economic Opportunity Act (1964); Higher Education Act (1965).

NORTH AMERICAN FREE TRADE AGREEMENT

DATE: Approved November 20, 1993
CATEGORIES: Business, Commerce, and Trade; Foreign Relations; Treaties and Agreements

This agreement reduced barriers to the flow of goods, services, and investment among Canada, Mexico, and the United States.

Approval of the North American Free Trade Agreement (NAFTA) in 1993 was one in a long series of policy actions reflecting a commitment by the United States government to relatively unrestricted international trade and finance. This commitment began in 1934, when, in the depths of the Great Depression, the United States adopted a policy of reciprocal trade agreements. Agreements were negotiated whereby the United States reduced tariffs on the products of other countries that agreed to the do the same for U.S. products. This helped trade to expand and gave each country an opportunity both to sell more exports and to buy more imports. At the end of World War II, this policy was extended by the formation of the General Agreement on Tariffs and Trade (GATT), which involved many countries negotiating at once. GATT negotiations involved a series of "rounds," with the Uruguay round ending in new agreements in 1994.

FREE TRADE VS. PROTECTION

Policy toward international trade has always been controversial. Most economists argue that relatively free international trade encourages each country to specialize in the products it can produce most efficiently. Advocates claim that competition is intensified and innovation encouraged, allowing consumers to benefit from lower prices and higher productivity. Such benefits were evident in products such as automobiles (after the 1950's) and electronic products (after the 1970's). However, within each country there are industries that believe they would not be able to compete with imports. U.S. companies producing clothing and shoes, for example, have complained that they are undersold by imports from low-wage countries such as China. One reason that wages are low in China, however, is that labor productivity has typically also been low there.

As NAFTA was being developed, many firms and labor unions opposed the liberalization of trade, arguing that competition from imports would reduce job opportunities. These issues were strongly debated in the presidential election of 1992. President George H. W. Bush had initiated and encouraged the formulation of NAFTA, and Democratic candidate Bill Clinton supported it, but Independent candidate H. Ross Perot strongly opposed NAFTA. He claimed there would be a "giant sucking sound" as U.S. jobs were transferred to Mexico. Many environmentalists also opposed NAFTA, claiming that Mexican products had another unfair advantage because requirements for environmental protection were lax in Mexico. Some libertarian groups opposed NAFTA on the basis that it did not really provide free trade, because of the substantial bureaucratic involvement required to carry out its many complex provisions.

Supporters of NAFTA argued that many U.S. business firms would gain by improved access to Mexican markets. For example, privatization of the Mexican telephone system in 1991 created profit opportunities for U.S. firms who were among the world leaders in this high-tech sector. U.S. firms producing motion pictures, recorded music, television programs, and computer software received much revenue from sales to other countries and often were damaged by intellectual piracy. NAFTA offered them the prospect of improved protection of their intellectual property rights. Pro-NAFTA forces also argued that the treaty would increase the prosperity of the Mexican economy, increasing wage levels and decreasing the large flow of Mexican immigrants across the southern border of the United States. They also pointed out that the economies of Canada and Mexico were far smaller than that of the United States, and thus were unable to flood U.S. markets with goods.

APPROVAL AND PROVISIONS

The treaty was first approved in Canada, where it was supported by the ruling Progressive Conservative Party, completing legislative approval June 23, 1993. In the U.S. Congress, there was considerable opposition, but strong lobbying by President Clinton secured the treaty's approval on November 20, 1993. In Mexico, support by the dominant Institutional Revolutionary Party of President Carlos Salinas de Gortari assured relatively easy approval on November 22, 1993.

As finally approved, the agreement was a long and complex document. It had four major types of provisions. First, NAFTA reduced, and promised to eliminate, all tariffs (taxes on imports) and most nontariff barriers (such as quantitative quotas on imports) among the three countries. These liberalizations were to be spread over fifteen years, but two-thirds of Mexican imports to the United States and half of U.S. exports to Mexico were duty-free or became so immediately. Government contracts were to be open to competitive bidding by firms from all three countries.

Second, NAFTA provided rules to protect investment and intellectual property rights. NAFTA expanded Canadian and U.S. companies' ability to set up or buy a business in Mexico and made it easier for them sell out if they wanted to quit. U.S. and Canadian banks were given greater freedom to invest in Mexican banks. Restrictions on bringing profits back were removed. Protection of intellectual property rights involved patents, copyrights, trademarks, and computer software. U.S. firms strongly desired protection against people copying books, records, videotapes and audiotapes, and software without permission or payment of royalties. This had been more of a problem in Mexico than in Canada.

Third, NAFTA reduced barriers to trade in services, such as banking and finance, transportation, telecommunications, and audiovisual activities. Mexico extended temporary work permits to service providers from Canada and the United States.

Last, NAFTA provided administrative procedures to settle disputes over the way each country applied the rules. Special commissions were created to exert influence over environmental policies and over labor-market conditions.

IMPACT

NAFTA did not have a large immediate impact on economic relations between the United States and Canada, since their trade, services, investment, and intellectual property conditions were already on a relatively harmonious basis. For the first year after NAFTA's adoption, both the United States and Mexico appeared to benefit. U.S. export sales to Mexico and imports from Mexico increased substantially. Mexico benefited from substantial capital inflow, increasing production capacity, and improving technology. In December, 1994, however, Mexico was hit by a financial crisis that resulted in a devaluation of the Mexican peso by about one-half. The International Monetary Fund attributed the panic to a reaction by Mexican investors to a large government deficit and declining foreign reserves. Inflation in Mexico had been running at a rate of nearly 200 percent per year. Feeling the peso was overvalued, investors sold Mexican securities and used the proceeds to buy dollars and other foreign currency.

Previous NAFTA opponents pointed to the panic as justification for their views, although the panic could not be directly traced to NAFTA. The panic led to severe economic depression in Mexico. As Mexican prices and incomes fell, Mexicans reduced their purchases of imports and U.S. export sales to Mexico fell by 40 percent in the spring of 1995. NAFTA did help cushion the impact of the crisis on the Mexican economy. Export-oriented areas, such as the city of Juarez, found their sales to the United States greatly increased. In 1995, there was a large inflow of direct investment by U.S. firms eager to buy or build factories and take advantage of the momentarily inexpensive Mexican property, labor, and materials.

Controversy over the impact of NAFTA has continued since its inception, with labor and liberal interests generally against the agreement and conservative interests generally for it. In 2001, the Economic Policy Institute, a nonprofit think tank devoted to "the economic condition of low- and middle-income Americans," founded by academicians including economist Lester Thurow and former U.S. secretaries of labor Ray Marshall and Robert Reich, noted that all fifty U.S. states had experienced a net loss of more than 766,000 "actual and potential jobs" under NAFTA as of the year 2000. At the same time, U.S., Canadian, and Mexican government officials continued to hail the agreement as a success in lowering labor costs and increasing returns to companies and their investors. While the long-term effects on the economies of these nations remained to be seen, it appeared at the beginning of the twenty-first century that the agreement placed individual workers at a disadvantage when it came to job security and collective bargaining. The debate over NAFTA's impact formed only part of a much larger discussion that had begun in 1994 at the Summit of the Americas. At that meeting, the heads of state of thirty-four democracies of the Western Hemisphere proposed the Free Trade Area of the Americas, an agreement to unite the economies of the Western Hemisphere into a single free trade zone by progressively removing all barriers to trade and investment.

Paul B. Trescott

SOURCES FOR FURTHER STUDY

Belous, Richard S., and Jonathan Lemco, eds. *NAFTA as a Model of Development.* Washington, D.C.: National Planning Association, 1993.

Cameron, Maxwell A., and Brian W. Tomlin. *The Making of NAFTA: How the Deal Was Done.* Ithaca, N.Y.: Cornell University Press, 2002.

Deere, Carolyn L., and Daniel C. Esty, eds. *Greening the Americas: NAFTA's Lessons for Hemispheric Trade.* Boston: MIT Press, 2002.

Gereffi, Gary, David Spener, and Jennifer Bair, eds. *Free Trade and Uneven Development: The North American Apparel Industry After NAFTA.* Philadelphia: Temple University Press, 2002.

Gianaris, Nicholas V. *The North American Free Trade Agreement and the European Union.* Westport, Conn.: Greenwood, 1998.

Grayson, George W. *The North American Free Trade Agreement: Regional Community and the New World Order.* Lanham, Md.: University Press of America, 1995.

Hakim, Peter, and Robert E. Litan, eds. *The Future of North American Integration: Beyond NAFTA.* Foreword by Strobe Talbott. Washington, D.C.: Brookings Institution Press, 2002.

Kingsolver, Ann E. *NAFTA Stories: Fears and Hopes in Mexico and the United States.* Boulder, Colo.: Lynne Rienner, 2001.

MacArthur, John R. *The Selling of "Free Trade": NAFTA, Washington, and the Subversion of American Democracy.* Berkeley: University of California Press, 2001.

McKinney, Joseph A. *Created from NAFTA: The Structure, Function, and Significance of the Treaty's Related Institutions.* Armonk, N.Y.: M. E. Sharpe, 2001.

Weintraub, Sidney. *NAFTA: What Comes Next?* Westport, Conn.: Praeger, 1994.

Zangari, B. J., ed. *NAFTA: Issues, Industry Sector Profiles and Bibliography.* Commack, N.Y.: Nova Science, 1994.

SEE ALSO: Bretton Woods Agreement (1944); General Agreement on Tariffs and Trade of 1947 (1947); General Agreement on Tariffs and Trade of 1994 (1994).

BRADY HANDGUN VIOLENCE PROTECTION ACT

DATE: March 1, 1994
U.S. STATUTES AT LARGE: 107 Stat. 1536
PUBLIC LAW: 103-159
U.S. CODE: 18 § 921 et seq.
CATEGORIES: Crimes and Criminal Procedure; Health and Welfare

This legislation established a mandatory five-day waiting period and background check before a handgun could be purchased in the United States.

On November 30, 1993, President Bill Clinton signed the Brady Handgun Violence Protection Act into law—the first significant federal gun control legislation passed since 1968. Its passage came after a six-year campaign by James and Sarah Brady and Handgun Control, Inc., which was fiercely opposed by the National Rifle Association.

OUT OF TRAGEDY

James Brady had been active in Republican Party politics from the early 1960's. He had held posts in the administrations of presidents Richard Nixon and Gerald Ford. In 1980, he joined the presidential campaign of Ronald Reagan as director of public affairs. When Reagan became president in January, 1981, Brady was named White House press secretary. On March 30, 1981, a mentally disturbed young man shot at President Reagan and his entourage as they left a Washington, D.C., hotel at which the president had delivered a speech. Reagan was seriously wounded, as were a Washington police officer and a secret service agent. James Brady was the most seriously injured, with a gunshot wound to the head. For several days, Brady was near death. His recovery was long and painful. He was not allowed to go home for eight months and did not return to work for almost two years. Even then, he continued to suffer paralysis of the left side, problems with speech, and memory difficulties.

Sarah Kemp Brady was a Republican Party activist when she met James in 1970. They were married in 1973. At the time Brady was shot, they had a two-year-old son, Scott. Sarah helped her husband in his long recovery. In 1984, when Scott was five years of age, Sarah found him playing with a friend's loaded pistol. This event, along with her husband's experience, convinced her to become active in the gun control movement. She called Handgun Control, Inc., the most influential gun control advocacy group, and offered to help. From that point on, Sarah Brady became a tireless advocate for stricter gun control laws.

GUN CONTROL: PROS AND CONS

A proposed federal gun control law, called the Brady bill because of the activism of Jim and Sarah Brady, was first introduced in Congress by Democratic representative Ed Feighan of Ohio, on February 4, 1987. The main provision of the bill was a seven-day waiting period for the purchase of handguns. Polls at the time showed that the American public favored such a measure, but the bill was strongly opposed by the National Rifle Association (NRA). The position of the NRA was that any new gun control legislation violated the Second Amendment to the Constitution.

The Second Amendment is part of the Bill of Rights, which was ratified in 1791. It says simply, "A well regulated Militia, being necessary to the security of a free State, the right of the people to keep and bear Arms, shall not be infringed." Legal interpretations of the amendment have usually concluded that some restrictions on firearms are constitutional. During the 1930's, violence perpetrated by organized crime had led to the passage of the first federal gun control laws. These laws banned private ownership of submachine guns and banned the sale of firearms to known criminals. In 1939, in *Miller v. United States,* the Supreme Court found that these restrictions were constitutional, since such weapons had no relationship to the formation of a well-regulated militia. The next significant piece of federal gun control legislation was passed in 1968, in response to the assassinations of Martin Luther King, Jr., and Robert Kennedy. This law prohibited interstate sales of firearms and required gun dealers to keep records of sales.

DEFEATS BEFORE PASSAGE

The NRA worked throughout the 1970's and 1980's to repeal some provisions of the 1968 Gun Control Act. They had some success in 1986, when Congress voted to repeal the ban on interstate sales of rifles and shotguns. In 1987, the NRA mounted an intense lobbying campaign to defeat the Brady bill and spent approximately two million dollars in the effort. The Brady bill was to be voted on in the House of Representatives in September of 1988. Handgun Control, Inc. and the Bradys lobbied hard for it, and on September 7, a group of 120 uniformed police officers marched on the Capitol in support of it. However, the bill was defeated by a vote of 228 to 182.

The Brady bill was reintroduced in Congress in 1990, but it was never brought to a vote because of opposition from powerful members of Congress, including House Speaker Tom Foley (Democrat, Washington). The bill was introduced again in 1991. On May 8,

1991, the House of Representatives passed a bill requiring a seven-day waiting period for gun purchases. The Senate version, passed on June 28, called for a five-day waiting period. The compromise bill, incorporating the Senate requirements, was passed by the House on November 27, but Republican senators launched a fili-buster against it and it never came to a vote in the Senate. In 1992, supporters of the Brady bill once again tried to bring it up for a vote in the Senate, but were unable to get enough votes to end the filibuster.

PASSAGE AND PROVISIONS

By 1993, public support for gun control legislation had increased dramatically. A poll conducted in March of that year showed that 70 percent of all Americans and 57 percent of gun owners felt that there should be more restrictions on the sale of firearms. Passage of the Brady bill was favored by 88 percent of people in the United States. The bill was introduced in the House by Democrat Charles Schumer of New York on February 22, 1993, and in the Senate by Ohio Democrat Howard Metzenbaum on February 24. The NRA and Handgun Control, Inc. kept up their intensive lobbying efforts.

On November 10, 1993, the House passed the bill by a vote of 238 to 182. Ten days later, the Senate passed its bill by a vote of 63 to 36. There were significant differences in the bills passed by the two houses of Congress, and a conference committee negotiated for two days before presenting a conference report to both houses. On November 22, the House of Representatives passed the compromise bill by a vote of 238 to 187. In the Senate, minority leader Robert Dole (Republican, Kansas) threatened to block passage of the bill with a filibuster. Dole negotiated with Senate Majority Leader George Mitchell of Maine, and finally agreed not to block passage of the bill if the Senate would consider modifications to it early in the new year. The Senate passed the bill by voice vote on November 24. Jim Brady called it a "Thanksgiving present for the American people." The law went into effect on March 1, 1994.

IMPACT

Assessments of the effectiveness of the Brady bill after its first year of enforcement were mixed. The NRA and other antigun-control groups asserted that the law not only was a clear violation of the

Second Amendment but also was ineffective, because it did not keep criminals from buying guns illegally. They pointed to the fact that the Department of Justice prosecuted only four cases under the Brady bill it its first year. They also pointed out several loopholes that have allowed limitations on law enforcement record-keeping and have exempted pawn shops from some of the rules. Several judges found some provisions of the law unconstitutional, although it has remained in effect pending appeal.

The Bradys and other supporters of the bill maintain that it was a success. They pointed to government figures showing that seventy thousand convicted felons were prevented from buying guns under the law in its first year. They admitted that the bill was weak, but asserted that it was an important first step in stopping handgun violence. Jim Brady called his namesake bill "the end of unchecked madness and the commencement of a heartfelt crusade for a safer and saner country."

Deborah D. Wallin

SOURCES FOR FURTHER STUDY

Cozic, Charles P., ed. *Gun Control.* San Diego, Calif.: Greenhaven Press, 1992.

Davidson, Osha Gray. *Under Fire: The NRA and the Battle for Gun Control.* New York: Henry Holt, 1993.

Dickenson, Mollie. *Thumbs Up: The Life and Courageous Comeback of White House Press Secretary Jim Brady.* New York: Wiliam Morrow, 1987.

LaPierre, Wayne. *Guns, Crime and Freedom.* Washington, D.C.: Regnery, 1994.

Siegel, Mark A., et al. *Gun Control: Restricting Rights or Protecting People?* Wylie, Tex.: Information Plus, 1995.

SEE ALSO: National Firearms Act and Federal Firearms Act (1934); Omnibus Crime Control and Safe Streets Act (1968); Comprehensive Crime Control Act (1984); Violent Crime Control and Law Enforcement Act (1994).

VIOLENT CRIME CONTROL AND LAW ENFORCEMENT ACT

DATE: September 13, 1994
U.S. STATUTES AT LARGE: 108 Stat. 1796
PUBLIC LAW: 103-322
CATEGORIES: Crimes and Criminal Procedure

This law provided significant funds for hiring and training community police officers and set more severe punishments for a number of crimes.

The Violent Crime Control and Law Enforcement Act increased punishment for many federal crimes. One of the more controversial provisions of the act had to do with firearms ownership. The act bans the manufacture of certain types of "assault weapons" and limits the number of rounds weapons can hold. Because of this, the National Rifle Association opposed the bill, arguing that such restrictions impinge on the rights specified in the United States Constitution. Such opposition meant that the bill had to go through several revisions before being accepted by Congress and President Bill Clinton. The final bill also placed restrictions on the purchase of weapons, and it contained a provision that individuals who have been convicted of crimes of domestic violence are prohibited from purchasing weapons.

Besides addressing weapon ownership, the Violent Crime Control and Law Enforcement Act increased the penalties for a large number of crimes, specifically gang-related crimes, terrorism, illegal immigration, and fraud at the federal level. Terrorism and illegal immigration are both crimes that are under federal jurisdiction. While fraud and gang-related crimes are not necessarily under federal jurisdiction, the definition of these crimes was expanded under the act. For example, using telephone lines to commit fraud is a federal crime and therefore can be punished under the 1994 act's provisions. The act also dictates that individuals who have been incarcerated for sex crimes must notify the community to which they are moving following the term of incarceration.

One of the most controversial provisions of the act was the "Three Strikes, You're Out" provision. Under this part of the law, a defendant would receive mandatory life in prison if he or she had been conviced in federal court of a "serious violent felony" and also had two or more prior convictions in federal or state courts, at least one being a "serious violent felony." The other prior offense could be a "serious drug offense."

Finally, the act allocated a large amount of funding for research in criminal justice topics, especially domestic violence and community policing. Over eight billion dollars was set aside to hire and train more than 100,000 new police officers. These officers would be trained to work with community members to help reduce crime in their neighborhoods.

Christina Polsenberg

Sources for Further Study

DIANE Publishing Company, ed. *Violent Crime Control and Law Enforcement Act of 1994 (Public Law 103-322)*. Collingdale, Pa.: Editor, 1994.

Felde, Jon, Christopher Zimmerman, and Christine Wnuk. *States and the Violent Crime Control and Law Enforcement Act of 1994*. Denver, Colo.: National Conference of State Legislatures, 1995.

Reams, Bernard D., Jr., ed. *Omnibus Anti-Crime Act: A Legislative History of the Violent Crime Control and Law Enforcement Act of 1994, Public Law 103-322*. Buffalo, N.Y.: William S. Hein, 1997.

See also: Omnibus Crime Control and Safe Streets Act (1968); Organized Crime Control Act (1970); Racketeer Influenced and Corrupt Organizations Act (1970); Comprehensive Crime Control Act (1984); Brady Handgun Violence Protection Act (1994); Violence Against Women Act (1994).

Violence Against Women Act

Date: September 13, 1994
U.S. Statutes at Large: 108 Stat. 1902
Public law: 103-322
U.S. Code: 42 § 3796gg
Categories: Crimes and Criminal Procedure; Women's Issues

This act provided federal protection to the victims of gender-motivated violence.

The Violence Against Women Act of 1994, Title IV of the Violent Crime Control and Law Enforcement Act of 1994, was the result of four years of testimony before Congress and was drafted in response to what its chief legislative sponsor, Senator Joseph R. Biden, called a "national tragedy." In a 1991 report, for example, the Senate concluded after an investigation of the subject that violence perpetrated by men was at the top of the list of dangers to women's health in the United States, that every fifteen seconds a woman is battered, and that every six minutes a woman is raped.

Signed into law by President Bill Clinton in 1994, the act authorized $1.6 billion in grants over six years to assist state and local law enforcement officers and prosecutors in their efforts to reduce violent crimes against women, including domestic violence. The act also created a federal right to be free from gender-based violence and allowed victims of gender-motivated violence to bring suit for damages. Additionally, the act assured that protective orders against domestic violence obtained in one state would be given "full faith and credit" in other states. Finally, the act increased penalties for federal rape convictions.

Timothy L. Hall

SOURCE FOR FURTHER STUDY

Meyer-Emerick, Nancy. *The Violence Against Women Act of 1994: An Analysis of Intent and Perception*. Westport, Conn.: Greenwood Press, 2001.

SEE ALSO: Mann Act (1910); Family Violence Prevention and Services Act (1984); Violent Crime Control and Law Enforcement Act (1994).

NORTH KOREA PACT

ALSO KNOWN AS: Agreed Framework of 1994
DATE: October 21, 1994
CATEGORIES: Asia or Asian Americans; Foreign Relations; Treaties
and Agreements

The threat of North Korean nuclear arms prompted the United States
to develop incentives for the complete dismantling of that nation's nu-
clear program.

The isolated communist dictatorship of North Korea signed a pact,
or "agreement framework," with the United States on October 21,
1994, outlining a timetable for steps by each side that would end
in the complete dismantling of North Korea's nuclear weapons
program within ten years. In return, the United States promised to
reduce trade barriers, supply North Korea with oil to fill its energy
needs, and assist in the replacement of North Korea's old graphite
reactors with new, safer, light-water reactors.

Experts said the new reactors would be less suited to producing
weapons-grade plutonium, the raw material for making nuclear
bombs. However, U.S. officials admitted that the agreement posed
a risk that North Korea could discard the agreement during the
ten-year period and obtain fuel to make nuclear weapons. Sources
at the Central Intelligence Agency (CIA) asserted that there was a
better than even chance that North Korea had already developed a
nuclear weapon but believed that, without the pact, it would have
developed many more bombs—as many as one hundred over the
subsequent ten years.

WITHDRAWAL FROM NUCLEAR NONPROLIFERATION

Tension had grown between the United States and North Korea as
a result of North Korea's repeated refusal to allow international inspection of its nuclear facilities, which some U.S. experts believed
were being used to extract plutonium for nuclear bombs. This refusal was in violation of the Nuclear Nonproliferation Treaty, an
international agreement to prevent the spread of nuclear weapons that had been signed in 1968 by many countries, including

North Korea. Moreover, in defiance of International Atomic Energy Agency regulations, North Korea had removed eight thousand highly radioactive fuel rods from a major nuclear complex at Yongbyon. If the rods were reprocessed, which the North Koreans said was necessary for safety reasons, they would yield enough plutonium to make five nuclear bombs.

The United States responded to these violations by pushing for trade sanctions against North Korea, which in turn said it would interpret any U.S.-led embargo as an act of war. The standoff was eased by a peace mission in early summer, led by former U.S. president Jimmy Carter. The North Korean president, Kim Il Sung, agreed to open negotiations with U.S. government representatives. Kim also suggested a meeting with the South Korean president, Kim Young Sam, which would have been the first meeting between the two leaders since Korea was divided at the end of World War II. After a promising start, however, negotiations were halted by the sudden death in July of Kim Il Sung. They were resumed under the leadership of his chosen successor, his fifty-two-year-old son Kim Jong Il, and the agreement was signed.

THE PACT AND ITS PHASES

The agreement would take about ten years to be fully implemented, allowing at least five years before international monitors would carry out inspections to determine how much weapons-grade plutonium had been extracted by the North Koreans. It was expected to be at least eight years before all of North Korea's eight thousand plutonium-laden fuel rods could be removed from the country. This delay in the pact was criticized by South Korea and by some U.S. Republicans, who feared that North Korea would take Western aid money and later renege on the pact. The North Koreans feared that the United States' commitment to aid would evaporate as soon as North Korea relinquished its nuclear potential. To alleviate fears on both sides, President Bill Clinton's administration pointed to the pact's carefully synchronized steps. It also said that North Korea would not possess a functioning nuclear reactor until it fulfilled its side of the pact.

The pact was a three-phase plan. In the first phase, scheduled to begin at the time of signing the pact and expected to take five years to carry out, North Korea was to freeze its nuclear program while the United States and its allies undertook a massive aid effort to provide North Korea with new sources of energy. The North Koreans would not refuel their Yongbyon reactor and would stop building two larger reactors. The fuel rods already removed were to be properly stored and regularly inspected. In return for the North Korean freeze, the United States and its allies were to begin work on the first of two light-water reactors, at a cost of four billion dollars, most of which would be provided by South Korea and Japan. At this stage, no nuclear components of the reactor would be installed. Pending completion of the new reactors, the United States and its allies would provide up to half a million metric tons of free oil per year.

In the second phase, North Korea would allow monitors to inspect the two waste sites that were previously off limits, so that it could be determined how much weapons-grade plutonium had been removed. The North Koreans would also begin sending their rods to a third country. Removal of all the rods was expected to take up to eight years. In return, the United States was to complete work on the first light-water reactor, which would begin producing electricity.

In the third and final phase, the North Koreans were to dismantle the plants that were involved in its nuclear weapons program. In return, the United States and its allies would complete work on the second light-water reactor.

RENEWED TENSIONS

The progress of the pact after the signing was far from smooth. On December 17, 1994, a U.S. Army helicopter that had strayed five kilometers north of a demilitarized zone into North Korean air space was shot down by the North Koreans. One of the two pilots was killed; the second was held by the North Koreans before being released on December 30, after U.S. warnings that any further delay could jeopardize the pact. In early 1995, another problem was encountered. On March 8, North Korea threatened to jettison the agreement if the United States continued to insist that South Korea build the two new light-water reactors. Observers said that it would be humiliating for North Korea to obtain reactors from its long-term enemy, South Korea, because that would prove that South Korea was richer and more technologically advanced than North Korea. North Korea also feared that South Korea would somehow use the deal to gain control over North Korea. The

Clinton administration pointed out, however, that South Korea was the only country willing to take the lead in financing the light-water reactors.

Furthermore, the Clinton administration protested the diversion of some of the fifty thousand tons of heavy fuel oil supplied by the United States to North Korea for heating and electricity. Intelligence reports suggested that the oil was diverted by officials unconnected with the pact. This type of oil cannot be used to power planes and tanks in North Korea's army, but it may have been used in industrial sites. According to U.S. officials, the diversion meant either that North Korea's leadership could not control the implementation of the accord or that it had chosen not to do so. In either case, the incident fueled the fears of some analysts that the leadership of North Korea was unstable or uncertain.

Fears escalated in early April, 1996, when for three consecutive days heavily armed North Korean troops entered the demilitarized zone between North and South Korea. The zone had been established in 1953 as part of the armistice agreement ending the Korean War. The incursions followed an announcement by the North Korean government that it no longer recognized the demilitarized zone. A few days later, on April 16, President Clinton and South Korean president Kim Young Sam proposed "four-party" talks (among South Korea, North Korea, the United States, and the People's Republic of China) to bring about a permanent peace deal replacing the 1953 armistice.

Plenary sessions of the talks occurred in 1997 and 1998, and in 1998 South Korea's Kim Dae Jung announced his nonaggressive, pro-economic-cooperation Sunshine Policy toward North Korea, which was followed by ministerial talks between the two Koreas and, in September, by a ceremony inaugurating plans to rejoin the broken railway line between the two nations. On the nuclear front, the United States and North Korea had negotiated a method to store spent fuel from North Korea's five-megawatt nuclear reactor in canisters, a process completed in 2000.

On August 31, 1998, North Korea launched a Taepodong-1 ballistic missile, which was met by the United States with a renewed effort at diplomatic talks. On April 25, 1999, representatives of the United States, South Korea, and Japan announced the creation of a Trilateral Coordination and Oversight Group (TCOG) to coordinate policy; the group held meetings in 1999 and 2000.

In the summer and fall of 2002, in the wake of the September 11, 2001, terrorist attacks on the Pentagon and the World Trade Center, the United States was gearing up for a possible war with Iraq in the event that renewed U.N. weapons inspections in that country failed to prove Iraq's full compliance with previous U.N. resolutions that it dismantle its biological, chemical, and nuclear weapons programs. President George W. Bush had named North Korea, along with Iraq and Iran, as members of an "axis of evil" that might give aid to terrorists. U.S. intelligence had provided evidence that North Korea had been pursuing the manufacture of enriched uranium, which would be of use only in nuclear weapons rather than commercial nuclear energy programs—a violation of both the Nuclear Nonproliferation Treaty and the Agreed Framework. In the first week of October, U.S. State Department officials confronted North Korea with this evidence, which North Korea initially denied but then confirmed in a stunning admission. President Bush's response was low-key; he called the admission "troubling" but did not call on the United Nations to censure North Korea and did not threaten military action—a response that drew criticism from those who found parallels in the Iraq situation.

In November, 2002, the United States, South Korea, Japan, and the European Union cut off fuel oil shipments to North Korea. North Korea refused to indicate why it had made the admission but maintained that the 1994 agreement had been nullified by this retaliatory action. The United States was not willing to do the same, recognizing the Agreed Framework as its instrument for keeping North Korea in check. The South Korean government of President Kim Dae Jung, which had been pursuing a relaxed "sunshine policy" with North Korea, similarly responded with caution and expressed hopes that the breach could be resolved through diplomatic talks. After a September summit with Japan, North Korea's diplomatic relations with that nation were on hold over conflicts regarding Japanese aid and repatriation of kidnapped Japanese citizens. As the winter of 2002 set in, North Korea's citizens faced not only a lack of heat and energy but worsening impoverishment and geopolitical isolation as well.

Claire J. Robinson, updated by
Christina J. Moose

SOURCES FOR FURTHER STUDY
Albright, David. "How Much Plutonium Does North Korea Have?" *Bulletin of the Atomic Scientists* 50, no. 5 (September/October, 1994): 46-53.
Powell, Bill, and Russell Watson. "Headless Beast: North Korea After Kim." *Newsweek* 124, no. 3 (July 18, 1994): 18-23.
Tai Sung An. *North Korea: A Political Handbook*. Wilmington, Del.: Scholarly Resources, 1983.
Watson, Russell. "Home for New Year's Eve." *Newsweek* 125, no. 2 (January 9, 1995): 49.

SEE ALSO: Nuclear Nonproliferation Treaty (1968).

GENERAL AGREEMENT ON TARIFFS AND TRADE OF 1994

DATE: December 1, 1994
CATEGORIES: Agriculture; Business, Commerce, and Trade; Foreign Relations; Tariffs and Taxation; Treaties and Agreements

The most ambitious trade agreement to date, GATT was designed to facilitate free trade and increase exports worldwide.

On December 1, 1994, the U.S. Senate joined the House of Representatives in voting overwhelmingly in favor of what was widely considered to be the most far-reaching trade agreement reached to date. The General Agreement on Tariffs and Trade (GATT) slashed tariffs (taxes on imports) by an average of 40 percent in the 124 participating countries. Cuts in tariffs were expected to bring a boom in U.S. exports, leading to more jobs. In addition, American consumers would have access to cheaper imported goods. GATT, which had taken eight years to negotiate, represented a huge leap toward free trade worldwide.

A version of GATT had governed most international trade since 1948, but negotiations to expand the agreement began only in 1986. The new GATT was governed by a new organization, the

World Trade Organization, located in Geneva. This organization had more power over signatory nations than its predecessor, the GATT Secretariat, and had the authority to enforce agreements through the imposition of trade penalties.

The Senate's and House of Representatives' vote in favor of GATT sounded a rare note of unity between Democrats and Republicans. They were brought together by their confidence that the agreement would revitalize the economy. President Bill Clinton's administration estimated that the agreement would create half a million new jobs. The administration also predicted an annual increase of $150 billion in U.S. economic growth when the agreement was fully implemented, after ten years. Worldwide, the Organization for Economic Cooperation and Growth estimated that GATT's lower tariffs and higher import quotas (limits on amounts of goods permitted to be imported) would increase world income by $270 billion per year.

REASONS FOR THE AGREEMENT

Tariffs have been used by almost all nations in the world to protect their own farmers and native industries against competition from cheaper foreign goods. Increasingly, however, many economists have come to oppose such self-protectionist measures. They believe that free trade, without the barriers of tariffs, is the key to worldwide economic growth. The principles of free trade that inspired GATT hold that a country that is good at producing a given product will profit from exporting it to countries that are less efficient at producing that product. In return, a country can use the wealth it gains from exports to buy goods and services that are produced more efficiently elsewhere. It is theorized that, when each country focuses on what it does best, market forces of supply and demand organize distribution for maximum economic growth and consumers benefit from lower prices. However, governments have interfered with these market forces by imposing tariffs and strict quotas limiting the amounts of a product that can be imported, giving the product a false scarcity value that pushes up its price.

OPPOSITION AND RESISTANCE

Not all economists are convinced that promoting free trade through initiatives such as GATT is the answer to the world's economic problems. Some argue that free trade benefits developed nations more than developing nations, since the richer nations can import goods from countries where labor and materials are cheaper. Critics of this view cite the Asian nations as proof of the benefits of free trade for developing nations. During the early 1960's, these countries were in serious economic trouble. Those that favored free trade (Hong Kong, Taiwan, South Korea, and Singapore) experienced more growth than countries that did not (India, North Korea, and Vietnam). Manufacturing did tend to flow toward sources of cheap labor, but this tendency helped develop the local economy and raise the standard of living.

Concerns over the possible negative effects of GATT are not restricted to economics. Cultural conflicts have arisen from the agreement, such as a disagreement between the United States and Japan over rice. The Japanese have always banned the import of rice to protect their own rice crop, which occupies a central position in their culture and religion, but under GATT the Japanese agreed to allow the import of some rice. Although the conflict was resolved, the episode presented an important challenge to advocates of free trade: How far should a country's cultural traditions be compromised to facilitate world trade?

Resistance to GATT also came from within the United States. Critics expressed fears that the World Trade Organization could attack U.S. consumer protection laws (such as the labeling of food product ingredients), worker protection laws, and environmental regulations as trade barriers. Among those who raised questions about the power of the World Trade Organization were Republican Senator Bob Dole, consumer advocate and 2000 presidential candidate Ralph Nader, and various environmental lobby groups. Critics have presented many scenarios to back up their arguments. For example, if the United States decided on ethical grounds to ban the import of South Asian rugs made using child labor, countries that suffered from the decision could take their case to a panel of three World Trade Organization judges. If the judges ruled against the United States, then Congress or the state whose regulation was under challenge would have to decide whether to change that regulation. If the lawmakers refused, trade sanctions could be imposed against U.S. exports. As another example, environmentalists have expressed concern that under GATT, the United States could not impose its own stringent environmental laws on other nations. In 1991, under existing GATT rules whose enforcement provisions were far weaker than those ratified in 1994, the United States lost a case brought against one of its federal laws banning the importation of tuna caught in nets that also trapped dolphins. A GATT panel ruled that the United States could not impose its environmental restrictions on the rest of the world. Otherwise, the panel said, the United States could use those restrictions to keep out foreign competitors. In an attempt to allay fears about the World Trade Organization and its possible threat to U.S. sovereignty, President Clinton reached an agreement with Senator Dole to create a commission in the United States to review judgments that the organization makes against the United States.

Trade Affected

The main areas of trade affected by GATT and its stipulations are as follows. In agriculture, U.S. GATT negotiators were at odds for years with the European Community over agricultural issues. The Europeans wanted to maintain subsidies to their farmers, but the United States wanted subsidies eliminated because they gave an unfair advantage in the marketplace at high cost to consumers. GATT produced a compromise that stipulates that agricultural tariffs be reduced by 36 percent in industrial nations and 24 percent in developing nations.

Regarding intellectual property, GATT required all member countries to respect patents, trademarks, and copyrights. This requirement was expected to eradicate the pirated computer programs, records, videocassettes, and prescription drugs rampant in developing nations.

Regarding automobiles, restrictions on auto exports, such as those that the United States imposed on Japan, were eliminated. The agreement also banned the widespread practice of requiring high local content in some products, such as cars, a practice that protects local jobs but discourages imports. The agreement also limited the ability of countries to favor domestically owned factories at the expense of foreign-owned ones.

Finally, richer nations were required to phase out quotas on clothing imports over a ten-year period. Quotas were to be replaced by less restrictive tariffs. Some of the strongest opposition to GATT in the United States had come from textile states such as North Carolina and South Carolina, which feared that their industries would suffer as a result of cheap foreign imports.

It seemed inevitable that GATT would continue to provoke conflicts of nationalistic self-interest, but there is also hope that its ratification marked the beginning of a new era of increased global cooperation and trust between its signatory nations.

Claire J. Robinson

SOURCES FOR FURTHER STUDY

Boskin, Michael J. "Pass GATT Now." *Fortune* 130, no. 12 (December 12, 1994): 137-138.

Dentzer, Susan. "A New Tapestry of Protectionism." *U.S. News and World Report* 117, no. 22 (December 5, 1994): 83.

Harbrecht, Douglas. "GATT: Tales from the Dark Side." *Business Week*, no. 3404 (December 19, 1994): 52.

Nader, Ralph. "Drop the GATT." *The Nation* 259, no. 11 (October 10, 1994): 368-369.

Thomas, Rich. "Tempest over Trade." *Newsweek* 124, no. 23 (December 5, 1994): 50.

SEE ALSO: General Agreement on Tariffs and Trade of 1947 (1947); North American Free Trade Agreement (1993).

UNITED STATES RECOGNITION OF VIETNAM

DATE: Announced July 11, 1995
CATEGORIES: Foreign Relations

U.S. diplomatic recognition of Vietnam marked the end of the traumatic and divisive Vietnam War era.

President Bill Clinton, on July 11, 1995, announced the diplomatic recognition of the Socialist Republic of Vietnam by the United States. Recognition of Vietnam brought to a close a war that officially had ended more than twenty years before. In announcing his decision, Clinton said, "We can now move on to common ground. Whatever divided us before, let us consign to the past."

AFTERMATH OF THE VIETNAM WAR

Concerning Vietnam, moving away from the past had proved a long and agonizing process for the United States. The Vietnam War took the lives of more than fifty-eight thousand U.S. personnel between 1961 and the fall of Saigon on April 30, 1975. The United States had hoped that the peace agreement of January, 1973, which provided for a cease-fire, withdrawal of foreign troops, return of prisoners of war, and a peaceful reunification of Vietnam, might prevent a communist takeover of all of Vietnam.

North Vietnamese forces, however, remained in South Vietnam after the agreement and, after consolidating their areas of control, launched an offensive in March, 1975, that would lead, by the end of April, to complete victory and establishment of one Vietnam, with Hanoi as its capital. The final resolution of the war intensified United States resentment toward Vietnam and made reconciliation with the former enemy even more difficult. An embargo on trade with North Vietnam, imposed in 1964, was extended to all of Vietnam. Nevertheless, President Jimmy Carter, elected in 1976, took some first steps toward a rapprochement by lifting the prohibition on travel to Vietnam, beginning discussions with the Vietnamese government, and accepting Vietnam as a member of the United Nations.

These initial steps were halted by the Vietnamese demand in 1978 for reconstruction aid promised in the 1973 Peace Accords. Hostility between Vietnam and the United States was increased in the same year by a Vietnamese friendship treaty with the Soviet Union, recognition of the People's Republic of China (Vietnam's historic enemy) by the United States, and Vietnam's invasion of Cambodia. From the United States' perspective, improved relations with Vietnam henceforth were dependent on that nation's withdrawal from Cambodia, its recognition of an independent Cambodian government, commitment to basic human rights for its own citizens, and, most important, a strict accounting of all U.S. servicemen missing in action or taken prisoner in Vietnam.

ROADMAP TO DIPLOMATIC RECOGNITION

The Vietnamese agreement in 1989 to withdraw from Cambodia opened the way for a sequence of steps that ultimately would lead to normalization of relations. In 1991, President George H. W. Bush defined the incremental steps, known as the "Roadmap," that

Vietnam would have to take before the United States would grant diplomatic recognition. One of these steps, a peace agreement between Vietnam and Cambodia, was completed in October, 1991.

The United States reciprocated in 1992 by permitting U.S. companies to open offices in Vietnam. With the trade embargo still in effect, however, there was little incentive for companies to do so. The next significant development was Clinton's decision in 1993 to end U.S. opposition to international institutions and other nations making money available to Vietnam. Soon afterward, U.S. businesses were declared free to bid on projects funded by international financial institutions, so that they would not be shut out of business opportunities partially financed by U.S. dollars.

Throughout the early 1990's, the Vietnamese had been increasingly helpful in locating the remains of missing U.S. servicemen. Teams from the United States were permitted to search the Vietnamese countryside; and war records, including the archives of the war museum in Hanoi, were turned over to the United States.

LIFTING THE TRADE EMBARGO

One major step short of diplomatic recognition remained: lifting the trade embargo. Debate centered on several issues, including the economic implications of maintaining the trade embargo. The U.S. business community recognized Vietnam's resources, including oil reserves estimated to be the fourth largest in the world and a labor force with one of the highest literacy rates in Southeast Asia. It also was obvious that other nations were gaining significant investment advantages in the country. Impediments to foreign investments also were recognized, among them inadequate distribution capabilities, state control of businesses, and both a market philosophy and legal system still in flux.

The continuing communist nature of the government and restrictions on individual rights raised concerns with many persons in the United States, but others noted that the United States had long done business with a variety of repressive regimes, including China. From a geopolitical perspective, it was argued that an economically strengthened Vietnam would be a counterbalance to Chinese domination in the region.

The most emotional issue surrounding the trade embargo and diplomatic recognition of Vietnam was continuing uncertainty over the fate of U.S. troops still listed as missing in action or known to have been taken prisoner. The trade embargo was viewed by many as a means to pressure the Vietnamese government into cooperating on the prisoner-of-war/missing-in-action (POW/MIA) issue. On the other hand, many argued that improving relations with Hanoi would both reward the country for past cooperation and encourage future efforts.

On February 3, 1994, President Clinton announced an end to the United States' trade embargo against Vietnam. This decision, Clinton stated, had been based on only one criterion: "gaining the fullest possible accounting for our prisoners of war and our missing in action." The president continued:

> Today I am lifting the trade embargo against Vietnam because I am absolutely convinced it offers the best way to resolve the fate of those who remain missing and about whom we are not sure.

Lifting the embargo did not involve granting most favored nation trade status to Vietnam, so tariffs on Vietnamese goods imported into the United States remained high. In addition, U.S. businesses operating in Vietnam would not have the support afforded by a U.S. embassy.

DIPLOMATIC RECOGNITION

Diplomatic recognition was the next logical step, but it also excited controversy. The arguments for and against lifting the trade embargo, especially regarding POW/MIA issues, were also applied to normalization of relations. President Clinton's announcement on July 11, 1995, was boycotted by the American Legion and by several family groups, including the National League of Families of American Prisoners and Missing in Southeast Asia. Members of Congress were divided, arguing either that recognition acknowledged Vietnam's cooperation and would further the effort to reach as final an accounting as possible, or that it would remove the final incentive for Vietnamese cooperation.

As Clinton spoke, he was accompanied by politicians from both parties, including Republican Senator John McCain, a former prisoner of war, and Democratic Senator Bob Kerrey, who had lost part of a leg in combat during his tour of duty. "Never before in the history of warfare has such an extensive effort been made to resolve the fate of soldiers who did not return," the president said. He promised that "normalization of our relations with Vietnam is not the end of [that] effort."

RESPONSE

Prime Minister Vo Van Kiet of Vietnam greeted the resumption of diplomatic relations with an expression of gratitude to President Clinton and a promise that Vietnam would continue to help the United States resolve questions concerning the fate of the missing U.S. servicemen. The U.S. business community generally welcomed the president's decision but called for additional steps, such as granting most favored nation status to reduce tariffs and making insurance available from the Overseas Private Investment Corporation in order to protect U.S. investments.

Edward J. Rielly

SOURCES FOR FURTHER STUDY

Castelli, Beth. "The Lifting of the Trade Embargo Between the United States and Vietnam: The Loss of a Potential Bargaining Tool or a Means of Fostering Cooperation?" *Dickinson Journal of International Law* 13, no. 1 (Winter, 1995): 297-328.

Chang, Tim Tien-Chun. "Joint Ventures in Vietnam." *Commercial Law Bulletin* 9, no. 4 (July 1, 1994): 17-19.

Howes, Craig. *Voices of the Vietnam POWs*. New York: Oxford University Press, 1993.

Moss, George Donelson. *Vietnam: An American Ordeal*. Englewood Cliffs, N.J.: Prentice-Hall, 1990.

Sutter, Robert G. *Vietnam-U.S. Relations: The Debate over Normalization*. Washington, D.C.: Library of Congress, 1992.

U.S. Congress. House. Committee on Foreign Affairs. Subcommittee on Asian and Pacific Affairs. *U.S. Economic Embargo on Vietnam*. Washington, D.C.: Government Printing Office, 1993.

SEE ALSO: Amerasian Homecoming Act (1987).

COMMUNICATIONS DECENCY ACT

DATE: February 8, 1996
U.S. STATUTES AT LARGE: 110 Stat. 86
PUBLIC LAW: 104-104
U.S. CODE: 47 § 151
CATEGORIES: Communications and Media; Speech and Expression

> *Also known as Title V of the Telecommunications Act of 1996, this act revised earlier laws to mandate that telecommunication service providers be held criminally accountable if they failed to censor "indecent material."*

In 1995 Nebraska's Democratic senator J. James Exon responded to increased public concern over the growing use of telecommunications technologies to transmit pornography and to engage children in inappropriate contacts with adults by introducing a bill called the Communications Decency Act. Exon complained that the Internet contained "not simply nude pictures or 'cheesecake,' but the most debased, lewd material one can imagine." There is no valid reason, he said, that "these perverts should be allowed unimpeded on the Internet." His goal was to "help make the information superhighway safer for kids and families to travel."

PROVISIONS AND DEBATE

Exon's bill broadened the protections already existing in the Communications Act of 1934, and increased penalties for their violation. A key aspect of the law was its replacing of the term "telephone" with "telecommunications device" in order to encompass facsimile (fax) machines, computer modems, and other devices. The act made it a criminal offense to use interactive computer systems to send communications to specific persons, or to persons less than eighteen years of age, that depict or describe sexual or excretory activities or organs in manners that might be deemed patently offensive—as measured by local community standards. The law made violations punishable by prison terms and fines up to $250,000. The act specifically excluded from liability telecommunications and information service providers, system operators, and employers who do not knowingly participate in such violations themselves.

Immediately after the act's original bill was introduced to Congress, it met strong criticism from the American Civil Liberties Union (ACLU); the telecommunication, computer, and publishing industries; and such professional organizations as American Library Association; Human Rights Watch; Association of Publishers, Editors and Writers; American Booksellers Association; and American Society of Newspaper Editors.

PASSAGE AND COURT REACTION

On February 1, 1996, Exon's bill was passed overwhelmingly in both houses of Congress and became part of the Telecommunications Act of 1996, which President Bill Clinton signed into law a week later. Minutes after the president signed the act—the ACLU and nineteen other groups filed suit at a federal court in Philadelphia to block the new law by challenging its constitutionality. These groups argued that the law would criminalize forms of expression that were protected under the First Amendment.

On June 12, 1996, a federal court voted 3-0 to grant a motion for a preliminary injunction on the law's "indecency" provisions. The court also found that the act went too far in restricting the First Amendment rights of all computer users in its effort to protect children. On July 1 the Justice Department filed papers in Philadelphia asking the Supreme Court to let the law take effect, as President Clinton and a majority of senators and representatives intended. Conservative groups supporting the act promised to help Congress write new legislation if the lower court's ruling was allowed to stand.

Richard Keenan

SOURCES FOR FURTHER STUDY

Aufderheide, Patricia. *Communications Policy and the Public Interest: The Telecommunications Act of 1996.* New York: Guilford Press, 1999.

Kennedy, Charles H. *An Introduction to U.S. Telecommunications Law.* 2d ed. Boston: Artech House, 2001.

SEE ALSO: First Amendment (1789); Comstock Act (1873); Communications Act (1934); Foreign Agents Registration Act (1938); Communications Act Amendments (1960).

MEGAN'S LAW

ALSO KNOWN AS: Jacob Wetterling Crimes Against Children and Sexually Violent Offender Registration Act
DATE: May 17, 1996
U.S. STATUTES AT LARGE: 110 Stat. 1345
PUBLIC LAW: 104-145
U.S. CODE: 42 § 14701
CATEGORIES: Children's Issues; Crimes and Criminal Procedure; Health and Welfare

This law required communities to be informed of the whereabouts of sex offenders.

In some states persons convicted of sexual crimes were required to register their addresses with state or local police departments, but officials were not required to notify the community and those convicted of sexual offenses often failed to register. After seven-year-old Megan Kanka was kidnapped, raped, and killed in New Jersey on July 29, 1994, her parents and the nation were shocked that the person accused of the crime was a two-time sex offender who lived across the street. As a result, New Jersey adopted the New Jersey Sexual Offender Registration Act of 1994, requiring prison officials to notify communities when a sex offender has been released to live or work in a neighborhood. Similar laws were adopted by the remaining forty-nine states between 1994 and 1996.

On September 13, 1994, Congress enacted the Jacob Wetterling Crimes Against Children and Sexually Violent Offender Registration Act as part of its omnibus crime control act. This federal legislation required state prison officials to notify local police when a person convicted of sex offenses moves into a neighborhood. On May 17, 1996, Congress strengthened the law by requiring local law enforcement officials to make this information available to the community. This amendment became known informally as Megan's Law. States are allowed to decide how dangerous those accused of sexual offenses are and what type of notification is required. DNA, saliva samples, names, and addresses of convicted offenders are updated in a nationwide database system.

In some states the information on such persons is placed in a computerized online database, and journalists and photographers have accessed the information in order to provide publicity for the community. Nevertheless, some two thousand released sex offenders successfully challenged the constitutionality of the statute in U.S. District Court in New Jersey, and the district court ruling was appealed.

Michael Haas

SOURCES FOR FURTHER STUDY

Cohen, Fred, and Elizabeth Rahmberg-Walsh. *Sex Offender Registration and Community Notification: A "Megan's Law" Sourcebook.* Kingston, N.J.: Civic Research Institute, 1998.

Fodor, Megan Druss. *Megan's Law: Protection of Privacy.* Berkeley Heights, N.J.: Enslow, 2001.

SEE ALSO: Child Abuse Prevention and Treatment Act (1974); Parental Kidnapping Prevention Act (1980); Missing Children's Assistance Act (1984); Violent Crime Control and Law Enforcement Act (1994); Family Violence Prevention and Services Act (1984).

PERSONAL RESPONSIBILITY AND WORK OPPORTUNITY RECONCILIATION ACT

ALSO KNOWN AS: Welfare Reform Act
DATE: August 22, 1996
U.S. STATUTES AT LARGE: 110 Stat. 2105, 2268
PUBLIC LAW: 104-193
CATEGORIES: Health and Welfare

This act represented the most significant change in public welfare policies since the inception of Aid to Families with Dependent Children in 1935.

The Personal Responsibility and Work Opportunity Reconciliation Act of 1996 dramatically changed the impact of the welfare system on recipient families. The new welfare system demanded work in return for time-limited aid. Under this act, states were given broad discretion to design their own welfare policies, as long as most recipients were required to go to work and aid ended after two years. A maximum of five years of aid was to be granted over persons' lifetimes, and state spending on welfare was to be maintained at no less than 80 percent of what was spent in 1994. Some $14 billion was allocated for child care. Recipients' skills and needs were to be assessed formally, and Medicaid coverage was provided for at least one year after recipients began employment. There were also provisions for stringent child-support enforcement and possible job subsidies.

These provisions set out to make welfare a transitional program, to move recipients toward work and family independence. Proponents believed that long-term poverty would be reduced, improving the lives of millions of families. Opponents argued that public assistance would decline significantly without any guarantee of jobs, driving families deeper into poverty. The intensity of the debate highlighted the dramatic nature and significance of the act.

David Carleton

SOURCES FOR FURTHER STUDY

Duncan, Greg J., and P. Lindsay Chase-Lansdale, eds. *For Better and for Worse: Welfare Reform and the Well-Being of Children and Families.* New York: Russell Sage, 2002.

Weil, Alan, and Kenneth Finegold, eds. *Welfare Reform: The Next Act.* Washington, D.C.: Urban Institute Press, 2002.

SEE ALSO: Social Security Act (1935); Aid to Families with Dependent Children (1935); Family Support Act (1988).

DEFENSE OF MARRIAGE ACT

DATE: September 21, 1996
U.S. STATUTES AT LARGE: 110 Stat. 2419
PUBLIC LAW: 104-199
CATEGORIES: Health and Welfare; Women's Issues

This law was enacted to relieve states of any federal obligation under the U.S. Constitution to recognize same-sex marriages from other states.

Before the passage of the Defense of Marriage Act (DOMA) of 1996, issues of same-sex marriages had been prominent in public policy discussions. Although since the 1970's questions involving same-sex unions have come before various state courts, it was not until 1993 that the question of legal recognition emerged as part of a national debate. At its core was a 1990 same-sex marriage case in Hawaii, *Baehr v. Lewin* (852 P2d 44 Haw. 1993). In that case a same-sex couple, Baeher and Dancel, and other same-sex couples, applied for marriage licenses. When their requests were denied, they filed suit against the state. After an unsuccessful attempt in the lower court, the Hawaiian Supreme Court, in a groundbreaking decision on appeal in 1993, overturned the lower court and held that denial of marriage licenses to same-sex couples constituted a violation of the equal protection clause under the Constitution of Hawaii.

In rejecting the notion that the right to marry is a "fundamental right to privacy," the court concluded that by restricting the right to marry of same-sex couples only, the state had created a sex-based class, one that was forbidden by the constitution. Opponents of gay marriage decried this decision across the United States. In Hawaii, the state legislature moved to clarify its marriage law, stating that legal recognition of marriage should be granted only to opposite-sex couples. Across the United States, more than thirty state legislatures also moved to define marriage by excluding same-sex couples. The fear was not only that same-sex marriages were contrary to public policy but also that if legally recognized in Hawaii, then, under the "full faith and credit" clause of the U.S. Constitution, all other states of the Union would be required to recognize the legality of such marriages. While sixteen states ultimately enacted legislation in direct response to the Hawaii situation, in 1996 Congress acted to minimize developing state concerns on this matter.

PASSAGE AND PROVISIONS

In 1996, Congress passed the Defense of Marriage Act (DOMA). The act's expressed purpose was to relieve states of any federal obligation under the U.S. Constitution to recognize same-sex marriages from other states. Introduced simultaneously in the both houses as "a bill to define and protect the institution of marriage," the final act did two things. First, it amended the federal judicial code to provide that

> no State, territory, or possession of the United States or Indian tribe shall be required to give effect to any marriage between persons of the same sex under the laws of any other such jurisdiction or to any right or claim arising from such a relationship.

Second, it established a federal definition of "marriage" as only "a legal union between one man and one woman as husband and wife" and also defined spouse as only "a person of the opposite sex who is a husband or a wife." While the law does not impose a federal law on the states or bar states from legalizing same-sex marriages, it seeks to prevent the imposition of one state's definition of marriage on other states and on federal programs.

CRITICS AND SUPPORTERS

Introduced at the height of a presidential election year, DOMA was viewed by some critics as part of an election year politics. Robert Dole, the Republican candidate for the presidency in 1996, was one of the bill's cosponsors in the Senate, where it passed 85-14-1. A similar version sponsored by Bob Barr, a Republican from Georgia, overwhelmingly passed the House 290-133-10. President Bill Clinton signed the final version into law on September 21, 1996.

Alarmed by the case that made Hawaii the first state to legalize same-sex marriage in 1993, conservative supporters of DOMA argued that the traditional family has stood for five thousand years and should not be changed. Opponents and liberal supporters of same-sex unions argued that DOMA violates constitutional requirements and that states must recognize legal contracts made in other states; they also argued that DOMA furthers the politics of fear and division, inciting people in an area that is admittedly controversial.

The Defense of Marriage Act as enacted remained law as of 2002. Clearly it did not give states additional rights with respect to which marriages they need not recognize but only with respect to those whose divorces they need not recognize. Although arguments framed on the act's morality could not be litigated, the questions of whether DOMA was constitutional, within the powers of the Congress, or sound public policy still needed to be determined by the courts. In the meantime, same-sex couples remained ineligible for spousal benefits in states outlawing same-sex unions and remained ineligible for benefits and privileges reserved for opposite-sex couples under federal law.

Marc Georges Pufong

SOURCES FOR FURTHER STUDY

Eskeridge, William N. *The Case for Same-Sex Marriage: From Sexual Liberty to Civilized Commitment.* New York: Free Press, 1996.

_____. *Gaylaw: Challenging the Apartheid of the Closet.* Cambridge, Mass.: Harvard University Press, 2001.

Strasser, Mark P. *Legally Wed: Same-Sex Marriage and the Constitution.* Ithaca, N.Y.: Cornell University Press, 1997.

SEE ALSO: Cable Act (1922); War Brides Act (1945); Privacy Act (1974); Privacy Protection Act (1980).

INTERNET TAX FREEDOM ACT

DATE: October 21, 1998
U.S. STATUTES AT LARGE: 112 Stat. 2681
PUBLIC LAW: 105-277
U.S. CODE: 47 § 151
CATEGORIES: Communications and Media; Tariffs and Taxation

This law temporarily shielded consumers shopping on the Internet from taxation of fees imposed by Internet service providers as well as merchandise taxes not already in line with existing mail-order taxes.

The rapid growth of the Internet during the final decade of the twentieth century witnessed a corollary growth in sales transactions accomplished over the Internet. More and more Americans were obtaining access to the Internet, often by private Internet service providers. Once online, they discovered that the Internet provided the equivalent of a vast mail-order catalog, and they quickly took advantage of the new technology to shop. The rising tide of Internet transactions did not go unnoticed by state and local governments. Many of these determined to tax not only the transactions by which consumers were obtaining access to the Internet but also those transactions consummated by consumers once they arrived on the Internet. The Internet Tax Freedom Act had its genesis in fears that state and local governments, ever hungry for new tax revenues, would concentrate attention in a discriminatory fashion on the Internet.

PROVISIONS

The Internet Tax Freedom Act prohibits three forms of taxes. In the first place, it forbids state and local governments from taxing Internet access. Thus, when a consumer pays $19.95 per month for unlimited access to the Internet through a national provider such as America Online (AOL) or a local Internet service provider, governments may not assess a tax against this transaction. However, states that had already begun to levy such taxes against Internet access were "grandfathered"—that is, allowed to continue this taxation in spite of the act. In the second place, the act prohibits multiple taxation of a single Internet transaction. This provision assures that two states—for example, the state in which a business is located and the state in which a consumer is located—may not *both* attempt to tax the same consumer transaction. Finally, the act prohibits discriminatory taxes levied on Internet commerce. Thus, if a particular state does not tax mail-order transactions where a business has no retail outlet in the state where a consumer resides, the state may not tax Internet transactions with the same characteristics.

AMENDMENTS

On November 21, 2001, Public Law 107-75 amended the Internet Tax Freedom Act to extend its moratorium on Internet taxes until November 1, 2003. This extended moratorium reflected a continued desire by Congress to shield the Internet from particular forms of taxation. Nevertheless, the amendment, by failing to make the moratorium on Internet taxes permanent, also signified that Congress was reluctant to address definitively a tax issue affecting a fast-growing area of technological development.

Timothy L. Hall

SOURCES FOR FURTHER STUDY

Imparato, Nicholas, ed. *Public Policy and the Internet: Privacy, Taxes, and Contract.* Stanford, Calif.: Hoover Institution Press, 2000.

Wiseman, Alan E. *The Internet Economy: Access, Taxes, and Market Structure.* Washington, D.C.: Brookings Institution Press, 2000.

SEE ALSO: Communications Act (1934); Communications Act Amendments (1960); Digital Millennium Copyright Act (1998).

DIGITAL MILLENNIUM COPYRIGHT ACT

DATE: October 28, 1998
U.S. STATUTES AT LARGE: 112 Stat. 2860
PUBLIC LAW: 105-304
U.S. CODE: 17 § 112, 114
CATEGORIES: Business, Commerce, and Trade; Communications and Media; Copyrights, Patents, and Trademarks

The act was the first legislation to address copyright protection of intellectual property in electronic form.

The Digital Millennium Copyright Act of 1998 was the most sweeping reform of U.S. copyright law in a generation. The act was designed to comply with the 1996 World Intellectual Property Organization (WIPO) Treaties, which addressed copyright issues raised by the advent of global electronic communication.

THE CONCEPT OF COPYRIGHT

Copyright laws are designed to protect the "intellectual property" (words, music, and other original creative works) of individuals from theft and unauthorized use. Historically, works such as books, records, and other "hard copy" media have been relatively easy to protect from copyright theft, but during the 1990's the rapid development of the Internet, including e-mail and the World Wide Web, erected new obstacles to copyright enforcement by making it easy for Internet users to reproduce and distribute copyrighted information without compensating copyright owners. The spread of electronic communications worldwide made enforcement more difficult, because users were able to circumvent international copyright laws that were inconsistent and inadequate to address new technologies. Works most vulnerable to copyright infringement were recorded music and computer software programs, which were frequently exchanged by Internet users.

By the mid-1990's, mounting pressure from the entertainment and software industries prompted the United Nations to seek an international remedy to copyright infringement through the World Intellectual Property Organization (WIPO), a U.N. organization founded in 1893 to administer international copyright treaties. In December, 1996, at a WIPO conference in Geneva, Switzerland, more than sixty countries signed two international copyright treaties that are known collectively as the WIPO Treaties. The treaties emphasized that copyright applies on the Internet just as in the "offline" world, granting copyright holders the right to use passwords, encryption, and other technologies to restrict online access to copyrighted works.

PASSAGE AND PROVISIONS

The legislation that would become the Digital Millennium Copyright Act was introduced into the U.S. House of Representatives in July, 1997. After contentious debate and the defeat of competing bills in both houses, Congress passed the final version of the bill on October 12, 1998, and President Bill Clinton signed it into law two weeks later. In compliance with the WIPO Treaties, the Digital Millennium Copyright Act affirmed that copyright protection applied to online content, required that "webcasters" offering free music to Internet users pay licensing fees to record companies, and made it a crime in most cases to circumvent antipiracy measures built into commercial software. In addition, the act outlawed the use of computer programs that copy software illegally, limited the liability of Internet service providers for content transmitted through their servers, and reaffirmed the doctrine of "fair use," permitting academic and other nonprofit use of copyrighted materials.

REACTION

The Digital Millennium Copyright Act was welcomed by record companies and software firms but did not completely resolve the numerous issues surrounding the use of copyrighted materials online. Free music sites and online file-sharing networks continued to operate, often under the shadow of lawsuits, and libraries and academic institutions continued to argue that the act denied citizens the right to access information.

Michael H. Burchett

SOURCES FOR FURTHER STUDY

Grossman, George S. *Omnibus Copyright Revision Legislative History.* Reprint. Buffalo, N.Y.: William S. Hein, 2001.
Hawke, Constance S. *Computer and Internet Use on Campus.* San Francisco: Jossey-Bass, 2000.
Samuels, Edward. *The Illustrated Story of Copyright.* New York: St. Martin's Press, 2002.
Wilbur, Marcia K. *The Digital Millennium Copyright Act.* iUniverse .com, 2000.

SEE ALSO: Copyright Act of 1909 (1909); Copyright Act of 1976 (1976); Trademark Law Revision Act (1988); North American Free Trade Agreement (1993); General Agreement on Tariffs and Trade of 1994 (1994).

USA PATRIOT ACT

ALSO KNOWN AS: Uniting and Strengthening America by Providing
  Appropriate Tools Required to Intercept and Obstruct Terror-
  ism Act
DATE: October 26, 2001
U.S. STATUTES AT LARGE: 115 Stat. 272
PUBLIC LAW: 107-56
U.S. CODE: 18 § 175, 817
CATEGORIES: Military and National Security

*Quickly passed in response to the terrorist attacks of September 11,
2001, several provisions of this sweeping legislation were called into
question by civil libertarians.*

On September 11, 2001, anti-American extremists from the Middle
East used two civilian passenger jets to destroy the World Trade
Center towers in New York and a third to severely damage the Pentagon building. A fourth airplane, now thought to have been targeting the Capitol Building, was, with the aid of many heroic passengers, crashed in Pennsylvania before reaching its goal. In all,
approximately three thousand persons were killed. Shortly thereafter, anthrax-contaminated letters were sent to members of Congress and other U.S. citizens. As part of the resulting "war on terrorism," President George W. Bush asked Congress to eliminate
many restrictions on both domestic law enforcement and international intelligence agencies.

PASSAGE AND PROVISIONS

Only six weeks after the attacks of September 11, Congress overwhelmingly approved the USA Patriot Act (USAPA), a complex
antiterrorist bill of 342 pages. The House vote was 356 to 66, while
the Senate vote was 98 to 1. Civil libertarians strongly criticized the
legislation. The director of the national office of the American
Civil Liberties Union warned that it was "based on the faulty assumption that safety must come at the expense of civil liberties."

The USAPA significantly changed more than fifteen different
statutes. Several of its more important provisions reduced the judicial supervision of law enforcement authorities when gathering fi-

nancial records and conducting surveillance of telephone and Internet communication. By expanding the field of the Foreign Intelligence Surveillance Act of 1978 to include domestic crimes, the legislation authorized federal agents to monitor communications by certifying to a judge that the information to be obtained was "relevant" to an ongoing criminal investigation, without the requirement of probable cause. The act created a new crime of "domestic terrorism," with special provisions for secret investigations of such activities. It also encouraged the sharing of information among agencies involved in domestic law enforcement and foreign intelligence.

Other provisions of the USAPA dealt specifically with the rights of noncitizens. The U.S. attorney general was given broad new authority to detain noncitizens based on certification of "reasonable grounds to believe" that they endangered national security. In addition, once the attorney general designated a domestic group as a terrorist organization, he had the authority to deport any noncitizen associated with the organization, without any proof that the individual was personally engaged in terrorist activities.

IMPACT

The early application of the USAPA had its greatest impact on the detention and expulsion of noncitizens, especially Arabs and others from the Middle East. Several hundred individuals were detained in federal facilities on the basis of visa and immigration violations. On the issue of surveillance, there were indications that the USAPA might face significant resistance from the courts. In August of 2002, the Foreign Intelligence Surveillance Court rejected a request by the Department of Justice to allow broader cooperation between investigators of domestic crimes and international terrorism. The court identified more than seventy-five cases in which the Federal Bureau of Investigation had given misleading information when requesting electronic surveillance.

Thomas T. Lewis

SOURCES FOR FURTHER STUDY

Chang, Nancy. *Silencing Political Dissent: How Post-September 11 Anti-Terrorism Measures Threaten Our Civil Liberties.* New York: Seven Stones Press, 2002.

Cole, David, and James Dempsey. *Terrorism and the Constitution: Sacrificing Civil Liberties in the Name of National Security.* New York: New Press, 2002.

Parenti, Michael. *The Terrorism Trap: September 11 and Beyond.* San Francisco: City Lights Books, 2002.

Reams, Bernard D., Jr. *USA Patriot Act: A Legislative History of the Uniting and Strengthening of America, Public Law No. 107-56.* Buffalo, N.Y.: William S. Hein, 2002.

SEE ALSO: Violent Crime Control and Law Enforcement Act (1994); Aviation and Transportation Security Act (2001).

AVIATION AND TRANSPORTATION SECURITY ACT

ALSO KNOWN AS: Sky Marshals Bill
DATE: November 19, 2001
U.S. STATUTES AT LARGE: 115 Stat. 297
PUBLIC LAW: 107-71
U.S. CODE: 49 § 114
CATEGORIES: Military and National Security; Transportation

A reaction to the terrorist hijackings of September 11, 2001, this law mandated sweeping and expensive changes in airport security devices and personnel.

On September 11, 2001, two jetliners hijacked by terrorists plunged into and destroyed the Twin Towers of New York City's World Trade Center, leaving more than 2,750 people confirmed dead. A third jet flew into the Pentagon, adding more than 120 individuals to the day's terrorist casualties. A fourth crashed into a field in Pennsylvania, killing all 45 people aboard, after passengers apparently frustrated hijackers' attempt to use it as a flying weapon against another significant target in Washington, D.C., thought to be either the White House or, more likely, the Capitol.

These horrific events led to calls by the public for enhanced aviation security, and, within a little more than two months of September 11, Congress and President George W. Bush responded by passing and signing into law the Aviation and Transportation Security Act.

The most significant accomplishment of the act was to place airport security in the hands of the federal government. The Aviation and Transportation Security Act created a new administration within the Department of Transportation, called the Transportation Security Administration, to be administered by an undersecretary of the Department of Transportation. At least initially, the act required the federal government to assume responsibility for screening luggage and other passenger belongings for dangerous items. Furthermore, it provided minimum qualifications for screeners themselves, including the requirement that they be U.S. citizens, and mandated that the federal government take steps to conduct background checks not only on baggage-screening personnel but also on all persons with access to secure areas in the nation's airports. The act also stipulated that devices capable of detecting explosives in baggage be installed in the nation's airports within a little more than a year after the passage of the act.

The Aviation and Transportation Security Act also addressed inflight security issues. For example, it authorized the undersecretary of the newly created Transportation Security Administration to place U.S. marshals either on all airline flights or at least on those that posed high security risks. Moreover, to frustrate future attempts by terrorists to take control of airline cockpits, the act specified that cockpit doors be kept locked during flights and that they be fortified against attempts at forcible entry.

The massive upgrades to aviation security mandated by the Aviation and Transportation Security Act were expensive. Congress, recognizing the need for revenue to implement security changes, provided for a fee to be charged to airline travelers to cover the cost of these implementations. This fee would vary with the number of times a particular traveler boards planes in the course of a journey but was capped at five dollars per one-way trip. For the time being, Americans seemed willing to bear this cost.

Timothy L. Hall

SOURCES FOR FURTHER STUDY

Friedman, Thomas L. *Longitudes and Attitudes: Exploring the World After September 11.* New York: Farrar, Strauss and Giroux, 2002.
Henderson, Harry. *Terrorism.* New York: Facts On File, 2001.
Wallis, Rodney. *Combating Air Terrorism.* Washington, D.C.: Brassey's, 1993.

SEE ALSO: USA Patriot Act (2001).

BIPARTISAN CAMPAIGN REFORM ACT

ALSO KNOWN AS: Shays-Meehan Campaign Finance Reform Bill
DATE: March 27, 2002
U.S. STATUTES AT LARGE: 116 Stat. 81
PUBLIC LAW: 107-155
U.S. CODE: 2 § 431
CATEGORIES: Voting and Elections

The act attempted to eliminate what many saw as corruption of the political process by regulating "soft money" contributions to political parties and by prohibiting "issue ads" sixty days prior to an election.

Campaign finance reform became a hot-button political issue during the 1990's. Public figures such as senator and presidential hopeful John McCain (Republican of Arizona) made the issue a centerpiece of their political careers. Supporters of reform insisted that Congress had to rein in the power of money to influence and corrupt the political process. Opponents argued with equal vehemence that reform trespassed on free speech rights. In the spring of 2002, however, campaign finance reform leaped out of the domain of mere political argument and onto the pages of law. With the signature of President George W. Bush, the Bipartisan Campaign Reform Act of 2002 became federal law.

The Bipartisan Campaign Reform Act regulates campaign finance practices in two principal ways. First, it bans so-called soft money contributions from corporations and individuals to the national political parties and prohibits state and local parties from spending soft money on federal elections. "Soft money" refers to contributions made to political parties for so-called party-building activities—that is, activities intended to benefit the party generically as opposed to supporting a particular political candidate. Under existing federal law, soft money contributions were virtually unlimited. These were contrasted with "hard money" contributions, which might be used to support specific political candidates and which were severely limited by the terms of the Federal Election Campaign Act of 1971 (passed in 1972). Under the Bipartisan Campaign Reform Act, candidates are permitted to raise somewhat more "hard money" to offset the restrictions on "soft money." Second, the Act prohibits "issue ads" in the sixty days before an election. These, while not specifically calling upon voters to elect a particular candidate, have often been used in contested political races to sway potential voters toward one candidate or another.

On the same day President Bush signed the Bipartisan Campaign Reform Act into law, Senator Mitch McConnell (Republican of Kentucky), one of campaign finance reform's most implacable foes, brought suit challenging the constitutionality of the law. The National Rifle Association (NRA) filed a similar suit the same day. Moreover, in early fall of 2002, the Federal Elections Committee, charged with creating specific regulations to implement the general terms of the act, issued regulations that many observers viewed as weakening the effectiveness of the act. The impact of both developments remain unclear. The Supreme Court, in *Buckley v. Valeo* (1976), upheld provisions of the Federal Election Campaign Act of 1971 that restricted the amounts that supporters could contribute to a political campaign. It remained to be seen, however, whether the Bipartisan Campaign Reform Act, especially in its prohibition against issue ads, would be found to have violated freedom of speech.

Timothy L. Hall

SOURCES FOR FURTHER STUDY

Corrado, Anthony. *Campaign Finance Reform.* New York: Century Foundation Press, 2000.

Luna, Christopher, ed. *Campaign Finance Reform.* New York: H. W. Wilson, 2001.

Smith, Bradley A. *Unfree Speech: The Folly of Campaign Finance Reform.* Princeton, N.J.: Princeton University Press, 2001.

SEE ALSO: First Amendment (1789); Seventeenth Amendment (1913); Federal Corrupt Practices Act (1925); Twenty-third Amendment (1961); Federal Election Campaign Act (1972); Ethics in Government Act (1978); Twenty-seventh Amendment (1992).

U.S.-RUSSIA ARMS AGREEMENT

ALSO KNOWN AS: Moscow Treaty
DATE: Signed May 24, 2002
CATEGORIES: Foreign Relations; Treaties and Agreements

The treaty sought to reduce the number of active nuclear warheads to between seventeen hundred and twenty-two hundred by the end of 2012.

With the breakup of the Union of Soviet Socialist Republics into fifteen "new" sovereign states and the concomitant end of the Cold War in the early 1990's, the United States and the new Russian Federation sought to move into an era of closer relations. Although what came to be called START I had been signed in 1991, this new era brought about another treaty proposal, known as START II, although START II was never ratified by the U.S. Senate. START II was the first arms control treaty that would have substantially reduced the number of nuclear weapons in Russia and the United States. Continuing on this path in 1997, the two countries agreed on a framework of new negotiations that was to create START III. Due to political problems faced by the presidents of both countries, these negotiations never materialized.

In 1999 Russia elected a new president, Vladimir Putin, and in 2000 George W. Bush was elected president of the United States. Both presidents desired a reduction in the number of nuclear weapons, although for different reasons. Russia faced economic hardship and had been reducing the size of its armed forces since the demise of the Soviet Union. The expense of keeping its nuclear arsenal intact was beyond the funds available. Thus Russia desired to decrease the number of weapons systems in order to stabilize governmental expenditures. However, it was reluctant to make massive cuts unilaterally. In the United States, President Bush had stated during his campaign that he would like to decrease the size of the nuclear arsenal. After taking office in 2001, he sought to assess the military strength of the United States and decided that some significant changes should be made. In November, 2001, President Bush announced that the United States would reduce its nuclear arsenal to between seventeen hundred and twenty-two hundred warheads. This announcement essentially began the process of negotiating a new treaty. In December, 2001, President Putin stated that he was in basic agreement with President Bush.

It took until May 13, 2002, to negotiate the details of what is a relatively short treaty. While the impetus for the treaty was the decision by President Bush to cut the number of nuclear weapons, the details relied on negotiations that had taken place for START I, II, and III. The Moscow Treaty, as it is called, is a very simple but flexible document that commits both nations to reduce the number of active nuclear warheads to between seventeen hundred and twenty-two hundred. This must take place by December 31, 2012. It recognizes that the START I treaty remains in force. The number of warheads mandated by the treaty would be about one-third the number of active warheads in each country's 2002 arsenal. Counting warheads, rather than delivery vehicles, was first proposed in 1997. Exactly how each country will verify the compliance of the other will be negotiated by the Bilateral Implementation Commission. The treaty was to be in force through December 31, 2012.

Donald A. Watt

SOURCES FOR FURTHER STUDY

Rumsfeld, Donald H. "Transforming the Military." *Foreign Affairs*, May/June, 2002.

Talbot, Strobe. *The Russia Hand: A Memoir of Presidential Diplomacy.* New York: Random House, 2002.

SEE ALSO: START II Treaty (1993).

HOMELAND SECURITY ACT

DATE: November 19, 2002
PUBLIC LAW: 107-296
CATEGORIES: Civil Rights and Liberties; Government Procedure and Organization; Military and National Security

The Homeland Security Act instituted the most sweeping reorganization of federal government since passage of the National Security Act more than fifty years earlier.

On September 11, 2001, the United States experienced the worst attack on its territory since the bombing of Pearl Harbor on December 7, 1941, when hijackers later identified as members of the terrorist organization Al-Qaeda flew passenger airliners into the World Trade Center towers in New York City and into the Pentagon in Washington, D.C., killing approximately three thousand innocent civilians from many nations. A fourth jet crashed in Pennsylvania when passengers resisted the hijackers; it is now thought to have been targeting either the White House or the Capitol Building.

President George W. Bush and Congress responded over the next year with legislation that culminated in the Homeland Security Act of 2002, which President Bush signed into law on November 25, 2002. This massive reorganization of the federal government was spurred by the need to ensure national security at the borders and within the country against anticipated future attacks.

PROVISIONS

The act created the Department of Homeland Security (DHS) to function as a clearinghouse for intelligence for protection against terrorist attacks. In so doing, the new department would oversee approximately 170,000 workers from twenty-two federal agencies, including the Border Patrol, the Coast Guard, the Customs Service, the Federal Emergency Management Agency, the Immigration and Naturalization Service, the Secret Service, the Transportation Security Administration, and the Animal and Plant Health

Inspection Service's border inspection section. The new agency was to be organized into four divisions: Border and Transportation Security; Emergency Preparedness and Response; Chemical, Biological, Radiological, and Nuclear Countermeasures; and Information Analysis and Infrastructure Protection. Although the Federal Bureau of Investigation and the Central Intelligence Agency were not brought under DHS, it was expected that these law enforcement and intelligence agencies would work closely with the new department. President Bush nominated former governor of Pennsylvania and head of the former Office of Homeland Security Tom Ridge to head the new department.

The law thus imposed a huge and complicated reorganization on the existing structure of federal government, and although it required that the new department be operational within a year of its signing (by the end of November, 2003), both members of Congress and White House officials predicted that it would take at least two years for the reorganization to take place and be running smoothly.

ISSUES AND CONTROVERSIES

Many doubts surrounded the new law, not the least of which concerned the logistical problems posed by such massive reorganization. Critics and supporters alike expressed their concerns over diversion of resources, interagency turf battles, national security during the transition, failure to appropriate resources to cities, and labor rights of the workers who would be transferred. President Bush fought for and succeeded in securing a great deal of flexibility in hiring and firing employees in the new department.

Two issues in particular worried critics: First, the final bill was passed with liability protections for drug companies that manufactured vaccines that would be used to shore up defenses in the event of biological attacks. Second, the new law created an exemption to the Freedom of Information Act, which provided that information that companies give to the government "related to the security of critical infrastructure or protected systems" would automatically be withheld from the public. Such concerns were given little hearing the the lame-duck session of Congress that passed the bill 90-9. As one of the most vocal critics of the bill, Senator Robert Byrd (Democrat, West Virginia), said only a few hours prior to the law's passage on November 19:

There have been no hearings on this bill. . . . And we are being asked to vote on that 484 pages tomorrow. Our poor staffs were up most of the night studying it. They know some of the things that are in there, but they don't know all of them. It is a sham and it is a shame. We are all complicit in going along with it.

Christina J. Moose

SOURCES FOR FURTHER STUDY

Bremmer, L. Paul, and Edwin Meese. *Defending the American Homeland: A Report of the Heritage Foundation Homeland Security Task Force.* Washington, D.C.: Heritage Foundation, 2002.

Friedman, Thomas L. *Longitudes and Attitudes: Exploring the World After September 11.* New York: Farrar, Straus and Giroux, 2002.

Lee, Nancy, Lonnie Schlein, and Mitchel Levitas, eds. *A Nation Challenged.* New York: New York Times, 2002.

Rather, Dan. *What We Saw: The Events of September 11, 2001, in Words, Pictures, and Video.* New York: Simon and Schuster/CBS News, 2002.

SEE ALSO: National Defense Act (1916); National Security Act (1947); North Atlantic Treaty (1949); Internal Security Act (1950); Freedom of Information Act (1966); War Powers Resolution (1973); USA Patriot Act (2001).

THE DECLARATION OF INDEPENDENCE

In Congress, July 4, 1776
The unanimous declaration of the thirteen
United States of America

When in the Course of human Events, it becomes necessary for one People to dissolve the Political Bands which have connected them with another, and to assume among the Powers of the Earth, the separate and equal Station to which the Laws of Nature and of Nature's God entitle them, a decent Respect to the Opinions of Mankind requires that they should declare the causes which impel them to the Separation.

We hold these Truths to be self-evident, that all Men are created equal, that they are endowed by their Creator with certain unalienable Rights, that among these are Life, Liberty, and the Pursuit of Happiness—That to secure these Rights, Governments are instituted among Men, deriving their just Powers from the Consent of the Governed, that whenever any Form of Government becomes destructive of these Ends, it is the Right of the People to alter or to abolish it, and to institute new Government, laying its Foundation on such Principles, and organizing its Powers in such Form, as to them shall seem most likely to effect their Safety and Happiness. Prudence, indeed, will dictate that Governments long established should not be changed for light and transient Causes; and accordingly all Experience hath shewn, that Mankind are more disposed to suffer, while Evils are sufferable, than to right themselves by abolishing the Forms to which they are accustomed. But when a long Train of Abuses and Usurpations, pursuing invariably the same Object, evinces a Design to reduce them under absolute Despotism, it is their Right, it is their Duty, to throw off such Government, and to provide new Guards for their future Security. Such has been the patient Sufferance of these Colonies; and such is now the Necessity which constrains them to alter their former Systems of Government. The History of the present King of Great Britain is a History of repeated Injuries and Usurpations, all having in direct Object the Establishment of an absolute Tyranny over these States. To prove this, let Facts be submitted to a candid World.

He has refused his Assent to Laws, the most wholesome and necessary for the public Good.

He has forbidden his Governors to pass Laws of immediate and pressing Importance, unless suspended in their Operation till his Assent should be obtained; and when so suspended, he has utterly neglected to attend to them.

He has refused to pass other Laws for the Accommodation of large Districts of People, unless those People would relinquish the Right of Representation in the Legislature, a Right inestimable to them, and formidable to Tyrants only.

He has called together Legislative Bodies at Places unusual, uncomfortable, and distant from the Depository of their public Records, for the sole Purpose of fatiguing them into Compliance with his Measures.

He has dissolved Representative Houses repeatedly, for opposing with manly Firmness his Invasions on the Rights of the People.

He has refused for a long Time, after such Dissolutions, to cause others to be elected; whereby the Legislative Powers, incapable of Annihilation, have returned to the People at large for their exercise; the State remaining in the meantime exposed to all the Dangers of Invasion from without, and Convulsions within.

He has endeavoured to prevent the Population of these States; for that Purpose obstructing the Laws for Naturalization of Foreigners; refusing to pass others to encourage their Migrations hither, and raising the Conditions of new Appropriations of Lands.

He has obstructed the Administration of Justice, by refusing his Assent to Laws for establishing Judiciary Powers.

He has made Judges dependent on his Will alone, for the Tenure of their Offices, and the Amount and Payment of their Salaries.

He has erected a Multitude of new Offices, and sent hither Swarms of Officers to harass our People, and eat out their Substance.

He has kept among us, in Times of Peace, Standing Armies, without the consent of our Legislatures.

He has affected to render the Military independent of and superior to the Civil Power.

He has combined with others to subject us to a Jurisdiction foreign to our Constitution, and unacknowledged by our Laws; giving his Assent to their Acts of pretended Legislation:

For quartering large Bodies of Armed Troops among us:

For protecting them, by a mock Trial, from Punishment for any Murders which they should commit on the Inhabitants of these States:

For cutting off our Trade with all Parts of the World:

For imposing Taxes on us without our Consent:

For depriving us, in many Cases, of the Benefits of Trial by Jury:

For transporting us beyond Seas to be tried for pretended Offences:

For abolishing the free System of English Laws in a neighbouring Province, establishing therein an arbitrary Government, and enlarging its Boundaries, so as to render it at once an Example and fit Instrument for introducing the same absolute Rule into these Colonies:

For taking away our Charters, abolishing our most valuable Laws, and altering fundamentally the Forms of our Governments:

For suspending our own Legislatures, and declaring themselves invested with Power to legislate for us in all Cases whatsoever.

He has abdicated Government here, by declaring us out of his Protection and waging War against us.

He has plundered our Seas, ravaged our Coasts, burnt our Towns, and destroyed the Lives of our People.

He is, at this Time, transporting large Armies of foreign Mercenaries to compleat the Works of Death, Desolation, and Tyranny, already begun with circumstances of Cruelty and Perfidy, scarcely paralleled in the most barbarous Ages, and totally unworthy the Head of a civilized Nation.

He has constrained our fellow Citizens taken Captive on the high Seas to bear Arms against their Country, to become the Executioners of their Friends and Brethren, or to fall themselves by their Hands.

He has excited domestic Insurrections amongst us, and has endeavoured to bring on the Inhabitants of our Frontiers, the merciless Indian Savages, whose known Rule of Warfare is an undistinguished Destruction, of all Ages, Sexes and Conditions.

In every stage of these Oppressions we have Petitioned for Redress in the most humble Terms: Our repeated Petitions have been answered only by repeated Injury. A Prince, whose Character is thus marked by every act which may define a Tyrant, is unfit to be the Ruler of a free People.

Nor have we been wanting in Attentions to our British Brethren. We have warned them from Time to Time of Attempts by their Legislature to extend an unwarrantable Jurisdiction over us. We have reminded them of the Circumstances of our Emigration and Settlement here. We have appealed to their native Justice and Magnanimity, and we have conjured them by the Ties of our common Kindred to disavow these Usurpations, which would inevitably interrupt our Connections and Correspondence. They too have been deaf to the Voice of Justice and of Consanguinity. We must, therefore, acquiesce in the Necessity, which denounces our Separation, and hold them, as we hold the rest of Mankind, Enemies in War, in Peace, Friends.

We, therefore, the Representatives of the united States of America, in General Congress, Assembled, appealing to the Supreme Judge of the World for the Rectitude of our Intentions, do, in the Name, and by Authority of the good People of these Colonies, solemnly Publish and Declare, That these United Colonies are, and of Right ought to be, Free and Independent States; that they are absolved from all Allegiance to the British Crown, and that all political Connection between them and the State of Great Britain, is and ought to be totally dissolved; and that as Free and Independent States, they have full Power to levy War, conclude Peace, contract Alliances, establish Commerce, and to do all other Acts and Things which Independent States may of right do. And for the support of this Declaration, with a firm Reliance on the Protection of divine Providence, we mutually pledge to each other our Lives, our Fortunes, and our sacred Honor.

THE CONSTITUTION OF THE UNITED STATES OF AMERICA

We the People of the United States, in Order to form a more perfect Union, establish Justice, insure domestic Tranquility, provide for the common defence, promote the general Welfare, and secure the Blessings of Liberty to ourselves and our Posterity, do ordain and establish this Constitution for the United States of America.

ARTICLE I.

SECTION 1. All legislative Powers herein granted shall be vested in a Congress of the United States, which shall consist of a Senate and House of Representatives.

SECTION 2. The House of Representatives shall be composed of Members chosen every second Year by the People of the several States, and the Electors in each State shall have the Qualifications requisite for Electors of the most numerous Branch of the State Legislature.

No Person shall be a Representative who shall not have attained to the Age of twenty five Years, and been seven Years a Citizen of the United States, and who shall not, when elected, be an Inhabitant of that State in which he shall be chosen.

Representatives and direct Taxes shall be apportioned among the several States which may be included within this Union, according to their respective Numbers, which shall be determined by adding to the whole Number of free Persons, including those bound to Service for a Term of Years, and excluding Indians not taxed, three fifths of all other Persons. The actual Enumeration shall be made within three Years after the first Meeting of the Congress of the United States, and within every subsequent Term of ten Years, in such Manner as they shall by Law direct. The number of Representatives shall not exceed one for every thirty Thousand, but each State shall have at Least one Representative; and until such enumeration shall be made, the State of New Hampshire shall be entitled to chuse three, Massachusetts eight, Rhode Island and Providence Plantations one, Connecticut five, New-York six, New Jersey four, Pennsylvania eight, Delaware one, Maryland six, Virginia ten, North Carolina five, South Carolina five, and Georgia three.

When vacancies happen in the Representation from any State, the Executive Authority thereof shall issue Writs of Election to fill such Vacancies.

The House of Representatives shall chuse their Speaker and other Officers; and shall have the sole Power of Impeachment.

SECTION 3. The Senate of the United States shall be composed of two Senators from each State, chosen by the Legislature thereof, for six Years; and each Senator shall have one Vote.

Immediately after they shall be assembled in Consequence of the first Election, they shall be divided as equally as may be into three Classes. The Seats of the Senators of the first Class shall be vacated at the Expiration of the second Year, of the second Class at the Expiration of the fourth Year, and of the third Class at the Expiration of the sixth Year, so that one third may be chosen every second Year; and if Vacancies happen by Resignation, or otherwise, during the Recess of the Legislature of any State, the Executive thereof may make temporary Appointments until the next Meeting of the Legislature, which shall then fill such Vacancies.

No Person shall be a Senator who shall not have attained to the Age of thirty Years, and been nine Years a Citizen of the United States, and who shall not, when elected, be an Inhabitant of that State for which he shall be chosen.

The Vice President of the United States shall be President of the Senate, but shall have no Vote, unless they be equally divided.

The Senate shall chuse their other Officers, and also a President pro tempore, in the Absence of the Vice President, or when he shall exercise the Office of President of the United States.

The Senate shall have the sole Power to try all Impeachments. When sitting for that Purpose, they shall be on Oath or Affirmation. When the President of the United States is tried, the Chief Justice shall preside: And no Person shall be convicted without the Concurrence of two thirds of the Members present.

Judgment in Cases of Impeachment shall not extend further than to removal from Office, and disqualification to hold and enjoy any Office of honor, Trust or Profit under the United States: but the Party convicted shall nevertheless be liable and subject to Indictment, Trial, Judgment and Punishment, according to Law.

SECTION 4. The Times, Places and Manner of holding Elections for Senators and Representatives, shall be prescribed in each State by the Legislature thereof; but the Congress may at any time by Law make or alter such Regulations, except as to the Places of chusing Senators.

The Congress shall assemble at least once in every Year, and such Meeting shall be on the first Monday in December, unless they shall by Law appoint a different Day.

SECTION 5. Each House shall be the Judge of the Elections, Returns and Qualifications of its own Members, and a Majority of each shall constitute a Quorum to do Business; but a smaller Number may adjourn from day to day, and may be authorized to compel the Attendance of absent Members, in such Manner, and under such Penalties as each House may provide.

Each House may determine the Rules of its Proceedings, punish its Members for disorderly Behaviour, and, with the Concurrence of two thirds, expel a Member.

Each House shall keep a Journal of its Proceedings, and from time to time publish the same, excepting such Parts as may in their Judgment require Secrecy; and the Yeas and Nays of the Members of either House on any question shall, at the Desire of one fifth of those Present, be entered on the Journal.

Neither House, during the Session of Congress, shall, without the Consent of the other, adjourn for more than three days, nor to any other Place than that in which the two Houses shall be sitting.

SECTION 6. The Senators and Representatives shall receive a Compensation for their Services, to be ascertained by Law, and paid out of the Treasury of the United States. They shall in all Cases, except Treason, Felony and Breach of the Peace, be privileged from Arrest during their Attendance at the Session of their respective Houses, and in going to and returning from the same; and for any Speech or Debate in either House, they shall not be questioned in any other Place.

No Senator or Representative shall, during the Time for which he was elected, be appointed to any civil Office under the Authority of the United States, which shall have been created, or the Emoluments whereof shall have been encreased during such time; and no Person holding any Office under the United States, shall be a Member of either House during his Continuance in Office.

SECTION 7. All Bills for raising Revenue shall originate in the House of Representatives; but the Senate may propose or concur with Amendments as on other Bills.

Every Bill which shall have passed the House of Representatives and the Senate, shall, before it becomes a Law, be presented to the President of the United States; If he approve he shall sign it, but if not he shall return it, with his Objections to that House in which it shall have originated, who shall enter the Objections at large on their Journal, and proceed to reconsider it. If after such Reconsideration two thirds of that House shall agree to pass the Bill, it shall be sent, together with the Objections, to the other House, by which it shall likewise be reconsidered, and if approved by two thirds of that House, it shall become a Law. But in all such Cases the Votes of both Houses shall be determined by yeas and Nays, and the Names of the Persons voting for and against the Bill shall be entered on the Journal of each House respectively. If any Bill shall not be returned by the President within ten Days (Sundays excepted) after it shall have been presented to him, the Same shall be a Law, in like Manner as if he had signed it, unless the Congress by their Adjournment prevent its Return, in which Case it shall not be a Law.

Every Order, Resolution, or Vote to which the Concurrence of the Senate and House of Representatives may be necessary (except on a question of Adjournment) shall be presented to the President of the United States; and before the Same shall take Effect, shall be approved by him, or being disapproved by him, shall be repassed by two thirds of the Senate and House of Representatives, according to the Rules and Limitations prescribed in the Case of a Bill.

SECTION 8. The Congress shall have Power To lay and collect Taxes, Duties, Imposts and Excises, to pay the Debts and provide for the common Defence and general Welfare of the United States; but all Duties, Imposts and Excises shall be uniform throughout the United States;

To borrow Money on the credit of the United States;

To regulate Commerce with foreign Nations, and among the several States, and with the Indian Tribes;

To establish an uniform Rule of Naturalization, and uniform Laws on the subject of Bankruptcies throughout the United States;

To coin Money, regulate the Value thereof, and of foreign Coin, and fix the Standard of Weights and Measures;

To provide for the Punishment of counterfeiting the Securities and current Coin of the United States;

To establish Post Offices and post Roads;

To promote the Progress of Science and useful Arts, by securing for limited Times to Authors and Inventors the exclusive Right to their respective Writings and Discoveries;

To constitute Tribunals inferior to the supreme Court;

To define and punish Piracies and Felonies committed on the high Seas, and Offenses against the Law of Nations;

To declare War, grant Letters of Marque and Reprisal, and make Rules concerning Captures on Land and Water;

To raise and support Armies, but no Appropriation of Money to that Use shall be for a longer Term than two Years;

To provide and maintain a Navy;

To make Rules for the Government and Regulation of the land and naval Forces;

To provide for calling forth the Militia to execute the Laws of the Union, suppress Insurrections and repel Invasions;

To provide for organizing, arming, and disciplining, the Militia, and for governing such Part of them as may be employed in the Service of the United States, reserving to the States respectively, the Appointment of the Officers, and the Authority of training the Militia according to the discipline prescribed by Congress;

To exercise exclusive Legislation in all Cases whatsoever, over such District (not exceeding ten Miles square) as may, by Cession of particular States, and the Acceptance of Congress, become the Seat of the Government of the United States, and to exercise like Authority over all Places purchased by the Consent of the Legislature of the State in which the Same shall be, for the Erection of Forts, Magazines, Arsenals, dock-Yards and other needful Buildings;—And

To make all Laws which shall be necessary and proper for carrying into Execution the foregoing Powers, and all other Powers vested by this Constitution in the Government of the United States, or in any Department or Officer thereof.

SECTION 9. The Migration or Importation of such Persons as any of the States now existing shall think proper to admit, shall not be prohibited by the Congress prior to the Year one thousand eight hundred and eight, but a Tax or duty may be imposed on such Importation, not exceeding ten dollars for each Person.

The Privilege of the Writ of Habeas Corpus shall not be suspended, unless when in Cases of Rebellion or Invasion the public Safety may require it.

No Bill of Attainder or ex post facto Law shall be passed.

No Capitation, or other direct, Tax shall be laid, unless in Proportion to the Census or Enumeration herein before directed to be taken.

No Tax or Duty shall be laid on Articles exported from any State.

No Preference shall be given by any Regulation of Commerce or Revenue to the Ports of one State over those of another: nor shall Vessels bound to, or from, one State, be obliged to enter, clear, or pay Duties in another.

No Money shall be drawn from the Treasury, but in Consequence of Appropriations made by Law; and a regular Statement and Account of the Receipts and Expenditures of all public Money shall be published from time to time.

No Title of Nobility shall be granted by the United States: And no Person holding any Office of Profit or Trust under them, shall, without the Consent of the Congress, accept of any present, Emolument, Office, or Title, of any kind whatever, from any King, Prince, or foreign State.

SECTION 10. No State shall enter into any Treaty, Alliance, or Confederation; grant Letters of Marque and Reprisal; coin Money; emit Bills of Credit; make any Thing but gold and silver Coin a Tender in Payment of Debts; pass any Bill of Attainder, ex post facto Law, or Law impairing the Obligation of Contracts, or grant any Title of Nobility.

No State shall, without the Consent of the Congress, lay any Imposts or Duties on Imports or Exports, except what may be absolutely necessary for executing it's inspection Laws: and the net Produce of all Duties and Imposts, laid by any State on Imports or Exports, shall be for the Use of the Treasury of the United States; and all such Laws shall be subject to the Revision and Control of the Congress.

No State shall, without the Consent of Congress, lay any Duty of Tonnage, keep Troops, or Ships of War in time of Peace, enter into any Agreement or Compact with another State, or with a foreign Power, or engage in War, unless actually invaded, or in such imminent Danger as will not admit of delay.

ARTICLE II.

SECTION 1. The executive Power shall be vested in a President of the United States of America. He shall hold his Office during the Term of four Years, and, together with the Vice President, chosen for the same Term, be elected, as follows

Each State shall appoint, in such Manner as the Legislature thereof may direct, a Number of Electors, equal to the whole Number of Senators and Representatives to which the State may be entitled in the Congress: but no Senator or Representative, or Person holding an Office of Trust or Profit under the United States, shall be appointed an Elector.

The Electors shall meet in their respective States, and vote by Ballot for two Persons, of whom one at least shall not be an Inhabitant of the same State with themselves. And they shall make a List of all the Persons voted for, and of the Number of Votes for each; which List they shall sign and certify, and transmit sealed to the Seat of the Government of the United States, directed to the President of the Senate. The President of the Senate shall, in the Presence of the Senate and House of Representatives, open all the Certificates, and the Votes shall then be counted. The Person having the greatest Number of Votes shall be the President, if such Number be a Majority of the whole Number of Electors appointed; and if there be more than one who have such Majority, and have an equal Number of Votes, then the House of Representatives shall immediately chuse by Ballot one of them for President; and if no Person have a Majority, then from the five highest on the List the said House shall in like manner chuse the President. But in chusing the President, the Votes shall be taken by States, the Representation from each State having one Vote; A quorum for this Purpose shall consist of a Member or Members from two thirds of the States, and a Majority of all the States shall be necessary to a Choice. In every Case, after the Choice of the President, the Person having the greatest Number of Votes of the Electors shall be the Vice President. But if there should remain two or more who have equal Votes, the Senate shall chuse from them by Ballot the Vice President.

The Congress may determine the Time of chusing the Electors, and the Day on which they shall give their Votes; which Day shall be the same throughout the United States.

No Person except a natural born Citizen, or a Citizen of the United States, at the time of the Adoption of this Constitution, shall be eligible to the Office of the President; neither shall any person be eligible to that Office who shall not have attained to the Age of thirty five Years, and been fourteen Years a Resident within the United States.

In Case of the Removal of the President from Office, or of his Death, Resignation, or Inability to discharge the Powers and Duties of the said Office, the Same shall devolve on the Vice President, and the Congress may by Law provide for the Case of Removal, Death, Resignation or Inability, both of the President and Vice President, declaring what Officer shall then act as President, and such Officer shall act accordingly, until the Disability be removed, or a President shall be elected.

The President shall, at stated Times, receive for his Services, a Compensation, which shall neither be increased nor diminished during the Period for which he shall have been elected, and he shall not receive within that Period any other Emolument from the United States, or any of them.

Before he enter the Execution of his Office, he shall take the following Oath or Affirmation:—"I do solemnly swear (or affirm) that I will faithfully execute the Office of President of the United States, and will to the best of my Ability, preserve, protect and defend the Constitution of the United States."

SECTION 2. The President shall be Commander in Chief of the Army and Navy of the United States, and of the Militia of the several States, when called into the actual Service of the United States; he may require the Opinion, in writing, of the principal Officer in each of the executive Departments, upon any Subject relating to the Duties of their respective Offices, and he shall have Power to grant Reprieves and Pardons for Offenses against the United States, except in Cases of Impeachment.

He shall have Power, by and with the Advice and Consent of the Senate, to make Treaties, provided two thirds of the Senators present concur; and he shall nominate, and by and with the Advice and Consent of the Senate, shall appoint Ambassadors, other public Ministers and Consuls, Judges of the supreme Court, and all other Officers of the United States, whose Appointments are not herein otherwise provided for, and which shall be established by Law: but the Congress may by Law vest the Appointment of such inferior Officers, as they think proper, in the President alone, in the Courts of Law, or in the Heads of Departments.

The President shall have Power to fill up all Vacancies that may happen during the Recess of the Senate, by granting Commissions which shall expire at the End of their next Session.

SECTION 3. He shall from time to time give to the Congress Information of the State of the Union, and recommend to their Consideration such Measures as he shall judge necessary and expedient; he may, on extraordinary Occasions, convene both Houses, or either of them, and in Case of Disagreement between them, with Respect to the Time of Adjournment, he may adjourn them to such Time as he shall think proper; he shall receive Ambassadors and other public Ministers; he shall take Care that the Laws be faithfully executed, and shall Commission all the Officers of the United States.

SECTION 4. The President, Vice President and all civil Officers of the United States, shall be removed from Office on Impeachment for, and Conviction of, Treason, Bribery, or other high Crimes and Misdemeanors.

ARTICLE III.
SECTION 1. The judicial Power of the United States, shall be vested in one supreme Court, and in such inferior Courts as the Congress may from time to time ordain and establish. The Judges, both of the supreme and inferior Courts, shall hold their Offices during good Behaviour, and shall, at stated Times, receive for their Services, a Compensation, which shall not be diminished during their Continuance in Office.

SECTION 2. The judicial Power shall extend to all Cases, in Law and Equity, arising under this Constitution, the Laws of the United States, and Treaties made, or which shall be made, under their Authority;—to all Cases affecting Ambassadors, other public Ministers and Consuls;—to all Cases of admiralty and maritime Jurisdiction;—to Controversies to which the United States shall be a Party;—to Controversies between two or more States; between a State and Citizens of another State; between Citizens of different States,—between Citizens of the same State claiming Lands under

Grants of different States, and between a State, or the Citizens thereof, and foreign States, Citizens or Subjects.

In all Cases affecting Ambassadors, other public Ministers and Consuls, and those in which a State shall be Party, the supreme Court shall have original Jurisdiction. In all the other Cases before mentioned, the supreme Court shall have appellate Jurisdiction, both as to Law and Fact, with such Exceptions, and under such Regulations as the Congress shall make.

The Trial of all Crimes, except in Cases of Impeachment, shall be by Jury; and such Trial shall be held in the State where the said Crimes shall have been committed; but when not committed within any State, the Trial shall be at such Place or Places as the Congress may by Law have directed.

SECTION 3. Treason against the United States, shall consist only in levying War against them, or in adhering to their Enemies, giving them Aid and Comfort. No Person shall be convicted of Treason unless on the Testimony of two Witnesses to the same overt Act, or on Confession in open Court.

The Congress shall have Power to declare the Punishment of Treason, but no Attainder of Treason shall work Corruption of Blood, or Forfeiture except during the Life of the Person attainted.

ARTICLE IV.

SECTION 1. Full Faith and Credit shall be given in each State to the public Acts, Records, and judicial Proceedings of every other State; And the Congress may by general Laws prescribe the Manner in which such Acts, Records and Proceedings shall be proved, and the Effect thereof.

SECTION 2. The Citizens of each State shall be entitled to all Privileges and Immunities of Citizens in the several States.

A Person charged in any State with Treason, Felony, or other Crime, who shall flee from Justice, and be found in another State, shall on Demand of the executive Authority of the State from which he fled, be delivered up, to be removed to the State having Jurisdiction of the Crime.

No person held to Service or Labour in one State, under the Laws thereof, escaping into another, shall, in Consequence of any

Law or Regulation therein, be discharged from such Service or Labour, but shall be delivered up on Claim of the Party to whom such Service or Labour may be due.

SECTION 3. New States may be admitted by the Congress into this Union; but no new State shall be formed or erected within the Jurisdiction of any other State; nor any State be formed by the Junction of two or more States, or Parts of States, without the Consent of the Legislatures of the States concerned as well as of the Congress.

The Congress shall have Power to dispose of and make all needful Rules and Regulations respecting the Territory or other Property belonging to the United States; and nothing in this Constitution shall be so construed as to Prejudice any Claims of the United States, or of any particular State.

SECTION 4. The United States shall guarantee to every State in this Union a Republican Form of Government, and shall protect each of them against Invasion; and on Application of the Legislature, or of the Executive (when the Legislature cannot be convened) against domestic Violence.

ARTICLE V.

The Congress, whenever two thirds of both Houses shall deem it necessary, shall propose Amendments to this Constitution, or, on the Application of the Legislatures of two thirds of the several States, shall call a Convention for proposing Amendments, which, in either Case, shall be valid to all Intents and Purposes, as Part of this Constitution, when ratified by the Legislatures of three fourths of the several States, or by Conventions in three fourths thereof, as the one or the other Mode of Ratification may be proposed by the Congress; Provided that no Amendment which may be made prior to the Year One thousand eight hundred and eight shall in any Manner affect the first and fourth Clauses in the Ninth Section of the first Article; and that no State, without its Consent, shall be deprived of it's equal Suffrage in the Senate.

ARTICLE VI.

All Debts contracted and Engagements entered into, before the Adoption of this Constitution, shall be as valid against the United States under this Constitution, as under the Confederation.

This Constitution, and the Laws of the United States which shall be made in Pursuance thereof; and all Treaties made, or which shall be made, under the Authority of the United States, shall be the supreme Law of the Land; and the Judges in every State shall be bound thereby, any Thing in the Constitution or Laws of any State to the Contrary notwithstanding.

The Senators and Representatives before mentioned, and the Members of the several State Legislatures, and all executive and judicial Officers, both of the United States and of the several States, shall be bound by Oath or Affirmation, to support this Constitution; but no religious Test shall ever be required as a Qualification to any Office or public Trust under the United States.

ARTICLE VII.
The Ratification of the Conventions of nine States, shall be sufficient for the Establishment of this Constitution between the States so ratifying the Same.

Done in Convention by the Unanimous Consent of the States present the Seventeenth Day of September in the Year of our Lord one thousand seven hundred and Eighty seven and of the Independence of the United States of America the Twelfth. In Witness whereof We have hereunto subscribed our Names

Amendments to the U.S. Constitution

AMENDMENT I.

Congress shall make no law respecting an establishment of religion, or prohibiting the free exercise thereof; or abridging the freedom of speech, or of the press, or the right of the people peaceably to assemble, and to petition the Government for a redress of grievances.

[ratified December, 1791]

AMENDMENT II.

A well regulated Militia, being necessary to the security of a free State, the right of the people to keep and bear Arms, shall not be infringed.

[ratified December, 1791]

AMENDMENT III.

No Soldier shall, in time of peace be quartered in any house, without the consent of the Owner, nor in time of war, but in a manner to be prescribed by law.

[ratified December, 1791]

AMENDMENT IV.

The right of the people to be secure in their persons, houses, papers, and effects, against unreasonable searches and seizures, shall not be violated, and no Warrants shall issue, but upon probable cause, supported by Oath or affirmation, and particularly describing the place to be searched, and the persons or things to be seized.

[ratified December, 1791]

AMENDMENT V.

No person shall be held to answer for a capital, or otherwise infamous crime, unless on a presentment or indictment of a Grand

Jury, except in cases arising in the land or naval forces, or in the Militia, when in actual service in time of War or public danger; nor shall any person be subject for the same offence to be twice put in jeopardy of life or limb, nor shall be compelled in any criminal case to be a witness against himself, nor be deprived of life, liberty, or property, without due process of law; nor shall private property be taken for public use without just compensation.

[ratified December, 1791]

AMENDMENT VI.

In all criminal prosecutions, the accused shall enjoy the right to a speedy and public trial, by an impartial jury of the State and district wherein the crime shall have been committed; which district shall have been previously ascertained by law, and to be informed of the nature and cause of the accusation; to be confronted with the witnesses against him; to have compulsory process for obtaining witnesses in his favor, and to have the assistance of counsel for his defence.

[ratified December, 1791]

AMENDMENT VII.

In Suits at common law, where the value in controversy shall exceed twenty dollars, the right of trial by jury shall be preserved, and no fact tried by a jury shall be otherwise re-examined in any Court of the United States, than according to the rules of the common law.

[ratified December, 1791]

AMENDMENT VIII.

Excessive bail shall not be required, nor excessive fines imposed, nor cruel and unusual punishments inflicted.

[ratified December, 1791]

AMENDMENT IX.

The enumeration in the Constitution, of certain rights, shall not be construed to deny or disparage others retained by the people.

[ratified December, 1791]

AMENDMENT X.
The powers not delegated to the United States by the Constitution, nor prohibited by it to the States, are reserved to the States respectively, or to the people.

[ratified December, 1791]

AMENDMENT XI.
The Judicial power of the United States shall not be construed to extend to any suit in law or equity, commenced or prosecuted against one of the United States by Citizens of another State, or by Citizens or Subjects of any Foreign State.

[ratified February, 1795]

AMENDMENT XII.
The Electors shall meet in their respective states, and vote by ballot for President and Vice President, one of whom, at least, shall not be an inhabitant of the same state with themselves; they shall name in their ballots the person voted for as President, and in distinct ballots the person voted for as Vice-President, and they shall make distinct lists of all persons voted for as President, and of all persons voted for as Vice-President, and of the number of votes for each, which lists they shall sign and certify, and transmit sealed to the seat of the government of the United States, directed to the President of the Senate;—The President of the Senate shall, in the presence of the Senate and House of Representatives, open all the certificates and the votes shall then be counted;—The person having the greatest number of votes for President, shall be the President, if such number be a majority of the whole number of Electors appointed; and if no person have such majority, then from the persons having the highest numbers not exceeding three on the list of those voted for as President, the House of Representatives shall choose immediately, by ballot, the President. But in choosing the President, the votes shall be taken by states, the representation from each state having one vote; a quorum for this purpose shall consist of a member or members from two-thirds of the states, and a majority of all the states shall be necessary to a choice. And if the House of Representatives shall not choose a President whenever the right of choice shall devolve upon them, before the fourth day

of March next following, then the Vice-President shall act as President, as in the case of the death or other constitutional disability of the President.—The person having the greatest number of votes as Vice-President, shall be the Vice-President, if such number be a majority of the whole number of Electors appointed, and if no person have a majority, then from the two highest numbers on the list, the Senate shall choose the Vice-President; a quorum for the purpose shall consist of two-thirds of the whole number of Senators, and a majority of the whole number shall be necessary to a choice. But no person constitutionally ineligible to the office of President shall be eligible to that of Vice-President of the United States.

[ratified June, 1804]

AMENDMENT XIII.

SECTION 1. Neither slavery nor involuntary servitude, except as a punishment for crime whereof the party shall have been duly convicted, shall exist within the United States, or any place subject to their jurisdiction.

SECTION 2. Congress shall have power to enforce this article by appropriate legislation.

[ratified December, 1865]

AMENDMENT XIV.

SECTION 1. All persons born or naturalized in the United States and subject to the jurisdiction thereof, are citizens of the United States and of the State wherein they reside. No State shall make or enforce any law which shall abridge the privileges or immunities of citizens of the United States; nor shall any State deprive any person of life, liberty, or property, without due process of law; nor deny to any person within its jurisdiction the equal protection of the laws.

SECTION 2. Representatives shall be apportioned among the several States according to their respective numbers, counting the whole number of persons in each State, excluding Indians not taxed. But when the right to vote at any election for the choice of electors for President and Vice President of the United States, Representatives in Congress, the Executive and Judicial officers of a State, or the members of the Legislature thereof, is denied to any of the male inhabitants of such State, being twenty-one years of age, and citizens of the United States, or in any way abridged, except for participation in rebellion, or other crime, the basis of representation therein shall be reduced in the proportion which the number of such male citizens shall bear to the whole number of male citizens twenty-one years of age in such State.

SECTION 3. No person shall be a Senator or Representative in Congress, or elector of President and Vice President, or hold any office, civil or military, under the United States, or under any State, who, having previously taken an oath, as a member of Congress, or as an officer of the United States, or as a member of any State legislature, or as an executive or judicial officer of any State, to support the Constitution of the United States, shall have engaged in insurrection or rebellion against the same, or given aid or comfort to the enemies thereof. But Congress may by a vote of two-thirds of each House, remove such disability.

SECTION 4. The validity of the public debt of the United States, authorized by law, including debts incurred for payment of pensions and bounties for services in suppressing insurrection or rebellion, shall not be questioned. But neither the United States nor any State shall assume or pay any debt or obligation incurred in aid of insurrection or rebellion against the United States, or any claim for the loss or emancipation of any slave; but all such debts, obligations and claims shall be held illegal and void.

SECTION 5. The Congress shall have power to enforce, by appropriate legislation, the provisions of this article.

[ratified July, 1868]

AMENDMENT XV.

SECTION 1. The right of citizens of the United States to vote shall not be denied or abridged by the United States or by any State on account of race, color, or previous condition of servitude.

SECTION 2. The Congress shall have power to enforce this article by appropriate legislation.

[ratified February, 1870]

AMENDMENT XVI.

The Congress shall have power to lay and collect taxes on incomes, from whatever source derived, without apportionment among the several States, and without regard to any census or enumeration.

[ratified February, 1913]

AMENDMENT XVII.

The Senate of the United States shall be composed of two Senators from each State, elected by the people thereof, for six years; and each Senator shall have one vote. The electors in each State shall have the qualifications requisite for electors of the most numerous branch of the State legislatures.

When vacancies happen in the representation of any State in the Senate, the executive authority of such State shall issue writs of election to fill such vacancies: *Provided,* That the legislature of any State may empower the executive thereof to make temporary appointments until the people fill the vacancies by election as the legislature may direct.

This amendment shall not be so construed as to affect the election or term of any Senator chosen before it becomes valid as part of the Constitution.

[ratified April, 1913]

AMENDMENT XVIII.

SECTION 1. After one year from the ratification of this article the manufacture, sale, or transportation of intoxicating liquors within, the importation thereof into, or the exportation thereof from the United States and all territory subject to the jurisdiction thereof for beverage purposes is hereby prohibited.

SECTION 2. The Congress and the several States shall have concurrent power to enforce this article by appropriate legislation.

SECTION 3. This article shall be inoperative unless it shall have been ratified as an amendment to the Constitution by the legislatures of the several States, as provided in the Constitution, within seven years from the date of the submission hereof to the States by the Congress.

[ratified January, 1919, repealed December, 1933]

AMENDMENT XIX.

The right of citizens of the United States to vote shall not be denied or abridged by the United States or by any State on account of sex.

Congress shall have power to enforce this article by appropriate legislation.

[ratified August, 1920]

AMENDMENT XX.

SECTION 1. The terms of the President and Vice President shall end at noon on the 20th day of January, and the terms of Senators and Representatives at noon on the 3d day of January, of the years in which such terms would have ended if this article had not been ratified; and the terms of their successors shall then begin.

SECTION 2. The Congress shall assemble at least once in every year, and such meeting shall begin at noon on the 3d day of January, unless they shall by law appoint a different day.

SECTION 3. If, at the time fixed for the beginning of the term of the President, the President elect shall have died, the Vice President elect shall become President. If a President shall not have been chosen before the time fixed for the beginning of his term, or if the President elect shall have failed to qualify, then the Vice President elect shall act as President until a President shall have qualified; and the Congress may by law provide for the case wherein neither a President elect nor a Vice President elect shall have qualified, declaring who shall then act as President, or the manner in which one who is to act shall be selected, and such person shall act accordingly until a President or Vice President shall have qualified.

SECTION 4. The Congress may by law provide for the case of the death of any of the persons from whom the House of Representatives may choose a President whenever the right of choice shall have devolved upon them, and for the case of the death of any of the persons from whom the Senate may choose a Vice President whenever the right of choice shall have devolved upon them.

SECTION 5. Sections 1 and 2 shall take effect on the 15th day of October following the ratification of this article.

SECTION 6. This article shall be inoperative unless it shall have been ratified as an amendment to the Constitution by the legislatures of three-fourths of the several States within seven years from the date of its submission.

[ratified January, 1933]

AMENDMENT XXI.

SECTION 1. The eighteenth article of amendment to the Constitution of the United States is hereby repealed.

SECTION 2. The transportation or importation into any State, Territory, or possession of the United States for delivery or use therein of intoxicating liquors, in violation of the laws thereof, is hereby prohibited.

SECTION 3. This article shall be inoperative unless it shall have been ratified as an amendment to the Constitution by conventions in the several States, as provided in the Constitution, within seven years from the date of the submission hereof to the States by the Congress.

[ratified December, 1933]

AMENDMENT XXII.

SECTION 1. No person shall be elected to the office of the President more than twice, and no person who has held the office of President, or acted as President, for more than two years of a term to which some other person was elected President shall be elected to the office of the President more than once. But this Article shall not apply to any person holding the office of President when this Article was proposed by the Congress, and shall not prevent any person who may be holding the office of President, or acting as President, during the term within which this Article becomes operative from holding the office of President or acting as President during the remainder of such term.

SECTION 2. This article shall be inoperative unless it shall have been ratified as an amendment to the Constitution by the legislatures of three-fourths of the several States within seven years from the date of its submission to the States by the Congress.

[ratified February, 1951]

AMENDMENT XXIII.

SECTION 1. The District constituting the seat of Government of the United States shall appoint in such manner as the Congress may direct:

A number of electors of President and Vice President equal to the whole number of Senators and Representatives in Congress to which the District would be entitled if it were a State, but in no event more than the least populous State; they shall be in addition to those appointed by the States, but they shall be considered, for the purposes of the election of President and Vice President, to be electors appointed by a State; and they shall meet in the District and perform such duties as provided by the twelfth article of amendment.

SECTION 2. The Congress shall have power to enforce this article by appropriate legislation.

[ratified March, 1961]

AMENDMENT XXIV.

SECTION 1. The right of citizens of the United States to vote in any primary or other election for President or Vice President, for electors for President or Vice President, or for Senator or Representative in Congress, shall not be denied or abridged by the United States or any State by reason of failure to pay any poll tax or other tax.

SECTION 2. The Congress shall have power to enforce this article by appropriate legislation.

[ratified January, 1964]

AMENDMENT XXV.

SECTION 1. In case of the removal of the President from office or of his death or resignation, the Vice President shall become President.

SECTION 2. Whenever there is a vacancy in the office of the Vice President, the President shall nominate a Vice President who shall take office upon confirmation by a majority vote of both Houses of Congress.

SECTION 3. Whenever the President transmits to the President pro tempore of the Senate and the Speaker of the House of Representatives his written declaration that he is unable to discharge the powers and duties of his office, and until he transmits to them a written declaration to the contrary, such powers and duties shall be discharged by the Vice President as Acting President.

SECTION 4. Whenever the Vice President and a majority of either the principal officers of the executive departments or of such other body as Congress may by law provide, transmit to the President pro tempore of the Senate and the Speaker of the House of Representatives their written declaration that the President is unable to discharge the powers and duties of his office, the Vice President shall immediately assume the powers and duties of the office as Acting President.

Thereafter, when the President transmits to the President pro tempore of the Senate and the Speaker of the House of Representatives his written declaration that no inability exists, he shall resume the powers and duties of his office unless the Vice President and a majority of either the principal officers of the executive department or of such other body as Congress may by law provide, transmit within four days to the President pro tempore of the Senate and the Speaker of the House of Representatives their written declaration that the President is unable to discharge the powers and duties of his office. Thereupon Congress shall decide the issue, assembling within forty-eight hours for that purpose if not in session. If the Congress, within twenty-one days after receipt of the latter written declaration, or, if Congress is not in session, within twenty-one days after Congress is required to assemble, determines by two-thirds vote of both Houses that the President is unable to discharge the powers and duties of his office, the Vice President shall continue to discharge the same as Acting President; otherwise, the President shall resume the powers and duties of his office.

[ratified February, 1967]

AMENDMENT XXVI.

SECTION 1. The right of citizens of the United States, who are eighteen years of age or older, to vote shall not be denied or abridged by the United States or by any State on account of age.

SECTION 2. The Congress shall have power to enforce this article by appropriate legislation.

[ratified July, 1971]

AMENDMENT XXVII.
No law, varying the compensation for the services of the Senators and Representatives, shall take effect, until an election of Representatives shall have intervened.

[ratified May 7, 1992]

LEGAL RESOURCES

The reality of legal research is that no single volume of books contains the whole law applicable to a particular person or circumstance. Rather, different governments and different branches within these governments create law, and the products of this multiple creative work are scattered across innumerable volumes. One of the professional skills of attorneys is the ability to navigate these multiple sources of legal authority, but interested laypersons may profit from understanding at least the broad contours of the legal terrain.

PRIMARY SOURCES OF THE LAW

The first major division of legal authority has to do with the divisions among federal, state, and local lawmaking authorities. Authorities at each of these levels create law, with the higher authority sometimes but not always displacing laws of the lower authority. For example, according to the supremacy clause of the U.S. Constitution, when the federal government creates laws inconsistent with those of state or local governments, the federal law prevails. However, federal laws frequently leave room for state and local laws on the same subject. As a consequence, a given situation may be subject to the law of one or all of these authorities, and legal researchers must be prepared to consult resources available for each.

The second division of legal authority is among the various branches within government. Laws or legal rules may have their genesis in the legislative, executive, or the judicial branches of federal, state, or local governments. Legislatures create law in the form of statutes, which are ultimately collected in codes. Executives, at least at the federal level, create law in the form of executive orders or administrative regulations. Judicial branches create law in the form of case opinions and rules governing legal practice and procedure. Moreover, courts routinely interpret other legal materials, such as constitutions or statutes, and these interpretations are of sufficient importance that their content may be included in legal volumes containing constitutions or statutes. For example, a very common version of federal statutes is referred to as the United States Code Annotated and consists not only of statutes collected

Level	*Branch*	*Chief Source of Legal Authority*
Federal	Legislative (Congress)	United States Code or United States Code Annotated.
Federal	Executive branch	Executive orders and regulations enacted by federal departments and agencies and collected in the Code of Federal Regulations.
Federal	Judicial	Opinions in cases decided at the district court, court of appeals, and Supreme Court levels and collected in multivolume sets known as the *Federal Supplement*, *Federal Reporter*, and the *United States Reports*, respectively.
State	Legislative	Each state has a code of laws similar to the United States Code Annotated. Such codes include, for example, the Annotated California Code and the Code of Virginia Annotated.
State	Executive	State governors and other executive officials may produce executive orders comparable to those of the U.S. president. In addition, state administrative agencies generally promulgate regulations on a variety of subjects entrusted to them by state law.
State	Judicial	States have one or more levels of courts that produce published judicial opinions on questions of law. These opinions are collected in one or more "reporters," as they are called. In addition, West Publishing in St. Paul, Minnesota, a leading publisher of legal materials, collects opinions decided by the courts of states in various regions of the country into regional reporters, such as the *Pacific Reporter*, which includes cases decided by California and other western states, and the *Southern Reporter*, which includes cases decided by Mississippi courts and the courts of other southern states.

in the form of a code but also of references to case opinions that interpret the various provisions of the code.

Thus, a given legal problem may require that researchers consult legal authorities created by multiple branches of government within the federal, state, and local governmental systems. The preceding table attempts to summarize the key sources of legal authority for federal and state governments. In addition to the sources listed, the highest source of law for both federal and state governments is the U.S. Constitution. A copy of the U.S. Constitution is available in the United States Code Annotated and also at a number of sites on the World Wide Web, discussed below. In addition, state governments are subject to the authority of their respective state constitutions. Local governments produce laws as well in the form of municipal or county ordinances, but these laws generally lack the broad spectrum of lawmaking power as exercised by federal and state governments. Such laws enacted at the local level are generally available in local government offices and sometimes in public libraries.

FINDING PRIMARY LEGAL SOURCES

Primary legal sources, such as the United States Code and the various federal and state judicial opinions, are generally available from three sources. First, all the materials discussed in the table are published as multivolume hardback series. Some public libraries have copies of such items as the United States Code Annotated and the annotated code for the relevant state. To find a more complete collection of primary sources of the printed type, one must generally gain access to a law library. Local courthouses are generally the most likely place to find a law library with the resources described above.

Second, all the sources above, and many more, may be accessed remotely from the two leading computer databases of the law profession: Westlaw and Lexis. These databases charge a subscription fee and per usage fees and are thus financially out of the range of most individuals other than lawyers.

Third, and perhaps most important, many primary legal sources are available free of charge on the World Wide Web. Individuals may access these sites either through personal or job-related Internet connections or through Internet connections made available in many public libraries. The following section describes some of the legal resources available on the Internet.

ONLINE RESOURCES

The following list contains a variety of World Wide Web resources relating to the law. One of the realities of the World Wide Web is that information sites sometimes change their locations and sometimes cease to exist altogether. Thus, readers may find that some addresses no longer work. It is impossible to briefly summarize the varieties of legal materials now available online, but two kinds of Web sites will be of most assistance to those interested in researching the law: sites that serve as indexes to legal resources generally and sites devoted to particular legal topics. The first list below contains the World Wide Web addresses of several general legal information sites on the Web.

ABA Legal Research Selected Starting Points
www.abanet.org/lawlink/home.html
Links to legal materials maintained by the American Bar Association (ABA).

ABA Network
www.abanet.org
Web site maintained by the American Bar Association (ABA) providing a variety of legal information for both lawyers and the public.

Alan Gahtan's Canadian Legal Resources
gahtan.com/lawlinks
Collection of Canadian legal resources.

American Law Resources On-Line
www.lawsource.com/also/usa.htm
Extensive collection of legal resources.

CataLaw
www.catalaw.com
Searchable index of legal information.

Center for Information Law and Policy
www.law.vill.edu
Collection of legal Web resources maintained by the Villanova Law School.

Counsel Quest
www.CounselQuest.com
Internet legal resources locator.

FedLaw
www.legal.gsa.gov
Web site maintained by the U.S. General Services Administration (GSA) devoted to legal resources useful to federal lawyers and employees.

Law Lists
www.lib.uchicago.edu/~llou/lawlists/info.html
A guide to electronic discussion groups concerning the law.

LawInfo Com
www.lawinfo.com
Referral site for lawyers and a variety of legal resources.

Legal Information Institute
www.law.cornell.edu
One of the Web's most exhaustive collections of legal materials maintained by the Cornell Law School.

Legal List
www.lcp.com/The-Legal-List
An outline of and introduction to legal resources on the Internet.

Library of Congress
lcweb.loc.gov/homepage/lchp_txt.html
Indexes to the holdings of the Library of Congress, on-line exhibits, and a variety of resources, including some legal materials.

Thomas
thomas.loc.gov
Detailed information about federal legislation maintained by the Library of Congress.

U.S. House of Representatives Internet Law Library
law.house.gov
General information source for federal law.

World Wide Web Virtual Library: Law
www.law.indiana.edu/law/v-lib/lawindex.html
General Web resources indexed by the Indiana University School of Law, Bloomington.

GOVERNMENT AGENCIES AND OFFICES
The next category of Web sites includes those maintained by various governmental agencies and offices that are generally devoted to a particular legal topic. Governmental agencies and offices frequently make available to the public legal information relevant to their operations.

Agriculture Department
14th and Independence Avenue SW
Washington, DC 20250
(202) 720-2791
www.usda.gov
Federal agency that supports agricultural production.

Bureau of Alcohol, Tobacco, and Firearms
650 Massachusetts Avenue NW
Washington, DC 20226
(202) 927-7777
www.atf.treas.gov/mailpage.htm
Collects taxes on and generally regulates alcohol, tobacco, and firearms.

Central Intelligence Agency
Public Affairs Staff
Central Intelligence Agency
Washington, DC 20505
(703) 482-0623.
www.odci.gov/cia
Provides intelligence information on issues relating to national security and conducts counterintelligence operations.

Consumer Product Safety Commission
East West Towers
4330 East West Highway
Bethesda, MD 20814
(301) 504-0580
www.cpsc.gov
Federal agency charged with protecting the public from unsafe products.

Customs Service
1301 Constitution Avenue, NW
Washington, DC 20229
(202) 927-1350
www.customs.ustreas.gov
Assesses and collects duties on imported goods.

Education Department
600 Independence Avenue SW
Washington, DC 20202-0498
(800) USA-LEARN
www.ed.gov
Federal agency that supports education in the United States.

Environmental Protection Agency
401 M Street SW
Washington, DC 20460
(202) 260-7963
www.epa.gov
Federal agency with responsibility for administering environmental laws.

Equal Employment Opportunity Commission
1801 L Street NW
Washington, DC 20507
(202) 663-4900
(800) 669-4000
www.eeoc.gov
Site operated by federal commission that enforces civil rights laws relating to employment.

Federal Bureau of Investigation (FBI)
J. Edgar Hoover Building
935 Pennsylvania Avenue NW
Washington, DC 20535-0001
(202) 324-3000
www.fbi.gov
Information on federal law enforcement.

Federal Trade Commission
CRC-240
Washington, DC 20580
(202) 382-4357
www.ftc.gov
Agency that registers complaints about credit reporting agencies and debt collection agencies and handles other issues relating to credit.

Fish and Wildlife Service
C Street NW
Washington, DC 20240
(202) 208-5634
www.fws.gov
Federal office with responsibility for conserving and enhancing fish and wildlife and their habitats.

Food and Drug Administration
5600 Fishers Lane
Rockville, MD 20857
(301) 443-1544
www.fda.gov
Federal agency with regulatory authority over food, cosmetics, and medicines.

Government Printing Office
Washington, DC 20402
(202) 783-3238
www.access.gpo.gov
Site of the government office that prints, binds, and distributes the publications of the U.S. Congress and the executive departments and offices of the federal government.

Health and Human Services Department
200 Independence Avenue SW
Washington, DC 20201
(202) 619-0257
www.os.dhhs.gov
   Principal federal agency with responsibility for protecting health of citizens and providing essential services, especially to those of limited means.

Housing and Urban Development Department
451 7th Street SW
Washington, DC 20410
(202) 708-3600
www.hud.gov
   Generally regulates housing matters in the United States.

Immigration and Naturalization Service
425 I Street NW
Washington, DC 20536
(202) 514-4316
www.ins.usdoj.gov
   Source of information relating to becoming a U.S. citizen.

Internal Revenue Service
1111 Constitution Avenue NW
Washington, DC 20224
(800) 829-1040
www.irs.ustreas.gov
   Determines, assesses, and collects taxes in the United States.

Justice Department
950 Pennsylvania Avenue NW
Washington, DC 20530-0001
(202) 514-2001
www.usdoj.gov
   Chief arm of federal law enforcement.

Labor Department
200 Constitution Avenue, NW, Room S-1032
Washington, DC 20210
(202) 219-8211
www.dol.gov
Federal agency charged with enhancing job opportunities and ensuring the adequacy of workplaces.

National Park Service
1849 C Street NW
Washington, DC 20240
(202) 208-6843
www.nps.gov
Federal office that regulates the use and preservation of national parks.

Occupational Safety and Health Administration (in the Labor Department)
200 Constitution Avenue
Washington, DC 20210
(800) 321-6742
www.osha.gov
Federal office with responsibility for preventing accidents and illnesses in the workplace.

Official Federal Government Web Sites (maintained by the Library of Congress)
lcweb.loc.gov/global/executive/fed.html
List of sites maintained by various federal agencies and offices.

Secret Service
1800 G Street N
Washington, DC 20223
(202) 435-5708
Protects the president of the United States and other public officials; investigates certain commercial crimes, including counterfeiting.

Securities and Exchange Commission
450 Fifth Street NW
Washington, DC 20549
(202) 942-7040
www.sec.gov
Federal agency with responsibility for administering federal securities laws and protecting investors.

Social Security Administration
Office of Public Inquiries
6401 Security Boulevard
Room 4-C-5 Annex
Baltimore, MD 21235
(800) 772-1213
www.ssa.gov
Federal office that administers the Social Security program.

State Department
2201 C Street NW
Washington, DC 20520
(202) 647-4000
www.state.gov
Chief agency for the implementation of U.S. foreign policy.

Treasury Department
1500 Pennsylvania Avenue NW
Washington, DC 20220
(202) 622-1100
www.ustreas.gov/menu.html
Federal agency that regulates currency, taxes, customs, and related matters.

White House
Washington, DC 20520
(202) 456-7041
www.whitehouse.gov/WH/Welcome-plain.html
Site providing a variety of information on the U.S. presidency.

LEGAL ORGANIZATIONS

Many nongovernmental organizations also provide information to the public on particular legal topics. The following list includes a number of such organizations.

ABA Center for Professional Responsibility
American Bar Association
541 North Fairbanks Court
Chicago, IL 60611-3314
(312) 988-5304
e-mail: ctrprofresp@abanet.org
Web site: www.abanet.org/cpr/home.html
Promotes the study and discussion of ethics relating to lawyers and judges.

Alliance for Justice
2000 P Street, NW, Suite 712
Washington, DC 20036
(202) 822-6070
e-mail: alliance@afj.org
Web site: www.afj.org
National association of environmental, civil rights, mental health, women's, children's and consumer advocacy organizations.

American Bar Association
750 N. Lake Shore Drive
Chicago, IL 60611
(312) 988-5000
e-mail: info@abanet.org
Web site: www.abanet.org
National association of lawyers.

American Inns of Court
127 South Peyton Street, Suite 201
Alexandria, Virginia 22314
(703) 684-3590
Web site: www.innsofcourt.org
Association of lawyers, judges, law teachers, and students dedicated to increasing professionalism in the practice of law.

Association of Trial Lawyers of America
1050 31st Street NW
Washington, DC 20007
(800) 424-2725
e-mail: help@atlahq.org.
Web site: www.atlanet.org
Association of plaintiffs' lawyers and others devoted to the cause of injured persons and other victims.

Better Business Bureau
Council of Better Business Bureaus, Inc.
4200 Wilson Boulevard, Suite 800
Arlington, VA 22203-1804
(703) 276-0100
Web site: www.bbb.org
Organization devoted to promoting fair and ethical business practices.

Conflict Resolution Center International
204 Thirty-seventh Street
Pittsburgh, PA. 15201-1859
(412) 687-6210
e-mail: crcii@conflictnet.org
Web site: www.conflictres.org
Organization that promotes nonviolent dispute resolution.

Electronic Privacy Information Center
666 Pennsylvania Avenue SE, Suite 301
(202) 544-9240
e-mail: info@epic.org
Web site: www.epic.org
Public interest research institute devoted to issues of privacy.

False Claims Act Legal Center
1220 19th Street NW, Suite 501
Washington, DC 20036
(800) 873-2573
e-mail: ams@taf.org
Web site: www.taf.org/taf
Organization that promotes whistle-blowers' suits against individuals and entities that have defrauded the U.S. government.

National Crime Prevention Council
1700 K Street NW, Second Floor
Washington, DC 20006-3817
(202) 466-6272
Web site: www.ncpc.org
  National organization dedicated to crime prevention.

National Fraud Information Center
P.O. Box 65868
Washington, DC 20035
(800) 876-7060
e-mail: fraudinfo@psinet.com
Web site: www.fraud.org
  Organization that assists consumers in obtaining advice about telephone solicitations and reporting possible telemarketing fraud to law-enforcement agencies.

National Lawyers Guild
558 Capp Street
San Francisco, CA 94110
(415) 285-5067
e-mail: nlgsf@igc.apc.org
Web site: www.emf.net/~cheetham/gnawld-1.html
  National association of progressive lawyers.

National Organization for Victim Assistance
1757 Park Road NW
Washington, DC 20010
e-mail: nova@try-nova.org
Web site: www.try-nova.org
  Nonprofit organization that seeks to further victims' rights.

National Paralegal Association
P.O. Box 406
Solebury, PA 18963
(215) 297-8333
e-mail: admin@nationalparalegal.org
Web site: www.nationalparalegal.org
  Organization for paralegals and those interested in a paralegal career.

SELECTED RESEARCH CENTERS
The following is a list of selected centers devoted to research on particular topics. Since the titles of the centers reflect the centers' concentration, the list does not describe each organization. A few centers have e-mail addresses and/or Web sites, which have been included when available.

ABA Center on Children and the Law
1800 M Street, NW
Washington, DC 20036
(202) 331-2250
e-mail: ctrchildlaw@abanet.org
Web site: www.abanet.org/child

American Indian Law Center
P.O. Box 4456, Station A
Albuquerque, NM 87196
(505) 277-5462

Arizona State University Center for the Study of Law, Science, and Technology
College of Law
P.O. Box 877906
Tempe, AZ 85287-7906
(602) 965-2554
e-mail: rosalind.pearlman@asu.edu
Web site: www.asu.edu/law/lawscien.htm

California Center for Judicial Education and Research
2000 Powell Street, 8th Floor
Emeryville, CA 94608
(510) 450-3601

Center for Dispute Settlement
1666 Connecticut Avenue NW, Suite 501
Washington, DC 20009

**Center for Information Technology & Privacy Law,
John Marshal Law School**
315 South Plymouth Court
Chicago, Illinois 60604
(312) 987-1419
e-mail: cil@jmls.edu
Web site: www.jmls.edu/info

Center for Law and Computers, Chicago-Kent College of Law
565 West Adams
Chicago, Illinois 60661
(312) 906-5300
e-mail: clc@chicagokent.kentlaw.edu
Web site: www.kentlaw.edu/clc

Center for Reproductive Law and Policy
120 Wall Street
New York, NY 10005
(212) 514-5534

Center for Women Policy Studies
2000 P Street NW, Suite 508
Washington, DC 20036
(202) 872-1770

College of William and Mary Institute of Bill of Rights Law
Marshal-Wythe School of Law
Williamsburg, VA 23185
(804) 221-3808
Web site: www.wm.edu/law/programs/ bill_of_rights.htm

Columbia University Center for the Study of Human Rights
1108 International Affairs Building
New York, NY 10027
(212) 854-2479
e-mail: cshr@columbia.edu
Web site: www.columbia.edu/cu/humanrights

Crime Control Institute and Crime Control Research Corporation
1063 Thomas Jefferson Street, NW
Washington, DC 20007
(202) 337-2700

Florida State University Center for Employment Relations and Law
College of Law
Tallahassee, FL 32306
(904) 644-4287

Freedom Forum First Amendment Center
Vanderbilt University
1222 16th Avenue South
Nashville, TN 37212
(615) 321-9588
e-mail: info@fac.org
Web site: www.freedomforum.org

Georgetown University Anne Blaine Harrison Institute for Public Law
111 F. Street NW
Washington, DC 20001
(202) 662-9600

Harvard Legislative Research Bureau
Harvard Law School
Cambridge, MA 02138
(617) 495-4400

Judge David L. Bazelon Center for Mental Health Law
1101 15th Street NW, Suite 1212
Washington, DC 20005
(202) 467-5730

Loyola University of Chicago National Center for Freedom of Information Studies
820 North Michigan Avenue
Chicago, IL 60611
(312) 915-7095

Marine Law Institute University of Maine School of Law
246 Deering Avenue
Portland, Maine 04102
(207) 780-4474
e-mail: bbsmith@payson.usmacs.maine.edu
Web site: www.law.usm.maine.edu/mli/mli.htm

Marquette University National Sports Law Institute
1103 West Wisconsin Avenue
Milwaukee, WS 53233
(414) 288-5815
e-mail: munsli@vms.csd.mu.edu
Web site: www.mu.edu/law/sports/sports.htm#institute

Meiklejohn Civil Liberties Institute
P.O. Box 673
Berkeley, CA 94701-0673
(510) 848-0599
e-mail: mcli@igc.apc.org

N. Neal Pike Institute on Law and Disability, Boston University School of Law
765 Commonwealth Avenue
Boston, MA 02215
(617) 353-2904
e-mail: pikeinst@bu.edu
Web site: www.bu.edu/pike/home.html

National Center for Juvenile Justice
710 Fifth Avenue, Suite 3000
Pittsburgh, PA 15219-3000
(412) 227-6950
e-mail: ncjj2@nauticom.net
Web site: http://www.ncjj.org

National Center on Women and Family Law
799 Broadway, Room 402
New York, NY 10003
(212) 674-8200

National Council on Crime and Delinquency
684 Market Street, Suite 620
San Francisco, CA 94105
(415) 896-6223

National Immigration Law Center
1636 West 8th Street, Suite 215
Los Angeles, CA 90017
(213) 487-2531

National Women's Law Center
1616 P Street NW
Washington, DC 20036
202-328-5160
Web site: http://www.protectchoice.org/ leadernwlc.html

Vermont Law School Environmental Law Center
Chelsea Street
South Royalton, VT 05068
(802) 763-8303
Web site: www.vermontlaw.edu/elc/elc.htm

—Timothy L. Hall

CATEGORIZED INDEX

DISABILITY ISSUES

EDUCATION

GOVERNMENT PROCEDURE AND ORGANIZATION

VOTING AND ELECTIONS

WOMEN'S ISSUES

SUBJECT INDEX

Abolitionist movement, 154, 274, 479

Abortion controversy, 1123, 1352, 1455

Abrams v. United States (1919), 57, 133, 453

Abzug, Bella S., 1234

Acheson, Dean, 794

Acid rain, 843, 1494

Adams, John, 128, 148

Adams, John Quincy, 165, 171

Adams-Onís Treaty (1819), 169

Addyston Pipe and Steel Co. v. U.S. (1899), 355

Adkins v. Children's Hospital (1923), 704

Administration on Aging, 957

Administrative Procedures Act (1946), 1002

Adoption Assistance and Child Welfare Act (1980), 1218

Advertising practices, 686

Affirmative action, 980, 1167

Africa, Cold War in, 1370

African Americans. *See* Categorized Index

Age discrimination, 929

Age Discrimination Act (1975), 957, 1285, 1453, 1501

Age Discrimination in Employment Act (1967), 1026, 1285, 1484

Agee, Philip, 1401

Aging issues. *See* Categorized Index

Agins v. City of Tiburon (1980), 81

Agnew, Spiro, 1021

Agreed Framework of 1994. *See* North Korea Pact

Agricultural Adjustment Act (1933), 555, 575

Agricultural College Act. *See* Morrill Land Grant Act of 1890

Agricultural Marketing Act (1929), 551

Agriculture. *See* Categorized Index

Aid to Families with Dependent Children (1935), 647, 962, 1121, 1458

Air Commerce Act (1926), 530

Air Force, U.S., 775

Air Pollution Control Act (1955), 789, 839, 1132

Air Quality Control Act (1967), 1132

Aircraft Noise Abatement Act (1968), 1060, 1203

Airline Deregulation Act (1978), 1343

Alabama claims (1871), 311

Alaska Federation of Natives, 1153

Alaska Lands Act. *See* Alaska National Interest Lands Conservation Act

Alaska National Interest Lands Conservation Act (1980), 956, 1380

Alaska Native Brotherhood, 1153

Alaska Native Claims Settlement Act (1971), 1151, 1382

Alaska Pipeline, 1153

Alaska Statehood Act (1958), 1380

Alaskan natives, 1151, 1189, 1383

Albertson v. Subversive Activities Control Board (1965), 799

Albright, Horace M., 442

Aldrich, Nelson W., 365, 427

Aldrich Plan, 427

Aleuts, 1456

Alien Act (1798), 127

Alien and Sedition Acts. *See* Sedition Act of 1798

Alien Enemies Act (1798), 127

Alien land laws (1913), 421

Allen v. Board of Elections (1969), 974

Allison, William, 327

Allotment policy, 347

Alternative Motor Fuels Act (1988), 1462